Praise for *On*

"Foster unpacks the evolution of governance and delivers a clear road map for building high-performing boards in today's complex and unpredictable world. A must-read for anyone committed to excellence in board leadership."
—Hubert Joly, Chairman and CEO (Retired), Best Buy

"In the ever-evolving world of public company leadership, having a playbook like *On Board* is an invaluable asset."
—Rob Lynch, CEO, Shake Shack

"Foster thoughtfully defines the role of directors in this vital and balanced 'how-to' examination of how effective boards should operate."
—Stuart Miller, Executive Chairman, Co-CEO, and former CEO, Lennar

"Using real-world examples, Foster masterfully deciphers the complex matrix of corporate governance today in this astonishing overview of the governance landscape."
—Melissa Sawyer, Partner, Global Head of Mergers & Acquisitions Group, and Cohead of Corporate Governance Practice, Sullivan & Cromwell

"This fast-paced and very readable guide is a valuable addition to the Wall Street canon."
—Bill Cohan, *New York Times* Best-Selling Author—*Power Failure*

"Good governance is the foundation of a great company. This playbook clearly fleshes out the essence of good governance. I would recommend it to entrepreneurs, directors, and public company executives alike."
—Harvey Jones, Director, Nvidia

"Foster's book is a master class in corporate governance even for experienced directors and for everyone interested in how firms make decisions. The book offers both the lens and the focus for board success."
—Glenn Hubbard, Dean Emeritus and Russell L. Carson Professor of Finance and Economics, Columbia Business School

"I highly recommend this insightful book. Foster not only educates the reader on the foundations and legal obligations but illuminates proper governance as a strategic asset that can drive long-term success."

—Jeremy London, Executive Partner, Skadden, Arps, Slate, Meagher & Flom

"I wish I had read this book before I joined my first board. The governance principles, ideas, and real-world perspective shared are excellent."

—Rob Steele, Vice Chairman (Retired), Procter & Gamble

"This very complete but readable book provides a contemporary history of what drives today's good governance and has detailed descriptions of how to implement good governance. It should be required reading for everyone concerned about or involved in the governance and leadership of any organization."

—Steve Rattner, Chairman and Chief Executive Officer, Willett Advisors

"Having worked with Foster, I have experienced firsthand his wisdom on corporate governance. His book offers a valuable study on the evolution of modern corporate governance and how directors can better understand the board's role and its performance potential."

—Jordan Brugg, CEO, Spencer Stuart

"This is the ultimate insider's guide to corporate boards of directors, including real-world examples of what *really* happens inside boardrooms."

—Scott Ullem, CFO, Edwards Lifesciences

"Stories and anecdotes make complex governance concepts relatable and easy to comprehend, ensuring that readers can immediately apply the lessons to real-world scenarios."

—Mei-Wei Cheng, President and CEO (Retired), Siemens Northeast Asia and China, and Former Chairman and CEO, Ford Motor Company China and General Electric China

On Board

HOW TO OVERSEE COMPANIES WITH CARE AND LOYALTY

On Board

The Modern Playbook for Corporate Governance

Jonathan F. Foster

Radius Book Group
New York

Radius Book Group
A Division of Diversion Media and Communications, LLC
www.RadiusBookGroup.com

Copyright © 2025 by Jonathan F. Foster

All rights reserved, including the right to reproduce this book or portions thereof in any form whatsoever. No part of this publication may be reproduced or transmitted in any form or by any means, electronic or mechanical, including photocopying, recording, or any other information storage and retrieval, without the written permission of the author.

For more information, email info@radiusbookgroup.com.

First Radius Book Group Edition: June 2025
Hardcover ISBN: 9798895150788
Trade Paperback ISBN: 9798895150146
eBook ISBN: 9798895150153

Manufactured in the United States of America
10 9 8 7 6 5 4 3 2 1

Cover design by Pete Garceau
Jacket design by Elizabeth Kingsbury
Interior design by Scribe Inc.

Radius Book Group and the Radius Book Group colophon are registered trademarks of Radius Book Group, a Division of Diversion Media and Communications, LLC.

This book contains the opinions and ideas of the author. There is no business, financial, legal, governance, or other professional advice or services offered. The comments, suggestions, and strategies that follow may not be suitable for every individual, situation, or company and are not warranted or guaranteed to produce any particular results.

For Roni, Rebekah, and Jack . . .

Contents

Section I

Why This Book and a Historical Perspective

    1. On Board   3
    2. How We Got to Now   7

Section II

What Do Directors Do and How Do Directors Do It?

    3. The Core of the Corporate Directors' Role   19
    4. The Three Major Board Committees   45
    5. Board Leadership   69

Section III

In What Context Must Directors Work?

    6. Mergers, Acquisitions, and Sales of Companies   89
    7. The Rising Influence of Activist Investors   117
    8. The Growing Impact of Institutional Investors   137
    9. Distressed Companies and Financial Restructurings   155
    10. Environmental, Social, and Governance Issues   179

Section IV

What Can Directors Do to Promote Long-Term Success?

    11. New Directors: Recruiting, Diversity, and Onboarding   199
    12. The Chief Executive Officer   215
    13. Risks and Crises   229
    14. Keeping a Board Fresh and Sharp   243
    15. Looking Forward and Recommendations   253

Acknowledgments	259
Appendix: Interviews	263
Notes	269
Index	327
About the Author	339

Section I
Why This Book and a Historical Perspective

Chapter 1
On Board

It all started with the summary blurbs in the two columns on the left side of the front page of the *Wall Street Journal* some 50 years ago—the hard copy newspaper, of course. My father helped run and then owned a small manufacturing company in New Hampshire and would bring the *Journal* home from the office at night.

Even in a time before the internet and social media, it still seemed late to be reading about the day's business news when the day was largely over. So my father promised that if I read the front page of the *Journal* each evening for a few weeks, he would buy me my own copy that would be delivered at home with the midday mail for me to read after school. I took him up on the offer.

The *Journal*'s stories confirmed my sense that as fun as life in New Hampshire seemed as a young teenager, Wall Street was a lot more exciting. That excitement has never left me. I ended up with a short stop in public accounting at what is now PwC and have spent the past 30-plus years largely in mergers and acquisitions (M&A) advisory work, including at Lazard, where I became a managing director, and at a firm I started and where I continue to be active, Current Capital Partners.

About 25 years ago, I joined my first board of directors and then my second, both small public companies, and I got to see what it was like to be involved in corporate governance firsthand, not just as an outside advisor, and to share in the responsibility for a company's performance, good or bad.

Shortly after the 2007–9 recession, I joined the board of Masonite, a building products manufacturer that had emerged from a restructuring under Chapter 11 of the US Bankruptcy Code. An investment firm, Centerbridge, was a minority investor entitled to one board seat. Given my background and relationship with a number of people at Centerbridge, they nominated me for their seat.

At my first board meeting, there was consideration of who would join and then who would be chair of the audit committee. I raised my hand for both and remained audit chair for some 15 years, until Masonite was sold in 2024 to Owens Corning for approximately $4 billion. During that time, I helped see Masonite through a listing on the New York Stock Exchange (NYSE), a chief executive officer (CEO) transition, two changes of the chief financial officer (CFO), and a more than 10 times increase in annual earnings before interest, taxes, depreciation, and amortization, or EBITDA.

I was not quite sure how to be an effective audit committee chair when I took on the role, but I did know how to learn. I called my friend Steve Key, an experienced director, the former head of the New York City office of the accounting firm Arthur Young (which later became Ernst & Young), and the former CFO of Textron and Conagra. Just a few weeks later, I sat with him on the porch of his Victorian home in Providence, Rhode Island.

Steve started by explaining to me the importance of a great culture, which he described as "the beliefs and behaviors that determine how an organization's employees and management interact and handle inside and outside transactions. Normally, this is a by-product of great leadership," Steve added, "and is focused on delivering value to the customer and returns to the investor." He said that the audit committee must work within this culture and underscored the benefit of putting together a work plan for the entire year.

Steve noted that two of the most critical tasks that lead to committee success are a strategic overview of what the accounting and finance area must do over the next several years to support operations in realizing its strategic objectives and a review of the key people in the accounting and finance functions. Over the rest of the afternoon, Steve gave me a detailed course on how to be an effective audit committee chair. It is a course I have long wanted to expand upon in many directions and share with others.

I have now been on more than 50 corporate boards ranging from small private companies to distressed companies to public companies, including Fortune 500 companies. I have been a nonexecutive chair as well as a member and head of the three major board committees and a member of various other board committees.

I certainly have not seen it all, but I have seen a lot.

I still remember my first major board meeting as an investment banker back in 1990, when I was the junior member of the Lazard team advising Wheelabrator on its merger with Waste Management. Michael Dingman, who later renounced his US citizenship and moved to Nassau, was the swashbuckling CEO of Wheelabrator, which had evolved from the Henley

Group, which had previously been spun off from Allied-Signal under Dingman's leadership with a motley collection of assets. I looked over at one point, and while I had been on the edge of my seat for an hour just taking it all in, Dingman's eyes were shut tight, and he seemed to be asleep.

That same year over the Christmas holiday period, in a separate deal, the United Airlines pilots acquired control of the airline. Again, as the young associate on the Lazard team, I sat in a large conference room in the Regency Hotel in New York City, where the "power breakfast" originated, as the United board approved this deal. My recollection is that just one director asked just one question: "Will our free first-class tickets continue to be available after the transaction closes?"

As I will show in the pages ahead, corporate governance has improved a lot. Of course, more improvements are necessary. I am convinced that good governance can be the difference between success and failure for a business. While this book is focused primarily on directors and boards of publicly traded companies, good governance is important for private companies and, indeed, any organization.

This book looks at the evolution of modern corporate governance and the key issues for directors to understand and address. From the core responsibilities of care and loyalty to specific issues when considering a potential sale of a company; to environmental, social, and governance (ESG) topics; to CEO succession and more, my hope is that this book will be a guide for anyone who wants to better understand the role of a board and how it can function most effectively in today's dynamic, global corporate world.

Corporate governance is often overlooked, especially with so much focus on celebrity CEOs and the 24/7 business news cycle. But little is more important to a business than good governance, even if we often only notice when a board fails spectacularly in its duties. To hopefully avoid these spectacular failures and experience only rising stock prices—as we all wish for—I hope you will read on.

Chapter 2
How We Got to Now

In the chapters that follow, it should become clear that a good governance playbook in today's increasingly complex, fast-changing corporate environment is based on several core tenets.

First, the board oversees management, and management runs the company day-to-day. Some use the expression "noses in, fingers out." In other words, directors should be involved in major issues but not in the details—those should be left to management.

Second, the days of the CEO running the board and the company virtually unfettered are largely over. A lot more is expected of directors than ever before, with increasingly stringent rules put in place by the Securities and Exchange Commission (SEC) and the major stock exchanges as well as case law and pressure from large institutional investors, governance advisory firms, activists, and others. At the same time, directors should "stay in their lane" and not overstep their oversight role.

Third, various strategic steps, such as M&A, including sales of assets and companies and leveraged buyouts (LBOs), as well as restructurings, are a significant part of the corporate landscape and have profound impacts on a board's roles, responsibilities, and potential legal risks.

Lastly, we are living in a time when a corporation's role is being debated as perhaps never before. There is a constant and continuing debate over ESG issues and whether corporations should be striving to maximize long-term *shareholder* value or look to broader *stakeholders* as well (not only shareholders but employees, communities, and other constituents).

Some 100—or even as few as 50—years ago, it was more often than not the case that directors were in large part figureheads, frequently just agreeing with management, largely unaccountable, and lacking real responsibility for oversight. Frank Carlucci—who worked for four presidents, including as national security advisor and secretary of defense in President Ronald Reagan's second term, and then went on to another successful career at the private equity firm Carlyle Group, from which he retired as chair in 2003, and died in 2018—sat on 14 public company boards in 1996, according to company proxy statements. Today, institutional investors and governance advisory services generally limit individuals to no more than 5 public company boards at once.

These were also times when business largely focused only on business, usually with little concern for ESG issues, including diversity or interests outside the company. It was not that many decades ago, maybe five, that there was tremendous corporate stability, where big leverage, big transactions, and big restructurings were infrequent. It was, in many respects, a far simpler time to be a board member.

Jim McCann, the founder and chair of 1-800-FLOWERS, who has grown the company into a billion-dollar business and is a member of other corporate boards, has noticed the change: "Governance has evolved dramatically over the last five decades and certainly since I began serving on boards. As a lifelong learner, I embraced the steep learning curve I faced, as it became clear to me that governance is an area that is vital to the success of a company."

McCann is not alone. Daniel Slifkin, a litigation partner at the law firm Cravath, now in its third century, and formerly the head of the firm's litigation department, has noticed the changes as well. "There's been an increase in professionalism and just general attention," he told me.

To appreciate and understand corporate governance today—and all of the issues to come in this book—requires a review of the history of modern transactions and related topics that have driven the evolution of corporate governance to its current state. As Charles Dickens wrote in *David Copperfield*, "It's in vain to recall the past, unless it works some influence upon the present." Indeed, the past does inform modern corporate governance. Therefore, we will start with how we have come to understand the best practices for the work and responsibilities of directors today.

Tracing the History

Corporate governance has been a topic of concern, though not a defined field of study, ever since there was the possibility of conflict between investors and managers—which brings us all the way back to the 16th and 17th centuries with enterprises such as the East India Company.[1] Adam Smith noted in *The Wealth of Nations* that "the managers of other people's money" were not inclined to exercise control with the "same anxious vigilance with which the partners in a private copartnery [company] frequently watch over their own."[2] In other words, management was not going to look out for investor interests as carefully or thoroughly as owners would.

In 1914, Supreme Court Justice Louis D. Brandeis published a collection of essays titled *Other People's Money and How the Bankers Use It*, in which he argued that small investors were powerless to control their investments and even managers had grown relatively powerless due to the enormous size of the corporations of the time and the inefficiencies that resulted. He lamented the loss of small businesses and was afraid of how growing consolidation might hurt the public.[3] To an extent, he was asking for a regime of corporate governance that did not exist at that time.

Our modern sense of corporate governance probably began in 1932, when Adolf A. Berle and Gardiner Means published *The Modern Corporation and Private Property*. This may have been the first work to define the concept of corporate governance as the management of concerns that arise between ownership and control: what it means for ownership and control to be separated, who is most impacted, and whether they should in fact be separated at all.[4]

The book coincided with what some have called a move from "entrepreneurial capitalism" to "managerial capitalism" where corporate control is exercised by professional managers, not equity owners.[5] The SEC was created at this point as well, in the wake of the Great Depression, ostensibly to protect investors. However, the Securities Exchange Acts of 1933 and 1934—the 1934 act launched the SEC—contain few references to directors.[6] For decades, managerial capitalism flourished with relatively little board oversight of senior executives. There was an understanding that corporate governance was a subject worth studying, but management teams operated without the checks and balances from directors that we take for granted today.[7] It was not until the 1970s that the SEC and others really started to address corporate governance concerns.

The 1970s and '80s: The First Wave of Corporate Governance Reform

A 1968 study of directors recognized that it was unwise "to assume all is well at the corporate pinnacle," pointing to director absenteeism and exceedingly brief board meetings.[8] Myles Mace of Harvard Business School wrote a seminal piece in 1971 that criticized boards of public companies for rarely engaging in meaningful evaluations of executive performance and only contemplating the dismissal of the CEO in the event of a crisis.[9]

At about the same time, issues of corporate governance started to land on people's radar screens and in the news as never before. The *New York Times* covered the resignation of former Supreme Court Justice Arthur Goldberg from his seat on the board of Trans World Airlines (TWA) in 1972 after unsuccessfully attempting to institute more oversight of management's actions. Goldberg tried to "establish an independent committee of outside directors to review the actions and recommendations of management . . . [arguing] that non-officers on the Board should be allowed to meet independently and have the authority to hire an autonomous staff of technical specialists."[10] It was reported that Goldberg believed this should be the case not just at TWA but everywhere.[11]

"Exorbitant executive payouts, disappointing corporate earnings, and ill-considered acquisitions," as one history describes it, led the SEC to take a firmer hand in corporate oversight in the mid-1970s.[12] In 1973, the chair of the SEC, G. Bradford Cook, announced his intention to establish guidelines for directors. He said in a speech, "Directors are fiduciaries and have an affirmative responsibility to act fairly and honestly to seek to assure that their corporations do the same. They owe this responsibility not only to their own shareholders but to all public investors who buy, sell or hold their company's securities."[13] This was the beginning of corporate governance as we have come to know it.

In 1974, the SEC investigated a case where three outside directors of a bankrupt railroad, Penn Central, were said to have failed to discover executive misconduct and thus misrepresented the company's finances.[14] The result of the SEC investigation was a report that promised new rules for directors. "The Commission," reads the report, "taking a look at the future, has paid increasing attention to the role, the qualifications, the responsibilities, and the independence of corporate directors, which appear to be called for. . . . The staff report points up the critical importance of the whole subject of the responsibility of directors, the greater utilization of public and independent directors, the professionalization of their function, providing staff support for directors and judging their performance not on the basis of hindsight but on the basis of the reasonableness of their judgments in the circumstances and at the time it was exercised."[15]

Around the same time, a number of US companies were discovered to be paying bribes to foreign officials—and their outside directors were found to be completely unaware, despite the knowledge of senior executives.[16] The SEC forced a number of the companies involved to make board-level changes, such as adding independent directors and creating an audit committee, and then pushed the NYSE to require all companies listed on its exchange to have an independent audit committee, which happened starting in 1976.[17] In 1977, the SEC held six weeks of hearings regarding corporate governance in an attempt to understand the full landscape of issues.[18]

But the reforms did not go much further at the time, despite the chair of the SEC in the late 1970s, President Jimmy Carter's appointee Harold Williams, making speeches generally saying that an ideal board would be composed exclusively of outside directors, but for the CEO, and would have an audit committee, nomination committee, and compensation committee. These were his own views, but they were not the law, even with Senator Howard Metzenbaum of Ohio introducing in Congress a bill that would have largely codified these steps in the Protection of Shareholders' Rights Act of 1980.[19]

The 1970s and early 1980s really were the time when sentiment began to shift, and it was finally recognized that a board had a unique role to play and should not just be rubber-stamping management's desires and decisions. In addition to the SEC, the rise of activist investors encouraged improved governance. The first round of activists often sought to break up or sell companies, using their own money to purchase blocks of shares for leverage to gain board seats and influence outcomes. They were focused on simply pushing companies to reduce inefficiencies and maximize profits.[20]

More attentive governance was being encouraged against the backdrop of a societal push from stakeholder capitalism—where companies were in many cases motivated to produce solid returns for shareholders but, at the same time, to be good corporate citizens serving employees, customers, and the community—to shareholder capitalism, where many investors were concerned that companies were not doing everything it took to maximize stockholders' returns and wanted to move business in the direction of economic profit above all.

The Chicago school of free market economists, led in many respects by Milton Friedman, sought to reframe the goal of the corporation as solely to make money for shareholders. In his influential 1970 *New York Times* article "The Social Responsibility of Business Is to Increase Its Profits," Friedman wrote that corporate executives were failing in their duties to shareholders if they pursued any aim that did not absolutely maximize profits. Quoting from his book *Capitalism and Freedom*, he wrote, "There is one and only one social responsibility of business—to use its resources and engage in activities designed to increase its profits so long as it stays within the rules of the game, which is to say, engages in open and free competition without deception or fraud."[21]

The motivation for the piece was that he and others felt that executives were wasting efforts—and money—on trying to control pollution, fight inflation, train the unemployed, and more.[22] And so a new group of more aggressive investors rose up and pressured numerous boards of companies that were seen to be poorly managed and underutilizing assets to maximize value—while certainly capturing some of this value for themselves.

This was the start of the boom in activism as well as M&A, including LBOs—much of this driven by the advent of high-yield debt financing. Corporate raiders of the 1970s and 1980s, such as Carl Icahn (still active today), looked to gain positions in companies and then attempt to strong-arm them to take actions they believed would increase (often short-term) shareholder value.[23]

Indeed, takeover offers were received by nearly half of all major US corporations during the 1980s.[24] This drove many companies to adopt anti-takeover or defense strategies, including the so-called poison pill pioneered by Marty Lipton, a founding partner of the law firm Wachtell Lipton, who continues to be a valued counselor to boards and management teams today. In general, when an unfriendly party acquires a specified ownership percentage in a company, a poison pill permits the other existing shareholders to acquire substantial stock in the company at a significant discount to the market price, thus making an acquisition much more expensive for the aggressor.

Michael Milken of the firm Drexel Burnham Lambert was a pioneer of the LBO by developing high-yield bonds or those with a rating below investment grade—sometimes referred to as "junk bonds"—to finance corporate takeovers. Milken is perhaps the most important financier of our generation. Today, the global high-yield market is over $5 trillion. Parenthetically, Milken was eventually convicted of violating securities laws and served about two years in prison. He was later pardoned by President Donald Trump.

Private equity firms have played a major role in encouraging and facilitating corporate efficiency and value maximization, notwithstanding criticisms about their cost-cutting and resulting negative impacts on workforces and communities. They typically raise equity funds that, combined with taking on substantial debt, help them purchase companies in partnership with these companies' senior executives and then seek to increase value and ultimately exit, usually through the sale of the company or an initial public offering (IPO). For example, today a leading asset management firm with some $600 billion under management, KKR was launched in 1976. Other private equity firms—including Wesray, Blackstone, and Apollo—followed.

Institutional investors—in some cases under the umbrella organization of the Council of Institutional Investors, organized in 1985—pushed for directors to be more independent of management and align their interests with shareholders, not company executives. At the same time, courts—especially in Delaware, where the majority of large public companies are incorporated—became more aggressive about seeing that directors fulfilled their two basic duties: the duty of care, or the requirement that directors inform themselves appropriately before making decisions, and the duty of loyalty, or the requirement that directors not have material conflicts of interest.

Boards became critical to overseeing management more effectively in order to satisfy more demanding shareholders. This was, in many ways, the first wave of corporate governance as a driving force in business, working to overcome economic complacency and provide that companies were acting in efficient, justifiable ways guided by an independent, engaged board. But as the years passed—and the booming stock market of the 1990s and early 2000s hid some failures in the boardroom—there was once again a need for action and reform.

2008–Present: The Second Wave of Corporate Governance Reform

Scandals at Enron, WorldCom, and other companies in the early years of this century, coupled with the global financial crisis of 2007–9, made it clear that more change was needed and perhaps not entirely in the same direction as the first wave of reform. Corporate governance has more recently included the rise of calls for enhanced director independence, the separation of the roles of chair of the board and CEO, and genuine consideration of ESG issues, which have changed the landscape for directors and management teams.

In our current environment, *long-term* shareholder success is now the stated mission of the most influential voices in the business world, from academics, to the Delaware courts, to the National Association of Corporate Directors (NACD), with over 24,000 members. I was on the National

Association of Corporate Directors' 2015 Blue Ribbon Commission on Long-Term Value Creation, which argued for exactly this approach.

Admiral Mike Mullen is a retired US Navy admiral who served the country as the 17th chair of the Joint Chiefs of Staff under Presidents George W. Bush and Barack Obama. Since retiring from the military, he has served on a variety of boards, including at General Motors and Sprint. "What drove me crazy," he told me, "were the demands on total shareholder return every quarter. The impact of analysts on CEO behavior is extraordinary, even probably more so than the analysts realize, to increase [short-term] returns."

It is true that a long-term approach—often marked by investing in broader stakeholders such as a company's community—takes valuable resources. But a company committed to a wide variety of stakeholders can potentially create value for its shareholders, even in the short-term, by making these investments—by, for instance, attracting higher-quality employees excited about the company's role in the world and generating positive press that can lead to more business opportunities.

Of course, it is hard to decide what an appropriate expenditure is, for example, in a community project. I was involved with a company whose leaders wanted to contribute $5 million to restore a local park. It was a small expenditure for this large company. However, I wondered if we should contribute perhaps $2.5 million, $5 million, or even more than that. These are difficult decisions; unlike capital expenditures on new company projects, the amount of an effective but not excessive investment in community projects cannot often be analyzed with hard numbers.

In my experience, management objectives and shareholder interests have become more aligned. Managers should absolutely continue to run the day-to-day business activities, and directors should provide informed oversight. Shareholders hold boards accountable through regulatory oversight, activism, commentary by governance advisory firms, proxy voting, litigation, and other efforts. There are exceptions to good governance, and we will discuss some examples of major governance failures such as at the iconic US aircraft manufacturer Boeing.

Marty Lipton told me in an interview, "The major changes in the expectation of boards and directors have reflected business problems, legislation, and regulation. Changes come more slowly from legislation and regulation; they come more quickly if they are necessary to facilitate the operations of companies. Directors have become serious shepherds of their responsibilities, not to mention that there's been a significant amount of litigation over the last 50 years that has held directors liable for problems they should have dealt with."

I share this historical overview to show that while corporate governance has been transformed over the past 50 years or so, there continue to be major oversights, and the role of a director is more complex and more important than ever before. Unless you know the history of how we arrived at where we are, you will not understand the issues we still face. Without appreciating the past, we risk failing to continue to improve governance and even reversing the progress in recent decades—hurting businesses, the economy, and society more broadly.

Section II
What Do Directors Do and How Do Directors Do It?

Chapter 3
The Core of the Corporate Directors' Role

On May 20, 2011, Vice Chancellor Donald F. Parsons of the Delaware Court of Chancery released an opinion that may not have made headlines beyond the world of attorneys, investment bankers, and corporate directors but certainly had a significant impact on these audiences. At issue in the decision in *In re Smurfit-Stone Shareholder Litigation* was whether the board of Smurfit-Stone, a publicly traded Fortune 500 manufacturer of paperboard and paper-based packaging, had fulfilled its fiduciary duties in approving a sale to Rock-Tenn, a competitor in the paper and packaging business.

The plaintiffs claimed that the board had rushed through the transaction without seeing that it was maximizing shareholder value, engaged in exclusive negotiations with Rock-Tenn without adequately canvassing the market, agreed to restrictive deal protections, permitted members of the management team with conflicting interests to participate in the negotiations, and relied on a financial advisor with no industry experience.

Smurfit-Stone had recently emerged from a Chapter 11 bankruptcy reorganization with a new 11-person board, including 8 independent directors, selected in a process driven by the former major debtholders of the company who were now significant shareholders. These directors had worked to quickly become familiar with the company's management, businesses, competitive position, strategic challenges, financial position, market perception, and other issues. They had retained Goldman Sachs to advise on several topics, including a significantly underfunded pension obligation. The company was in the midst of a search for a new CEO and a new CFO; it had substantial overhead compared to the competition, driven in part by a dozen paper mills, some of which were not particularly cost competitive, and three separate headquarters due to a previous business combination as well as the opening of an office in Atlanta near a major competitor, Georgia-Pacific, from which it had hired a number of executives.

Given these issues and uncertainties, particularly a CEO with a short-term contract and a widely known search underway for his replacement, it was not surprising that the board received an unsolicited takeover offer—from a major private equity firm that had teamed with a senior executive who would become the CEO if the offer were successful. The board immediately formed a special committee of independent directors—because the CEO was conflicted as a potential seller of his stock and a buyer or investor in the newly acquired company if he stayed on in some capacity—and retained outside advisors: Lazard as its investment bank and Wachtell Lipton as legal counsel.

The Lazard team was led by Bill Lewis and the low-key but powerful Barry Ridings. Lewis was a senior M&A banker who had run Morgan Stanley's M&A business and then decamped to Lazard before moving to Apollo, while Ridings, along with his friend and Bermuda neighbor, Terry Savage, had built one of Wall Street's leading restructuring advisory practices and had advised Smurfit-Stone on its restructuring. Steve Rosenblum led the Wachtell Lipton team. He had been at Wachtell Lipton, one of the leading law firms for M&A, since the late 1980s, and in his trademark dark suits, white shirts, and red ties, Steve was known for his thoughtful advice and long work hours.

The unsolicited proposal from the private equity firm was rejected for offering a price too low. However, on December 23, 2010, the board was met with another unsolicited offer, this time from Rock-Tenn and its proven, acquisition-minded CEO, Jim Rubright. Given that every board is obligated to maximize shareholder value, all public companies are essentially for sale at some price, and the board was open to listening.

Rock-Tenn's interest was strategic and logical. It had completed and successfully integrated two substantial acquisitions. Importantly, Rubright later explained to me that he had determined that the containerboard industry had been rationalized so that supply and demand were generally in balance, but he expected demand would increase significantly with the economy strengthening and e-commerce accelerating. He went on to say that Smurfit-Stone had emerged from its restructuring with an improved cost structure and strong earnings in its first quarter as a new public company, and an acquisition would help bring more price discipline to the market. "I preached price, not volume," he told me.

Rock-Tenn was working with an investment banking team led by John Church of Wachovia, now Wells Fargo. Church, currently a vice chair in investment banking at Morgan Stanley, had covered paper and packaging companies for years and had Rubright's trust.

The process played out quickly—19 days from the initial approach to the announcement of a $3.5 billion deal—but not without careful consideration by both parties. Smurfit-Stone set up a transaction committee of three directors to be able to meet and react faster than the entire board could; of course, all directors were kept well informed and were responsible for ultimately deciding whether or not to recommend a transaction to shareholders. Rubright said, "[Rock-Tenn] never felt rushed. We had done two deals that went well and had a strong executive team and superb advisors. I always focus on the critical issues, and the other issues are not that important." There were numerous meetings for due diligence and contract negotiations as well as board meetings for both companies.

The Smurfit-Stone board discussed whether to contact potential financial and other corporate buyers, but it was clear to the directors that there were a limited number of potential acquirers, and they should have all been well aware of the opportunity to make their interest known given the prior bankruptcy. Ultimately, the Smurfit-Stone board, advised by Lazard and Wachtell Lipton, decided that the final price offered by Rock-Tenn—$35 per share, paid 50 percent in cash and 50 percent in Rock-Tenn common stock, a 27 percent premium to the Smurfit-Stone stock price before rumors of a potential sale started—was attractive and approved the execution of a definitive agreement and public announcement.

Very quickly, the Smurfit-Stone board was sued in the Delaware Court of Chancery, and while the outcome should have been clear to anyone who knew the facts, no one ever wants to be sued. A significant issue in the case was the standard to which the board was to be held. Board actions are typically evaluated under the business judgment rule: Was the process reasonable and were the actions taken in good faith? However, in the seminal *Revlon v. MacAndrews & Forbes* case (*Revlon*) that addressed a situation where a company was sold for 100 percent cash and the shareholders did not have a "tomorrow" in which to participate in the company's future success, the court held that the standard of scrutiny is higher, requiring a board to make a reasonable effort to obtain the highest possible value for the company.

The details of *Revlon* will be explored later, but with the consideration for Smurfit-Stone being a mixture of cash and stock, there was some uncertainty as to which standard was appropriate. In the end, the standard was irrelevant to the verdict.

Vice Chancellor Parsons wrote in his opinion, "Plaintiffs have not shown a reasonable probability of success on their claim that the Board breached its fiduciary duties by approving the Rock-Tenn merger. . . . [Regardless of the governing standard,] the result would be the same."[1] He went on to state, "I reject Plaintiffs' contention that the Board and Special Committee were not adequately informed when they authorized the signing of the Merger Agreement."[2] He also wrote, "There were a number of pieces of information to support $35 per share as a fair price."[3]

Indeed, each of the plaintiffs' claims was dismissed.

The deal went on to be overwhelmingly approved by the shareholders, with more than 91 percent of the Smurfit-Stone shares that voted at the company's shareholder meeting voting for the transaction.

To complete the story, in 2015, Rock-Tenn combined with another competitor, MeadWestvaco, to form WestRock. Then, in late 2023, WestRock completed a deal with Smurfit Kappa to create Smurfit WestRock, the largest containerboard producer in the world with annual revenue of some $34 billion.[4] Interestingly, Smurfit Kappa was the international business of what was originally Jefferson Smurfit Corporation before it merged with Stone Container in 1998 and became Smurfit-Stone.

Vice Chancellor Parsons's opinion was of particular interest to me because I was one of the eight independent directors who had been appointed to the Smurfit-Stone board upon the company's emergence from Chapter 11. I was also a member of the special committee and the transaction committee and deposed prior to the trial. I was confident that our board was unconflicted, well informed, and well advised, and that it made the value-maximizing decision. I was pleased that our board decided not to settle with a plaintiff whose claim was uninformed and weak but to let the court decide—and we won resoundingly.

The experience continues to be a stark reminder to me that the duties of a director matter. There are real stakes in terms of dollars and, in some cases, in terms of people's lives. I contrast my Smurfit-Stone experience with the news that has emerged in recent years from Boeing, the major American company that has been manufacturing airplanes for more than a century and is ranked about 50th on the most recent Fortune 500 list.[5]

The Boeing board, while filled with directors successful in a range of roles and enterprises, was found culpable in fatal plane crashes in 2018 and 2019. "Rather than prioritizing safety," wrote Vice Chancellor Morgan T. Zurn of the Delaware Court of Chancery, the directors "lent their oversight authority to Boeing's agenda of rapid production and profit maximization."[6] Indeed, Zurn continued, "not only did the Director Defendants act inconsistently with their fiduciary duties, but they also knew of their shortcomings."[7] The board did not escape liability here; it wound up agreeing to pay $237.5 million to shareholders, although it should be noted that the money was paid by the company's directors and officers (D&O) insurance policy, not the directors themselves.[8] In January 2024, in the wake of another incident where a door plug failed on an Alaska Airlines Boeing 737 MAX 9, the board found itself under new scrutiny.[9]

Given these two contrasting examples, what are the key responsibilities of a director, and how can a director effectively execute them?

The Responsibilities of a Director

A board is elected by the shareholders to oversee management. The board members do not manage the company. The CEO, the CEO's direct reports, and employees throughout the organization manage it on a day-to-day basis. In their oversight role, directors are responsible, in general, for hiring, evaluating, compensating, and sometimes terminating the CEO; considering and ultimately approving corporate strategy; evaluating and signing off on capital allocation (investments in capital expenditures, debt repayment, acquisitions and returns of capital to shareholders through dividends and/or share repurchases); and reviewing financial controls and financial statements, capital structure, and compliance matters.

I spoke with Jed York, the principal owner and CEO of the San Francisco 49ers football team, which has won five Super Bowls, tied for second-most in NFL history. York has a unique vantage point as an owner and CEO. His view is that "a board's role is obviously governance—but beyond that, it needs to help guide the CEO and executive team to see things that they might not see when they're in the battle on a daily basis."

Corporate strategy is critical, as it guides the company forward. I think of corporate strategy as a thoughtful, long-term plan to achieve the company's objectives, which are often, in general, to increase market position, revenues, earnings, margins, and cash flow. But strategy can be defined differently depending on the business.

Several years ago, *Vanity Fair* ran a feature piece titled "How Chef Mario Carbone Built the Most Celebrity-Studded Restaurant on Earth."[10] Mario and his cofounders of Major Food Group, Jeff Zalaznick and Rich Torrisi, in a little more than a decade have developed one of the leading hospitality companies, with more than 40 restaurants, private venues, and hotels. Mario told me that, for him, "[strategy] starts with the story—it starts with who we are and why we are important. We set a stage, we craft our story, and we tell that identical story over and over every single night. There's really no ambiguity after having a meal at Carbone: 'I had dinner in a Martin Scorsese set last night and ate a veal parm the size of a hubcap.'"

Management should develop the strategy, but the directors are the representatives of the shareholders empowered to question, challenge, and ultimately approve the strategy. Directors also need to see that, while executing that strategy, the company's senior executives are acting in the shareholders' best interest. In other words, a director is a coach, not a player.

Len Elmore agrees. He was an All-American basketball player at the University of Maryland and played for ten years in the National Basketball Association (NBA). Elmore is also an attorney, having been both a prosecutor and in private practice; he now teaches at Columbia University. He explained that a coach's role is "analogous" to a director's role, and a player's role is "analogous" to an executive's role: "As a coach you don't run the plays. A director is not going to undertake the duties and responsibility of management. However, directors can provide insights and be a sounding board for executives."

"At the board level, you're worried about long-term return on capital," adds Doug Oberhelman, the former chair and CEO of Caterpillar, a Fortune 100 company, and a former board member of Exxon Mobil and a current director of Bombardier. "You're worried about cash flow over time. You're worried about debt levels over time. You're worried about customer satisfaction over time, the very basics at a high level. And those are really the questions you probe on."

At the same time, directors should not go too far. Paula Sneed, a former senior executive at Kraft and a member of numerous boards, including Charles Schwab, shared a similar perspective: "As board members, we are there to add value to the thinking the executives have already done."

Naren Gursahaney, a former CEO and corporate director, having led ADT and ServiceMaster as well as having served as a director of various companies, agrees: "The board's job is oversight, insight, and foresight. You need to have a healthy respect for the line and understand that when it comes time to make decisions, that's what you hired management to do. If you think they do it poorly, then your job is to change management."

For organizations very broadly, governance is critical. For example, Ron Klain has had a distinguished career in both the public and private sectors, including, among other positions, serving as the 30th White House Chief of Staff under President Joe Biden from January 2021 to February 2023 and now as the chief legal officer of Airbnb, the world's largest hospitality company, with a market value of some $100 billion.

Talking about governance in the White House as Chief of Staff, Klain explained, "I'd say you're COO [chief operating officer] of the White House, and in some ways COO of the federal government. The president is the chair of the board and in some ways the entire board himself. What you're trying to do is muster the organization to achieve his or her goals and objectives."

Governance is very important to provide safe, quality care for sick patients too. Initially spurred by a family tragedy, Beth Daley Ullem is a nationally recognized governance expert and patient advocate for safety and quality in health care. She told me, "In health care, your purpose is to care for people in their most vulnerable and sick state. I think that is often lost in the boardroom [of health care organizations], and there's a real opportunity for boards to understand how their oversight can deliver on that promise to patients. Boards have a responsibility to the community to make sure that every patient is safe, every patient gets good care, and every patient is treated with respect."

Mario Carbone believes that governance is imparting a consistent vision throughout any organization: "It's about giving our people all the resources and tools to make sure that they understand who we are and why we're special so that in that moment when I'm not around and someone's making a decision, they're going to understand the guardrails and principles of what we're looking to do."

Of course, not all boards are effective. In the wake of the accounting scandal at Enron that came to light in 2001, Michael H. Sutton, former chief accountant for the SEC, testified in front of a US Senate subcommittee, saying, "We would like to believe that Enron is an anomaly, that the governance issues raised are isolated to this case, but they are not. While Enron has become a poster child for a system out of control, the underlying concerns about the diligence of Boards of Directors and audit committees reach far more broadly into our corporate and capital market culture."[11]

Speaking about the issues facing boards today, Charles Elson, founding director, Weinberg Center for Corporate Governance; retired Woolard

Chair in Corporate Governance, University of Delaware; and a well-known voice on "good governance," told me, "The problem remains that boards are made of human beings, and human beings don't like confrontation in front of people that they know and like. Boards still find it difficult to make those hard decisions from time to time based on that very fundamental human quality." Of course, the goal—and the owners' or shareholders' expectation—is to have committed directors who act with diligence and concern. But people are indeed human, and no one is perfect; this is why the courts do not expect perfection, and their standards are about acting in good faith, employing a reasonable process, and using sound business judgment.

In general, from a legal perspective, we talk about two core duties of a director: the duty of care and the duty of loyalty. Care relates to using reasonable diligence, and loyalty refers to putting the best interests of the company ahead of any other considerations. Scholars have argued that there are not just two duties but perhaps three, adding good faith to the usual two, or even as many as five distinct duties—care, loyalty, objectivity, good faith, and rationality, according to Julian Velasco, professor of law at the University of Notre Dame.[12] I have also heard some attorneys describe disclosure as a duty.

I cannot imagine any director disputing the need for objectivity, good faith, and rationality in the performance of the role, but I believe that it is reasonable to consider these added duties as elements of care and loyalty. Without objectivity and rationality, it is hard to argue you have fulfilled the duty of care, and good faith goes to both care and loyalty. Of course, there are various disclosure requirements for companies, and disclosures by directors are important to determine whether there are any potential conflicts.

There is no rulebook for how a director should fulfill his or her duties. However, there is case law, as well as "best practices" and "custom and practice," for how directors should meet their responsibilities, and key to that is understanding the duties of care and loyalty.

The Duty of Care

The duty of care was well articulated by the Delaware Supreme Court in 1985 in *Smith v. Van Gorkom* (*Van Gorkom*), where shareholders of TransUnion Corporation sought rescission of a merger, arguing that the board's approval was not the product of an informed business judgment.[13]

"The determination of whether a business judgment is an informed one turns on whether the directors have educated themselves 'prior to making a business decision, of all material information reasonably available to them,'" the court stated, in part quoting from a 1971 case.[14] "Fulfillment of the fiduciary function requires more than the mere absence of bad faith or fraud. Representation of the financial interests of others imposes on a director an affirmative duty to protect those interests and to proceed with a critical eye in assessing information."[15]

In practice, this means paying attention. Directors, particularly of large public companies, usually have impressive backgrounds. However, regardless of your résumé, serving on a board is a major responsibility that requires thoughtful work and a significant commitment of time while remembering that you oversee but do not manage. Fulfilling the duty of care means that you carefully read, digest, and question information relevant to a topic and decision, and you do not just skim it on the flight to the meeting. I remember a presentation by a consultant to a distressed company that showed a critically low amount of cash at the holding company where the debt sat. No explanation was provided concerning how much of the subsidiaries' cash could be upstreamed to make debt payments. So I asked.

As Peter McCausland, former chair and CEO of the industrial gas distributor Airgas and a former member of a number of boards, told me, "You have to have the courage to speak up and say, you know, I'm not sure. I'd like to postpone this and not take the next step until we have more information."

Fulfilling the duty of care means staying abreast of the important aspects of the company's business, strategy, financial performance, capital structure, and legal and compliance issues as well as asking questions and continuing to probe until the answers are satisfactory. That is the job. This is why a board exists.

The Duty of Loyalty

The duty of loyalty is about acting in good faith for the benefit of the company and its shareholders, not for oneself. The 1939 Delaware Supreme Court case *Guth v. Loft* laid this out quite clearly.[16] Charles G. Guth was president of Loft, a candy company. While serving in his role at Loft, Guth acquired the formula and trademark for Pepsi-Cola and formed the Pepsi-Cola Corporation. But Guth did not keep the two ventures separate. He used Loft's "money, credit, facilities and personnel in the furtherance of the Pepsi venture" for his own benefit, not to benefit the company—a clear conflict.[17]

As the court wrote, "Corporate officers and directors are not permitted to use their position of trust and confidence to further their private interests. . . . If an officer or director of a corporation, in violation of his duty as such, acquires gain or advantage for himself, the law charges the interest so acquired with a trust for the benefit of the corporation, at its election, while it denies to the betrayer all benefit and profit. . . . [The rule] demands of an officer or director the utmost good faith in his relation to the corporation which he represents."[18]

The duty of loyalty does not require the absolute absence of conflicts of interest. While that was once the case, the law has evolved: "Directors are allowed to engage in interested transactions, provided that the transactions are sanitized by the approval of either fully informed directors or shareholders ex ante, or the courts ex post. If a transaction is sanitized by director or shareholder approval, it usually is found not to involve a conflict of interest and is reviewed under the business judgment rule."[19]

In practice, satisfying the duty of loyalty involves asking yourself a simple question and answering it honestly: Am I looking out for the best interests of the company and its shareholders? Directors must make sure that they do not have any disqualifying conflicts, are not doing anything that is self-serving or could be construed as self-serving, and are completely focused on making a decision for the benefit of the organization and its constituencies. And directors must consider whether circumstances change such that while they were not previously conflicted, they might be at a later time.

According to Daniel Slifkin of Cravath,

> A true conflict is when you can't exercise your independent judgment, that you feel in some way torn between two positions—whether you're going to just do what the CEO wants because he's your friend as opposed to doing what's right by the company, for instance. But optics are important here too. They're important to the court. Just because you're friendly with the CEO shouldn't be a conflict. But you need to be very open about what relationships you have, and it's always best to be open and allow shareholders to vote if something could be seen as a significant conflict.

"It's common sense that if a director has a conflict, and they know when they do, that they alert other directors to that fact so that at least people are put on notice to deal with a problem," adds Andre Bouchard, a partner in the litigation department at the law firm Paul, Weiss and the former chancellor of the Delaware Court of Chancery who presided over a number of high-profile disputes when he led the court from 2014 to 2021.

Leo E. Strine Jr. was the chief justice of the Delaware Supreme Court from 2014 to 2019 as well as Bouchard's predecessor as chancellor of the Delaware Court of Chancery, and he is now of counsel at Wachtell Lipton. He adds, "Identifying potential conflicts is an exercise in self-awareness and sometimes an uncomfortable one. But it's when you don't identify conflicts and don't figure out ways to address them that alleviate the concern that you get into trouble. That's why I always say that the first 24 to 96 hours of, say, a deal process usually generates over half the litigation risk."

Delaware courts have affirmed that while directors may be indemnified for violations of the duty of care, indemnification cannot be extended to acts of bad faith such as violations of the duty of loyalty.[20] The logic, according to a 1988 law review article by Deborah A. DeMott of Duke Law School, is that while, on the one hand, if not for some level of indemnification, directors "run the risk of liability for damages greatly in excess of the economic benefits they receive from serving the corporation,"[21] on the other hand, indemnifying directors when they fail to act in good faith goes a step too far. Directors can, of course, also be officers of the company. It is becoming standard in Delaware for companies to indemnify officers for duty of care violations too.

Andy Rossman is managing partner of the law firm Quinn Emanuel's New York office and chair of the firm's M&A litigation practice. Quinn Emanuel is the largest law firm dedicated solely to business litigation and arbitration. Rossman told me, "I have very few instances where directors are actually personally liable from their own pockets as opposed to being protected by indemnity and insurance. Though the way you mitigate the risk is to be actively involved—and have evidence of it. Hire the experts that you need to hire to get the advice that you need, both legal and financial, and make sure that the board minutes reflect it. I think too frequently the inclination is to have the minutes be very bare bones. Courts like to see directors actually show their work."

In fact, there are no requirements concerning how board minutes should be prepared or what content must be included. I have found that different general counsels and outside attorneys have varying perspectives on how detailed they should be. But what Rossman says is consistent with my view. I believe that board minutes should be detailed enough to explain what was covered and to be useful in litigation. They should reflect the substance of the various topics discussed and note the significant questions and answers. The presentations provided should be included in an appendix. Any follow-up issues that the board asks management to address should be noted, and, of course, the additional information requested should be considered at a future meeting with later board meeting minutes reflecting that.

The Delaware Courts

The rulings I cited in explaining the two core duties of care and loyalty—and of course the *Smurfit-Stone* and *Boeing* opinions—all come, as do Chancellor Bouchard and Chief Justice Strine, from the Delaware court system, which plays a critical role in establishing the expectations for director behavior and deserves a closer look. Delaware is the legal home for so many corporations—more than 70 percent of the Fortune 500,[22] nearly 80 percent of the companies that completed IPOs in 2022, and more than one million companies in all.[23]

Delaware's Court of Chancery—a separate court for corporation law, with judges rather than juries and with written opinions to explain its rulings—dates back to 1792, and while the reason for its initial creation has been lost to history, the effect has been to create a virtuous cycle pushing more and more companies to incorporate in Delaware.[24] The well-developed case law, in combination with a flexible set of statutory provisions that make doing business easier and friendlier than in most other jurisdictions, generally means that the rules are clear, judges are informed, and businesses can act with substantial predictability to limit risk.

Lewis S. Black is the author of a 2007 pamphlet for the Delaware Department of State titled *Why Corporations Choose Delaware*. In it, he writes, "Most Delaware corporations never find themselves involved in lawsuits in the Court of Chancery. On the other hand, one experienced general counsel I know takes a practical approach. He told me that, if his corporation is going to be sued anyway, he would far prefer to litigate in the Court of Chancery where he is assured a level playing field and a knowledgeable judge."[25]

William T. Allen was the chancellor of the Court of Chancery from 1985 to 1997. Allen, who died in 2019, wrote influential opinions setting the standards for director responsibility in mergers, hostile takeovers, and many other situations.[26] Known as the jurist who "saved corporate law" according to an article written shortly after his death, Allen authored many of the cases that appear in this book, including *In re Caremark Derivative Litigation* (*Caremark*), *Unocal v. Mesa Petroleum* (*Unocal*), and *Revlon*.[27] Allen is credited by former justice of the Delaware Supreme Court Jack B. Jacobs as making the Delaware courts the "national institutional expositor of corporate law . . . inform[ing] a multitude of constituencies—including the legal academy, the corporate bar and their board clients, and his fellow jurists—of the true import and continued relevance and application of ancient principles of equity."[28]

The case for Delaware was articulated in depth in a 2000 law review article by Jill E. Fisch of the University of Pennsylvania Law School. Delaware business law is not substantively better or different than other states, she argues—"state corporation statutes contain relatively little substantive variation . . . [and] corporate codes tend toward uniformity"—but the distinction in Delaware is how agile the Court of Chancery and its judges are as business and related issues evolve and change.[29]

"Delaware courts anticipate the effect of business developments and try to develop responsive legal principles," she insists.[30] As the world changes, business needs change quickly, and having a court system able to navigate changes promptly is a huge benefit.

For all of these reasons, Delaware usually continues to be the default site of incorporation and corporate dispute management. "Certainly, folks in my generation have benefited from our Delaware forefathers who laid the groundwork for having a business-friendly environment attracting corporations to come to the state," says Mike Allen (no relation to William T. Allen), director (partner) at Richards Layton & Finger, the largest Delaware law firm. "They set up the Court of Chancery with the assurance that you're going to get expert judges, you're not going to be subject to a jury trial, and you'll get predictable results that transactional folks can plan around. Coupled with the wealth of case law that has developed over the last 50 years, I think that's really what makes Delaware special."

"Some of the other advantages are structural," Allen continues. "The pace at which the Secretary of State's office can turn around filings, a lot of the mechanical things that become very important if you're trying to do a closing, the nimbleness of the Delaware Secretary of State to assist, all of those are helpful. And the folks in Delaware recognize how important the business franchise is to the state, so there is, not surprisingly, a real focus by members of the bar to constantly improve and refine our statutory regimes to address issues that come up in terms of practice."

Daniel Slifkin of Cravath agrees. "Delaware has extremely fine systems for resolving disputes. I just came off an emergency dispute," he told me. "The court said, 'I'm going to give you a trial within three months,' and they did. There are systems in place in Delaware among the judges, among the lawyers, among the people who practice there, whether Delaware counsel or not, to get things done in a very rapid manner against a backdrop of a very established law. Other jurisdictions don't have that."

Allen walked me through an example where a few of his clients over the years had been public companies that needed to do reverse stock splits in order to keep their share prices high enough not to be delisted from a stock exchange. "That sort of a reverse split is a neutral transaction," he explained, or one where value does not change—the outstanding shares are reduced, and the stock price adjusts higher. For example, if a company has a $1 stock price and 100 shares and the shares are reverse split or reduced to 10 shares, the stock price at that moment should go to $10. "But under the Delaware statute, as with most amendments to the certificate of incorporation, the vote of a majority of the outstanding shares was required." The problem was that many retail investors usually did not vote, so a quorum, and a majority vote, was very difficult to accomplish. Delaware recognized this was a problem and amended the statute to require 51 percent of the votes cast rather than 51 percent of the outstanding shares. "It's a great example of something Delaware could tackle and quickly get to what I think is a good and fair result," Allen explained.

All of this said, there have been recent challenges to Delaware's primacy. Increasing concerns have been expressed that some recent opinions from the Delaware courts, particularly for controlled companies such as Tesla in the Elon Musk compensation case (described in chapter 4) and those involving, among others, the investment bank Moelis as well as TripAdvisor and Match.com, have changed the so-called controller law that has been in place for several generations. This has, to some extent, undermined confidence in the consistency of the Delaware courts and the practicality of Delaware as a good home for corporations.

In a 2024 case involving the dating website Match.com, the Delaware Supreme Court continued to show concern about controlling stockholders, ruling that the entire fairness standard should be applied in a wider range of deals involving controlled companies.[31] While this may be friendly to minority investors, it also inspired concern from entrepreneurs who have substantial stakes in some publicly traded companies registered in Delaware.

Also in 2024, Vice Chancellor J. Travis Laster issued an opinion in *West Palm Beach Firefighters' Pension Fund v. Moelis & Co.* (*Moelis*) finding that a stockholder agreement giving the founder, chair, and CEO of Moelis, Ken Moelis, substantial governance rights, including influence over director nominations, violated Delaware law. Though these provisions are quite common and would have been valid if part of the company's certificate of incorporation, Vice Chancellor Laster deemed them invalid under Delaware law. This was understood to give shareholders an enhanced opportunity to challenge provisions that grant particular investors special rights.[32]

As Chief Justice Strine told me, "I don't expect you're going to have existing companies leave over this, but a lot of the most innovative companies start as controlled companies, so I think it is a serious issue."

In response, in July 2024, Delaware governor John Carney signed into law a series of amendments that effectively overturned *Moelis*, providing that companies have the authority to enter into these types of shareholder agreements without having to amend their charters or articles of incorporation.[33] Many board members and executives had been disappointed in the *Moelis* ruling, as it called into question the enforceability of stockholder agreements that were in place. Now stockholder agreements approved by boards are generally enforceable as long as they do not violate a company's charter.[34]

However, some have criticized these amendments, arguing that they were rushed, went beyond merely overturning *Moelis*, and permit boards to contract away key responsibilities without shareholder input or support.[35] Importantly, in 2025, statutory amendments were signed into law by Governor Matt Meyer that provide safe harbor from liability for conflict-of-interest transactions, including with controlling stockholders, with approval by independent directors or disinterested stockholders. Further, the amendments narrow the scope of what books and records are subject to inspection by stockholders.[36]

For its part, Nevada has passed business-friendly legislation designed to attract corporations with broad protections for officers and directors.[37] Shareholders of TripAdvisor voted to reincorporate in Nevada, though 56 percent of the vote was controlled by the company's chair and CEO. While TripAdvisor argues otherwise,[38] this move has been challenged in court as a self-interested transaction that may end up with the controlling shareholder owing monetary damages to the minority shareholders due to the differences in rights between the legal regimes in the two states.[39] However, in February 2025 the Delaware Supreme Court reversed the Court of Chancery and, in a 5–0 opinion, ruled that the business judgment standard, not the more onerous entire fairness standard, applies when evaluating potential breaches of fiduciary duty claims regarding a company's reincorporation in another state.[40]

Elon Musk moved the incorporation of his privately held company SpaceX to Texas in early 2024, bitter after losing in a Delaware Court of Chancery dispute over his compensation package at Tesla.[41] "If your company is still incorporated in Delaware," he wrote, "I recommend moving to another state as soon as possible."[42]

There are indeed significant differences between Delaware law and, for instance, Nevada law. Nevada, unlike Delaware, does not declare that maximizing shareholder value is the standard. Nevada statutes also do not preclude corporations from limiting director liability for breaches of the duty of loyalty in cases where directors derive personal benefits, and unlike in Delaware, there is no heightened standard beyond business judgment to evaluate change-of-control situations.[43] Nevada also permits jury trials in corporate law cases.[44]

Despite some visible but limited criticisms, with Delaware's established judicial system and predictability, Delaware generally remains the forum of choice for corporations today. "I don't think that you're going to be in a better place in other jurisdictions where there's a lot of uncertainty," says Allen. "They don't have the body of case law. In some cases, you might get a jury trial or be in front of a judge who's never seen a corporate case before. I think that Delaware is still the best place to be."

Rossman agrees:

> I think Delaware is important, and that will continue. I think it's an interesting time for Delaware because there's been perhaps more focus than ever on the power and decision-making of that court, and it has come under scrutiny in some high-profile cases, but what makes Delaware if not unique then at least special is you've got a super high-quality judiciary in terms of their acumen, their level of attention, their speed of important business decisions, and you've got an extremely well-developed body of law. It should be the most predictable, because it has had the occasion to have very lengthy opinions about very important topics that come up again and again and again.

While Nevada and Texas are often mentioned as potential states in which to incorporate, "Maryland has a good judiciary," Chief Justice Strine told me. "People are talking about New York. I have historical confidence in my state and that it will continue to display one of its key historical strengths: listening to its constituents."

It should be noted that a 2024 report by Trivariate Research found that the state of incorporation "tells investors nothing about a company's future stock returns," with no difference in the average beta-adjusted performance of stocks for companies incorporated in one state that switch to another.[45] The firm's CEO and founder Adam Parker was previously the director of Global Quantitative Research at Morgan Stanley.

There are significant differences in corporate law in states such as Delaware and Nevada that could very well change corporate behavior—quite possibly for the worse when it comes to shareholder interests. "I don't want to isolate a single jurisdiction," notes Chancellor Bouchard, "but the notion that institutions—sophisticated shareholders—are going to want to be in a jurisdiction where there are not some legitimate boundaries, especially loyalty-based boundaries, is hard to imagine. There's no corporate law if there's not a duty of loyalty."

Standards for Decisions

Courts most often use the business judgment rule to evaluate board decisions. In general, this shields directors from personal liability when they have acted in good faith—even when their decisions prove unsound or incorrect when examined after the fact.[46] The justification for this rule is straightforward. It would be beyond challenging for a court to determine whether directors made the "correct" or "optimal" business decision.[47] Putting directors at risk of being second-guessed would punish risk-taking, stifle technological advancement, and cripple the kind of business activity that has the potential to generate attractive shareholder returns.[48] The system has therefore evolved to look at process, not outcome, at least in the absence of gross negligence.[49]

Slifkin explains, "Business judgment essentially means the directors will be given space by the law to make mistakes. You can do what you think is best for the company and not be concerned that if you make a mistake and it doesn't quite go that well, then you'll get sued [and be found liable]." Rossman adds, "Highly qualified directors and management are in a better position to evaluate that than the judge. That's the idea."

It is helpful to look at a few recent circumstances where the business judgment rule has been violated and the directors' duties have been found to have been breached. *Marchand v. Barnhill* is a 2019 Delaware case in which directors of Blue Bell Creameries were sued for breaches of their duties of care and loyalty in allegedly failing to forestall a listeria outbreak in which three people died.[50] The complaint in the case argued that despite years of compliance failures at the company's facilities and a growing number of positive tests for listeria, "Blue Bell's board had no committee overseeing food safety, no full board-level process to address food safety issues, and no protocol by which the board was expected to be advised of food safety reports and developments."[51]

Indeed, as the situation worsened, "instead of holding more frequent emergency board meetings to receive constant updates on the troubling fact that life-threatening bacteria was found in its products, Blue Bell's board left the company's response to management."[52]

The Delaware Supreme Court—overturning a Court of Chancery decision—found that the good faith standard of the business judgment rule was not met, given that "no reasonable compliance system and protocols were established as to the obviously most central consumer safety and legal compliance issue facing the company . . . resulting in the death and injury of company customers."[53]

The decision in the Blue Bell case emerged from a previous case, the 1996 Court of Chancery decision in *Caremark*,[54] where the court found that holding directors liable for failing to oversee a corporation requires that "(a) the directors utterly failed to implement any reporting or information system or controls; or (b) having implemented such a system or controls, consciously failed to monitor or oversee its operations thus disabling themselves from being informed of risks or problems requiring their attention."[55]

The Court of Chancery's ruling in the Blue Bell case found that the reporting system in place satisfied this standard—ruling that because there was some semblance of a monitoring system in place, the board could not be held liable—but the Delaware Supreme Court demanded more. "We are not examining the effectiveness of a board-level compliance and reporting system after the fact," the court ruled. "Rather, we are focusing on whether the complaint pleads facts supporting a reasonable inference that the board did not undertake good faith efforts to put a board-level system of monitoring and reporting in place."[56] The Supreme Court found that the particular facts here showed that the Blue Bell board did not undertake the effort required by *Caremark* and that even though the threshold for board liability is high, the board fell short: "If *Caremark* means anything, it is that a corporate board must make a good faith effort to exercise its duty of care. A failure to make that effort constitutes a breach of the duty of loyalty."[57]

Another informative example is the *Boeing* case mentioned at the start of this chapter. In the wake of airplane crashes in 2018 and 2019 killing everyone on board, shareholders sued the Boeing directors, alleging "complete failure to establish a reporting system for airplane safety . . . [and] turning a blind eye to a red flag representing airplane safety problems."[58]

At Boeing, no board committee was tasked with overseeing airplane safety. Also, its audit committee—which had risk under its purview—did not specifically address safety as a risk, as it addressed just risks of a directly financial nature. Safety was not a regular board agenda item or included in board reports. Even as the *New York Times* and the *Wall Street Journal* reported safety lapses, the board paid little attention and did not investigate. Drawing heavily on the Blue Bell case, the Court of Chancery found that "directors knew the board should have had structures in place to receive and consider safety information" and allowed the case to go forward.[59] Ultimately, the Boeing directors agreed to a $237.5 million settlement—which was paid by the D&O liability insurance.[60] The current and former directors did not admit to any wrongdoing in the settlement.[61]

"Any of these companies that got themselves into oversight issues generally had bad boards," explains Charles Elson. "But when you have a scandal and the board is replaced, you often get a decent board. The problem is when you have a scandal, and the board isn't replaced. That's when you have real issues." The Boeing board, according to governance expert Nell Minow, quoted in the *Los Angeles Times*, "took no action after the first crash [in 2018]."[62] Boeing's board has now turned over more than 50 percent of its directors since its initial tragic safety failures and crash, but this has been seen by many as too little, too late.[63]

Boeing did replace its CEO after the 2018–19 events, though it was with the board's chair at the time, Dave Calhoun. As will be discussed later, he ended up stepping down as CEO in 2024 after another series of challenges at the company, replaced later in the year by Kelly Ortberg, an external hire with deep experience in the aerospace industry.[64]

The business judgment rule is not always the relevant standard. There are, in some cases, more onerous standards that are required. In the M&A context, we will examine the *Revlon* standard in chapter 6, under which, in circumstances where a decision has been made to sell the company and the selling shareholders have no meaningful, ongoing interest in a newly combined company, the board must make a reasonable effort to obtain the highest immediate value—as opposed to the ability to consider long-term value under the business judgment rule.

Also, in the case of a "controlling or dominating shareholder standing on both sides of a transaction"—a conflict, as discussed under the duty of loyalty—courts will apply the entire fairness test, which is a much more involved test than the business judgment rule.[65] Entire fairness involves process and price. As the Delaware Court of Chancery explained in *Weinberger v. UOP* (*Weinberger*), regarding a transaction between a parent company and its subsidiary, "When directors of a Delaware corporation are on both sides of a transaction, they are required to demonstrate their utmost good faith and the most scrupulous inherent fairness of the bargain."[66]

"The concept of fairness," the court goes on to explain, "has two basic aspects: fair dealing and fair price. . . . All aspects of the issue must be examined as a whole since the question is one of entire fairness."[67] I refer to the requirements as "process and price."

This is a fact-based inquiry that goes well beyond the business judgment rule. Usually, when there is an apparent conflict, it is dealt with through an independent special committee and/or shareholder approval. This will generally allow the standard to remain the business judgment rule. If entire fairness applies, both the process by which the board approved the decision and the price that was obtained must be deemed fair. This can be difficult to show, so efforts are typically made to see that the business judgment standard, not entire fairness, applies.

Slifkin explains, "Entire fairness is a circumstance where you really have to be concerned that everything you do is going to be scrutinized by the court. Entire fairness is really difficult to work with, but it shouldn't be impossible to win because otherwise it has a chilling effect. I do think there's a big space for business judgment. Otherwise, you may be too risk averse. If you're in a situation of entire fairness, you may not take appropriate risks. The people who take risks fuel the economy. Businesses spin their wheels unless they're prepared to take risks."

I was an expert witness for Larry Ellison and a co-CEO who was another director of Oracle in a 2022 case in the Delaware Court of Chancery that helps illustrate the line between business judgment and entire fairness. In *In re Oracle Corporation Derivative Litigation*, certain shareholders of Oracle, one of the largest computer software companies in the world, alleged that the company, in which founder Ellison owned approximately 28 percent of the stock, overpaid in its acquisition of NetSuite, in which Ellison owned approximately 39 percent of the stock.[68] "Ellison, a corporate fiduciary," wrote the court, "withdrew from Oracle's consideration of the NetSuite acquisition just before the initial presentation to the Oracle board, and . . . the remaining directors empowered a special committee to conduct the negotiation of any acquisition of NetSuite. This is adequate to cleanse Ellison's conflict as a director and officer standing on both sides of the transaction."[69]

Had Ellison been found to be a "controller" of the company—exercising sufficient power such that the remaining directors were coerced beyond their ability to exercise their business judgment—the transaction would have been analyzed under the entire fairness standard. Here, Ellison "did not have hard control of Oracle. He did not exercise control generally in regard to Oracle's operations. He did not attempt to assert control in the transaction by which Oracle acquired NetSuite, and as a director and officer abstained from participation in the transaction. He was . . . a holder of potential control over a transaction in which he was interested. . . . [But] Ellison was not a controller," the court determined, "and business judgment applies."[70] The court found for Ellison and the other director on all allegations.

This ruling highlights the importance of keeping potentially conflicted parties uninvolved in transactions and forming independent special committees in conflict situations.

Being a Director, in Practice
A Good-Faith Effort
The reality is that there are neither comprehensive legal requirements nor a uniformly agreed-upon approach for what a director must do beyond the duties of care and loyalty and various standards explained earlier. Fundamentally, the core of the role is to act in good faith. Often, acting in good faith means recognizing our own limitations. There is no expectation that directors have to act alone. On the contrary, it is entirely appropriate—and good practice—for directors to rely on information provided by management as long as it seems reasonable and is carefully reviewed. In addition, it is well accepted that directors can use outside advisors on whom the directors reasonably believe they can rely, such as investment bankers, lawyers, accountants, and others. For example, in the potential sale of a company, it is customary, and very often the case, that directors rely on an investment

bank for valuation work and guidance. Board members do not need to have all the necessary skills for a given decision to act appropriately, but they must be able to identify the needs, hire experts for help, and carefully consider the decisions to be made.

Seeking and using outside advice must be done thoughtfully and in good faith. To blindly accept the advice of advisors could be just as dangerous as failing to seek the advice. As Slifkin notes, "A director can't just rely upon the reputation of whatever institution it is. They should ask questions, tough questions—What work do you do for the company? What work have you done for this CEO? How are you going to be compensated for this?"

Ron Lumbra, a partner at the executive search firm Heidrick & Struggles, told me, "The very best directors bring wisdom, judgment, and first-class decision-making. Underneath that, in many cases, there's subject matter expertise, but when you really look at directors who help, it's sound decision-making, not necessarily the subject expertise."

I have seen situations where there is a perceived skills gap on the board or an opening for a new director, and the CEO or an outside director insists that a board needs an expert in a particular area where the company has challenges. In today's world, that sometimes means there is a push to find a cybersecurity expert. This may well be valuable, but going back to the analogy that directors are coaches, not players, it is most important to have that cybersecurity expert on the management team. After all, if you have great cybersecurity coaches but no high-quality cybersecurity players, you will do terribly on the field. In addition, if individuals are no longer active day-to-day in a particular field, expertise can diminish rapidly.

Effective board members may well have particular value to add in a given area, but they should be able to participate thoughtfully in discussions and be well informed to vote on a wide range of issues. Directors should be literate, not necessarily experts, in many areas, such as the industry, financial statements, supply chains, information technology, cybersecurity, and major legal issues. I would add that sometimes an industry expert can fracture the board by having detailed conversations with the executive who heads that area, and you can sense the other directors tuning out. It is important to keep the discussions at a level where the entire board is able to engage. Of course, all directors have the same obligations and legal liability.

Agendas, Questions, and Meetings

Another element of an effective board is driving a value-added agenda. As the Blue Bell case and *Boeing* sadly illustrate, important business issues do not always make it to the agenda, and if management is not bringing up topics that the board believes should be addressed, it is incumbent on a board to insist that they are surfaced and thoroughly discussed. The chair or lead independent director—I will talk more in chapter 5 about board leadership—should set the agenda with the CEO. However, any director should suggest any topic that he or she believes should be discussed.

"It was hard for me to keep my mouth shut when I saw certain things," Admiral Mullen told me, "having been a CEO equivalent or being in command. I learned over time to not say 'this is how it ought to be done' and instead ask questions: 'What do you think about this?' or 'How are you approaching this particular issue?'"

An informed, committed board knows what the major risks to the company are, and most boards oversee a thoughtful, dynamic risk evaluation and mitigation process, whether through a risk committee, an audit committee, full board reporting, or other mechanisms. It is not the board's responsibility to manage risks, but it is absolutely its responsibility to oversee the management of risks.

There are also no rules as to what must or even should happen in or between board meetings. Not surprisingly, expectations can differ widely among CEOs, broader management teams, and individual directors. A board typically has four or five meetings per year. It has traditionally been four, but a fifth meeting—without the pressure of near-term business concerns, quarterly earnings, estimated annual results, the ever-growing compliance burden, and ESG issues—can help the board tackle larger, longer-term, more strategic issues such as a long-range plan.

A typical quarterly meeting lasts the better part of two days—often committee meetings the first day, starting perhaps just after an optional directors' lunch with management, followed by dinner, which might include an outside speaker (such as an industry consultant, analyst, or banker); a detailed board meeting the next day, with an executive session or time with just the directors; and time for just the independent or nonmanagement directors to meet, all wrapping up in the midafternoon.

A strategic planning meeting is usually a bit different. It could include detailed presentations by each business unit leader, a company SWOT (strengths/weaknesses/opportunities/threats) analysis, and a comprehensive long-term business plan. "There should be a regular drum beat of strategy," Admiral Mullen told me, "a place in the governing structure each year to set a strategy. I think it is such a foundational part of a good organizational construct. And you have to keep updating it. You don't necessarily get your strategy right the first time. The world changes, or life changes, so you update it. But you do need to have it in the first place."

"I don't know that the board is responsible for developing the strategy," adds Gursahaney, "but certainly our job as directors is to critique and stress-test the strategy, to make sure that the strategy is sound, well grounded, and data driven."

No matter the type of meeting, a prepared, thoughtful board will have digested the materials before the session starts, ask thoughtful questions, and challenge assumptions. At the end of the meeting, there should be an endorsement of any key decisions proposed or—also a good outcome—an agreement to have another meeting to address various questions and perhaps analyze other scenarios before the board signs off on the topic(s) at issue.

Finding Sufficient Time
With the growing challenges that all companies face—from global competitiveness, to increased risks, to an ever-growing compliance burden, to greater demands by a range of constituencies from employees to environmental activists—there almost always ends up being a need for more meeting time. Meetings need to provide the opportunity to discuss strategy and how to effectively tell the company's story to the public markets as well as time for longer executive sessions, first with any management directors and then with just the nonmanagement directors.

One quirk that I find in a typical two-day board meeting is that the agenda often wraps up in the early afternoon on the second day. The directors usually have, and certainly should have, committed the entire day to the meeting, so I would prefer to see the usual schedule go through the late afternoon.

Chief Justice Strine argues that we could be using directors' time more effectively. "Right now we just add more and more. We never get rid of anything," he told me.

> We never restructure anything. I'm not sure it's as effective as it can be, because no one steps back and asks if we could do this differently.

For example, I think the independent directors especially should spend more time with each other and actually shape meeting agendas. I think that they should in fact be meeting at the beginning of the board meeting [not just at the end, which is more typical]. Also, with things such as Zoom, we can do things better. Independent directors can meet in advance and get some checklist items done electronically so when they come in, they're as useful and informed as possible.

Director and Management Interactions

Beyond board meetings, there is typically contact between directors and the CEO, if not with other senior executives as well. I have been on boards where CEOs will proactively reach out to each director periodically to discuss key issues or brainstorm new ideas, particularly in areas where certain directors have valuable experience.

Some directors believe they should not talk to a member of the management without asking the CEO first. I have never heard a high-quality CEO expect this "preapproval." While the entire senior team typically reports to the CEO, the board, which is charged by the shareholders with overseeing management, cannot possibly do its job well without access to the senior team and a good relationship with these leaders. I always discuss with the CEO any concerns, key learnings, or new ideas that have emerged from conversations with the team.

As a director, I want to add value where I can but not waste anyone's time. You may think that you are the smartest person in the room. You may or may not be. But you cannot be an effective director if you are unable to gain a consensus with your peers on the path forward that you advocate. You need to preserve your capital so that you can have influence when it matters and hopefully move the group to your way of thinking.

University of Pennsylvania Wharton School professor and author Adam Grant writes about disagreeing productively—expressing interest and asking questions.[71] Specifically, he argues that debating ideas with respect is the way to achieve productive results and that conflict is not necessarily a bad thing as long as it does not get personal.[72]

In my view, it is good for directors to have different perspectives and different opinions. If all directors had the same view, the board would add much less value; there would even be an argument that there would be no reason to have a board. It is just important to keep in mind that an effective director does not need to talk too much, ask questions that have already been answered in written materials, dive into details of day-to-day operations rather than strategic issues, or be particularly opinionated.

Klain explains that the relationship between management and the board is critical: "The board's going to meet for a day or two each quarter, and then they're gone, so the question is how management reacts to the board's direction. Some places there's very dynamic interaction that makes the board very effective. If you don't have a good dynamic between the board and management, the board's never going to be that effective because there's nothing they can do to be ever-present."

Ken Freeman is a very successful leader who, among other roles, is the former CEO of Quest Diagnostics, a former partner at the leading global investment firm KKR, and the former interim president of Boston University after he was the dean of the business school; he remains dean emeritus and a business school professor there. I vividly remember a board dinner over a decade ago where Freeman, the chair, feeling that too many directors were making too many comments that were extending board conversations into far too many details and taking us off track, asked the independent directors (all but the CEO) to stay behind after the dinner. He said, quite simply, "I just want to remind you that you don't have to say something to show everyone how smart you are. See you tomorrow." That was and is terrific advice.

I always say what I think when I believe it is additive. But it is not a bad thing to make just a few thoughtful comments over the entirety of a board meeting rather than a few too many.

Chapter 4
The Three Major Board Committees

The existence of board committees dates back to the 1940s, when, following a scandal at McKesson & Robbins, a leading pharmaceuticals company, the SEC began to recommend that every board have an audit committee.[1] In 1938, one of McKesson & Robbins's creditors noticed some oddities in the company's books and questioned the value—or even the existence—of the company's inventories. The SEC investigated and discovered that the company's president, Philip Coster, was a convicted felon using a fake name and that the company's foreign operation was a sham, funneling almost $3 million over 12 years to Coster and his three brothers (also working at the company under false names), concealed with a variety of forged invoices and contracts as well as made-up memoranda to support these falsifications.[2]

The company's auditor, Price Waterhouse and Company (now PwC), insisted it had followed professional standards in relying on the documents provided. The SEC came to the same conclusion—which made it quite obvious that the existing standards were nowhere near sufficient. After all, in this case, $9 million in fictitious receivables and $10 million in fictitious inventories—some 20 percent of the $87 million of assets on the company's balance sheet—had been hidden and not found in over a decade of audits. The SEC issued a report recommending far more rigorous auditing, and the modern-day audit committee began.[3]

From there, committees have grown in importance, and their workloads have increased dramatically, particularly in the wake of the financial scandals at Enron and WorldCom in the early 2000s. These debacles led to the passage of the Sarbanes-Oxley Act (Sarbanes-Oxley), which sharpened the rules for audit committees and added other requirements. Then the global financial crisis or Great Recession in 2007–9 led to the passage of the Dodd-Frank Wall Street Reform and Consumer Protection Act (Dodd-Frank), which created, among other things, increased requirements for compensation committees. The NYSE now requires its companies to have an audit committee, a compensation committee, and a nominating and governance committee, each composed of independent directors. NASDAQ requirements are similar but allow for situations where there is not a separate nominating and governance committee—although this rarely is the case.[4]

However, even without the regulatory requirements, committees are a logical and effective way for boards to operate efficiently, give directors the opportunity to engage where their skills and interests are most relevant, and help boards make well-considered, timely decisions. While committee chairs report regularly to the entire board regarding their committees' work and the entire board must vote to approve most major decisions, committees are where much of the detailed board work happens.

I should take a moment here to discuss the definition of "independence" for a director, since it is important to note that the audit and compensation committees must be composed entirely of independent directors under NYSE rules, and a special committee must have directors who are all independent of the conflicted person or issue that drove the establishment of the committee.

Under NYSE rules, an independent director is "affirmatively determined" by the board to have no "material relationship" with the company, either directly or through another organization that has a corporate relationship. There are bright-line disqualification rules, including if the director is (or has been in the past three years) an employee of the company; if an immediate family member is an executive officer; if the director or immediate family member has received more than $120,000 from the company during any 12-month period within the last three years, not including director fees, pension payments, and deferred compensation for prior service; or if the director or an immediate family member is a partner or employee of the company's auditor or works on the company's audit.[5] There are somewhat more stringent independence rules for members of the audit and compensation committees.

I will discuss the three required committees in this chapter, but it should also be noted that boards may and often do have additional committees, permanent and temporary, tailored to the needs of the company and particular circumstances. Indeed, an estimated 75 percent of S&P 500 company boards have at least one committee beyond the three core committees, including finance, risk, compliance, technology, sustainability, public policy, science, and other committees.[6]

Nearly one-third of S&P 500 companies have an executive committee that usually includes the CEO and a few board members and generally meets more often than the entire board to provide timely input on a range of issues and decisions.[7] In addition, and as discussed, special committees may be formed to address conflict transactions, and transaction committees may be formed to react in a timely manner to a pending major deal.

I have served as a member, and also as chair, of the three core committees and as a member of various other committees. I cannot imagine that a significant public company board could function well without effective committees. From an audit committee that reviews financial statements and approves quarterly and annual SEC filings, to a compensation committee that leads the determination of compensation for the CEO and other senior executives, to the nominating and governance committee that leads the effort to nominate directors for election by the shareholders, these committees do much of the critical if sometimes mechanical work necessary for a well-functioning board and a well-governed company.

Audit Committee

The primary responsibilities of the audit committee are to oversee the company's internal controls, financial statements, internal and external (or independent) audit functions, and often other accounting, finance, capital structure, compliance, and risk topics. Following the McKesson & Robbins scandal, audit committees became more and more standard for public companies. In 1972, the SEC "endorsed" the establishment of independent audit committees.[8] In 1974, the SEC required any company with an audit committee to reveal the names of its members.[9] And in 1978, the NYSE made audit committees a requirement for its listed companies.[10]

In 2002, Sarbanes-Oxley was passed in the wake of the financial scandals at Enron, which became the largest bankruptcy in US history in 2001, and WorldCom, whose bankruptcy quickly eclipsed Enron's in 2002.[11] Sarbanes-Oxley established standards regarding auditor independence, created requirements for executive officers to remove themselves from the auditing process, mandated an annual report from management regarding the effectiveness of the internal financial controls of the corporation, required that CEOs and CFOs certify the accuracy of the company's financial statements, increased criminal penalties for financial crimes, and created a new entity—the Public Company Accounting Oversight Board (PCAOB)—to oversee accounting firms under the authority of the SEC.[12]

Sarbanes-Oxley also tightened the requirements for audit committees, requiring that listed companies have them and, as mentioned earlier, mandating that each member be independent—and for members of this committee not to accept any consulting, advisory, or other fees from the company. This law also provides that the independent auditing firm reports to the audit committee. It added a requirement that at least one member of the audit committee be a "financial expert," as defined by the statute.[13] In addition, all members of the audit committee must be financially literate, as determined by the board, or must become financially literate within a reasonable period of time after their appointment, according to NYSE rules.[14]

The Sarbanes-Oxley definition of "financial expert" is rather general, requiring a person to have "thorough education and experience as a public accountant or auditor or a principal financial officer, comptroller, or principal accounting officer of an issuer, or from a position involving the performance of similar functions," an understanding of generally accepted accounting principles and financial statements, experience in the preparation or auditing of financial statements (or experience actively overseeing those engaged in such activities), familiarity with internal accounting controls, and an understanding of audit committee functions.[15] Potential audit committee members complete a questionnaire prepared by management, often with assistance from an outside law firm, as to whether they have the required skills and experience; there is no test or other inquiry.

Often, the membership of the audit committee is made up of individuals with backgrounds in accounting or finance, such as active or former CFOs and accountants. I have also seen effective audit committee members with other backgrounds such as operating executives comfortable with controls, accounting, and financial statements as well as treasurers and investment bankers. As with other committees, the chair typically has the most active role. As of 2021, data from Spencer Stuart showed that 62 percent of audit committee chairs had a financial background, whether as a CFO, another corporate finance executive, an accountant, or a banker.[16] To my surprise, just 26 percent of directors overall were considered to qualify as financial experts.[17]

Admiral Mike Mullen has served on audit committees and highlighted their critical importance: "You want to find out what's going on in the company? It's all coming through there. And you want to find out where the problems are? They're all coming through there too."

It is unquestioned that Sarbanes-Oxley has had an enormous impact on corporate governance. Writing for the Harvard Law School Forum on Corporate Governance in 2022 and reflecting on Sarbanes-Oxley after 20 years, Michael W. Peregrine, partner at the law firm McDermott Will & Emery, and Charles Elson of the University of Delaware cited the act's success in increasing our societal focus on corporate responsibility, the importance of the audit function, the necessity to pay attention to director competencies on the board, and the critical need for director independence. "Perhaps more thematically important," they write, "was the [continued] gentle shift in corporate control from the CEO to the board."[18]

Hopefully, an auditor's ultimate conclusion on a client's annual financial statements is an "unqualified" opinion, under the standards issued by the PCAOB, that "the financial statements, taken as a whole, are presented fairly, in all material respects, in conformity with the applicable financial reporting framework."[19] Despite some criticism that Sarbanes-Oxley has created a false sense of confidence that "clean opinions" mean that all financial risk has been appropriately addressed—unrealistic, of course—and that the Sarbanes-Oxley regulations failed to identify the problems with the risky financial instruments that led to the 2007–9 financial crisis, Peregrine and Elson still describe "a drastic reduction in the number of public company financial accounting scandals since its enactment."[20]

There is also criticism—not unfair—that Sarbanes-Oxley has added significant costs to being a public company, since the reporting requirements do not apply to private companies (though the enhanced penalties—significant fines and jail time for altering or destroying financial documents—do apply regardless of whether a company is public).[21] A study by the consulting firm Protiviti found that the average company spends more than $1.7 million annually on Sarbanes-Oxley compliance costs—largely outside consultants along with internal employees—and that even the smallest companies surveyed (with less than $500 million in annual revenue) are spending, on average, nearly $1 million.[22]

Audit committees' responsibilities are delineated in their charters and generally include oversight of internal controls, financial statements, and related SEC filings as well as other topics such as risk. Typically, once per quarter, armed with a draft of either the Form 10-Q (a quarterly financial report to the SEC) or the Form 10-K (an annual filing with the SEC that includes the company's financial statements, management's discussion and analysis of financial results, and related information), a proposed earnings press release, and a draft presentation and script for a conference call with investors, the audit committee members read and comment on this information and have a meeting with the senior accounting, tax, compliance, treasury, and internal and independent auditor personnel to review and discuss significant issues in the quarter or year as well as these materials. The conversations may also include a discussion of emerging technical and regulatory issues that have the potential to impact future financial statements. Ultimately, the committee will usually approve the SEC filings and sometimes the press release and investor conference call materials, depending on how the committee works with management, before the SEC documents are filed. Details, problems, and issues that arise unexpectedly and require the audit committee's attention can include internal controls failures, potential write-offs of assets, claims of harassment, and theft of company property.

While the independent auditing firm issues an annual opinion on the company's internal controls and financial statements, management is responsible for preparing the financial statements. The auditing firm may also provide certain consulting services that do not run afoul of rules that compromise independence; these services can include tax advice and due diligence on potential acquisitions, among other services. It is helpful for the board and management to have a strong relationship with the external audit firm. There will likely be difficult issues to address, and the firm's senior team members and colleagues can be important advisors and thought partners.

During what I call my "sabbatical from Wall Street," I was the COO and CFO of ToysRUs.com, the then-new online business of the iconic toy retailer. When I arrived, the financial systems and reporting, as well as the information technology, had major challenges. Frustrated that there were numerous consultants helping us but limited progress, I asked one of the team members at Ernst & Young (EY), the auditor, if there was a senior person who could help organize and accelerate the efforts. A few days later, in walked Mark Manoff, who was immediately a valuable partner.

Manoff spent 39 years at EY in many leadership roles, lastly as Americas vice chair of markets and a member of EY's executive board and operating committee, before retiring. He believes that a strong relationship between the audit committee and the independent audit firm is "based on competency and trust and an independent view." It should include "candid dialogue between the audit committee members, senior management, the outside auditors, and the internal auditors and having everyone be clear that it's all for the betterment of the organization and shareholders—but that dialogue can only occur if the parties have the right competencies and styles."

Internal audit, or an audit function provided by company employees, has a broader purview, especially today. Manoff summarizes it well: "The purpose of an internal audit function is to help ensure that the company's system of internal control is operating effectively. It means providing an independent [of management] view of the systems and operating procedures and internal controls and addressing issues associated with that." Expectations for internal audit can vary but typically include an annual risk assessment; review, improvement, and testing of financial controls; audits of locations such as factories or stores and documents such as expense reports; and investigations including those concerning allegations of theft, harassment, and related problems.

Manoff explains what I have increasingly seen: "The risk universe is getting broader and more complex whether it's around artificial intelligence, cybersecurity, other technologies, the supply chain, or geopolitical risks." Therefore, internal audit is increasingly taking a broader look at how the company can protect against numerous, varied, more threatening risks.

As mentioned, it is required that the independent auditing firm reports to the audit committee, and it is a "best practice" that the head of internal audit reports to the audit committee. However, the management team, particularly the CFO and chief accounting officer, works closely with the external and internal auditors. In addition, it is only practical that the auditing firm is managed administratively by the CFO and the head of internal audit by the CFO or general counsel.

Beyond these core responsibilities, audit committees have also broadened their portfolio. Some audit committees have expanded their name, such as to "audit and finance," to reflect that the committee often oversees capital structure, financing, pension plans, compliance, and risk. In fact, the audit committee often—particularly in cases where there is not a separate committee devoted to these issues—takes on responsibility for risk broadly, including ESG risks, cybersecurity, artificial intelligence–related concerns, and potential geopolitical issues.[23]

I have been on 18 audit committees and chaired 10, including two Fortune 500 audit committees. It has generally been thought that the audit committee takes the most time of any of the committees, and the data bears this out: in 2021, audit committees met more frequently than other committees, an average of 8.4 times each year as compared to 6.2 times per year for the compensation committee and 4.7 times per year for the nominating and governance committee, according to research from Spencer Stuart.[24]

Audit committees should remain vigilant in their oversight of controls, financial statements and related information, and the independent and internal auditors. However, now, more than two decades past Sarbanes-Oxley, the general expectations for the audit committee are reasonably straightforward. This contrasts with the two committees to follow, where there is currently more change to and expansion of their responsibilities.

Compensation Committee

In broadest terms, the compensation committee is responsible for the compensation of senior or so-called C-level executives (given that many senior executives often have titles that start with "chief" such as "chief" financial officer, "chief" human resources officer, etc.) at the company. The SEC, the NYSE, and NASDAQ all require a compensation committee to exist. As mentioned, under NYSE rules, this committee must be composed entirely of independent directors, with added independence requirements for this committee on top of the basic rules explained earlier, including that boards should "consider whether [the] director receives compensation from any person or entity that would impair his/her ability to make independent judgments about [the] company's executive compensation."[25]

NASDAQ rules are very similar except that the committee is permitted to have just two independent directors, and CEOs are prohibited from attending meetings where their compensation is being discussed.[26]

Regardless of the stock exchange rules, it is certainly appropriate that senior management's compensation is approved by independent directors and that investors appreciate that these directors are not beholden to any of these senior executives.

The compensation committee is generally charged with reviewing and approving goals related to CEO compensation, evaluating the CEO's performance in light of these goals, determining the CEO's compensation, and approving compensation for non-CEO executive officers.[27] In addition, it must consider the risks of a company's compensation plans.[28] Executive officers are generally defined as a company's CEO; president; principal financial officer; principal accounting officer or controller; any vice president in charge of a significant business unit, division, or function; and anyone who performs equivalent policy-making functions.[29]

When considering C-level compensation, there should be a focus on incentive-based pay. Compensation packages can be complex for senior executives at many companies, involving not just an annual cash salary but typically also an annual cash bonus based on performance and a long-term equity grant that can be determined in a variety of ways. The bonus and equity are considered "at risk" or "incentive" compensation because they are based not just on "showing up for work" but rather on the company's performance. In larger public companies, it is not unusual for 90 percent or more of a CEO's compensation to be at risk.

Of course, opinions may vary on what performance-based compensation is and is not. Take the simple example of a CEO of a large, liquid public company with a strong track record and balance sheet that is well covered by equity analysts. Assume that this executive's salary and annual cash bonus are 10 percent and 20 percent, respectively, of total compensation for a given year. Assume further that the CEO's long-term equity grant, when awarded, is 70 percent of the value of the year's total compensation. The final assumption is that 50 percent of the equity grant vests equally over three years—time-vested shares—and 50 percent vests and is realized at the end of three years based on the performance of the company compared to the performance of a group of comparable companies. Is the entirety of the annual bonus and equity grant incentive-based and therefore all but the salary (meaning 90 percent of the year's compensation) at risk? Or, given that the shares that are time-vested will undoubtedly increase or decrease in value but are likely to remain very valuable, are they not 100 percent incentive compensation?

The first step in the process of determining compensation is deciding on a peer set of companies for pay purposes. These are usually 12 to 20 companies that can certainly be in the same or similar industries but, most importantly, should be ones from which the company would seek to recruit senior executives and that have annual revenues ranging from 0.5 to 1.5 times the company's annual revenue. Size is relevant, as research shows that executive compensation is correlated with company size.[30]

Once you have identified the peer set of companies, you look at the salaries, target bonuses, and equity grants for the executives. The compensation committee usually considers the mean and median as well as the different quartiles for the peer set. The majority of committees usually seek to pay executives at the median. Sometimes, such as with a first-time CEO, you might start that person at, say, the 25th percentile and expect to move him or her up as performance merits it. Sometimes, if the executive has a long record of success, you may decide instead to pay at perhaps the 75th percentile.

The annual bonus formula should be set at the beginning of the year. Metrics such as for the annual bonus should be tied to the company's goals, sometimes with an adjustment factor (e.g., up or down by perhaps 10 percent for safety performance). One-time items can be added back or subtracted as well. Some bonus formulas are simple and may be based just, for instance, on EBITDA. Others may have multiple metrics that can include revenue growth, operating margin, free cash flow, and more. Bonuses will typically have a "cut-in" or threshold at which some bonus is paid, a target amount where 100 percent of the intended bonus is paid, and a maximum point where 150 percent to 200 percent of the target bonus is paid. The cut-in is often about 80 percent of the prior year's metric(s).

However, I am often reluctant to pay a bonus where the bonus year's metrics do not exceed the prior year's results. After all, a bonus is not salary; a bonus should be paid only for good performance. And if bonus metrics are down compared to the prior year, the shareholders, for whom the board and management work, have probably seen their stock decline in value, making it potentially awkward to award incentive compensation. Of course, this has to be weighed against the performance of the various executives, the desire to retain them, and compensation paid to executives in similar roles at companies in the peer set. Data provides important context for the determination of a bonus plan, but the compensation committee must ultimately decide what to do.

Equity is usually the largest component of senior executives' compensation opportunity. Doug Benham is the former CEO of Arby's and has served on more than a dozen corporate boards. He is now a trustee (essentially a director) of AMH, a real estate investment trust that is a leading owner, operator, and developer of single-family rental homes with some 60,000 properties, where he is chair of the human capital and compensation committee. "It's all about how you incent long-term performance by the management team and align them as closely as possible to create shareholder value," he told me.

While annual bonus metrics such as a given year's EBITDA should drive annual performance, metrics for equity such as total shareholder return

(TSR), or the change in stock price including any dividends paid that are assumed to be reinvested in the stock, should drive long-term shareholder value.

Equity can come in various forms, such as stock, stock options, stock appreciation rights (SARs), restricted stock, restricted stock units (RSUs), and performance stock units (PSUs). Usually issued annually, grants can consist of one or more forms of equity. They typically vest in part based on time and in part based on performance.

Stock is, of course, simply shares in the company immediately owned by the employee. This component is not often used. Stock options provide an opportunity to purchase shares of the company's stock at a fixed or strike price typically equal to the company's closing price on the grant date for a period of time, often 10 years. Stock options are much less widely used today than previously, in part because they are thought to encourage excessive risk-taking. If the stock price does not exceed the strike price by the time the options can no longer be exercised or expire, they are worthless. Therefore, there can be an incentive to act in a way that will cause the stock price to have a short-term peak, at which point the options can be exercised and the stock sold, with no long-term consequences for the executive if the price then falls. This can, of course, fail to serve the long-term interests of the company and its shareholders.

SARs give an employee the right to receive the cash or stock equivalent of the increase, if any, in the company's stock price over a specified period of time. Restricted stock is company stock that is not yet owned by the grantee. Note that, importantly, the holder here is subject to the same ups and downs as shareholders, closely aligning incentives.

RSUs are the SARs equivalent for restricted stock, with the holder entitled to receive the value—in either cash or stock—of the company's stock at a particular point in time. The incentives are similar to those of restricted stock.

PSUs are similar to RSUs, except that such equity vests at a specified future date, generally based on a comparison to an index or peer set, and they can be worth more, less, or the same amount at the vesting date compared to the grant date, depending on performance.

PSUs are increasingly used. Benham explained to me his view: "This sounds simplistic, but what it comes down to is an analysis of TSR as benchmarked against your peer set of companies. It's important where a CEO stands versus the peer group, because you can have a low or even negative shareholder return, but it could be great compared to everybody else."

The feeling that negative shareholder returns should still yield rewards for the CEO and other senior executives is not universal. Howard Ungerleider recently retired after a career at Dow, lastly as president and CFO as well as a member of the company's senior executive committee. He is now an operating advisor at the private equity firm Clayton, Dubilier & Rice (CD&R) and argues, "If you're generating a negative return, by definition you're destroying value. Why do you deserve anything?" Sometimes, PSU holders are limited to earning up to only the target amount if the TSR over the measurement period is negative.

The equity components of executive compensation are now most frequently a mix of RSUs and PSUs. In a 2021 survey, Deloitte and the National Association of Stock Plan Professionals found that 86 percent of US public companies grant RSUs, compared to just 3 percent in 2000,[31] and option grants have fallen to just 5 percent.[32] At the same time, incentive pay has become an increasing percentage of overall executive pay, particularly for CEOs. According to the Economic Policy Institute, the stock-related components of CEO pay made up 73 percent of CEO compensation in 2016 but rose to 82 percent by 2021, and that increase explained nearly 95 percent of the growth in CEO compensation over that time.[33]

There has traditionally been a widespread school of thought that only senior executives—perhaps the C-level but in no case further down in an organization than through the vice presidents—understand and appreciate stock compensation. How deep into the employee base to provide equity as part of the compensation program is a decision driven by company culture and the CEO—with input, if not approval, from the compensation committee.

Earlier, I mentioned the sale of United Airlines to the pilots' union. Shortly after the transaction, the pilots' union contract was expiring, and the economy had softened. I recall that the pilots did not recognize the potential value of their equity and pushed very hard for major pay increases, regardless of the effect on shareholder value—which would have affected them in a significant way. Among other experiences, this made me generally supportive of limiting how deep into an organization ownership is allocated.

Pete Stavros is a partner and co-head of global private equity at KKR as well as the founder and chair of Ownership Works, a nonprofit seeking to "establish employee ownership as the new standard of socially responsible business and investing" and through employee ownership create better places to work with more invested employees and ultimately greater financial results.[34] His work has made many people, including me, rethink the point of view that equity should be limited to the top tier of management. Stavros's model is for all employees to become owners of the company.

It is a challenge to get companies to implement this, Stavros admits: "CEOs are already drowning in priorities, from improving earnings and growing the business, to M&A and integration, to DEI [diversity, equity, and inclusion] topics, sustainability, and decarbonization—and so many other issues. Then we throw on top of it the idea of making everyone an owner, which administratively in and of itself is not that easy and involves teaching employees about the business, teaching financial literacy, driving employee engagement, and measuring it all in a way that recognizes the very real outcomes . . . it's very challenging."

But the rewards can be substantial. "If you get broad-based ownership right, those other things become easier," Stavros continues. "[A lack of employee ownership is] not just bad for companies; it's bad for human beings. Today, much of the workforce is bouncing around from thing to thing to thing. They're not building skills or wealth, and companies are having to constantly rehire and train their workforce. Instead, we could change the culture."

Indeed, in May 2024, Blackstone announced that it would provide equity to most employees at its portfolio companies in the US, echoing the approach KKR committed to for new investments in 2022. Other major private equity firms, including Apollo, Ares, Silver Lake, and TPG, also have committed to shared ownership for at least some of the companies in which they invest.[35]

In the United Airlines situation, Stavros believes that there were mistakes: "Stock for workers—but not for CEOs, of course—should always be a free and incremental benefit, not a trade for wages or pension or 401K or any of that. This is equity, it's risk, there's no guarantee—but it costs you nothing, and the way we're going to get paid back is by getting you more engaged."

Sometimes, one or more nonfinancial metrics may be used to help determine the incentive bonus and/or equity component or to modify one or both incentive plans, such as by increasing or decreasing them by, say, 10 percent, perhaps based on safety or ESG performance—or perhaps given the attainment (or not) of certain strategic goals such as increasing sales backlog or selling one or more noncore assets.

In early 2024, Boeing increased the percentage of its bonus plan metrics focusing on safety and quality to make up 60 percent of incentive compensation rather than the 25 percent level where it previously stood.[36] Metrics include employee safety, work done out of sequence on the assembly line, and necessary rework.[37]

Matt Turner is president of Pearl Meyer Executive Compensation and has over 30 years of experience working on senior management pay. "I think it may be an overreaction," he told me. "Down the line they may find it difficult to revert to a normal weighting. It is rare to see safety at more than 25 percent, with 15 to 20 percent most common where these types of incentives are used. I have seen modifiers where financial results factors are limited if safety falls below some threshold or if there is a major incident."

Determining an incentivizing, value-enhancing pay package is not something the committee needs to do alone. In my view, the committee should always engage the help of a compensation consultant. Under NYSE and NASDAQ rules, there is guidance that permits the use of compensation consultants.[38] The SEC has annual disclosure requirements for these consultants, including their identity and the scope of their assignments, and under Dodd-Frank, companies must also disclose any conflicts of interest regarding the compensation consultant.[39]

I have found that a good compensation consultant is able to provide excellent data, some aggregated and some proprietary, to help establish effective metrics and, along with colleagues, will be active with a significant number of companies and can thus offer an experienced perspective on various issues. "We see ourselves as helping the committee find the solutions that best allow a management team to execute a particular business strategy," Turner told me. "Salary is table stakes. We think it's just as important to get the right balance between short-term and long-term incentives so the executives are driven to deliver results on an annual basis as well as position the company for long-term sustainability and health." He added, "You've got to [ultimately] answer to investors."

David Wise is vice chair of rewards at Korn Ferry, working with management teams and compensation committees on these issues. "For me, short-term incentives are a balance between results today and building the foundation for tomorrow, all within a year's time horizon," he told me. "A long-term incentive is fundamentally different, because it is the piece that at the end of the day should align with investors, sponsors, and the interests of other important constituencies. So the short-term incentive is more about strategy execution. The long-term incentive is about alignment with outcomes for investors."

However it is done, directors have to use their judgment and tailor a compensation program to maximize short-term and long-term results just as Turner and Wise say, with long-term shareholder value being paramount. For example, I joined the board and compensation committee of Chemtura, a specialty chemicals company, when it exited Chapter 11 and began trading on the NYSE in 2010. Among other things, we wanted to incentivize management to sell lower-quality businesses if that increased shareholder value. Over time, a number of less-attractive businesses were sold, margins increased, and Chemtura became a more focused company. The compensation committee and board did not add smaller companies to our peer set and eliminate larger ones as businesses were sold and annual revenue decreased. In 2017, Chemtura was sold to a strategic buyer, Lanxess, for $2.7 billion. I believe that our approach to compensation was effective, importantly because, from the company's emergence from bankruptcy until the sale, the company's annual revenues fell from about $2.4 billion to $1.7 billion, but the stock price approximately doubled.[40]

The SEC requires a compensation discussion and analysis in the annual proxy statement that explains the rationale behind all material elements of executive compensation.[41] Assuming that directors follow a reasonable process, they are generally insulated from any liability from compensation decisions.

This does not mean there is, or should be, unlimited latitude for compensation choices. The 2006 Delaware case *In re Walt Disney Derivative Litigation* concerned whether the Disney board breached its duties when it granted former president Michael Ovitz a $130 million severance package. The court distinguished between "best practices" and the threshold for the exercise of due care.[42]

In a "best case" scenario, the court held, the compensation consultant would have provided committee members with information on the compensation Ovitz would have received under a range of potential circumstances. This should have formed the basis for their deliberations. Instead, they received a term sheet with far fewer details—but the fact that they relied on the consultant and were reasonably informed as to the magnitude of the potential payout was ruled to be enough to protect them. There was no bad faith found, and so the business judgment rule applied.[43] I wonder if today, with directors and senior executive compensation rightly under more scrutiny, the court would have reached the same decision. I doubt it.

Boards should, of course, strive to meet best practices and not just do the minimum to avoid legal liability. Chancellor William Chandler of the Delaware Court of Chancery, despite finding that the board had complied with its duties, was critical of its process:

> [Disney's chair and CEO Michael] Eisner's actions in connection with Ovitz's hiring should not serve as a model for fellow executives and fiduciaries to follow. . . . His lapses were many. He failed to keep the board as informed as he should have. He stretched the outer boundaries of his authority as CEO by acting without specific board direction or involvement. He prematurely issued a press release that placed significant pressure on the board to accept Ovitz and approve his compensation package in accordance with the press release. To my mind, these actions fall far short of what shareholders expect and demand from those entrusted with a fiduciary position. Eisner's failure to better involve the board in the process of Ovitz's hiring, usurping that role for himself, although not in violation of law, does not comport with how fiduciaries of Delaware corporations are expected to act.[44]

On Eisner's side, the focus was on the outcome, not the commentary. Eisner's attorney, Gary Naftalis, said that his client was pleased: "We always believed that there was no basis for this case."[45]

Nonetheless, Chandler felt that his words had an impact. Looking back on his career when he retired in 2011, Chandler said, "The Walt Disney derivative litigation probably will be remembered by corporate law experts as having the greatest impact on boardroom governance. That case established tougher standards and higher expectations for corporate compensation committees, as well as for compensation consultants hired by boards."[46]

These issues continue to make news. In January 2024, Chancellor Kathaleen McCormick of the Delaware Court of Chancery struck down Elon Musk's $55 billion compensation package for his position as CEO of Tesla.[47] Shareholders had sued, claiming that there were director conflicts, a lack of reasonableness and rationale, and inadequate disclosure.[48] The chancellor found there was no true independence of many of the directors from Musk, and thus the decision needed to be evaluated under the more onerous entire fairness standard, where both the decision-making process and the valuation must be fair, rather than the business judgment rule where the courts generally defer to management's informed judgment. Under such an analysis, the court found that the compensation grant failed and should be canceled.[49]

In June 2024, just a few months after the court's ruling, there was a shareholder vote on the issue, and 72 percent of the voting shares—including large institutions such as Vanguard—in fact voted in favor of restoring Musk's initial compensation package, valued at that point at $47 billion due to a decline in Tesla's stock.[50] Musk's response to the criticism has been to reassure shareholders, emphasizing that he cannot sell any of the stock for five years. "It's not actually cash, and I can't cut and run, nor would I want to," he said at Tesla's annual meeting.[51]

Nonetheless, in December 2024, the chancellor upheld her earlier ruling.[52] Therefore, Musk cannot be paid under the plan. Among other options, a new plan can be put in place, and the ruling can be appealed to the Delaware Supreme Court. It remains to be seen what happens next.

Another important element in public company executive compensation is a vote, known as Say-on-Pay, introduced in the Dodd-Frank legislation. This requires publicly traded companies to give their shareholders an opportunity to vote on executive compensation at least once every three years, albeit the vote is nonbinding.[53] While the idea that shareholders should have input on executive pay makes sense, in practice it is not clear that Say-on-Pay has had much effect on executive compensation.

The 2007–9 financial crisis initially made Say-on-Pay an appealing option in the political arena, but the reality is that only some 2 percent of votes fail,[54] and in cases where the vote is low, it is not clear whether the problem is executive pay as much as it is an indication of disappointing stock price performance. In their 2018 article, Professors Jill E. Fisch, Darius Palia, and Steven Davidoff Solomon write, "Although shareholders at a few issuers have rejected compensation plans, shareholders at the overwhelming majority of issuers vote to approve executive compensation, and the average percentage of votes in favor exceeds 90%. The link between say on pay and Chief Executive Officer (CEO) compensation is unclear."[55]

"Shareholders appear to care a lot about performance," the authors continue, "and, to an extent, they are using say on pay to punish executives for poor performance rather than for excessive pay. As a result, the say on pay vote may be counterproductive to the extent that it heightens an executive's incentives to focus on short-term stock price at the potential cost of working to enhance firm value."[56]

There have been some high-profile Say-on-Pay failures. In 2023, for example, Netflix shareholders voted no on Say-on-Pay for the second year in a row.[57] After the failed vote in 2022, the company had shifted most of its executive compensation to stock and performance bonuses, but the vote was still negative in 2023.[58] Indeed, the majority of companies whose shareholders vote negatively make similar changes, shifting more executive pay to stock or variable compensation.[59]

The data supports the idea that failed votes do change compensation practices. Therefore, Say-on-Pay is having some effect.[60] But given how few companies have low or failed votes, Say-on-Pay does not appear to have done much to affect executive compensation more broadly.

Turner believes there has been some positive impact from Say-on-Pay: "I think there has been an improvement in the relationship between how senior executives in the US are paid and the value created for shareholders and certainly more accountability for the goals that are being set. Say-on-Pay forces board members to actively listen to what shareholders are saying. If there's a downside, in addition to the additional time and attention that companies need to spend on disclosure and regulatory requirements, perhaps this may put a bit of a damper on creativity."

Wise is a bit more skeptical: "The optimist in me says that Say-on-Pay has helped shine a light onto listed company pay practices and on the signals embedded within an executive pay program. The pessimist in me says it's become an end unto itself to not fail one's Say-on-Pay vote, and that has shifted the focus from a pay program that might be right for the business to a pay program that institutional investors find not problematic. But you've got to have enough resilience to sometimes buck the market practice."

It should be noted that 2023 saw Apple CEO Tim Cook's pay fall by 40 percent, citing "balanced shareholder feedback," an example of Say-on-Pay perhaps having a concrete impact.[61]

Another intended guardrail on CEO pay was the additional Dodd-Frank requirement that companies disclose the ratio of CEO compensation to the median compensation of all of the company's employees.[62] This calculation is complex, and it is hard to compare the ratio fairly across many industries.

I believe that the CEO pay ratio is largely the result of politics and not thoughtfulness on executive compensation. We can look at an example: take two CEOs—A and B—who both are top performers and receive very similar total compensation. Assume that CEO A runs a manufacturing company where the vast majority of employees are in low-cost countries, while CEO B leads a technology company with primarily highly skilled, US-based workers. The workforces and thus ratios for these two companies are not comparable—and yet the required disclosures will show the pay ratio to be much higher for CEO A than CEO B, making it appear as if there is more pay inequality in Company A than Company B.

Some will argue that you can compare the CEO pay ratio for leaders in similar industries, but it is hard to find very strong comparability between workforces. And the difference between "good" and "bad" is not always clear. Is a 50:1 ratio good when competitors are at 300:1? Or are both ratios high? What is a desired range of pay ratios?

It is also the case that the impact of a top CEO and other executives can be very significant, and even at the highest levels of pay, compensation, while perhaps eye-popping in nominal dollars, may well be a very small fraction of the value created if compensation plans are well constructed.

In any event, CEO pay has increased tremendously over time, as has the CEO pay ratio, climbing from 21:1 in 1965, to 61:1 in 1989, to 307:1 in 2019, to 351:1 in 2020.[63]

More and more, compensation committees are broadening their portfolios and even changing their names. As of 2022, 84 percent of S&P 500 companies' compensation committees have added at least one nontraditional responsibility to their charters, and 49 percent have changed their names.[64] Committee names such as "development and compensation committee" or "human capital/talent and compensation committee" reflect these added duties, which can include such mandates as succession planning, pay equity (equal pay for similar roles regardless of background), training and development, DEI, employee engagement, and corporate culture and ethics.[65]

Human capital management, not just compensation, is a tremendously important area on which boards should be focused. As Admiral Mullen told me, talking about his service in the military and experience in the corporate world, "I succeeded through people. I feel very strongly that the human resources leader at a company needs to be at the table, as impactful as the

CEO." Understanding how to develop the most effective mix of people in order to drive success is always a challenge, and it goes beyond compensation.

This broader concern is increasingly reflected in committee charters. A sometimes overlooked role of board members is how to help develop the company's executives. But it is not just the senior executives. As one example, the charter for Levi Strauss's compensation and human capital committee lists the following responsibility: "Review annually the development, implementation and effectiveness of the Company's policies and strategies relating to its human capital management function, including but not limited to those policies and strategies regarding culture, recruiting, retention, career development and progression, talent planning, and diversity and inclusion. The Committee shall review periodically reports on the Company's compensation, workforce and workplace management and training programs as they may request from time to time."[66]

This is typical of where compensation committees are heading. In their article "The Expanded Role of the Compensation Committee," Ani Huang and Richard R. Floersch of the HR Policy Association write about a "perfect storm" of factors driving this expanded compensation committee role: an increased focus on talent by institutional investors, companies being expected to address societal problems previously left to government, regulatory pressure from the SEC regarding human capital disclosures, and the social justice movement pushing DEI to the forefront.[67]

Wise agrees: "The remit of the compensation committee really has broadened to become the human capital committee, with compensation as one part of a human's value proposition for what it takes to be successful and happy and satisfied at work." Wise points to how compensation metrics have broadened—to include elements such as the safety incentives added by many companies, including Boeing, and climate metrics—as evidence that thinking about these issues has evolved:

> Five years ago, you didn't see these metrics in compensation programs. Over the last few years, you've seen their representation skyrocket in the design of public company pay programs. In many cases, that is being done for virtue signaling: this is a moment in time where companies want to show their commitment to it, want to make progress on it, and therefore like many critical initiatives, they put it into the incentive for a period of time. And then my guess is that some companies will move on to other priorities because they've accomplished

a lot and it's part of the routine or because other things just become more visible and important. The beauty of incentive programs is that if we name it and measure it and set a goal around it, it probably will get done because that's how humans are wired.

In summary, Wise shared with me what he feels are the keys to a successful compensation committee: "Number one, a fundamental understanding of how the company makes money and an appreciation for the role that people and how they're rewarded play in enabling that strategy. Number two, a balanced approach between investor and public optics and what is fundamentally right for the business. And number three, a productive relationship with the management team that finds a balance between understanding that they're human beings with needs and desires and the board's underlying commitment to investors." I fully agree.

Nominating and Governance Committee

Many have traditionally thought of the nominating and governance committee as the least demanding of the three major committees—but even if this might have been the case in the past, it is increasingly not today. The greater demands on directors mean that more care needs to go into recruiting, onboarding, and evaluating new directors, and ESG issues also increasingly fall to this committee.

Under each umbrella term—nominating and governance—falls an important set of responsibilities. On the nominating side, while I believe that the selection of a new director should be a decision made by the entire board and not just the members of this committee, it is efficient for this committee to run the recruitment process, often assisted by an executive search firm. Finding a new director should involve assessing the skills and talents of the sitting directors and what expertise may be missing or should be increased. Diversity across various dimensions, including experience, perspective, gender, race, and ethnicity, is also an important consideration.

It is unquestionable that diversity has come to the forefront of discussions about board composition over the past generation. Vicki L. Bogan, Ekaterina Potemkina, and Scott E. Yonker of Cornell University write, "The business case for board diversity focuses on the fact that demographically homogeneous boards have the risk of insularity and may not be well positioned to operate in an increasingly dynamic global environment with a diverse global workforce. In fact, there exists academic evidence that boards comprised of individuals with heterogeneous backgrounds leads to better corporate outcomes."[68]

The *New York Times* noted in early 2022 that the killing of George Floyd in 2020 prompted real change quite quickly: "The outpouring of anger and frustration that followed [Floyd's killing] . . . prompted many companies to pledge to make changes to address racial injustice and inequity. . . . Directors who are Black, Asian, Hispanic, Middle Eastern or from another non-white ethnic group occupy 4,500 board seats among companies in the Russell 3000 stock index, 25 percent more than they did at the end of 2020 and nearly 50 percent more than at the end of 2019."[69] That amount of change between 2019 and 2024 is significant, and there has been progress on the management side as well. In 2024, among the 671 unique companies in the Fortune 500 and S&P 500, 13.5 percent of CEOs and 13.8 percent of CFOs were nonwhite, up from 4.3 percent and 2.9 percent, respectively, in 2004.[70] Women composed 9.4 percent of sitting CEOs and 17.8 percent of CFOs among those same companies in 2024, up from just 1.3 percent and 5.2 percent, respectively, in 2004.[71] Of course, these percentages are still very low.

California passed a law in 2018 requiring boards to have at least two or three female directors by 2022 depending on board size; that law was struck down in 2022 as unconstitutional.[72] However, several large institutional investors, including BlackRock and State Street, had announced expectations that boards should be sufficiently diverse, with State Street saying it will vote against the nominating and governance committee chairs of companies without at least one minority board member.[73] Internationally, some countries have passed laws concerning board diversity; in France, for example, there is a requirement that boards must have a certain percentage of women, rising to 40 percent by 2030.[74]

However, largely Republican politicians and conservative groups have been pushing back against various diversity initiatives for some time. With President Trump having already issued numerous executive orders to, among other things, lessen diversity efforts, and with the Republicans controlling both houses of Congress, more executive orders and memoranda; new laws, regulations, and litigation; as well as increased activism, shareholder proposals, and general pressure are expected to continue to drive a reduction. For example, BlackRock's 2025 proxy voting guidelines have no requirements for board diversity. Previously, they indicated that boards should have 30 percent diverse members, including at least two women and one director from an underrepresented group.[75]

It is logical that a board reflects in a significant way its workforce and customers. I was a director of a women's health company. We had both women and men on the board. When a new director was sought during my tenure, we decided to consider only women.

I believe that diversity is critical to board credibility and effective decision-making. At the same time, any director must be fully qualified. In addition, diversity on the board should not excuse a lack of diversity in the C-suite or among broader management. Many business leaders are celebrating that women now run more than 10 percent of Fortune 500 companies,[76] and JetBlue made headlines in 2024 for appointing Joanna Geraghty as the first female CEO of a major US airline,[77] but these efforts are not enough.

Of course, diversity efforts on the board side need to be balanced with other priorities as well. I remember one circumstance when I was the nominating and governance chair and had a respectful but rather heated argument with a CEO for whom I had the highest regard over the search requirements for a board seat on an already reasonably diverse board where we were lacking a specific, important skill set among the directors: someone well versed in technology and able to contribute to the board of a global company. I was convinced that finding a person with the requisite knowledge and experience, as well as good chemistry with our sitting directors, should be the priority—with diversity an important consideration but not the primary one. The CEO, all of whose direct reports at that time were white males, thought that finding a diverse candidate should be a requirement. I urged that we needed to look holistically at every possible candidate and, at the same time, make diversification of the C-suite a priority too.

Ultimately, we found a diverse director with the technology skill set that we sought, and over time, diversity came to executive management as well. We completed this search successfully, in part, by expanding our recruiting from the often-typical candidate specification for a chief technology officer to a search where we identified target technology companies and considered successful executives in these organizations, including those a few levels below ones that reported to the CEO.

Leaders should tap diverse networks and look beyond the kinds of people who have typically occupied senior roles. At the same time, it may well take a generation or more to create a sufficiently large pool of qualified diverse director and senior management candidates to provide the ability for all boards and C-suites to be truly diverse.

In addition to skills, experience, and diversity, it is also important to consider carefully how potential new directors will likely work with the rest of the board and the management team. Chemistry is critical if hard to evaluate. One simple but sometimes overlooked step is that any "finalist" for a board seat should meet with each of the sitting directors. Although these will all be successful people, references should be checked carefully too.

In my view, it is important to remember that a CEO reports to the board, and thus the independent directors on the committee—and not the CEO—need to drive the director recruitment process. Certainly, the CEO's input on desired skill sets and potential new directors should be sought, and the CEO should meet with any director candidates that the committee and other directors believe are "finalists" and add his or her view on these candidates.

On the governance side, there are various topics for the nominating and governance committee to consider. For example, this committee should look at the company's potential defenses in the case of an unsolicited offer that undervalues the company; these may include a shareholder rights plan, or poison pill, as well as perhaps restricting the ability for shareholders to act by written consent and call a special meeting of shareholders. In addition, this committee usually reviews the reports and recommendations by governance advisory firms, including on topics such as whether to vote for or against individual directors, Say-on-Pay, and various other matters at annual meetings. Where there may be challenges, such as a director being reelected but by a small margin or a lower than approximately 90 percent affirmative vote on Say-on-Pay, the committee should develop a strategy to address any shortcomings.

Similar to the compensation committee, the nominating and governance committee's responsibilities and name are changing at many companies. For example, more than one-third of companies in a 2022 survey of 300 executives at publicly owned companies with annual revenue greater than $500 million reported that they had placed some ESG-related oversight responsibilities in the hands of the nominating and governance committee.[78]

With or without the added responsibilities of ESG oversight, there are many important issues for the nominating and governance committee to consider that make its work very important, even if it does not always get the attention it deserves.

Chapter 5
Board Leadership

Individual board members, and of course board committees, are important for board success. But I believe the board's leader is a key element for board success too. In this chapter, I will describe the role of the board leader and discuss the leadership positions that include the chair, which can be structured in different ways, and the lead independent director. I will also discuss the issue of a company's CEO as board chair or not; this question inspires vigorous debate from proponents on both sides.

The Importance of Board Leadership

Just as the roles of directors and board committees have become more complex and critical over the past few generations, the importance of strong leadership on corporate boards has grown substantially also. The number of stakeholders putting demands on most boards—such as institutional investors, activists, employees, and the public—is significant, and their demands cannot always be reconciled with each other. Important, difficult decisions have to be made, and companies are increasingly dependent on having not just an effective CEO and engaged directors but also an effective board leader.

The board leader sets the agenda (with the CEO), provides guidance and support to management, and seeks to ensure good governance, working to facilitate an effective board that interacts well with and properly oversees management. Importantly, the board leader should engage all directors in the dialogue and encourage those with particular expertise to be especially helpful in these areas. The board leader increasingly engages directly with shareholders, usually about governance and often alongside the CEO and CFO.

The CEO, on the other hand, is the operational leader of the organization, driving strategy and execution of the business plan. The CEO is ultimately responsible for the company's financial results and satisfying the demands of stakeholders. The executives who report to the CEO include business unit leaders, staff leaders (such as the CFO and general counsel), and often others, including, for instance, a head of diversity.

"An effective chair," according to INSEAD professor Stanislav Shekshnia, writing in the *Harvard Business Review*, "provides leadership not to the company but to the board, enabling it to function as the highest decision-making body in the organization." This is different from how we think about leadership in general. "To be effective," Shekshnia concludes, "chairs must recognize that they are not commanders but facilitators. Good chairs recognize that they are not first among equals. They are just the people responsible for making everyone on their boards a good director."[1]

That said, the chair's relationship with the CEO is also critical. Jim Citrin is a prominent recruiter of CEOs. He leads Spencer Stuart's CEO practice, co-leads the board practice, and is on the firm's board; he has worked on more than 850 executive searches and succession assignments. An expert on leadership and professional success, Citrin has authored seven books and has nearly one million followers on LinkedIn, where he addresses leadership and career strategy issues. "The chair or leader's relationship with the CEO is something really worth focusing on," he told me, "because getting it right adds so much value to the company, and getting it wrong creates real toxicity."

The Various Board Leadership Models

There are four general board leadership models—an independent chair; a combined chair and CEO; an executive chair; and a nonexecutive, nonindependent chair (often the company's former CEO or a senior professional at a major investor). In cases where there is not an independent chair, there is almost always a lead independent director.

For the S&P 500 as of 2022, the breakdown looks like this:

Independent chair: 36 percent
Combined chair and CEO: 43 percent
Executive chair: 15 percent
Nonexecutive, nonindependent chair: 7 percent
Note: Percentages add to 101 due to rounding[2]

The first two are the prevalent board leadership positions and have the clearest roles. An independent chair is the board leader and does not have a management role in the company. As Bob Byrne, a director of numerous companies, including the former independent board chair of Masonite, the door manufacturer where I also served as a director, explained to me,

> As chair, I'm most attentive to trying to make sure that the board is well informed. My biggest concern is that the board only gets to see what management wants to show them. So I'm always trying to know enough about the company and have enough conversations with the CEO and his direct reports to know what's going on so that I can see if something's happening within the company that the directors should know about. I want our agenda to be as relevant as it can be, with the information we want to see, not just what management thinks it should be.

There is much more discussion about the independent chair versus the combined chair and CEO role later in the chapter. But it is first worth looking at a harder role to define: the executive chair. A company with an executive chair—meaning the chair role is held by a person who is not the CEO but is considered the most senior company executive—can be a complex one. In May 2023, the investment bank Lazard announced that Peter Orszag would step into the role of CEO, and the longtime previous chair and CEO, Ken Jacobs, would be named executive chair. I spoke with Jacobs, whom I have known for many years since he went to Lazard as a vice president from Goldman Sachs and I was a young associate at Lazard, about his new role and how the responsibilities would be split: "The CEO has all of the executive responsibility. He needs time to run the firm, and so my executive chair role is 100 percent focused on clients unless the CEO asks for help on firm matters. The executive chair title helps in terms of client effectiveness, and the role is well defined, with the parameters understood by all parties. It's all about roles and defining them well."

In November 2024, Lazard announced that Jacobs would become senior chair and senior advisor to the board and give up his board seat. Orszag added the chair role to his CEO position, and Dan Schulman, a Lazard board member and former CEO of PayPal, replaced Richard Parsons as the lead independent director of Lazard.

Dave Brandon, the former president and CEO of Domino's Pizza, athletic director at the University of Michigan, and then the CEO of

Toys"R"Us, explained to me his view that the decision to have an executive chair can be driven by issues regarding the company's CEO:

> When I stepped down as CEO of Domino's, I made a deal to stay on as nonexecutive chair of our board, and that role required one level of engagement. But it was very different when we made a change in the CEO, and because the new CEO had no public company CEO experience, we decided to reposition my role as an executive chair. I didn't have an office at the company before, but now I have an office. I rejoined the company as an employee, I participate in the bonus plan, and I'm more actively engaged. I have much more regular meetings with the CEO, and I participate in more activities, particularly around quarterly earnings communications and investor days. My goal is to put our new CEO in a position where I set him up for success by lending him the experience that I have.

More and more boards have been using the executive chair role to help with the transition to a new CEO. According to a 2023 report from Spencer Stuart, "In the past several years, we have seen an uptick in the share of boards appointing an executive chair to smooth the transition from a successful long-time CEO to an internal candidate or to provide continuity following an external CEO appointment. Almost half of incoming S&P 1500 CEOs—43 percent—were appointed alongside an executive chair."[3]

In many cases, the executive chair's service is temporary, just a few years. The theory is that the support and advice from the executive chair to the CEO and other constituencies are valuable. Spencer Stuart's research, however, shows that the executive chair model does not lead to improved corporate performance. Fifty-four percent of the time when there is an executive chair, the company in fact underperforms its peers.[4] The cause of this underperformance—by an average of 14 percent—is unclear, however.

As with Jacobs and Brandon, executive chairs are often former CEOs—though not always. A former CEO who remains on the board, particularly as executive chair, can cause challenges. The NACD cautions against having a past CEO serve as the chair for any significant amount of time. "The past CEO can find it difficult to transition from a day-to-day, hands-on management role to a more lofty governance role," the NACD writes. "If the executive chair is a recent CEO who has been successful and continues to exercise influence in the running of the company, the current CEO may lack the clear operating authority needed to be effective."[5]

Larry Berg, co-owner of the Los Angeles Football Club (a Major League Soccer franchise) as well as a senior partner at the private equity firm 26North and former senior partner at Apollo, spoke to me about the role of an executive chair: "If a CEO is newer, they are more likely to accept it. I do think that in situations where the chair has more experience and more gravitas than the CEO, I like having an executive chair."

Steve Sterrett is a Hoosier, born, bred, and educated in Indiana, where he was a senior manager at the "Big Four" accounting firm PwC and CFO of Simon Property Group, the largest owner of shopping malls in the country. Sterrett was lead director and is now nonexecutive chair of Berry Global, a major packaging company that announced in November 2024 that it had agreed to combine with Amcor in a 100 percent stock transaction to create a global leader in health care and consumer packaging solutions with some $35 billion in total enterprise value.[6] I am a longtime director of Berry and chair of the audit committee. I will join Sterrett on the Amcor board when the transaction closes. Sterrett is also the lead trustee (director) for Equity Residential, which owns or has investments in more than 300 properties with some 80,000 apartments across the US. Given all of that, he has a very well-informed perspective on board leadership and finds the executive chair structure worrisome. "I don't like it," he told me. "It strikes me as someone who wants to put one toe in the water toward life after being the CEO, but they're not quite ready yet. I fear it sets up the current CEO to fail. If it's for a six-month or nine-month period and then you're going to roll off the board, I can live with that. But I would think you could do your transition planning in a way that doesn't require giving someone the title of executive chair. After all, where does that person's authority start and stop?"

Sometimes it works well, such as at Morgan Stanley, where, in January 2024, the firm named Ted Pick as CEO, replacing the longtime, very successful CEO James Gorman—who became executive chair to help with the transition, announcing he would step down and retire from the firm before the end of 2024, which he did.[7]

Contrast this with the situation at Starbucks, where founder Howard Schultz was CEO at three different times as well as chair and executive chair at various times. He "retired" in 2023 with the title of "lifelong chair emeritus." "I am never coming back again because we found the right person," Schultz said after his third stint as CEO of the company.[8] And while Starbucks has an incredible brand, it is hard to see how Schultz's successors would have felt free of his influence.

Schultz's chair emeritus role may not completely avoid these issues. While the role, in general, is an honorary one and does not have voting power, a chair emeritus may still be looked to for advice and have influence. In Schultz's case, it seems to have been hard for him to step away. In early 2024, he made news with a *Wall Street Journal* headline reading, "Howard Schultz Is Back-Seat Driving Starbucks. That's a Problem for His Successor."[9] "Schultz wrote a LinkedIn post," the article went on to report, "that read like an open letter to shareholders criticizing how [then new CEO Laxman] Narasimhan and his senior leaders were running the business. On the heels of the company's weak earnings report, the 70-year-old declared that Starbucks had to improve service to its U.S. customers. He challenged executives to tie on one of the chain's signature green aprons and better root themselves in the coffee giant's history and culture."[10]

Alas, after just 18 months and with the company's stock having fallen some 20 percent, Narasimhan was replaced by the board with Brian Niccol, former CEO of Chipotle. Starbucks' market value increased by $20 billion on the announcement. According to the *New York Times*, Schultz "was consulted" on the hiring of Niccol.[11]

It can be challenging for a new CEO when there is an executive chair who previously held the CEO role. To that end, a very experienced executive and director told me that his company's executive chair, who is the former CEO, and the current CEO are both excellent, but it is awkward when directors ask operating questions first of the executive chair, not the CEO.

Peter Crist has almost 50 years of executive recruiting experience. He began in 1977 with Russell Reynolds Associates; then launched Crist Partners, which was acquired by Korn/Ferry, where he was vice chair and chair of the Global Board Services practice; and next started Crist Kolder Associates, where he remains active. He is also a director and past chair of Wintrust Financial. Crist believes that in almost all cases, the exiting CEO should not remain involved as executive chair for exactly these reasons.

Crist sees only one situation where the structure works well: "If you do have a young pony who needs and wants to have the retiring CEO stick around to be available on the board to help strategically on acquisitions or something strategy-wise, then I'm OK about that. But only if the incoming CEO embraces it. Typically, when you have a new CEO, get rid of the old CEO. Be nice, but don't allow people to linger."

It can be the case that a chair is the former CEO or a representative of a major shareholder: a so-called nonindependent, nonexecutive chair. While the nonexecutive chair is not the most senior operating executive, a former CEO or major shareholder in this position can cause the same challenges discussed with the executive chair.

An independent chair and a combined CEO and chair are very different options and in many ways can define management's relationship with the board. Having an independent chair is seen as a best practice in corporate governance; it is also recommended by the major governance advisory firms. However, as indicated earlier, in 2022, 43 percent of the S&P 500 companies had a combined chair and CEO.

In virtually every case where the chair is not independent, there is an additional role that is important: the lead independent director. As a practical matter, the lead independent director generally runs meetings of the nonexecutive or independent directors and is often the primary representative of the independent directors when dealing with the CEO, although all directors should, of course, have a strong relationship with and full access to the CEO. The lead director also often interacts with the chair on board agendas and works most closely with the chair on major topics such as senior personnel issues and potential major transactions.

Marty Lipton developed the lead independent director concept with Harvard Business School professor Jay Lorsch in 1992, seeking to combine the advantages of having one overall corporate leader with the advantages of more independent leadership on the board.[12]

"I think it's subtle," 1-800-FLOWERS's Jim McCann told me. "Sometimes I think people can overimagine the role of the chair, and I think it's much more like the lead independent director."

The NACD literature indicates that the chair has the authority to call director meetings, but the lead director can merely suggest to the chair that a meeting should be called. In addition, the chair sets the meeting agenda, while the lead director advises on what the agenda ought to be. And the chair represents the company to external stakeholders, whereas the lead director typically does not.[13]

There is in fact substantial debate over whether a lead director—as opposed to an independent board chair—is sufficiently empowered and influential when the chair and CEO are the same individual.[14] To me, the major differences in these two positions fall into three categories: the power to shape the board's agenda, the visibility to shareholders, and the sense of true board leadership.

The Ira M. Millstein Center for Global Markets and Corporate Ownership at Columbia University (Millstein Center) exists to engage with corporate leaders and help strengthen governance.[15] The center is named for Ira Millstein, who was a senior partner at the law firm Weil and still active in his late 90s before passing away in early 2024. Millstein was a counselor to numerous boards over the course of his career, including General Motors, Westinghouse, Walt Disney, and more, and was called "a venerable lawyer who crusaded for greater independence by corporate boards of directors" by the *New York Times*.[16]

On the topic of lead directors, one Millstein Center report argues, "The lead director is better than nothing. But on a scale of 1 to 10, having a [nonexecutive] chairman is 10, and having a lead director is about a 4."[17] According to this report, a lead director "doesn't have the same sort of effect [as a chair] in terms of shaping the dialogue and moving the strategy forward."[18]

Doug Oberhelman, former CEO of Caterpillar, has worked within a number of different board leadership models and agrees that the lead independent director position lacks much power: "I'm the lead director at Bombardier. And all that role is really about is running the private sessions of the directors. There's little [board] management role whatsoever."

Sterrett concurs: "You might pipe in a little bit as the lead independent director, but as the board chair, you really want to make sure that all the voices and all the perspectives are heard. You need the influence to be able to do that."

And yet some see it a different way. Naren Gursahaney, former CEO of ADT and ServiceMaster and an experienced director, has had experience with both structures. "To me it's form over substance," he told me. "Having been a nonexecutive chair and serving under a nonexecutive chair and then being in another company where we have a lead director, I'm not sure that the lead director behaves any differently than the nonexecutive chair does."

Having a lead independent director, though typical for boards without independent chairs, is not an NYSE or NASDAQ requirement. For the NYSE, a nonmanagement director is required to preside at executive sessions, but NASDAQ has no corresponding rule.[19] So while it is a "best practice" to have a lead independent director in cases where the chair is not independent, there is no law or regulation that mandates this.

The concern for many, including me, is that a lead independent director often lacks substantial influence, which leads to the question that drives the rest of this chapter and much of the discussion about board leadership: Should the CEO also be the board chair, or should there be an independent chair?

The Move toward—and the Argument in Favor of—Independent Chairs

Over the past 30-plus years, the trend has been clear: more and more companies have an independent board chair and split the roles of chair and CEO. While 43 percent of companies still had a combined chair and CEO in 2022, this is a huge decline from a generation ago. In 1989, a survey of 661 large US companies found that more than 80 percent had one individual holding both the CEO and chair titles.[20]

Institutional and activist shareholders have led some of the push in this direction. In 2022, Meta (formerly Facebook) shareholders sought to remove cofounder and CEO Mark Zuckerberg from the chair role while keeping him as the CEO and designating a new, independent chair of the board.[21] This was the fourth year in a row that such a move was attempted and the fifth time in six years, with these proposals backed by large institutional shareholders, including AllianceBernstein, Goldman Sachs, JPMorganChase, and Vanguard. Indeed, in May 2019, a majority of 68 percent of shareholders in number voted to split the roles.

Proponents pointed to the company's privacy scandals, proliferation of hate speech, and what they claimed was a lack of effective governance.[22] "Facebook is willing to allow a certain level of hate speech, political misinformation, and divisive rhetoric so it can make more money," Michael Frerichs, the Illinois state treasurer, told the *Wall Street Journal* in 2021. "That is exactly why the board's governance structure must change."[23] Given these comments, I am reminded that while I discussed that a low Say-on-Pay vote may well reflect disappointment with a company's financial and/or stock price performance, not disapproval of executive compensation decisions, sometimes wanting to strip a chair and CEO of the chair position can be driven by poor performance or other missteps—not governance concerns.

"It's Corporate Governance 101 that you separate the chair from the CEO," Natasha Lamb of the sustainable investment firm Arjuna Capital told S&P Global Market Intelligence during the efforts to take Zuckerberg's leadership of the board (but not the company) away.[24]

And yet the proposals to oust Zuckerberg failed each time due to Meta's dual-class share structure. Zuckerberg controls 58 percent of the vote through his Class B shares—which have ten votes each, while the widely held Class A shares have just one vote each.[25] Insulated from shareholder pressure, Zuckerberg has kept both roles.

Even without a prominent founder who is chair and CEO, it is very difficult to pass a proposal to separate the chair and CEO roles. In fact, just three of these types of proposals have passed since 2016 out of some 50 proposals each year, and the average support has been less than one-third of votes cast.[26] Some suggest that the lead independent director role has softened the appetite for separating the chair and CEO roles.

However, most institutional investors support the separation of the chair and CEO positions.[27] Activists, too, generally argue that it strengthens the independence of the board and increases accountability for the CEO. Put simply, leading the board and leading the company are separate, though related, jobs. Steve Girsky, CEO of Nikola and a veteran of public boards, points out the challenges of one individual trying to do both jobs well: "I don't think there is any upside to putting them together. It's just extra work for the CEO, and I'd rather see them focus on the business."

By separating the two positions, a company can clearly distinguish between managing the board and managing the company. In a *Harvard Business Review* article, Joseph Mandato and William Devine write, "A board chair leads the board's effort to excel at advising on strategy, monitoring performance, overseeing finance and controls, and evaluating management. A CEO establishes within the company a shared set of values, practices, and goals that enables the company to execute its strategic plan and build a meaningful future. To grow, a company needs both of these roles performed thoroughly and well."[28]

In addition, a CEO who is also the chair provides an awkward reporting structure: the CEO typically reports to the board, and the chair, of course, leads the board; so if the chair and CEO are the same person, the CEO technically reports to himself. As Charles Elson told CNBC, "It doesn't make much sense to have the person who's being monitored by the board to chair the group monitoring them."[29]

Sterrett agrees: "In a perfect world, it is probably better governance to separate them. We've all seen organizations that have a very strong personality at the top, and I think while it's possible for a lead independent director to exercise influence—and I think actually it's mandatory in that situation for a lead independent director to exercise influence—I think there is a higher likelihood of ultimate success if the lead independent director has the title of chair."

Fred Lynch was president and CEO of Masonite for 12 years, where Bob Byrne and I sat on the board. He is now an operating partner at the private equity firm AEA and has served on a number of boards. "I've acted as a CEO twice now," Lynch told me. "You really want to make sure that the board members are providing you with independent thinking. And if there are difficult board members, having an independent chair means that the CEO can go to the chair and tell them they need to go fix the problem. The CEO doesn't have to burn bridges to do that if they aren't also chair of the board."

Indeed, the Boeing safety debacle, which I discussed in chapter 3 in the context of directors and the duty of care, illustrates the risks of keeping the two roles in the hands of one individual. Joseph Mandato and William Devine write about Boeing in their *Harvard Business Review* article arguing for board chairs to be independent: "Beneath all the reporting on fatally flawed airplane design . . . there lies an organizational leadership truth. . . . Be wary of giving the CEO job and the board chair job to one person."[30]

Boeing's apparent failure to take adequate safety precautions "might have benefitted from a board chair initiating a closed executive session that considered [chair and CEO Dennis] Muilenburg's fixation on global and interplanetary aspirations [at the expense of safety]," Mandato and Devine write.[31] Indeed, in Boeing's case, the ultimate result of the alleged lapses thus far is that in March 2024, the board found itself under continued scrutiny following an incident where four missing bolts from a door plug caused a cabin panel to blow off an airplane during a flight. The company announced significant changes in senior management, including that CEO Dave Calhoun would retire at the end of 2024, a search for a new CEO would be performed, and the head of the company's commercial airplanes division would be replaced.[32]

More broadly, quoting five-time technology CEO Sam Gerace, the article explains that "organizationally the chairperson should not be the CEO, simply because organizations move in the direction of the questions that they ask. If you have a chair and a CEO, one and the same, there are questions that might not get asked."[33]

There is also potentially an issue, and at a minimum awkwardness, when it comes to the CEO performance evaluation and succession planning. While the compensation committee typically oversees the CEO evaluation process with input from the entire board and the nominating and governance committee typically manages CEO succession, also with the entire board involved, these processes can be awkward when the CEO is the head of the board. In this situation, too, the CEO is being evaluated and the successor contemplated by the board that he or she leads.

The major governance advisory firms both come down on the side of separating the two roles, as do major institutional investors such as BlackRock. However, they do not go so far as to insist that shareholders vote against unitary structures.[34] Institutional Shareholder Services (ISS), the largest governance advisory firm, states in its proxy voting guidelines for 2025 that shareholders should "generally vote for shareholder proposals requiring that the board chair position be filled by an independent director."[35] Glass Lewis, another important proxy advisory firm, has highlighted the difficulty of replacing an ineffective CEO when that CEO is also chair. "We believe that the presence of an independent chairman fosters the creation of a thoughtful and dynamic board," the firm adds, "not dominated by the views of senior management."[36]

The SEC has not taken a position. It requires disclosures about the board leadership structure and the role of a lead independent director, if applicable, but not disclosure about why the chair and CEO roles have or have not been separated.

The US is in a different place than most of the rest of the world on this issue. The question of whether there ought to be separation of the chair and CEO is barely an issue in many countries, where regulations often require that there is independence. The UK Corporate Governance Code mandates that the roles of chair and CEO not be held by the same person and that there should be a clear division of responsibilities between the person running the board and the person running the business.[37]

This UK approach emerged in the early 1990s, when the Cadbury Committee was formed to examine best practices in the wake of a series of corporate collapses blamed on a lack of board oversight.[38] Its report recommended the separation of the chair and CEO, and in 1993, the London Stock Exchange required companies to either do this or disclose why they had not. Now nearly all UK companies have a separate chair and CEO.[39] This generally holds true in Canada, Germany, the Netherlands, Australia,

Belgium, Singapore, and South Africa, among many other nations.[40] In fact, as of 2021, 76 percent of jurisdictions around the world either require or encourage the separation of the CEO and board chair roles compared to 36 percent in 2015.[41] The US has been slower to make the shift.

Nevertheless, not everyone finds these arguments compelling, and in fact, a significant set of voices takes the opposite position, insisting that a company and its shareholders are more effectively served when there is a combined chair and CEO.

Arguments against Separation

The arguments against separation center on the idea that combining the roles of chair and CEO results in clear accountability, coordinated leadership, and the ability to act quickly and decisively. This, or so goes the argument, leads to better corporate results.

Indeed, the chief argument against separation is that there is no evidence—despite a number of studies—that separation actually leads to improved outcomes. "The lack of an evident relationship between board leadership structure and firm performance exhibits a 'level of consistency . . . unusual in any literature,'" write Ryan Krause and Matthew Semadeni in their 2013 piece looking at stock price returns and analyst ratings, and research since then has not been any more persuasive.[42]

As Jamie Dimon wrote in the 2023 JPMorganChase Annual Report, "[There is a] constant battle by some proxy advisors who try to split the chairman and CEO role when there is no evidence this makes a company better off—in fact, today, lead directors generally hold most of the authorities previously assigned to the chairman."[43]

David F. Larcker and Brian Tayan of the Stanford Graduate School of Business explain further: "Separation can lead to duplication of leadership, impair decision making, and create internal confusion, particularly in times of crisis. It can also make the recruitment of a new CEO difficult if qualified candidates expect to hold both titles. This is especially true when the new CEO is an external hire. . . . Most research finds that the independence status of the chairman is not a material indicator of firm performance or governance quality. . . . [and after a company changes its structure, there is] no evidence that this decision impacts subsequent performance."[44]

Oberhelman agrees: "If you're really under strife and things are bad, you probably ought to have a split. But when the company is running well, what happened at Caterpillar when we split was that everybody was confused.

For a year, customers didn't know who the boss was, and employees didn't know who the boss was. Chair and CEO are two different jobs. But if you have an engaged board and a presiding or lead director, it works fine. The lead director will run the private sessions, and he will help on board succession. But I believe in one person in charge."

I also spoke with Dr. Jonathan Rich, an Iowa native with many patents and executive successes to his credit who, among other roles, is the former chair and CEO of Berry Global, the former chair of Pactiv Evergreen, and a former director, then CEO, and then (after leaving the CEO role) chair of Lumileds. He insists that a CEO can feel like a "second-class board member" when not the chair. "If the CEO is not good at leading the board," he told me, "he is probably the wrong CEO." Rich explains that the roles are different—"the CEO is responsible for execution and increasing value, and the chair is responsible for setting strategy with the board and determining capital deployment"—but that they end up being complementary when held by the same person: "No one knows more about strategy and capital deployment than the CEO, so he is well positioned to take on both roles if it's the right person with the right demeanor."

Chief Justice Strine concurs: "I think as long as you have a strong lead independent director, I don't see any reason why the CEO can't be chair." He adds, "If you're a strong leader, you should be willing to hear diverse voices. You should be willing to have your management team have some genuine debates and listen to your board and not come with everything prebaked." Of course, not all leaders are strong, and not all leaders want to hear and carefully consider alternative views.

Finding Common Ground

The reality is that there probably is not one optimum answer for every situation. All companies are different and go through different stages. All individuals are unique and have different competencies and demeanors. Even as someone who believes separation is generally preferable, largely because running the board and running the company are two different positions, and there are risks in the CEO being the head of the group (board) to whom he or she reports, I believe that it would be overly prescriptive to mandate that every company separates the roles.

Matteo Tonello of The Conference Board has written about the three most important indicators of board effectiveness as determined through observations and interviews with directors where in some cases the chair and CEO roles were combined and in others they were separated.[45] These three indicators are the ability to manage dissent, generate a productive group discussion, and facilitate a positive board culture (especially between the board and management).[46]

These qualities can exist when there is duality—when the chair and CEO roles are combined—and they can exist when the top roles are separate; the presence or absence of them depends on the nature of the individuals and the board's dynamics. But it is also the case that these are not necessarily the kinds of qualities that are evaluated in the search for a CEO; if the CEO is also going to be the board chair, attention must be paid to whether the necessary skill set is present.

"It's circumstantial," Jim McCann told me. "You have to look at where the CEO is in their tenure. Are they new to the job or new to the company or new to the industry, where they would benefit by having a more seasoned manager of the board?"

It has understandably been argued that if the CEO is not the board chair, the chair must understand the pressures facing the CEO and the complexities of the role. Michael Useem and his Wharton School of the University of Pennsylvania colleagues make the case that the people best positioned to understand the demands on a CEO are CEOs themselves. "As the number of active or former CEOs chosen for board seats continues its dramatic decline," they explain, "we believe CEO experience is an increasingly important asset [for board leadership]."[47]

I acknowledge that understanding the challenges that CEOs face is critical, but I do not agree that you have to have been a CEO to appreciate them. I like to compare this to the idea that you do not have to have been an all-star player to be a great coach, and in fact, many exceptional athletes have not been great coaches. Michael Jordan is one of the most phenomenal basketball players ever to squeak his shoes on the hardwood and has been extraordinarily successful in business, including as a team owner and pitchman for various consumer products—but his short tenure as a head coach in the NBA was not successful. At the opposite end of the spectrum, Gregg Popovich, the head coach of the San Antonio Spurs since 1996, the longest-tenured head coach in the NBA (though currently sidelined with health issues), and a five-time NBA champion as head coach, played college basketball but never played in the NBA. There are ways to understand well the pressures that a CEO faces, such as by being an experienced senior executive or a proven investment banker or attorney, just as many winning coaches have understood how athletes "tick" and how to motivate them without having been top players themselves.

It is interesting to note that there is fluidity in some companies' decisions on the chair position, and it can well be dependent on the particular CEO's competencies and experiences. Companies sometimes split the roles when a new CEO joins and then combine them again later once the CEO has gained experience and proven effective. In Larcker and Tayan's 2016 Stanford report, it was found that 78 percent of separations were associated with a succession event, but 34 percent of the companies in their sample recombined their chair and CEO roles after "permanently" separating them during the 20-year review period.[48]

As one example from the Stanford report, the electronics retailer Best Buy split the roles for more than a dozen years after founder and chair Richard Schulze stepped down as CEO in 2002 but remained chair until 2012. When Schulze's successor as chair, who was not the CEO, retired, the company gave the board chair position to then CEO Hubert Joly, recombining the roles that had been separated.[49] The price of Best Buy stock roughly doubled in the three years between when Joly was made CEO in 2012 and when he took the chair role, too, in 2015. From 2015 until he dropped the CEO role and became executive chair in 2019, the stock nearly tripled. He then served for a year as executive chair before leaving the company.

Unlike many iconic retailers, such as Toys"R"Us and Bed Bath & Beyond, Best Buy is one of the few major success stories in recent years when it comes to companies in the physical or store-based retail sector. Joly focused on building strong employee relationships and driving excellent customer service as well as adding new functions such as the Geek Squad to provide technical support and help—leading to tremendous growth in the share price.[50] Best Buy split the chair and CEO roles again after his departure and today has an independent board chair.

This kind of back-and-forth is not unusual. Board leadership structures in the Stanford study were not found to be terribly stable, with just one-third of companies making no changes over the 20-year period of examination and the companies that made no changes fairly evenly split between ones that combined the roles and ones that maintained them as separated.[51]

There are also practical considerations with these decisions. Separation of the titles or taking the chair role from the CEO can be perceived as an insult. "From a succession perspective it became difficult," Gursahaney told me, describing a situation he went through on a board. "We didn't want the next person to feel like he was getting less of the job than his predecessor had, so in cases like that, it becomes hard for the chair status to go away."

Consider Dimon's continued status as chair and CEO of JPMorganChase. Some of the company's shareholders made a case for why Dimon should be stripped of his responsibilities as chair in 2012 and 2013. However, the shareholders ultimately chose the security of the status quo, worrying that Dimon would resign if his role as chair was taken away, leaving the company without its proven leader. In 2012, then President Barack Obama even defended Dimon's performance in the midst of his fight to retain his position as chair. President Obama called JPMorganChase "one of the best-managed banks there is . . . [and] Jamie Dimon, the head of it, is one of the smartest bankers we got."[52] Home Depot cofounder Kenneth Langone came to Dimon's defense in 2013 as well: "'He should be both,' Langone . . . said in an interview, calling it 'nuts' to consider splitting Dimon's titles. 'He's probably the finest CEO across any business in America.'"[53] Dimon is an example of a uniquely proven executive who may be a logical choice to hold the two roles at once.

Sometimes, the chair and CEO issue can be industry specific. For a long time, most CEOs in financial services were also the chair. Therefore, high-quality CEO candidates generally expected to be the chair, and boards usually agreed while putting in place a strong lead independent director. Of course, things change, as with Morgan Stanley deciding to keep Gorman as executive chair for a period of time when he retired.

The choice to maintain or recombine the chair and CEO roles may have roots in the economic environment. During the 2008 recession, the percentage of S&P companies with combined positions temporarily plateaued at around 60 percent rather than continuing its downward trend. Boards perhaps feared that separating the two roles could cause distracting change in a very difficult environment.

Interestingly, I was involved in a CEO search where the retiring CEO was the chair too. Our ultimately preferred candidate, who took the job, said that he did not want the chair role but preferred to spend 100 percent of his time running the company.

When a board chooses to combine the roles of chair and CEO, the lead independent director is critical. I have seen situations work where the chair is independent and others where the chair is not. No structure is always perfect. But understanding the needs of the company and seeing they are being met by its board leadership are always vital.

Section III
In What Context Must Directors Work?

Chapter 6
Mergers, Acquisitions, and Sales of Companies

There is perhaps no more important time for board members than when the company on whose board they serve is considering a merger, major acquisition, sale of a substantial business unit, or, of course, sale of the entire company. The duties of care and loyalty discussed earlier are paramount, as directors must determine if the transaction is in the best interest of the shareholders and maximizes value. This is usually a complex decision with many issues, objective and subjective, that must be carefully considered and ultimately decided upon.

Of the public companies on whose boards I have sat, in every case where the company was sold, the directors were sued or threatened with a lawsuit. In fact, there is a saying that seems fairly accurate, or at least it did until recently: "Any time you sell a public company, there will be a lawsuit." Indeed, 82 percent of M&A deals involving public companies valued at over $100 million resulted in shareholder suits as recently as 2018—over 400 lawsuits in all, with 142 challenged deals and an average of 3.1 suits filed per deal—and that was down from an average of 90 percent and 4.7 lawsuits per challenged deal between 2009 and 2015, respectively.[1] The numbers have fallen since then due to the Delaware Court of Chancery's 2016 ruling in the *In re Trulia Stockholder Litigation* case that limited nuisance litigation. As Mike Allen explained to me, the Court of Chancery realized this was effectively a merger tax and not something the Delaware courts wanted to enable, so they worked hard to cut down on the nuisance suits and limit plaintiffs to legitimate issues.

At first, litigation simply moved to federal courts, but subsequent decisions have helped curb lawsuits there as well, and in 2022, shareholder suits challenging M&A deals were down 92 percent compared to the five-year average—with the trend continuing in 2023, with just four related filings in the first half of the year.[2]

Shareholders sometimes feel that a deal does not maximize value, and perhaps the plaintiff's bar sees an opportunity for a profitable settlement. Even with courts seeking to curb nuisance lawsuits of this type, it is still the case that legitimate complaints—where appropriate standards and custom and practice may have not been followed or merely where informed parties have very different views—can create real risk. A carefully considered process by a well-informed, well-advised board cognizant of the appropriate standard for the decision, as well as an indemnity from the company for the directors' actions along with D&O insurance, should leave the board well protected.

Given my experience in this area as an investment banker, corporate director, and expert witness in corporate litigation, including in cases in the Delaware Court of Chancery involving officers and directors of Tesla and Oracle regarding large acquisitions with alleged conflicts, I have developed a seven-step methodology for a board to follow in considering and approving a sale of the company or major acquisition that is consistent with custom and practice. I will share this later in the chapter, but to fully understand the implications for directors in major transactions, it is useful to first examine briefly the history of M&A and how much of the law regarding directors' duties and responsibilities has in fact emerged through M&A transactions and the ensuing legal actions that have required the courts to articulate and define principles and standards that did not previously exist.

A Brief History of M&A

M&A has been around in the modern sense for about 130 years, beginning with the economic expansion of the late 1890s. It was a time of technological growth and process innovations that drove economies of scale to develop in major industries such as steel, oil, mining, and the railroads.[3] There were benefits to becoming larger, and combined with new state legislation regarding incorporations and the beginning of trading in industrial stocks on the NYSE, horizontal consolidation ("merging to form monopolies," as Columbia University's George Stigler described it three-quarters of a century ago) led to the creation of behemoths, including Standard Oil Company of New Jersey and the United States Steel Corporation.[4]

There are generally two types of M&A deals: strategic and financial. A strategic, or corporate, transaction is when a corporate buyer seeks advantages such as to grow revenue, improve market share, add new products, enter new markets, and realize cost savings by eliminating duplicative efforts and revenue synergies from driving more sales through opportunities that the business combination provides.[5] A financial deal is led by investors such as private equity firms. These buyers are typically looking to invest in companies they can improve in some way or ways—investing more capital to facilitate organic growth, making complementary acquisitions, reducing operating costs, and so on—and sell for a profit in the future.[6] Of course, an initial or platform acquisition by an investment firm often leads to add-on acquisitions that can be considered strategic deals, and it is also the case that corporate or strategic acquirers certainly have financial motives for deals as well.

Perhaps counterintuitively, sometimes a financial buyer outbids a corporate buyer. After all, a corporate buyer should have a lower cost of debt and equity capital as well as savings and synergies to realize. However, the public markets typically discourage public companies from being as leveraged as private equity–owned companies, and there are substantial tax advantages with debt (interest is tax deductible subject to certain limits) that lower the average cost of deals with substantial debt.

Generally, funding for strategic deals is cash and/or stock and, for financial deals, is new debt raised from lenders and equity contributed by investors or limited partners in investment funds.

The early history of M&A was exclusively strategic deals such as the oil and steel transactions mentioned earlier. In the 1920s, the next wave of M&A focused on the consolidation of gas and electric utilities, highlighted by the purchase of Brooklyn Edison by Consolidated Gas in 1928. Horizontal energy acquisitions enabled economies of scale, though this resulted in a number of monopolies that caused the US government to intervene and prohibit anticompetitive behavior, giving teeth to the Sherman Antitrust Act, originally passed in 1890.

The Great Depression slowed merger activity for years, and we can jump to the 1980s—dubbed the "Deal Decade"—and the emergence of corporate raiders, hostile takeovers, and financial deals as the next significant developments in M&A. High-yield or "junk bond" financing became readily available, and LBOs—more about them later—took off. Whereas acquisitions had previously involved companies where boards and management teams were willing to make deals, corporate raiders such as Carl Icahn moved to engineer hostile takeovers, without, at least initially, the consent of the sellers' boards, through tender offers, proxy fights, and other efforts.

M&A deals have grown dramatically in frequency and dollar volume over the past four decades, driven not only by more availability of financing and LBOs but also by larger companies seeing M&A as a desirable way to grow as well as by companies looking beyond local borders, moving M&A global.[7] In the 1970s, there were just four M&A deals valued at more than $1 billion; since 2000, there have been over 200 deals valued at over $20 billion each. Today, a $1 billion M&A transaction is not particularly noteworthy. In 1985, there were 2,309 M&A deals in the US valued at a total of just over $300 billion.[8] By 2021, there were 25,170 deals valued at almost $3.5 trillion, a more than ten times increase.[9]

In one of the largest deals ever, AOL acquired Time Warner in 2000, a $182 billion transaction that is seen as perhaps the worst in M&A history. As the world moved from dial-up internet to high-speed broadband, AOL was left behind. "New" Time Warner suffered from the collapse of the dot-com bubble shortly after the deal and the implosion of the online advertising market. The two companies' cultures were never able to meld effectively, and AOL was spun off in 2009.[10]

With large deals now commonplace, the M&A advisory business, including ideas and deal execution provided by global banks and boutique firms, has become a multibillion-dollar industry. But the biggest players are less well known than the "rainmakers" in the later decades of the last century. In the 1980s and '90s, it seemed that most Fortune 500 CEOs and virtually everyone in the financial services industry knew the most prominent M&A bankers, such as Felix Rohatyn at Lazard, Bob Greenhill at Morgan Stanley, and Geoff Boisi at Goldman Sachs.

I worked for Rohatyn earlier in my career. He was a remarkable immigrant success story, having escaped from Nazi-occupied France as a child and eventually rising to become Wall Street's preeminent investment banker. "I had no idea what an investment bank did," Rohatyn wrote in his autobiography about the start of his career. "But I did need a paycheck."[11]

As an advisor, Rohatyn was a key player in many complex transactions, including the merger of Loews Corporation with Lorillard Tobacco, the acquisition of Loral by Lockheed Martin (where I was on the Lazard team and had yet another vacation canceled when the firm was hired in December to advise Loral), and the acquisition of Paramount Communications by Viacom. Rohatyn compared his work to that of a surgeon: "I get called when something is broken. I'm supposed to operate, fix it and leave as little blood on the floor as possible."[12]

I still remember his trademark button-down shirts, the two heavy wooden doors he sat behind before you entered his rather spartan office, the slide rule that he would use to check your numbers, and how he left for the day with a cardboard file of papers under his arm to walk a dozen blocks home.

At the same time, over the past few decades, the number and size of internal company M&A departments have increased dramatically. Today, every public company that I know has at least one internal M&A person, and many large companies have more than 10 people in this function. M&A has become less of a "black box" known well only by a very limited group of senior bankers, and information that was previously difficult to source has become democratized thanks to technology and databases. Key issues such as whether the target fits with the company's strategy and the savings and synergies that an acquirer should be able to deliver can often be more effectively addressed by company personnel than outside advisors.

Gary Matt and I met as young bankers in the mid-1980s. He went on to be a managing director in M&A at Lehman Brothers and then Barclays; he is now vice president of corporate development at Thermo Fisher Scientific, the world leader in serving science, with a market capitalization of some $200 billion. In the three years ending in June 2024, Thermo Fisher Scientific acquired companies with a total enterprise value of more than $25 billion.

Matt explained to me, "The task for any company is to do the work to gain conviction on what an acquisition or divestiture would mean to their company. This requires a thorough and thoughtful evaluation on an operational and financial basis. It also means a consideration of the effect on all of the company's stakeholders: shareholders, customers, employees, regulators, et cetera. Based on that judgment, a good decision on value and whether to transact can be made."

Internal M&A groups can be particularly valuable in strategic and post-deal execution considerations. Advisors can be very additive due to their market knowledge, experience in related transactions, and access to the opinions of other market participants. In fact, part of the rationale of investment banks organizing their M&A efforts into industry groups in the mid-1990s was to provide clients with industry viewpoints and industry information, not just strong technical expertise. In an increasingly sophisticated and competitive M&A environment, companies can undoubtedly benefit from both an internal M&A team and investment bankers, outside counsel, and consultants.

Van Gorkom and the Duty of Care

Under most circumstances, as discussed in chapter 3, board actions are evaluated under the business judgment rule: Was the process reasonable and were the actions taken in good faith by independent directors? However, business judgment—the deferral to boards provided they act in good faith—is not always the standard when a company is involved in an M&A transaction. Problematic M&A transactions have been the impetus to move beyond business judgment in certain situations. In chapter 3, we examined the duty of care, addressed in the 1985 Delaware Supreme Court case *Smith v. Van Gorkom* (*Van Gorkom*), where shareholders sought rescission of an M&A deal. It is worth giving the transaction and case a closer look here to understand clearly what sparked the duty of care and how the court's decision to hold the board liable for its actions went on to shape expectations about director behavior going forward.

In *Van Gorkom*, shareholders of Trans Union, a holding company whose cash flow was largely generated by its railcar leasing business, argued that the board's approval of a sale to Marmon Group was not the product of an informed business judgment.

In 1980, Jerome Van Gorkom, the defendant in *Van Gorkom*, had been the CEO of Trans Union for nearly 18 years and was spending much of his time trying to solve what seemed to him an intractable problem. The company was entitled to an increasing dollar amount of investment tax credits but did not have sufficient taxable income to fully utilize them.[13] In order to generate the income necessary, the company had completed many acquisitions and lobbied Congress to make the unused tax credits reimbursable to the company as cash. He was unsuccessful and sought another solution.[14]

Donald Romans, the CFO of Trans Union, had seen an article in the press about burgeoning LBOs, or acquisitions typically made by investment firms with a little equity and a lot of debt. According to the court, Romans "ran the numbers . . . to determine the cash flow needed to service the debt that would 'probably' be incurred in a leveraged buy-out, based on 'rough calculations' without 'any benefit of experts.'"[15]

At the meeting where Romans presented his initial findings, Van Gorkom expressed that he—approaching 65 years of age and mandatory retirement—would be willing to accept $55 per share for the 75,000 shares he owned (just approximately 0.5 percent of the outstanding shares of the company). Nearing retirement, he simply wanted to do a deal. And while $55 per share was a significant premium over the $29.50 to $38.25 range that the company had been trading at during the course of the year, no effort was made to bring in advisors to help determine the actual value of Trans Union—and this was ultimately the problem that led to the lawsuit and to the articulation of the duty of care. As the Delaware Supreme Court wrote, "Apart from the Company's historic stock market price, and Van Gorkom's long association with Trans Union, the record is devoid of any competent evidence that $55 represented the per share intrinsic value of the Company."[16]

Van Gorkom approached an acquaintance, Jay Pritzker, the cofounder of Hyatt Hotels and an eventual billionaire who acquired hundreds of companies over the course of his career. Van Gorkom asked Pritzker if he might be interested in buying the entire company at $55 per share. Three days later, Pritzker made a $55 cash offer through his holding company, Marmon Group, and Van Gorkom called an emergency board meeting.

The initial reaction by the rest of the board was negative. Trans Union CFO Romans believed that the price was too low and that there would be "adverse tax consequences of an all-cash deal for low-basis shareholders."[17] He also worried that allowing Pritzker to buy so many shares at the market price (part of the proposed deal was to allow Pritzker to acquire one million shares at the market price immediately) would effectively act as a "lock-up" preventing other offers.[18]

In a 20-minute presentation by Van Gorkom to the board, he explained that a 90-day waiting period, where Trans Union would be free to receive other offers (but not actively shop the company), would be sufficient to establish that $55 was a fair price. The board dropped its objections and voted to approve the transaction. Immediately following the announcement of the sale, the reaction of senior management was very negative, with key officers threatening to resign. Indeed, according to the court, there was an "'en masse' revolt . . . [with the] head of Trans Union's tank car operations (its most profitable division) [informing] Van Gorkom that unless the merger were called off, fifteen key personnel would resign."[19]

While never made public, it has been said that there was another serious offer for Trans Union but that it never progressed due to various factors. The sale to Marmon was ultimately approved by the holders of 70 percent of the outstanding shares, but litigation was brought. While the Delaware Court of Chancery applied the business judgment rule—deferring to the board and saying that it acted appropriately—on appeal, the Delaware Supreme Court disagreed and defined a duty of "due care and prudence" that directors must follow.[20]

As noted in chapter 3, the Delaware Supreme Court in *Van Gorkom* explained that "a director's duty to exercise an informed business judgment is in the nature of a duty of care," defining this duty as "an affirmative duty to protect [the stockholders' financial] interests and to proceed with a critical eye in assessing information."[21]

"On the record before us," the court went on to say, "we must conclude that the Board of Directors did not reach an informed business judgment . . . [and] at a minimum, were grossly negligent in approving the 'sale' of the Company upon two hours' consideration, without prior notice, and without the exigency of a crisis or emergency."[22]

Lacking valuation analysis or a legitimate market test, the board was found to have breached the fiduciary duty of care to stockholders, and the case now stands as the articulation of this duty of care that directors must fulfill.[23] Furthermore, the court held the directors liable for the difference between the fair value of the share price and the deal price—these monetary damages assessed to directors being perhaps the most significant legacy of the case. In the end, the case was sent back to the Court of Chancery, and the directors settled before the court made its ruling, agreeing to pay $23.5 million, $10 million of which was covered by insurance and the rest of which Pritzker agreed to pay even though he was not involved in the lawsuit.

The impact of *Van Gorkom* was indeed profound. Three years later, Stephen Radin of the law firm Weil wrote that the decision "shocked the corporate world," citing a *New York Law Journal* article that called it a "'distinct threat to the ability of companies to attract responsible directors.'"[24] "Particularly startling to many," Radin continued, "was the dramatization that individuals serving on corporate boards could be held liable for monetary damages for conduct undertaken in good faith."[25]

Others were more sanguine, arguing that the facts in *Van Gorkom* were so egregious as to make the case stand alone; this was not so much a change in the law as the application of existing law to an outlier situation. Radin cited a former Delaware Supreme Court justice in saying that "'a board of directors, without any significant particularized internal or external advanced study, and without prior agenda notice, cannot rely on the protection of the business judgment rule in approving a $700 million sale of 100% of the corporation in a two-hour meeting.'"[26]

The cases that followed *Van Gorkom* largely supported those who said this would not in fact revolutionize director liability. Radin found that in 18 of

24 cases that arose in the three years after *Van Gorkom* alleging duty of care violations, courts did not find fault in the board members' actions, and in the six where they did, injunctive relief was the remedy, not monetary liability for directors.

What did happen as a result of the case is that 33 states, including Delaware, very quickly passed statutes to largely prevent monetary damages from being assessed to directors. In Delaware, the General Assembly enacted a provision protecting directors from monetary liability for any actions arising from a breach of their duty of care, as long as the corporation's shareholders approved the inclusion of such a provision in the certificate of incorporation. "In essence," wrote Bernard Sharfman in a 1988 article, "Delaware lawmakers gave shareholders of Delaware corporations the opportunity to veto the [*Smith v.*] *Van Gorkom* decision if they found it was not in their best interests."[27]

"And veto they did," Sharfman goes on to write. "Out of a sample of one hundred Fortune 500 companies, ninety-eight . . . adopted an exculpatory provision."[28] Many states followed Delaware's lead and either raised the standard of culpability by law or allowed shareholders to specify in a company's certificate of incorporation that directors would not be held liable for monetary damages in situations where the duty of care was violated except in very limited circumstances (such as acting in bad faith).[29]

This may seem to imply that we can disregard *Van Gorkom*, but of course, that is not the message. It is true that directors are typically not going to be held personally liable for duty of care violations. But significant duty of care violations can certainly be violations of good faith. Are directors acting in good faith if they make hasty, ill-considered decisions and fail to consider the full scope of information available to them? Law professor John A. Humbach wrote in the *New York Law School Law Review* about how protecting directors from liability when making good-faith judgments is necessary in recruiting directors but does not protect them in every situation: "It is one thing to make defrauders and self-dealers give back their ill-gotten gains; it is something else again to force people who make good-faith mistakes in judgment to dig into their own personal assets to indemnify others whom they were only trying to serve."[30]

It would be an overstatement to say that Jerome Van Gorkom went down in infamy for his actions in this case; it is likely that few observers have ever given him much thought. But it is, in large part, thanks to *Van Gorkom* that the courts defined and board members now understand the duty of care.

Revlon and "Enhanced Scrutiny"

It is not the case that business judgment and entire fairness are the only standards at play in M&A transactions. The 1986 *Revlon* case, from the Delaware Supreme Court, established a higher standard, known as "enhanced scrutiny," when the sale of a company is all but inevitable. In this case, the court ruled that the board has one specific fiduciary obligation: to maximize value for shareholders.

This standard emerged in the context of the purchase of Revlon by Ronald Perelman, then the CEO of Pantry Pride and a budding activist. The Revlon board did not want Perelman—ultimately five-times-married and a billionaire, but ironically he was reportedly liquidating assets in 2022 in the wake of Revlon's bankruptcy reorganization, where he lost his majority stake in the company[31]—as Revlon's new owner, fearing his plan to break up the company, and rejected his initial offer in mid-1985 of as much as $45 per share (which was approximately the stock price at the time).

Perelman had initially tried to befriend Revlon CEO Michel Bergerac, attempting to charm him into supporting and even joining his takeover effort. But Bergerac rebuffed Perelman—and Perelman decided to take on the company anyway, later bad-mouthing Bergerac as living "the biggest life of any C.E.O. in America."[32] As the *New York Times* wrote in 2022, "People from Mr. Perelman's team will tell you he is one of the most generous people they have ever met. People from the opposing one will tell you he is vicious. . . . Expensive watches are given to employees, trees are planted in parks to honor friends' dead relatives, and wars ensue with those who cross him."[33]

Perelman and his company, Pantry Pride, made a hostile cash offer for Revlon at $47.50 per share, a modest premium over the $45 stock price at the time, and as the Revlon board advised shareholders not to accept the offer or any subsequent ones, Perelman raised his bid over the next few weeks to $53 per share.

At this point, the Revlon board was under pressure and started to search for a friendly suitor. It began discussions with the private equity firm Forstmann Little for a deal at $56 per share, and with the advice of probably the most prominent M&A lawyer since the advent of contemporary deals, Marty Lipton, Revlon adopted two antitakeover steps to try to prevent Perelman's unwanted efforts: it planned to repurchase 5 million shares (of nearly 30 million outstanding shares), and it put in place a "poison pill" allowing shareholders to exchange each share of Revlon for a note in the principal amount of $65 with a 12 percent interest rate and a one-year maturity if anyone acquired 20 percent or more of Revlon's shares.[34]

The "poison pill" is said to have been invented by Lipton in the early 1980s as a defense against the growing issue of hostile takeovers by unwanted outsiders. With it, if a hostile bidder acquires a designated percentage of a company's shares, shareholders gain the right to exchange their shares for a premium, buy shares at a discount, or do something similar that will drive up the price for an unfriendly suitor.

Poison pills hypothetically make companies unable to be acquired at an economically rational price. Therefore, it has been argued that this is bad for shareholders, since it locks in current management and can prohibit shareholders from selling their stock at a premium.[35] It is actually the case that poison pills are often effective as threats to prevent premature actions, and even at the height of their use, they were rarely triggered; typically, takeovers at what is seen to be fair value are usually agreed upon. It was reported that between 1997 and 2001, "for every company with a poison pill that successfully rebuffed an unwanted advance and remained independent, 20 pill-protected companies accepted takeover offers."[36]

Aside from poison pills, companies have another important defensive protection. Section 203 of the Delaware Corporate Code, enacted in 1988, delays a hostile takeover for three years unless the acquirer buys 85 percent of the target company's shares in a single tender offer, a stipulation that can discourage bidders for less than the entire company and can sometimes result in more amicable negotiations between the potential acquirer and the target company.[37]

The reality is that the real value of the poison pill is in the threat rather than the use of it. In fact, not a single pill was triggered in the US until December 2008, when Versata Enterprises triggered a pill adopted by Selectica.[38] The Delaware Supreme Court upheld the board's right to use this defense mechanism, establishing that the poison pill defense was appropriate in cases where the pill genuinely protects a legitimate corporate interest, represents a disinterested business judgment, is put in place after a careful process is followed, and does not make a successful proxy contest realistically unattainable.[39]

By 2010, the popularity of pills had diminished significantly, dropping to their lowest level in two decades. Pressure from shareholders, proxy advisory firms, and other parties drove the decline. In 2005, 54 percent of S&P 1500 companies had adopted pills that would be triggered if a party acquired the required percentage of the companies' stocks; by 2010, that number had declined to just 28 percent.[40] Data from 2020 shows that roughly 200 companies—down from over 2,200 two decades ago—still had an active poison pill in place.[41] Many others have a pill "on the shelf," ready but not in place until and unless a threat arrives.

Lipton has said that he invented the poison pill not to prevent takeovers but to level the playing field and give the target's board time to make a rational decision.[42] On a crisp October afternoon in 2023, I was fortunate to sit with Lipton, in his 90s but still engaged, in his office in Midtown Manhattan. It was not lost on me that he was in a dark suit, crisp white shirt, and tie—on a Friday. I had heard that he still dressed traditionally, so I had too. "The poison pill was an effective means of defense for 30 years," Lipton told me, "but the power of the institutional investor has rendered it less effective today when it comes to defending a company. It's still useful in certain situations, but ISS and the Council of Institutional Investors have deterred companies from using it as a prophylactic. For the most part, corporations now have decided not to have one until they are either attacked or feel the hot breath of being attacked."

In the *Revlon* case, the Revlon board ultimately settled on a deal with Forstmann Little at a price only slightly greater than Perelman's bid and worth less when considering the time value of money, as Perelman was proposing a tender offer that would close promptly, whereas the LBO would require financing, a shareholder meeting, and a vote as well as other steps that would take a number of months. The LBO also included a very strict no-shop provision (a prohibition on contacting or even responding to other potential buyers; a typical no-shop usually at least permits the seller to respond to unsolicited interest) and a lock-up option (a commitment to sell various assets at agreed prices) for Forstmann Little.[43]

As Professor Zachary Gubler writes, the provisions incorporated in the deal "effectively ended bidding for Revlon since Perelman could not compete with those agreements in place," and this "was particularly problematic in a situation like Revlon's where it was inevitable that the company was going to be broken up. . . . In that context, the court determined that '[t]he directors' role changed from defenders of the corporate bastion to auctioneers charged with getting the best price for the stockholders at a sale of the company.'"[44]

The deal protections, in other words, meant that value could not be maximized, and the board had acted improperly. The Delaware Supreme Court stopped the sale to Forstmann Little, and Perelman acquired Revlon for $58 per share. "The decision is important," wrote the *New York Times* just after the ruling, "because it established that while it may be perfectly legal to set up certain roadblocks, such as poison pills, to give directors more time to bargain, it appears to be illegal for directors to construct too many roadblocks and to chill bidding rather than make bidding possible."[45] "How Ronald O. Perelman accomplished this feat," the *Times* went on to say, "demonstrates that, in this era of the corporate raider, virtually no company is safe from takeover—regardless of the array of legal and financial roadblocks that it may erect."[46]

Perelman took Revlon public in 1996 and continued to own a majority of the company's stock—85 percent—until Revlon entered bankruptcy in 2022. The company emerged from bankruptcy in April 2023 with Perelman no longer a shareholder for the first time in almost four decades.[47]

It should be noted that the *Revlon* standard requires reasonableness, not perfection. Professor Clark W. Furlow explains that "[the issue is] whether the board made a reasonable, rather than a perfect, decision. If the board's decision is one of several reasonable alternatives, it should be approved by the court even if the judge thinks a different course of action would have been better."[48]

It should also be noted that maximizing value does not always mean accepting the highest nominal price. Boards are permitted to and should take into account factors such as the risk that a transaction will not close due to antitrust or other considerations as well as noncash elements of the deal. A board may rightly choose an offer where the due diligence is completed, financing is committed, and there are no apparent regulatory hurdles over an offer that is slightly higher but has a significant risk of not closing.[49] In *In re Dollar Thrifty Shareholder Litigation*, for example, the Delaware Court of Chancery found that, in a proposed merger with Hertz, the board of the rental car company Dollar Thrifty had not violated its duties in declining a last-minute higher bid, having concluded that the new bidder lacked the resources to finance the deal.[50]

I remember that Rohatyn used to dislike incentive fees for investment bankers, or a higher fee if a higher price was realized for a company, because he did not want even the optics of a fee structure to distract from advising a client to accept the "best deal" rather than the "highest price."

Subsequent cases have established that *Revlon* applies in three scenarios: (1) when a corporation initiates an active bidding process to sell itself or effect a breakup of the company, (2) when a company abandons its long-term strategy in response to a bidder's offer and seeks an alternative transaction involving a breakup, or (3) when approval of a transaction results in a sale or change of control.[51] It should be noted that *Revlon* is sometimes misunderstood to apply in situations where a board is just considering a sale. This is not the case. It is only the case that a board should be sensitive to the "*Revlon* Duty" if a sale of the company is imminent, because its process will be reviewed under the *Revlon* standard if a sale ultimately occurs.

Rob Kindler is global chair of the M&A group at the law firm Paul, Weiss and was formerly vice chair and global head of M&A at Morgan Stanley, managing director and global head of M&A at JPMorganChase, and a partner at the law firm Cravath. He even had a license plate on his car for some time that read "MNA GUY." "*Revlon* applies when there's going to be a change of control," Kindler summarized, "and when there won't be another opportunity to sell the company."

Enhanced scrutiny does not only apply in a sale of a company. Under the *Unocal* standard, articulated in the 1985 case *Unocal v. Mesa Petroleum*, an enhanced level of scrutiny is applied when companies adopt defensive measures against threats to control. In this situation, boards must show that they had "reasonable grounds for believing that a danger to corporate policy and effectiveness existed" and show that the chosen defensive measure was "reasonable in relation to the threat posed."[52] The *Unocal* framework was used by the Delaware Supreme Court in *Moran v. Household International* (and then later the *Versata v. Selectica* case) to uphold the right of companies to deploy poison pills.[53]

There are many examples of how poison pills and *Revlon* duties have played out in practice. The industrial gas distributor Airgas is an important example of a large company that fought off a hostile takeover and later was sold for a much higher price, ultimately benefiting shareholders. Peter McCausland started Airgas in 1982, buying one gas distributor for $5 million. He realized that the industry was largely populated by small companies and that Airgas could consolidate the industry through acquisitions and become a much stronger, more valuable company.[54] As the *Philadelphia Inquirer* wrote in 2007 after the company purchased a packaged gas business, "It's the 355th acquisition by chief executive officer Peter McCausland, a former mergers-and-acquisitions attorney who had the keen insight in the early 1980s that the gas business was ripe for consolidation."[55]

In 2009, Airgas was approached by Air Products, a competitor. "McCausland took the offer to the board," wrote the *New York Times* in 2016, "which rejected it as undervaluing the company. . . . In February 2010, Air Products went hostile with its $5 billion bid to shareholders [approximately $60 per share]."[56]

It was a very real threat. But Airgas had two important protections: a poison pill, which effectively stopped any single shareholder from building up a stake greater than 15 percent of the company without approval from the directors, and a staggered board (more on that in chapter 7), meaning that only 3 of the 11 directors were up for election in any given year.

Air Products was very aggressive. To get past the poison pill, it needed to find a way to gain a majority on the board. To do that quickly, Air Products aimed to move the next two Airgas annual meetings closer to each other on the calendar. Over McCausland's objections, Airgas shareholders voted with Air Products to remove McCausland and two other directors from the board at the first meeting and then voted to move up the next meeting.

Nevertheless, the fight was not over. Experienced director Paula Sneed was on the board of Airgas at the time. "When we had to bring the new Air Products directors onto the board and some of our long-standing board members were exited, it was a crisis period for us," Sneed explained to me. "But the board did something smart. Understanding the power of a united board, we worked very deliberately to bring the new members onboard, spending time and energy explaining to them what we knew to be the right thing for the Airgas shareholders. What won the battle for us was the new board members voted with the legacy Airgas board members as opposed to standing alone and creating tension in the boardroom." Indeed, the board—despite now including three Air Products nominees—unanimously rejected Air Products' offer as "clearly inadequate."[57]

It is worth noting that regardless of who nominates a director for a board seat—be it the company, an investor, or an activist—directors are elected by the shareholders and are responsible to all of them, not just to an investor, activist, or other party. This is how Airgas was able to prevail in this scenario. The Air Products nominees voted with the legacy Airgas directors and not in the way Air Products imagined they would.

The offer from Air Products at the time the board voted it down was $70 per share, up from the $60 initial bid. The fight appeared to be over. However, Air Products returned three years later and tried again. McCausland shared his story with me:

> I met with the Air Products CEO, who had a banker's book telling me that if I cared about my shareholders, we needed to sell to him. And then he ripped out a page, and it showed the overlap between the shareholders of Airgas and Air Products. And we had an 84 percent overlap, so if something was going to be a winner for Air Products, even if it wasn't right for Airgas, we were going to lose. We gave a presentation on why the institutional investors should vote for us and against Air Products. They listened to us, but then they said, "Peter, we're a large shareholder for an index fund. So we're a large shareholder of both companies. But because Air Products is a bigger company, we have a much larger stake in Air Products. I see what you're arguing, but even if it's a bad deal for Airgas, it's a good deal for Air Products, and so it's a good deal for us on balance."

McCausland did not give up. Exhausted from the fight and cognizant of the threat from Air Products, he ended up finding a buyer in Air Liquide, a French company that made an offer for $143 a share, more than double what the Air Products offer had been a few years earlier.

Daniel Neff is a partner, former co-chair, and now a member of the executive committee at Wachtell Lipton and a leading M&A attorney with a long history of defending companies from activists and hostile attacks. Neff and Wachtell Lipton advised Airgas in fending off Air Products. "Airgas was a classic takeover defense," Neff explained to me.

> We were capable of doing it, because we had a staggered board. But we lost the first of what was going to be two elections and meetings. Between the first and second annual meeting, we got a court decision that slowed down the hostile bidder [the Delaware Supreme Court rejected Air Products' attempt to force Airgas to hold its next shareholder meeting early]. That pause enabled the company to [gain the votes of the Air Products–nominated directors and] end up being sold four years later for so much more. We had an extremely strong feeling that great value would be lost if the

company were forced to be sold at the time the hostile bidder was trying to buy.

"It's been a fabulous deal for Air Liquide," McCausland told me. "And I'm glad, because that means it's been a good deal for my colleagues."

A more recent example of a poison pill situation is at PGT Innovations, a maker of impact-resistant windows and doors. The company rejected an initial $33 per share, $2.2 billion cash takeover bid in 2023 from Miter Brands, a competitor with backing from Koch Industries.[58] PGT had adopted a poison pill nine months earlier, justifying it at the time with concerns over an investor starting to build up a stake in the company. At Masonite, where, as I mentioned earlier, I was a director and chair of the audit committee for more than a decade until the company was sold to Owens Corning in 2024 for approximately $4 billion, there was clear strategic logic to extend its product offerings into those that PGT provided. Shortly after Miter's offer, Masonite announced an offer for $41 per share that the PGT board originally welcomed. Miter then increased its offer to $42 per share, and PGT recommended that its shareholders accept that proposal. The competitive process, facilitated in part by the poison pill, helped the PGT shareholders realize more value than they likely otherwise would have.

The 2015 Delaware Supreme Court case *Corwin v. KKR Financial Holdings* added an important clarification to *Revlon* situations, ruling that even when it comes to deals where *Revlon* would apply, once a transaction is approved by a fully informed, uncoerced majority of the disinterested stockholders, the standard of review reverts to the business judgment rule.[59]

In *Corwin*, shareholders filed a challenge after a stock-for-stock merger between KKR and KKR Financial, arguing that because KKR Financial's primary business was financing KKR's LBO activities and because KKR Financial was managed by an affiliate of KKR, not by independent management, KKR was the controlling stockholder of KKR Financial and the merger should have been subject to the entire fairness standard. The court held that shareholders were informed about the relationship between the two companies, KKR Financial had an independent board entitled to exercise its judgment, and "the business judgment standard of review was invoked because the merger was approved by a disinterested stockholder majority."[60]

Finally, I should note that there is a limit to *Corwin*'s power to avoid challenges to a deal once the disinterested shareholders approve it: the right under the Delaware General Corporation Law for stockholders to inspect corporate records under Section 220 if the stockholder declares a proper purpose "reasonably related to such person's interest as a stockholder."[61]

Activists have made wide use of Section 220 in recent years, hoping to find evidence of corporate mismanagement. In *Lavin v. West Corporation*, a 2017 Delaware Court of Chancery case, West Corporation sought to use the *Corwin* decision to stop shareholders from exercising a Section 220 demand to see records, claiming that because the company's merger with Apollo had been approved by a majority of disinterested shareholders, "the stockholder vote 'cleansed' any purported breaches of fiduciary duty."[62]

The court held that *Corwin* would not "stand as an impediment to an otherwise properly supported demand for inspection"[63] and that even a fully informed stockholder approval of a transaction would not foreclose the right of shareholders to review corporate information. West Corporation's argument was rejected, and the company was forced to allow inspection of its records. The practical implication of this decision is that directors should always exercise due care, and these obligations do not stop even if the disinterested shareholders approve a particular action.

Weinberger, "Entire Fairness," and the Duty of Loyalty

The enhanced scrutiny required by *Revlon* presumes good faith and a lack of conflicts of interest, which, of course, brings to mind the other overarching duty directors are obligated to abide by, as discussed previously in chapter 3: the duty of loyalty. While the duty of loyalty did not emerge from an M&A case (rather, it came from the double-dealing of Charles G. Guth, president of the candy company Loft, as explained in chapter 3), the way it applies in the M&A context is dealt with authoritatively in *Weinberger*, which came before the Delaware Supreme Court three years before *Revlon*, in 1983, and the development of a standard even more rigorous than enhanced scrutiny.

Enhanced scrutiny should not change a high-quality board's process, but the entire fairness standard—which we examine next—is Delaware's most onerous standard of review and one well beyond business judgment and enhanced scrutiny. Entire fairness requires that directors show the fairness of both the process and the price for the transaction that they approved.

In the *Weinberger* case, Signal had previously acquired 50.5 percent of the shares of UOP, a large petroleum company that was founded in 1914. When Signal wanted to buy the rest of the shares, the Signal board asked two of its directors, who were also UOP directors, to determine an appropriate price. Based on the results of a feasibility study, they found that up to $24 per share would be "a good investment."[64] Signal proposed to buy the remaining shares at $21 per share. Within four days, UOP received a fairness opinion from Lehman Brothers that $21 was fair to the UOP shareholders from a financial point of view, and a few days later, the UOP board met and approved the deal. The two directors who had done the initial study abstained from the vote, but they did participate in the deliberations and did not reveal the existence of findings in their report. UOP's board recommended that the shareholders approve the deal, which they did, but minority shareholders brought a suit challenging the transaction's fairness.[65]

The court articulated that review under an "entire fairness" standard was appropriate in cases where directors are interested in the transaction or an interested shareholder controls the board. The two-pronged standard that the court set out in *Weinberger* evolved from a 1952 Delaware Supreme Court case, *Gottlieb v. Heyden Chemical*, involving a board voting themselves stock options without stockholder ratification. The court in that case argued that by doing this, the board "assumed the burden of clearly proving their utmost good faith and the most scrupulous inherent fairness of the bargain."[66]

The entire fairness standard provided in *Weinberger* involves looking at fair dealing ("when the transaction was timed, how it was initiated, structured, negotiated, disclosed to the directors, and how the approvals of the directors and the stockholders were obtained") and fair price (the economic and financial considerations of the proposed transaction, "including all relevant factors: assets, market value, earnings, future prospects, and any other elements that affect the intrinsic or inherent value of a company's stock").[67] Here, the court ruled that entire fairness was not met because the feasibility study was hidden from UOP, and the UOP CEO did not even attempt to negotiate a price higher than the initial $21 per share offer. In addition, Signal rushed UOP to approve the deal when there was no business reason to do so. The Delaware Supreme Court remanded the case back to the Court of Chancery to consider the price aspect; the court ultimately decided that $22 would have been fair and ruled that the minority shareholders should be paid an additional $1 per share.[68]

In subsequent cases, it has been established that entire fairness is the appropriate standard when there are conflicts on the board. In summary, there are five scenarios where it applies: when (1) the board breaches its duty of care and the directors are not exculpated from liability, (2) a majority of the board has an interest in the decision or transaction that differs from the stockholders in general, (3) a majority of the board lacks independence from or is dominated by an interested party, (4) the transaction is one where the directors or a controlling stockholder stands on both sides, or (5) a controlling stockholder receives additional consideration to the detriment of the other stockholders.[69]

A special committee of independent directors can help avoid the entire fairness standard. The Delaware Court of Chancery, in *In re MFW Shareholders Litigation* (*MFW*), held that if a transaction is negotiated by a "special committee of independent directors fully empowered to say no, and approval by an uncoerced, fully informed vote of a majority of the minority investors [is obtained], the business judgment rule standard of review applies" rather than entire fairness.[70]

"*MFW* gave us the guideposts to get to business judgment," Mike Allen explains. "If you can check all the boxes, have the transaction negotiated by an independent committee of directors, and get a majority of the minority stockholder approval, then at least you have a pathway and you can make a business decision on whether that's a pathway you want to go down."

Special committees are effective when its director members are "disinterested and independent," meaning that they must disclose and not have any material financial or business relationships, or social or personal relationships, with the interested party or parties.[71] In the *Smurfit-Stone* case described in chapter 3, our independent special committee helped protect our board from being subject to the entire fairness standard when considering an LBO. There is usually an effort by a board and its advisors to avoid the entire fairness standard when considering a transaction, and there is usually an effort by a defendant in litigation to not be held to entire fairness when a plaintiff claims that is the appropriate standard. However, Kindler makes the point that "no one should be afraid of entire fairness. At the end of the day, after all, that's what you're trying to do anyway [follow a fair process and obtain a fair price]." That is true. But entire fairness is much harder to defend in litigation than business judgment.

The Special Case of Leveraged Buyouts

Earlier, I mentioned that LBOs are a specific type of deal: acquisitions that are made with substantial debt borrowed based on the target companies' assets and cash flows. Usually, these deals are executed by investment professionals at private equity firms with equity raised from investors in one or more funds and debt provided by various lenders. After closing, the firms seek to improve the companies, usually by growing revenues, enhancing margins, and increasing cash flows. Ultimately, the investors seek to exit, typically by selling or taking the companies public. LBOs have some history and governance implications that are well worth exploring.

One of the early LBO pioneers was Charles H. Dyson—later dubbed by *Forbes* as the "father of leveraged buyouts."[72] In 1954, having come up with a plan to buy a company using primarily debt, he secured $4.6 million from the First National Bank of Boston, combining it with $8,000 of his own money, to purchase Hubbard & Company, a maker of electric utility hardware, and launch his own Dyson Corporation. His son, John Dyson, is a successful financier who was, among other political appointments, Commissioner of Commerce of New York State. This put him in charge of economic development and tourism when the "I Love New York" campaign was founded. John Dyson remembered his father's first LBO in a conversation with me. "Dad would say, 'Well, yes, it's true I put up $8,000 of my own money to buy Hubbard, but that's because I only had $8,000! I had to go borrow $4 million from a bank in order to put the deal together. If I had the money to buy the company outright, I probably never would have thought of it.'"

Charlie Dyson had grown up in a poor family: his father was a union carpenter in New Jersey. He was offered a scholarship to Columbia, but because it was 1929 and the start of the Great Depression, he had to get a job instead and studied accounting at night and on weekends. After serving in World War II, Dyson was a vice president at Textron, an industrial conglomerate founded by a man named Royal Little, himself considered to be the "father of conglomerates." Dyson thought Little was buying the wrong kinds of companies, and Little eventually told him, "Charlie, you're driving me crazy. Why don't you start your own business?"

And that is exactly what Dyson did when he bought Hubbard in 1954. As John Dyson recalled, "He built companies by putting together groups of 5, 10 or even 15 smaller companies operating in similar areas of the economy, which provided them with better financing and additional capital to upgrade factories and find better sales resources—economies of scale. He didn't think taking over a company and shutting down factories was the right way to do things."

Aiming to do one acquisition each month, Charlie Dyson had little competition for years. Or at least until, in many ways, KKR launched the modern LBO industry. Jerome Kohlberg and his two protégés, Henry Kravis and George Roberts, founded the firm in 1976 after being at Bear Stearns, where they worked on some early LBOs. They realized that they could go out on their own and help owners and executives of a company profit and yet still maintain some control of their company. KKR had a vision of buying companies along with existing management as part of the investment group and taking on debt they could then pay down using the profits from operations. In this structure, current management would continue to run day-to-day operations—as opposed to probably losing control in a sale to a corporate buyer—under the supervision, guidance, and support of KKR.

As Daniel Gross writes in *Forbes Greatest Business Stories of All Time*, describing Kohlberg's first LBO in 1965 while at Bear Stearns, where the elderly owner of a gold-refining company, Stern Metals, wanted to maintain ownership in his company but also see liquidity from a sale, "The beauty of the deal to the family was that it had received millions for their company without relinquishing its leadership. The beauty of the deal to Kohlberg was that the very presence of the debt compelled all those interested in the deal, both the outside investors and the Stern family, to operate the company efficiently."[73]

KKR has become a publicly traded company with some $600 billion in assets under management and private equity investments in over 200 portfolio companies. Kohlberg has passed away, but Kravis and Roberts, both in their 80s, are still very much involved.[74]

LBOs have been said to compose as much as 35 percent of M&A activity at times but often much less.[75] They have ebbed and flowed with the economy, returning to prominence in the early 2000s but falling again during the financial crisis of 2007–9. LBOs surged once more, topping $200 billion in 2022.[76]

Blackstone was formed in 1985 by Steve Schwarzman and Pete Peterson. Peterson had been chair of Lehman Brothers, and Schwarzman was his mentee, chair of Lehman's M&A group. Today, Blackstone manages more than $1 trillion in assets, including private equity, real estate, and credit. Schwarzman, worth an estimated $50 billion, making him one of the nation's wealthiest individuals, is still active at Blackstone today—and the firm is the world's largest alternative asset manager.

Apollo was started in 1990 by Leon Black, Josh Harris, and Marc Rowan, former investment bankers at Drexel Burnham Lambert. It, too, is a broad-based investment firm with over $725 billion in assets under management in credit, equity, and real estate. Black resigned in 2021 due to his association with Jeffrey Epstein. Black admitted to a friendship with Epstein but denied any wrongdoing.[77] Rowan now serves as CEO. Harris has started another investment firm, 26North, and owns professional sports teams, including the Washington Commanders, Philadelphia 76ers, and New Jersey Devils.

In November 2023, the *Financial Times* wrote about how rising interest rates have slowed the LBO market: "Surging inflation and the consequent rise in interest rates have throttled most debt-backed, take-private buyouts. . . . Private equity managers have increasingly been driven to esoteric, highly risky forms of debt financing to keep the corporate show on the road."[78]

Certain institutional investors have lost some faith in the promise of high returns, especially as interest rates have increased substantially. And despite the promise of smart investors adding strategic value beyond what one can achieve as a passive market investor, some argue that private equity returns have been disappointing.

Of course, not all agree. The global investment manager Hamilton Lane, with almost $1 trillion in assets under management, finds that a majority of private equity funds have outperformed stocks over the past 20 years, with buyout transactions outperforming global public equities by an average of more than 10 percent annually.[79]

At the same time, there is a good argument that private equity is generally helpful to companies in a number of ways. Pete Stavros of KKR notes that private equity provides real value over the long term:

> We really don't care about quarterly earnings. We really don't care about one-year paybacks. And so we're building things for the long haul—which I think has increasingly been harder to do in public companies. The private equity model is such an efficient decision-making body, and it's such an efficient way to cascade change, whether it's climate related, for instance, or people related. A private equity firm has very few people who need to be convinced to do something that can impact hundreds of thousands if not a million people—and hundreds if not thousands of facilities—all over the world.

Sandra Horbach is a partner and chair of Americas corporate private equity at Carlyle, a global investment firm with some $450 billion in assets under management. Horbach previously spent 18 years at the private equity firm Forstmann Little, where she became the first woman to be named a partner at a major private equity firm, and she has been included in *Barron's* 100 Most Influential Women in Finance list since its inception. "I think private capital plays an increasingly important role," she told me, "and helps build and grow businesses. If you look at companies and how long from the time they take the first outside capital to when they are now going public, it continues to get longer and longer because people are seeing that there's a lot of value to be created during the period of private ownership."

Importantly, between 2005 and 2020, nearly 30,000 companies delisted from global markets,[80] and LBOs were very much a part of that activity. Therefore, it is important to understand the governance implications of LBOs.

The key conflict in an LBO that must be considered is that the CEO and management are typically sellers of the company and usually investors in or buyers of the company under new ownership too. Therefore, while you need management, especially the CEO and CFO, involved in the buyer's due diligence and to help the target company's advisors and board in the sale process, no management director (typically just the CEO) should be involved in board deliberations or a vote on the sale of the company.

There is an established process for boards to properly consider LBOs that usually includes a special committee of independent directors. It is critical that the special committee has thoughtful, informed directors on it and that the special committee and its advisors, not management, drive the deal. This should provide that a sale to a private equity firm is negotiated at arms' length and decided on by disinterested parties looking to maximize shareholder value and not in any way their own personal financial interests. Ideally, the committee should have the authority to reject an LBO or enter into definitive documentation with the private equity firm and recommend the sale to shareholders. Sometimes, special committees are just empowered to make a recommendation to the full board, which retains the final decision-making authority.[81]

The Board's M&A Process

While the duties of care and loyalty, as well as the standards of business judgment, enhanced scrutiny, *Revlon*, and entire fairness, provide guideposts for how a board should evaluate and either approve or reject M&A transactions, there is often the desire for specific guidance. Gregg Polle, vice chair of the M&A group at Bank of America, believes boards need to be "completely prepared in terms of really understanding what the company strategy is and how M&A may play into it." "For most boards," he continued in a conversation with me, "there are one or two or three really meaningful and transformational deals that the company would do, so you need to know who those companies are and be familiar with any potential issues that might arise so that when those windows open, you're ready to move quickly."

Given my experience in M&A advisory work, on corporate boards, and as an expert witness in corporate litigation, I have developed a methodology with seven steps that boards should follow to be consistent with custom and practice when considering a sale of a major business unit or the entire company: (1) evaluate strategic considerations, (2) retain qualified advisors, (3) consider potential buyers, (4) oversee due diligence, (5) determine valuation, (6) negotiate terms, and (7) complete the transaction. Step 3 should be modified when a board is considering an acquisition: for step 3, consider other target companies.

1. Evaluate Strategic Considerations

    There are various potential strategic reasons why a company may consider a sale, but ultimately, it is because the board believes that a sale will maximize long-term value for shareholders.

2. Retain Qualified Advisors

    Boards sometimes use external advisors, and certainly in the context of a significant M&A transaction, this can be very important. Financial and legal advisors can play critical roles, as can accounting, tax, and other consultants who can bring specialized expertise and a market-based perspective. Investment bankers often help boards and management teams with valuation, and lawyers often assist with negotiating definitive documentation.

3. Consider Potential Buyers

    Even if a company is approached by a logical buyer, it is important to at least consider other parties. While it is often the case that contacts are made with multiple potential buyers, that is not required.

4. Oversee Due Diligence

    In M&A, due diligence refers to the review of public and private information regarding the other party to the transaction (or both parties in the case of a merger). This helps identify potential risks in the deal and inform valuation.[82] There is no one-size-fits-all model for due diligence, but the process typically involves meeting and interviewing management and requesting information to enable (i) financial due diligence to understand the historical and projected financial performance as well as accounting and related details, (ii) strategic and operational due diligence to understand the target's strategy and business operations, and (iii) legal due diligence to identify any potential liabilities. In a potential sale of a company, management, overseen by the board, facilitates due diligence for one or more potential buyers.

5. Determine Valuation

    A key element of the financial advisor's efforts is typically to value the selling company. The financial advisor usually presents to the board the results of (at least) the three generally accepted valuation methodologies: an analysis based on comparable publicly traded companies, an analysis based on comparable M&A transactions, and a discounted cash flow analysis that calculates the present value of the target company's projected free cash flows. The bankers generally prepare and refine with management a financial model to, among other things, complete valuation and other financial analyses and compare potential deal structures and financing options.[83]

    Before the board approves a sale of the company, the financial advisor sometimes provides a "fairness opinion" indicating that, based on certain assumptions and work performed by the advisor, the consideration to be paid to the shareholders of the selling company in the transaction is fair to them from a financial point of view.[84]

6. Negotiate Terms

    Once the acquirer has made an offer, substantial due diligence has begun, and the parties appear to want to transact, negotiations over terms typically ensue. Both sides will, of course, attempt to improve the deal for their shareholders. Price and form of consideration (e.g., cash, stock, or a combination of both and perhaps an earn-out or contingent payment) are usually the most important issues for both parties, but other deal terms can be important, including the amount and timing of due diligence, representations and warranties in the contract, treatment of management and employees, how antitrust and other potential regulatory risks will be borne by the parties, and in the case of a public company target, the target's right (or lack of a right) to "go shop" for competitive offers during a specified period of time after announcement of the transaction.[85]

7. Complete the Transaction

    Finally, once the definitive documentation has been executed and the deal announced, the transaction must be completed. Key steps can include the finalization of any financing and receipt of any required consents and regulatory approvals. Sometimes, shareholder approval is also required. If a "go-shop" provision is involved, the target solicits offers from other parties; alternatively, if a "fiduciary out" is included in the final deal documents, the target can consider unsolicited offers from third parties, and if it finds one or more superior to the existing offer, the target company can terminate its agreement with the initial buyer and pursue an alternative offer.[86] The initial buyer may first have the right to match or improve upon any such offers. A buyer may seek to complete the acquisition through a tender offer, which can sometimes be completed more quickly than a merger, for which shareholder approval is required.

While no checklist, however carefully drawn up and followed, can ensure that litigation against a board will fail, following a careful process—and keeping detailed records of the process, such as thoughtful minutes of board meetings—is the most effective way to make well-informed, careful, documented decisions that should hold up to scrutiny from shareholders and courts.

The Value and Growth of M&A

Do M&A deals actually add value? A study by Bain in 2004 claimed that 70 percent of mergers did not add shareholder value, and CNN ran a headline with a related story insisting that "mergers fail more often than marriages."[87]

It is hard to believe that M&A has grown so dramatically if deals do not generally create value. Research published in 2016 by Professor Steve Kaplan at the University of Chicago Booth School of Business found that, on average, mergers do create value. "At the times when merger deals are announced," he writes, "the combined returns are usually positive both statistically and economically. On average, the overall value of both acquirer and acquired increases, which indicates that the market believes the announced deals will create value. This has been the case for the average acquisition going back 30 years, and it remains the case today."[88]

In a general sense, a 2017 McKinsey study suggests that acquisitions are not inherently good or bad but that M&A can create value if one or more of the following objectives are achieved and the acquirer does not overpay: improved target company performance, reduced excess industry capacity through consolidation, accelerated market access for the target's products, the ability to acquire technologies faster or cheaper than can be built, and/or the chance to exploit industry-specific scalability.[89]

New research released in 2024 found that, in contrast with the Bain study, 70 percent of takeovers in fact succeed. "Companies have gotten smarter about M&A," writes the *New York Times*, "acquirers are also getting more practice . . . [and] serial acquirers tend to have better returns."[90] In-house teams of specialists are able to do more diligence than companies did in the past, and "companies that did at least one deal a year [between 2012 and 2022] had 10-year total shareholder returns that were [130 percent] higher than businesses that did no deals."[91]

Gregg Lemkau, who had a long, successful career at Goldman Sachs, where his last role until 2020 was co-head of investment banking, and who is now the co-CEO of BDT & MSD Partners, a merchant bank with an advisory and investment platform, offered me an insightful summary of M&A's contemporary evolution and its impact on directors and corporate governance:

> M&A was virtually a cottage industry when I began my career in the 1990s. There was less than $300 billion worth of deals completed in 1990 compared to nearly $2 trillion in 2019. Some of that growth is due to the increased value of companies, of course, but much of it arises from companies' increased use of M&A as part of their core strategy as well as the development of private equity, which has grown dramatically.
>
> Pressure from activists has also exerted greater discipline on directors. Directors now have to think more about portfolio refinement, optimum capital structure, and how to drive value. Companies today regard M&A as an important element in their arsenal.
>
> Over the past 30 years, boards have become more professional and well advised, especially the boards of large US public companies. They have a deeper understanding of their fiduciary duties, and there is an abundance of Delaware case law to guide them. Things are obviously very different than they were three decades ago.

M&A is now a strategic consideration for most companies, as there can certainly be transactions that help maximize long-term value. Therefore, M&A should always be at least in the back of every director's mind—there are frequently opportunities to acquire and divest assets, and you never know when the opportunity for a transformational acquisition or a sale of the company may arise. Understanding the full scope of M&A governance issues is a core component of every director's job.

Chapter 7
The Rising Influence of Activist Investors

Activism, put simply, is the use of an ownership position to actively influence company policy and practice.[1] It can include efforts to force the election of new directors, a major stock repurchase, a substantial change in business strategy, the sale of a business unit or even the entire company, the abandonment of an announced acquisition, and other actions. These outcomes can be achieved through a variety of means, including dialogue with the board and management, letter writing, public demands, or even running a slate of directors not supported by the company for election at an annual meeting, which is called a "proxy fight." While some may consider efforts to advance ESG, political, and other concerns as activism, most activists seek to drive corporate actions directly related to increasing the target company's stock price; these activists and efforts are the focus of this chapter.

Having an activist campaign launched against your company is a major concern for directors today. Indeed, 2022 was "one of the most active years for shareholder activism," according to a study by David Kostin and Jenny Ma at Goldman Sachs, with investors launching 148 campaigns against 120 different public US companies.[2] Underperformers are, of course (and rightly), at the greatest risk. In looking at over 2,000 activist campaigns against Russell 3000 companies since 2006, Kostin and Ma found that there were four metrics that correlated with companies becoming targets as compared with their peers: slower sales growth, a lower trailing enterprise-value-to-sales multiple, a weaker trailing net income margin, and trailing two-year underperformance.[3]

But even young companies and outperformers have been attacked. "While some companies are less likely to be targets, no company is completely immune from an activist campaign," write Steve Klemash and David Hunker for the Harvard Law School Forum on Corporate Governance. "In recent years, activists have even targeted companies delivering impressive shareholder returns or companies that have only recently become public."[4]

Bloomberg's Activism Screening Model has found that 4.5 percent of companies in the Russell 3000 are hit by activist threats in a given year.[5] Lawrence Elbaum, co-head of Sullivan & Cromwell's Shareholder Activism practice and a partner in the firm's M&A group, explains that there are even more threats than this: "Suppose there are 300 publicly reported campaigns, everything from a public letter, nominating a director, making a bid for a company—there are probably another 100–150 campaigns a year that aren't public: behind the scenes agitators, celebrity activists, first-timers, and these may get resolved without any publicity whatsoever."

As Christopher Drewry, a partner at the law firm Latham & Watkins and global co-chair of the firm's Shareholder Activism & Takeover Defense practice, explained to me, "If you are sitting on a board and there is a major risk to your business like that, you're going to plan for that risk and be prepared for it."

I have been involved in nine situations where an activist approached the company in some manner, though not all have been made public. I was a member of the board of Lear, a Fortune 500 automotive supplier, in 2015 when an activist hedge fund, Marcato—which has since shut down[6]—sought to break the company up into two independent business units and have Lear execute a very large stock buyback. Marcato did not understand the value of Lear's two businesses being together and did not appreciate the substantial incremental costs if they were separated and managed independently. It could have been argued that Lear had a "lazy balance sheet" or an inefficient capital structure, as it had modest leverage and significant net cash.[7] It also had an undervalued stock that traded at a discount to its peers, and a stock repurchase should have increased earnings per share.

However, Marcato argued for as much as a $2 billion repurchase[8] that may have helped short-term shareholders through financial engineering but would have put substantial leverage on a company that had fairly recently emerged from a Chapter 11 bankruptcy reorganization and is in a highly cyclical business. This arguably made such a large repurchase shortsighted and not focused on maximizing long-term shareholder value. Ultimately, Marcato dropped its demand to split Lear into two companies, and Lear agreed to increase its buyback to $1 billion[9] and appoint one new director selected by Lear and approved by Marcato.

While activists may well approach companies with good intentions and even good ideas, their incentives are often not fully aligned with those of the company's board and management. An activist has a portfolio of investments and is rightly evaluated by its investors on the performance of its portfolio of investments or funds. While no investor wants to have a poor return on any one investment, an activist can be more aggressive with some number of investments when it knows that if they go poorly, there will likely be other investments that do well. It is very different for a board and management team that are responsible for just one company. Every director and executive should, as a valuable exercise, think from time to time as an activist would—but not necessarily act in such a manner.

This chapter summarizes the history of activism up to the present day, explains some key activist strategies and approaches, and then lays out a framework for board members to respond appropriately to activists and the governance implications that activism presents. As activism continues to grow, it is important for every board member to be aware of activists and how to thoughtfully respond to one or more aggressive shareholders that threaten or take action against the company.

The History of Activism

While the modern rise in shareholder activism has only taken hold in the past 40 years or so—with the emergence of corporate raiders in the 1980s—there were certainly agenda-driven shareholders before then who did their best to push companies in directions they saw fit. The first published case of shareholder activism occurred in 1926, when Benjamin Graham—who later became known as the "father of value investing," Warren Buffett's mentor, and the coauthor of the "investment bible," *Security Analysis*[10]—wrote a letter to the executives at Northern Pipeline, a company in which he held a small stake.

Graham, according to Walter Frick in *Harvard Business Review*, saw that the company owned millions of dollars of railroad bonds and other securities. He thought the securities should be sold and the profits distributed to shareholders as a dividend. "Running a pipeline is a complex and specialized business," the company responded, "about which you can know very little, but which we have done for a lifetime."[11]

Rather than give up, Graham spent the next year meeting with shareholders who owned at least 100 shares of the company and tried to enlist their support. He insisted that the shareholders were the owners of the company, and the managers were hired by them. This was not how the executives felt, of course. They believed investors did not understand their business, and their only contribution was the capital to fund it.[12] Graham got his way in the end. "The activist investor," *Harvard Business Review* writes, "was born."[13]

Activism took hold slowly over the next few decades. In 1942, the SEC amended its rules to require companies for the first time to enable shareholders to submit proposals for shareholder votes in a company's proxy statement, which is a document filed by a company with the SEC and ultimately sent to shareholders that provides information on issues to be considered and voted on at annual shareholder meetings. Corporate "gadflies"—activists who seek to push change through shareholder proposals—became common as the 1940s progressed and would confront management at shareholder meetings, often unsuccessfully.

Lewis and John Gilbert were early gadflies who attended more than 80 annual meetings each year, occasionally getting attention through stunts such as wearing a red clown's nose, in order to push companies to adopt shareholder reforms that are generally accepted today but were new at the time, such as holding annual meetings in more accessible locations, issuing postmeeting reports, limiting stock options for executives, and requiring companies' independent auditors to attend shareholder meetings.[14]

Their work continued for decades as, for example, they pushed a number of companies to adopt cumulative voting for directors that permits shareholders to cast all of their votes for one candidate, increasing the odds that minority shareholders can elect a director. As late as 1983, the Gilberts proposed a full 20 percent—198 of 972—of all resolutions proposed at annual meetings for public companies that year.[15]

However, through 1981, just two shareholder proposals not supported by management were approved.[16] But as deal volume exploded in the 1980s, large shareholders began to move from passive investors to more active participants.[17] Institutions and, at times, wealthy individuals, sometimes seeing that their holdings were so large that their shares could not be sold without significantly driving down a stock price, increasingly began to advocate for change.

Public pension funds started to submit proxy proposals focused on corporate governance issues, and then hedge funds such as Greenway Partners began to use shareholder proposals to force corporate restructurings and sales. This kind of activity grew throughout the 1990s and early 2000s, and by 2007, inflows to activist hedge funds had dramatically increased from $2.7 billion in 2000 to $55 billion in 2007.[18] Between 1995 and 2007, activist hedge funds significantly outperformed the stock market, bringing them more investors and more influence.[19]

Steve Wolosky, a shareholder activism pioneer and now chair emeritus of the Shareholder Activism practice at the law firm Olshan—which he cofounded more than 30 years ago—is well known for advising activists. He talked with me about the growth of activism over the course of his career:

> The corporate raiders of the world were in the infancy of activism in the early 1990s. There wasn't a tremendous focus on activism as a core philosophy or tool. But money follows performance. That fuels the growth. And modern communication has changed the whole world. The cost of communicating with shareholders used to be excessive. You had to mail the "fight letter" to everyone, and that was a tremendous amount of money. If you wanted to communicate, you issued a press release and hoped people read the *Wall Street Journal*. Access and communication have dramatically changed. I can draft a letter, and if I have the right mailing list, I push a button, and now I've communicated to 98 percent of the shareholder base.

A major contributing factor to the growth of activism has been the increased value, short-term oriented and financially engineered as it sometimes is, that activists have driven, with activist investors achieving an average return in 2023, for instance, of more than 20 percent.[20]

At the same time, there is evidence that activists who have a specific strategic change in mind—as opposed to campaigns that mostly address governance issues—yield stronger results. One study looking at 245 companies publicly targeted by activists in the US and Europe between 2017 and 2020 found that activist campaigns including an element of transformation—"where activists seek to promote strategic or operational change"—were associated with a two-year outperformance of 3.4 percent, and campaigns that included an M&A component outperformed the market by 2.8 percent over that same two-year period. On the other hand, campaigns that focused on governance demands underperformed by 2.0 percent.[21]

This data is not universally accepted. A 2023 review by the Capital Markets Advisory group at Lazard found that while activist campaigns led to five-day outperformance, "no [activist] group consistently outperforms the market over the first 12 months of a campaign."[22] "The conclusion," write the authors, "is that activists are certainly not always right, and management teams and boards should be confident challenging the notion that activism is always good for the public shareholder."[23]

In any event, there are, of course, examples of effective activism. In 2013, after a decade of lackluster performance, ValueAct, an activist firm, helped orchestrate the resignation of Microsoft CEO Steve Ballmer, who was replaced by Satya Nadella in early 2014. ValueAct urged Microsoft to focus on its existing software as well as its cloud infrastructure and to increase its dividend to shareholders. Microsoft's share price doubled over the next three years. Now the stock is up more than 10 times since Nadella took over, and in early 2024, Microsoft became just the second company to reach a market capitalization of $3 trillion.[24]

On the other hand, activist Bill Ackman spent two years from 2007 to 2009 trying to add himself to the board of the retailer Target and pushed the company to sell its credit card business and put the land underneath its stores into a real estate investment trust.[25] Management argued this was a distraction from the company's core business and spent over $20 million in a proxy battle, with shareholders ultimately rejecting Ackman's slate of directors. The stock price, albeit likely impacted by the 2007–9 financial crisis, fell.[26]

While results may be mixed, what cannot be denied is that activists have grown in both their preparation and the extent to which they articulate their push for change. Steven Gartner, retired chair emeritus of the law firm Willkie, led the firm from 2010 through 2020 and has represented activists in a number of proxy fights and campaigns as well as companies defending against activists. Gartner shared with me,

> The activists of the 1980s were in many cases there for a very quick buck. If you paid them to go away, they went away. That was basically the game. Today, it's very different. The big activists invest a massive amount of resources in trying to get to know a big company before they attack. If they come forward with a white paper, for instance, detailing what's wrong with the business, it is a very sophisticated piece. Often, the directors will look at that white paper and recognize that it's saying something they've been whispering to themselves all along and know they're right. The CEO has to go, or a particular division has been milking the company for five years and has to get wound down, or this business unit isn't strategic anymore and needs to be sold. Activists today simply bring a much higher level of credibility to the discussion.

It is perhaps indicative of this maturity of the activism business that Doug Oberhelman, the retired CEO of Caterpillar, agrees that activism "has changed from the early days where it meant throwing a bomb in and ruining a company for a 30 percent short-term stock gain to where now there's a lot more dialogue with management to make changes, and it really keeps management on their toes."

Key Players

Some think of activists in three general categories: economic activists such as Carl Icahn and Bill Ackman, whom I discuss in more detail later; governance activists such as Engine No. 1, which took action against Exxon, a topic of the coming chapter on ESG; and "vanity" activists such as the Gilberts, covered earlier in this chapter. No discussion of activists should start without Carl Icahn. He has become a billionaire by pressuring companies for the past 50-plus years to make more profitable use of their assets. Icahn's first raid was in 1985 on TWA, which had mixed results.

Icahn's reputation alone can now raise stock prices when he merely begins buying shares—even without any action to influence the company. This phenomenon, known as the "Icahn Lift," was the subject of a feature on CBS's *60 Minutes* and in other media profiles.[27] As a shareholder of Netflix, he made more than $2 billion in gains despite taking virtually no action.[28] It should be noted that in 2023, Hindenburg Research accused Icahn's public company of operating a Ponzi-like scheme in order to continue to pay shareholder dividends, causing the company's stock price to plummet in value. While Icahn has called the allegations false, this may call into question some of his success over the years.[29]

It has been said that Icahn's "archrival" is Bill Ackman, mentioned earlier in the Target example. Ackman, a multibillionaire, is the founder and CEO of Pershing Square Capital.[30] He has led successful activist campaigns at Wendy's (convincing the company to sell off its Tim Hortons brand), Canadian Pacific Railway,[31] and General Growth Properties, a shopping mall operator he helped turn around from near bankruptcy, among others.[32]

Dan Loeb and his hedge fund, Third Point, is another prominent activist. Loeb is known for shareholder letters that mock the performance of executives he is seeking to remove, a strategy that has worked in cases such as his two-year campaign against the board and management of Yahoo!

Jeff Smith is the CEO and cofounder of Starboard Value, an activist hedge fund launched in 2002. Smith was called "the most feared man in corporate America" by *Fortune* magazine,[33] and the fund has been involved in campaigns at Microsoft, Office Depot, Symantec, Smithfield Foods, Yahoo!, Macy's, Papa John's Pizza, and elsewhere.

Paul Singer is the founder and president of Elliott Investment Management, a multistrategy investment firm with about $70 billion of assets under management that has driven activist efforts at AT&T, Southwest Airlines, and many other companies.

Finally, Nelson Peltz—who prefers to call himself a "highly engaged shareholder" rather than an activist investor[34]—and his hedge fund, Trian, have been at the center of a number of battles and helped breathe new life into companies such as Disney, Snapple, Heinz, and Wendy's. At Pepsi, he sought to convince the company to spin off its beverage business from its snacks division to create "two leaner and more entrepreneurial companies."[35] He failed but still walked away with a 50 percent return on his investment in four years.[36]

Wolosky argues that individual personalities have become less important as activism has grown and matured. "If you look in the last few years," he told me, "the campaigns have been more about the issues than the personalities. I think that people have moved away from that. It's not about anything other than the fundamentals. You're going to win a campaign by putting together a great slate of directors and a platform that institutions can get behind."

The Impact of the SEC

The SEC has, over the years, impacted activism through a series of regulations, such as disclosure requirements once an investor buys a certain size stake in a company, the ability of multiple investors to work together, and more recently, the introduction of the universal proxy, which requires companies to list all board nominees—management and dissident—on one proxy card, permitting shareholders to vote not just for the company's or the activist's entire slate of directors but for any combination of director nominees they prefer.

As far as disclosure, sections 13(d) and 13(g) of the Securities Exchange Act of 1934 require investors who acquire more than 5 percent of a public company's shares to publicly file either a Schedule 13D or a Schedule 13G form with the SEC. Investors with an intent to obtain control of a company must file a Schedule 13D. Passive investors without an intent to seek control can file the much shorter 13G.

Until October 2023, activists had 10 days to make their public 13D disclosures, meaning they could accumulate shares in secret and communicate privately with institutional investors and others in order to build a larger position. That window was shortened to 5 business days by the SEC in October 2023. "In our fast-paced markets, it shouldn't take 10 days for the public to learn about an attempt to change or influence control of a public company," said Gary Gensler, the SEC chair at the time.[37]

In addition, the "universal proxy" took effect in August 2022.[38] Having one ballot makes it easier for investors to split their votes, and they can now, if desired, choose some nominees picked by the company and others by the activist. The expectation is that one ballot will make it more likely for a company to lose some board seats to activists but perhaps less likely for the company to lose a majority. Opponents worry that the new ballots will be confusing to shareholders.

It is not yet clear whether the universal proxy will impact fights between activists and companies in the long run, though early indications are that it is helping activists win more board seats. According to Barclays, activists won board seats in 80 percent of contested votes in the first half of 2023 as compared with 33 percent in the first half of 2022.[39]

Drewry offers an interesting hypothesis for this increase: "In 2023, over 90 percent of new board seats activists gained were through settlement, a tremendous increase because neither the company nor the activist knew what the impact of the universal proxy would be, and so that information gap had neither side feeling like it had leverage, which drove a lot of settlements." Nonetheless, Drewry represented a small public company in 2023 facing a change in control slate that went all the way to a shareholder vote—and did not lose a single seat. So even in the most difficult situations, the universal proxy does not make it impossible for companies to prevail.

The Rise of Activism Today

Since 2019, there have been up to 200 companies—even more in 2022—targeted each year by activists.[40] This is up from an average of 74 campaigns each year from 2005 through 2009.[41] The share of megacap companies (market capitalizations greater than $50 billion) has been rising in that mix, reaching 16 percent in the first quarter of 2023, the highest share on record. Motivated by the lure of outsized returns—though the statistical findings, especially when it comes to long-term gains, are mixed[42]—and the greater ease of information gathering and communication between shareholders enabled by technology, it appears that investors seeking change from the outside is not a trend that will slow anytime soon. A 2019 study by SquareWell Partners revealed that 87 percent of active managers say shareholder activism is a useful force in the market.[43] Activism—once associated just with the corporate raiders of the 1980s—is now often seen as a conventional strategy that unlocks shareholder value.

The 2007–9 financial crisis may well have been a turning-point event, moving activism into the mainstream. According to the *Wall Street Journal*, "In the wake of the crisis, many corporate executives took a more-conservative approach [than before], not wanting to be seen as risk-takers. They hoarded cash and avoided big spending."[44] Activists jumped in, and the number of campaigns has grown since.[45] Indeed, as of 2022, nearly 38 percent of directors of Russell 3000 companies have had experience with activist campaigns.[46] More than 50 percent of the public companies on whose boards I have sat have been approached by activists, in a few cases more than once.

Much recent activism has evolved from more financially oriented to strategically oriented, perhaps driven in part by the evidence that activism linked to strategic goals can yield higher returns. Financial activism generally means pressuring underleveraged companies to buy back stock in order to increase the stock price. While their pressures are usually couched in different language, these investors are often looking for quick gains.

Strategic activism, on the other hand, is focused on pushing companies to reorient their businesses, such as separating or selling one or more business units or making or not making a given acquisition, because activists believe that a certain path will maximize value—perhaps in the short-term, but possibly longer term as well.

Ele Klein, co-chair of the M&A and Securities group, co-chair of the Global Shareholder Activism group, and a member of the executive committee at Schulte Roth & Zabel, has seen this evolution play out. "I think the simple type of campaign of identifying issues with easy balance sheet type fixes," he told me, "doesn't exist as much anymore. Companies have gotten more sophisticated. This is a good that has come from the activist push. It has forced companies to actually think about things proactively and not just reactively. I think the whole market has evolved and become more mature, and that's a good thing. Activism is not a game. What activism is really about at its core is helping to hold underperforming companies accountable and make management responsible for that underperformance."

The strategic approach is well illustrated by the 2024 situation at Walt Disney. The company faced an activist threat from Trian, the investment vehicle led by Nelson Peltz, who argued, among other things, that Walt Disney needed to resolve CEO succession and increase its margins. In the midst of Peltz's efforts to gain Walt Disney board seats, the company found itself with an unusual ally: ValueAct, which, coincidentally, had been behind the ousting of Microsoft's CEO Steve Ballmer a decade earlier. ValueAct declared its support for Walt Disney's board nominees, and Walt Disney entered into a consulting agreement with it. "ValueAct Capital has a track record of collaboration and cooperation with the companies it invests in," said Walt Disney's CEO, Bob Iger. "We welcome their input as long-term shareholders."[47] ValueAct and other activists, including Blackwells, positioned themselves as Disney's (and Iger's) allies against the threat from Peltz—and both sides pushed for the board nominees of their choice. Even though Walt Disney emerged victorious, fending off the threat, the fight was very expensive and distracting for the company—with multiple sources estimating the cost at $70 million.[48] The cooperation between a company and an activist against a different activist is perhaps surprising, but it is indicative of the range of roles and potential impacts activists can have today.

Of course, the financial approach is not dead. It is often part of a strategic approach too. In November 2022, Berry Global, a leading packaging company where I am a director and, as I described, that has announced a merger with Amcor, entered into a cooperation agreement with Ancora Holdings and Eminence Capital, appointed three new directors, and formed a capital allocation committee. When faced with an activist threat, we listened to these shareholders and came to a mutually satisfactory agreement.[49]

One example that stands out among the many activist campaigns is the one in 2014 where Smith's Starboard Value won shareholder support to replace the entire board of Darden Restaurants, the owner of Olive Garden and other popular chains.[50] As the *New York Times* reported, "The resounding victory caps a one-year battle between Darden and a group of disgruntled investors who first called for Darden to create a separate company for its Red Lobster and Olive Garden chains and sell its real estate. Instead, Darden ignored their recommendations and just sold Red Lobster for $2.1 billion, resulting in a fierce war of words between the activist investors and Darden. Starboard Value then announced its plans to unseat the entire board, arguing that Darden's management had shown 'contempt for shareholder interest.'"[51]

Darden Restaurants adopted defensive measures to fight off the activists, including new bylaws that would make shareholder nominations of new directors more difficult. Starboard published a 300-page plan to increase the company's earnings, with granular recommendations down to criticism of how Olive Garden cooked its pasta. The arguments resonated, and Starboard Value won the votes to replace all of the Darden Restaurants directors.[52]

While activism at Darden Restaurants may be considered a success—the stock price is up some 300 percent since 2014—Ackman's battle with J.C. Penney is an example of how activist campaigns do not always yield the promised results. In 2010, Ackman acquired a $900 million stake in the company and gained himself a seat on the board. He pushed the company to replace its longtime CEO, Mike Ullman, with Ron Johnson, a former Apple executive. Sixteen months later, the stock had fallen by 50 percent, 19,000 employees had been laid off, and sales were down more than 25 percent. Ackman and the rest of the board fired Johnson and rehired Ullman—but just four months later, Ackman called for Ullman's ousting again.[53] It was the beginning of the end. Six years later, the stock price having never recovered, the company filed for bankruptcy.

The many examples of activists seeking to drive detailed change point to the idea that a convergence of activism and private equity has developed. Activists, more and more, want to participate in the running of companies they invest in—actively rather than passively. And while sometimes that works out, sometimes it does not.

Elbaum, who represents both activists and companies, sees some good in what activists do. "It gets information out there in the market," he told me, "and you want as much information about a company out there as you can so that the market prices everything in and gives you the most accurate valuation. I think activism can help promote the exchange of dialogue between management, directors, shareholders, and other constituencies."

"It is hard for activism to be harmful," Ackman has said. "If the ideas are good, they will happen. If they are bad, they won't get support."[54] But the *Wall Street Journal* wrote that "activism often improves a company's operational results, and nearly as often doesn't."[55]

Marty Lipton has been critical of activists for decades, and Wachtell Lipton has long been a highly regarded, popular choice to help companies defend against activists. "There are always companies that are not well-managed, pursuing a bad strategy," Lipton has said. "Those companies need to be turned around, but it is not necessary to have activists do it. The institutional investors should undertake to engage with those companies and convince them to turn around. If you promote activism, what you're doing is sending a message to every company that it should start thinking the way of the activist or otherwise it's going to be attacked, which means in a sense that you kill long-term strategies."[56]

Chief Justice Strine has criticized activism's short-term focus: "Activist hedge funds identify companies and take an equity position in them only when they have identified a way to change the corporation's operations in a manner that the hedge fund believes will cause its stock price to rise. The rise that most hedge funds seek must occur within a relatively short time period, because many activist hedge funds have historically retained their positions for only one to two years at most."[57]

The distraction that an activist threat can create can be very significant too. As Drewry told me,

> The cost in terms of distraction is extraordinarily high, and activists know that's their most effective tool and pain point. If you think about a normal board calendar, five meetings a year, if you have an activist fight that goes all the way, you're looking at as many as 20 board meetings during that fight, a C-suite spending 20 hours a week on the fight, and in the last weeks, flying around the country meeting with shareholders, it is a huge disruption, not to mention the personal burden on management, where I've seen senior leaders who are very used to stressful jobs throw in the towel and say this just isn't worth it.

"What Marty Lipton has been saying for years is that activism is a distraction to the board and doesn't let the board do their jobs," echoes Gartner. But he argues, "There are a lot of very weak boards out there. There is a lot of fat in corporate America that the activists take a slice at and say it's just something we ought to be better at. When you look at some of the campaigns today, they are not short-term fixes. They are strategic realignments of businesses."

One of Lipton's most ardent sparring partners over the value of shareholder activism has been Lucian Bebchuk, the James Barr Ames Professor of Law, Economics, and Finance and director of the Program on Corporate Governance at Harvard Law School. Bebchuk has disputed Lipton's insistence that activism does not have long-term benefits, including in a study of roughly 2,000 activist interventions over a 13-year period from 1994 to 2007.[58] The study did find higher stock returns and better operating performance for the companies subject to activist interventions when looking at a five-year time horizon (as measured by return on assets), but as explained earlier, the data is far from clear—and Lazard's more recent study pokes significant holes in Bebchuk's conclusion.

Governance Considerations

Boards and management teams should listen to an activist, as they should to any shareholder, but they should also be prepared and wary. It is important to not be forced into a given action because one small but noisy shareholder is being particularly aggressive. As Gartner told me from his decades of experience on both sides, activist and corporation, "The progress of boards over the last generation has been staggering in terms of sophistication and the willingness to engage with activists. A decade ago, if activists showed up, the standard operating procedure was to stiff-arm them and do whatever was necessary to resist their ideas, including having a proxy fight. Today, the first order of business is to meet with activists, hear what they have to say, and try to address the issues they raise quietly and peacefully." Drewry agrees, explaining, "You have to respect the fact that a particular investor, whether an activist investor or not, may be one of your larger shareholders, and you have to treat them with respect and consider their ideas."

Companies facing activists often hire a law firm, investment bank, and communications firm to help them. Drewry walked me through the steps he takes with a new client facing attack:

> The first thing I do is work through the annual meeting timeline, so we know when nominations go in, because that's when you're most vulnerable. I need to understand if shareholders can call a special meeting, act by written consent, and if it's a classified board. Understanding the defensive profile will let me know where the pain points are and how the activists can manipulate them. Activists are constantly developing new tactics, and we are constantly developing new bylaw language in response. And a company should of course have a rights plan—a poison pill—on the shelf. Facing a threat like this is a contentious, very challenging, very stressful period for both the board and management.

It should be noted that a poison pill is unlikely to be particularly effective against determined activists. It can make boards and management teams seem entrenched, and because most activists acquire stakes in their target companies below 10 percent, the threshold ownership percentage where a poison pill kicks in is often not met.

Muir Paterson is the global head of Strategic Shareholder Advisory in Citi's M&A group, where he advises corporate clients on activist and other situations. He previously helped grow Goldman Sachs's activist defense group and also worked as director of corporate governance for Wellington Management, an institutional investor, and was the cofounder of the special situations group at ISS, the leading governance advisory firm. This collection of experiences gives him a unique perspective. He explained to me the bankers' general role when advising a company faced with an activist: "Our role as advisor includes helping directors put themselves in the mindset of an investor. It's about the work that you do around the company and the board to figure out your value and your options, but it's also about understanding the shareholder army. It's understanding where your support base sits. It is often less about defense alone and more about the best way for the company to maximize value."

For a communications perspective, I spoke with Steve Lipin, the founder and CEO of the communications advisory firm Gladstone Place, who started his career as an M&A reporter at the *Wall Street Journal* and has three decades of financial communications experience. As he told me,

> In advance of any attack, you need a document outlining what you would say or do in the first 24 hours. Then you need to understand the potential criticisms of the company and how you would respond and have a constituent map or an understanding of the most important stakeholders you would need to communicate with during a fight. The final thing you need is a plan for what a contested election might look like. The communications strategy is critical to the success of a proxy contest, because it is largely a war of ideas and a public relations battle.

It is logical that *Corporate Board Member* writes that "the best strategy" for companies looking to resist activists "is, obviously, to perform better financially."[59] Drewry makes a similar point, adding, "What insulates companies from activism is a management team that is very forward leaning with the board on deeply evaluating strategic alternatives and then thoughtful about how they explain that to the shareholders."

It is important to be prepared for an activist attack and for a board and management to remain focused on maximizing long-term shareholder value. Experience has shown me that the following steps can help a company be ready for an approach from an activist:

1. See that the board and management are aligned on the company's strategy and key drivers of value as well as understand the company's valuation. You have to be informed and in agreement in order to present a unified front when faced with a threat from outside.
2. Engage with major shareholders at least annually, and certainly well before an activist appears, so that they understand the company's strategy and at least the CEO and CFO, if not the board leader as well, have a good working relationship with the primary owners of the company.
3. Monitor changes in investor holdings regularly and pay particular attention to new holders, especially those who have a history of activism.
4. Develop and update a plan to deal with an activist attack, including what advisors you plan to retain.
5. Try to have a new board candidate largely vetted and ready to join. This is a point emphasized by Drewry: "Many of the settlements with activists give them one new independent director board seat, and in a well-advised company, that can be someone the board already had prepared, so when the activists come, you can say we'll put your name in a press release and add this candidate who the board had identified and vetted. The activist can claim a victory, and it doesn't cost the board much."
6. Listen to the views of shareholders and be willing to adopt good suggestions—but also be unafraid to challenge any attacks head-on if you feel the proposals will not maximize long-term shareholder value.

A shareholder base that feels heard and knows senior management is much less likely to help derail an effective corporate strategy. Wachtell Lipton's Daniel Neff agrees: "When I get involved, the first thing I ask is, What do the stockholders think of management and of the board, and how ripe is the situation for an outside challenger? The ultimate determinant in an election contest is how you are doing with the voters."

Because it is so important, I want to repeat that even though I believe that a board should think like an activist as an exercise, it would be a mistake for a board and management team to act like an activist in all cases. There are major differences in the objectives of activists and management, as explained earlier. An activist seeks to increase value, usually for its vehicle, typically a fund that consists of multiple investments, to earn management fees and a percentage of the profits (known as a "carried interest") as well as to raise additional capital. However, a board and management team must never lose sight of the fact that they are charged with maximizing long-term shareholder value for just one company—even if that may put them at odds with the perhaps short-term goals of the activist coming after them.

While it is true that activists sometimes state that they are long-term investors, Neff believes it is important to be cautious: "Changes are made, and the stock price goes up, and then the activists inevitably disappear. That is not a good outcome in many instances. There are some companies where a bit of a kick in the pants can be desirable. But I think they are less and less. If the activists don't produce results in a short period of time, you end up with real tension. It's very hard to run a company with a 9- to 12-month time horizon and be better in the future." The board should not let activists have an inhibiting effect on actions that are in the best long-term interest of shareholders.

There are many defenses against unwanted activism. The first concerns staggered or classified boards: those composed of different classes of directors with different service terms that mean only a minority percentage of directors are up for election at each annual meeting. This makes overhauling a board a multiyear process, meaning that activists might be less likely to try, knowing a quick win is impossible. Bebchuk, through the Shareholder Rights Project, an organization he ran from 2011 to 2014, sought to move companies away from staggered boards toward annual elections in the hope of making activism through the pursuit of board seats faster and easier.[60] The effort, built on Bebchuk's belief that activism should be empowered as much as possible, was largely a success.

In 2000, 300 companies in the S&P 500 had staggered boards. By the end of 2013, just 60 boards were still staggered,[61] a number that has remained roughly consistent since then.[62] Bebchuk argued that staggered boards are associated with lower company valuations, lower gains for shareholders, value-decreasing acquisition decisions, and lower sensitivity of CEO turnover to company performance.[63]

Certainly, a staggered board provides a strong impediment to an activist being able to take board control quickly. Bebchuk's research found that between 1996 and 2000, not a single hostile bidder won control through a shareholder vote at one annual meeting where a company's board was staggered.[64] However, the data on company performance between those with staggered boards and those where all directors are elected each year is not so clear. A 2019 study showed that for the five years prior, S&P 500 companies with staggered boards saw an average total return of 125 percent versus 52 percent for the index as a whole, contradicting Bebchuk's work.[65] And a 2018 paper in the *University of Pennsylvania Law Review* looked at 2,961 companies over 23 years and found that staggered boards had no significant effect on company value.[66]

Nonetheless, the major governance advisory firms frown on staggered boards—and their lack of support means that staggered boards are unlikely to come back in any meaningful percentage any time soon. ISS and Glass Lewis have made the argument that entire boards should be elected every year—with ISS arguing that staggered boards are a "problematic" governance structure[67] materially adverse to shareholder rights[68] and Glass Lewis saying that it believes "staggered boards are less accountable to shareholders than boards that are elected annually" and that in its function as a takeover defense, a staggered board "entrenches management, discourages potential acquirers, and delivers a lower return to target shareholders."[69]

"A staggered board is the most effective defense," Elbaum says. "But if you don't have it now, you can't put one in."

While annual elections for every director appear here to stay, I have concerns. As discussed, the board is elected by the shareholders to oversee management and the maximization of long-term shareholder or stakeholder value. Therefore, it seems inconsistent that every director should be evaluated and elected or not elected every year.

A company can defend against efforts to quickly replace directors by limiting (in the company's certificate of incorporation or bylaws) the power of shareholders to call special shareholders' meetings and by creating advance notice provisions whereby shareholders seeking to nominate directors or bring up new business at a shareholders' meeting must provide written notice well in advance of any meeting.[70] Reasonable, unambiguous advance notice bylaws have been enforced by Delaware courts, though, if challenged, they are evaluated under the enhanced scrutiny standard.[71]

Of course, this defense is unlikely to last long, as a shareholders meeting is required once per year. "If the only way for your company to win a proxy fight against an activist is to leverage an advance notice bylaw, you might win in year one, but you will probably not ultimately win," Elbaum summarizes.

Companies may also eliminate the possibility of shareholder action by written consent. Under standard bylaws, shareholder actions may be taken by written consent, without a meeting or shareholder vote, making it possible for activists to appeal directly to shareholders and bypass shareholder meetings. In their certificates of incorporation, companies can change this default and require action to be taken at a meeting.[72]

These takeover defenses, along with the six steps listed earlier that can help a board prepare for a potential activist threat, provide the basic toolkit for boards looking to protect the interests of long-term shareholders. Ultimately, directors, senior executives, and shareholders should all have the same objective: maximize long-term shareholder value. Activism is not a problem when interests are aligned—shareholders can be instrumental as change agents—but can become one when the parties do not agree on how to get there or the activists are looking for something other than long-term success. Directors need to see that they are simultaneously looking out for the best interests of the company and its shareholders and properly reacting to any shareholders' concerns. It is a challenge that has only grown in recent years and will likely continue to grow.

Chapter 8
The Growing Impact of Institutional Investors

In the background, and increasingly the foreground, of much of the activism discussion in the previous chapter—and the growth of M&A discussed in chapter 6 as well as many other aspects of the capital markets—has been a set of investors that has grown significantly in size and influence over the past 50 years. I am referring to institutional investors, a broad category of investment firms, each with distinct goals, strategies, and time frames for their investments, but sharing the common feature that they invest on behalf of others. Because of their enormity, institutional investors can exert tremendous influence on shareholder votes in a large percentage of public companies and are a growing influence on corporate governance. Whether a board wants to engage with its institutional investors is irrelevant; it must engage with its institutional investors, usually an important ownership group, and understand their needs and concerns, or it may well find itself in the crosshairs of a key constituent.

Institutional investors is an umbrella term that covers banks, credit unions, pension funds, insurance companies, private equity firms, hedge funds, mutual funds, real estate investment trusts (REITs), and others. We can divide the institutional world between active managers (private equity firms, hedge funds, and the like) who make affirmative choices about the companies in which they invest and index funds that invest broadly and passively in the market. Institutions own approximately 80 percent of the shares, on average, of the companies in the Russell 3000 index, though there is some variation, with companies at the 25th percentile having 71 percent institutional ownership and companies at the 75th percentile being owned almost entirely—98 percent—by institutions (this data, which comes from a 2024 report, is from the fourth quarter of 2019, and the percentages have likely increased since then).[1]

The concentration of power these institutions hold is called a "problem of 12" by John Coates, the John F. Cogan Jr. Professor of Law and

Economics at Harvard Law School, where he also serves as deputy dean and research director of the Center on the Legal Profession, in his 2023 book *The Problem of Twelve: When a Few Financial Institutions Control Everything*.[2] "A 'problem of twelve,'" Coates writes, "arises when a small number of institutions acquire the means to exert outsized influence over the politics and economy of a nation."[3] "It's a notional number that captures the idea of 12 people sitting in a room that's about the size of a typical board," Coates said in an interview about the book. "There were 12 disciples. I'm sure there are other examples. It's just the idea of a small group of people."[4] According to Coates, "The Big Four index funds of Vanguard, State Street, Fidelity, and BlackRock control more than twenty percent of the votes of S&P 500 companies—a concentration of power that's unprecedented in America."[5]

Muir Paterson, global head of Strategic Shareholder Advisory in Citi's M&A group, adds, "The rise of the institutional investor is heavily influenced by index funds and their explosion in the past 20 or 30 years to more than 30 percent of the marketplace." Charles Elson of the University of Delaware expands by explaining that indexers became governance champions because "they couldn't sell their stock. There was nowhere to go. As indexers, they were stuck, and so they had to exert influence in some other way."

Indexing is a form of investing where you must own an entire index or group of companies. Therefore, you cannot sell the shares of a poorly performing company in a given index, so you are incentivized to encourage improved governance and push the company to take actions that you think will improve its stock price.

The theory behind indexing and its enormous growth is driven by academic studies and experiences that show that it is very difficult to "beat" the market, particularly after deducting transaction costs. Therefore, why not "own the market" or at least an index that addresses an investor's objectives, such as by putting money in a banking or other industry index? In addition, a large index fund can reduce transaction costs, particularly for smaller investors.

This chapter will look broadly at the rise of institutional investors and then take a closer look at the Big Four index fund providers as well as the proxy advisory firms ISS and Glass Lewis, whose policies and recommendations are substantial drivers of corporate actions and shareholder votes.

Most readers of the business press in recent years could not help but notice that institutional investors—most notably, BlackRock and its CEO,

Larry Fink—have driven more recent ESG behaviors and actions at large corporations; these issues will be discussed in chapter 10 on ESG, as will the shareholder versus stakeholder debate, where institutions and their shifting demands have driven various actions, reactions, and reappraisals.

Finally, in this chapter, I explain the governance implications of and offer recommendations for how boards should engage with institutional investors.

The Growing Size and Influence of Institutional Investors

There have been what we would recognize now as institutional investors for a century—the first modern mutual funds emerged in the 1920s from firms including State Street and Wellington—but their substantial influence has emerged only since the 1980s and '90s. While institutional investors held just 6 percent of outstanding corporate equity in 1950, that number jumped to 29 percent by 1980[6] and 76 percent by 2015[7] and has only continued to rise since then. It is not merely that institutions own the vast majority of shares; the concentration of power among a very small number of institutions is extraordinary. The largest 50 shareholders of the largest 20 US companies in 2016 (including Apple, Microsoft, General Electric, Coca-Cola, and 16 others) held an average of 44 percent of these companies' common stocks.[8] The largest 20 shareholders held 33 percent.[9] The largest 5 shareholders held an average of nearly 21 percent.[10] As of 2022, Vanguard alone owned more than 15 percent of 20 companies in the S&P 500 and was the number-one owner of 330 out of the 500 companies in this index.[11] It is no exaggeration to say that significant control of a large portion of our economy is concentrated in the hands of very few investment firms.

Pension funds have also been important in the growth and influence of the institutional investor. Private pension plan assets grew from $563 billion in 1980 to more than $13 trillion in 2021.[12] Government pension plans account for an additional $4 trillion.[13] In the 1980s, pension funds began to shift from their traditional position as passive shareholders to become more active. "Institutional shareholder activism by public pension funds basically began with their submission of proxy proposals in 1987," wrote Stuart L. Gillan of the SEC and Laura T. Starks of the University of Texas in 2000. "Although these funds could simply sell their holdings in underperforming companies (and many in fact do), often the holdings are so large that the shares cannot be sold without driving the price down and suffering further losses. More importantly, for many public pension funds, the fact that they index a large portion of their portfolios precludes selling underperformers. . . . The constraints on selling underperformers imposed by the indexing strategy have provided an important motivation for shareholder activism."[14]

The stage was set for this increased involvement by the Employee Retirement Income Security Act (ERISA), passed in 1974, which set minimum standards for private retirement and health plans to protect participants. Among its provisions, ERISA provided that managers of pension funds have a fiduciary duty to those covered by such plans. In 1988, the Department of Labor issued an opinion letter to Avon (referred to as the Avon letter) that made clear that included in those fiduciary responsibilities is the duty to vote at shareholder meetings.[15]

According to Kurt N. Schacht and Karina Karakulova of the CFA Institute (a not-for-profit organization that provides investment professionals with finance education and certifications), this caused fund managers to "[move] away from treating proxy voting as an afterthought. . . . [Avon] prompted not just ERISA funds but many public pension funds to pay attention, review the proxy issues, and submit votes that reflect the interests of investors. Proxy voting was not meant to be just a rubber-stamp for management's views, but rather the key to shareholder rights and better corporate accountability."[16]

At the same time, according to *Institutional Investor* in 1989, board service used to mean "coming to meetings, listening to reports, having lunch, and collecting your fee."[17] But pressure from institutional investors starting in the late 1980s pushed boards to be more independent, well informed, and effective.

Bill Ultan, managing director at the consulting firm Sodali, with over 30 years of experience helping companies with governance issues, told me, "When I started back in the mid-1980s, outside of hostile tenders and proxy fights, institutional investors did not have much interest in broader governance issues, their shareholder proposals were much more narrow in scope, and there was far more deference given to boards, with shareholders assuming that boards were doing what they were supposed to be doing."

The Securities and Exchange Commission Historical Society relays a story in its report on the moment when that began to change: "In 1986, GM bought out billionaire Ross Perot at a premium. This was an affront to institutional investors which did not get the same consideration. . . . When

CEO Roger Smith countered that, if investors did not like the way the company was managed, they could sell their shares, investors launched a revolt instead and worked with outside directors to replace management. This accomplishment served as a wakeup call to many companies."[18]

"Not everyone considered increasing shareholder power a good thing," the SEC Historical Society goes on to explain. "Some believed that institutions did not represent small shareholders and countered that their organized efforts drowned out small shareholder voices. Others argued that shareholder activists focused too much on share value, forcing management to emphasize short-term performance at the expense of the long-term health of the company. [But] despite these reservations, organized institutional shareholder power was here to stay."[19]

Ultan added, "Dale Hansen used to run CalPERS [the California Public Employees' Retirement System, which now has more than $500 billion of assets under management], and he was one of the first institutional investors who would attend annual meetings and submit proposals such as declassifying a board. He was a big part of institutional investors developing a greater awareness as to their power and ability to effect change."

The two important issues left to complete the discussion of institutional investors and the related corporate governance issues emerge from two relevant, important phenomena: the extraordinary rise of indexing and its concentration in a very few, very large players and the development of the highly influential governance, or proxy advisory, firms, mainly ISS and Glass Lewis. The governance advisory firms recommend corporate governance policies and how to vote on various issues that come before shareholders as well as offer related consulting services. This can help institutional shareholders with the daunting task of researching the governance issues at play in the approximately 4,000 public companies in the US. As a result, ISS and Glass Lewis have a significant influence on how institutional investors vote; it is estimated that these two firms have 97 percent of the proxy advisory market and that their recommendations are followed and can account for as much as an estimated 38 percent of shareholder votes.[20]

The Index Explosion

"Index funds have now gathered so much capital and concentrated so much ownership that they have enough voting power to strongly influence, if not determine, how public companies are governed," writes Coates. "We increasingly have an economy overseen by . . . roughly a dozen index fund managers."[21]

Passive or index funds have been shown to provide higher risk-adjusted returns than active investment funds because even if some active investors can outperform the market, selecting firms or funds that can consistently do so is very difficult. Given the dramatically lower costs—the median mutual fund charges 15 times the fee of an index fund—the case for index funds is even more powerful.[22]

The widespread acceptance of this reality has emerged over the past 50 years, from when indexing was called "Bogle's folly" after Vanguard founder Jack Bogle launched the idea in 1976. Bogle had been hired at Wellington Management after graduating from Princeton in 1951, having written his senior thesis on the topic of mutual funds—investment funds that pool money from a large number of investors in order to purchase securities. He rose up the ranks for nearly 25 years before leaving to start what he called "The Vanguard Experiment." He introduced the first index fund in 1976, collecting $11 million at launch for a fund that has now grown to over $9 trillion in assets under management.[23] In 1977, Vanguard stopped selling its funds through brokers and instead went directly to investors, saving them sales commissions. The company has led the entire industry to lower costs dramatically. Bogle died in 2019 and is widely credited as "the father of indexing."[24]

In Warren Buffett's 2016 shareholder letter, he praised Bogle:

> If a statue is ever erected to honor the person who has done the most for American investors, the hands down choice should be Jack Bogle. For decades, Jack has urged investors to invest in ultra-low-cost index funds. In his crusade, he amassed only a tiny percentage of the wealth that has typically flowed to managers who have promised their investors large rewards while delivering them nothing—or, as in our bet, less than nothing—of added value. In his early years, Jack was frequently mocked by the investment-management industry. Today, however, he has the satisfaction of knowing that he helped millions of investors realize far better returns on their savings than they otherwise would have earned. He is a hero to them and to me.[25]

From Vanguard's small beginnings, today more than 15 percent of the total US market is invested in passive index funds, and the Big Three index fund players—BlackRock, Vanguard, and State Street, ordered by size—have more than 20 percent of the voting power of the S&P 500 companies, rising to 25 percent if Fidelity is added to the list as well.[26] And because not all shareholders vote, these percentages can be even more meaningful. For example, assume for simplicity that a major corporation has 100 shares with 25 shares or 25 percent of the shares owned by the Big Three plus Fidelity. Assume further that small institutions and retail investors (individuals) own 15 shares or 15 percent of the company but do not vote on a given topic. Therefore, the Big Three plus Fidelity have almost 30 percent of the vote (25/(100 − 15)). In addition, these sophisticated, large investors can coordinate with each other in a way smaller investors just cannot, potentially allowing them to drive the change they want to see. Boards and management teams also know that disgruntled institutional investors may collaborate with activists to try to force changes too.

Ultan has seen all of this play out over his career:

> The emergence of index funds as the dominant asset managers strategically changes the dynamic for companies. These firms are not listening to quarterly earnings calls; they're not talking to your investor relations executives. They're not making buy-and-sell decisions. They engage purely from a portfolio risk assessment point of view, and that is what drives the changes they want to see. They've made the judgment that companies with classified boards have higher portfolio risk, or companies with a lack of diversity, or companies that are not focused on climate change. These concerns sometimes overlap with an investment approach, but that's not the goal. Still, you can't ignore them. These are huge shareholders with incredible sway on voting outcomes.

Experienced director Paula Sneed adds, "Over the past 20 years, the power of these firms has only gotten greater. Their annual letters about governance issues signal their views and how they will vote proxies. As a result, they have influence on corporate governance and strategy. They have a great deal of power."

The Big Three are in almost every major public company's top 10 shareholders, along with Fidelity, which has both index funds and actively managed ones. They largely engage with companies through what are known as stewardship teams. These teams exert influence in three ways. First, they set priorities that are published publicly, expecting that companies will act consistently with these mandates.[27] Second, they communicate with companies directly—State Street, for example, engaged with 1,533 companies in 2018, adding up to 70 percent of the firm's assets under management in the equity market, with BlackRock and Fidelity not far behind in terms of numbers and percentages.[28] Third, they cast shareholder votes, with Vanguard, for example, voting on almost 170,000 individual proposals in 2019.[29] Interestingly, research has shown that their votes are not necessarily consistent with the preferences of their underlying investors. "Currently, funds ignore the diversity of their investors while voting their shares, preferring to identically vote virtually all the shares they own.... They make no serious effort to [identify what shareholders prefer].... Simply ignoring that diverse preferences exist makes short work of them," writes Caleb N. Griffin, a professor at the University of Arkansas School of Law who has researched widely on issues of corporate governance and incentive effects and has testified before Congress on these issues.[30] "Their paternalism," he writes, "frustrates the ... spirit of their fiduciary obligations."[31]

For example, Griffin found that in the 2018–19 time frame he studied, the Big Three rarely supported environmental proposals despite widespread public support, they rarely supported efforts to address the gender pay gap despite public support, and they did not support "even one shareholder proposal related to data privacy, even though 81% of Americans believe [according to a 2019 Pew Research survey] that the risks of companies collecting their data outweigh the benefits and 79% of Americans are very or somewhat concerned about data privacy."[32]

Bogle was wary of the growing dominance of huge institutional investors such as BlackRock, State Street, and even the company he founded, Vanguard. Writing in the *Wall Street Journal* in 2018, he warned, "If historical trends continue, a handful of giant institutional investors will one day hold voting control of virtually every large U.S. corporation. Public policy cannot ignore this growing dominance, and consider its impact on the financial markets, corporate governance, and regulation."[33]

In the *New York Times* in 2022, columnist Farhad Manjoo quoted Harvard Law School professor Einer Elhauge, who has said that the concentrated ownership of the Big Three "poses the greatest anticompetitive threat of our time, mainly because it is the one anticompetitive problem we are doing nothing about."[34]

Having already discussed Vanguard, it is worth a closer look at BlackRock and State Street as well. BlackRock, founded in 1988 by a group led by Larry Fink, has become the largest asset manager in the world, with over $11 trillion in assets under management. Fink has written annual letters to the business community—addressed to the CEOs of BlackRock's portfolio companies until switching in 2023 to a letter to BlackRock shareholders—since 2012, highlighting issues of concern to BlackRock. These letters, issued publicly, have come to take on substantial influence and, in fact, according to a 2021 research study, have been successful in driving change.[35] Companies have altered their approaches and disclosures based on the content of Fink's letters.[36]

The shift in his letters from governance issues to ESG and broader shareholder and stakeholder topics will be discussed in more depth in chapter 10, but it is appropriate to mention that sustainability had become a big concern of Fink's—and thus much more of a consideration for most public companies due to BlackRock's power. Given the current political environment, this focus has waned; we will explore that further too.

State Street was founded in Boston in 1792. It is the second oldest continually operating US bank and the largest custodian bank in the world, servicing close to 10 percent of the world's assets, growing over the years in part, as with BlackRock, due to significant acquisitions.[37] A custodian bank holds the underlying assets, operating, according to the *New York Times*, "in a little-noticed corner of the financial world. They specialize in back-office financial tasks, using sophisticated technology to keep track of the securities positions of large investors like pension funds, hedge funds and charitable endowments."[38]

The three companies have done a tremendous amount to impact governance over the past generation, urging companies, for example, to increase board independence and diversity. Each year, BlackRock, for instance, releases an investor stewardship report, in which the firm says it intends to "provide further clarity to our clients, the companies they are invested in, and other stakeholders, about our voting activities."[39] The 2024 report highlights the driving principle behind BlackRock's voting decisions: "The majority of BIS' [BlackRock Investment Stewardship's] efforts are focused on corporate governance as, in our experience, sound governance is critical to the success of a company, long-term financial value creation, and the protection of investors' interests."[40]

Vanguard releases a similar annual report, explaining that the company does not seek to pursue public policy objectives but uses its position to push for change in four areas, according to its 2023 report: (1) board composition and effectiveness ("board members [should be] appropriately independent, capable, and experienced"), (2) board oversight of strategy and risk ("[boards should] have ongoing oversight of material risks to their company"), (3) executive pay ("the practices [should be] aligned with shareholders' long-term returns"), and (4) shareholder rights ("governance structures should allow shareholders to effectively exercise their foundational rights").[41]

State Street also releases an annual asset stewardship report. In 2022, the company listed its stewardship priorities as effective board oversight; climate risk management; human capital management; and diversity, equity, and inclusion (DEI).[42]

The three companies actually disagree on voting decisions over two-thirds of the time, according to Morningstar research, with each firm taking a unique voting stance on at least one ESG topic. Looking at 100 key resolutions between March 2021 and March 2023, Vanguard, for instance, voted against all 11 civil rights–related resolutions and against all 6 non-climate-related environmental resolutions, while BlackRock and State Street supported more than two-thirds of these. State Street supported 12 of 13 resolutions on human rights and ethical use of technology, while BlackRock and Vanguard supported just 4 and 1 of them, respectively. BlackRock supported significantly more resolutions on workplace equity than State Street or Vanguard.[43]

However, to focus exclusively on the Big Three ignores another important topic. The Big Three may well hold some 20 percent of the voting power at most big public companies, but a significant portion of the rest of the holders rely on governance advisory firms to help them make their voting choices.

The proxy advisory market is generally considered a duopoly: ISS and Glass Lewis. And their influence may be growing. Over recent years BlackRock has launched a Voting Choice program for its retail investors that allows them to vote following ISS's or Glass Lewis's recommendations instead of BlackRock's, and State Street and Vanguard have introduced similar pass-through voting plans, in part as a reaction to concerns that the Big Three have too much power over shareholder votes.[44]

But this trend may simply shift more influence to ISS and Glass Lewis, which, as stated earlier, already influence as much as an estimated 38 percent of shareholder votes. Therefore, it is important to look closely at these two firms.

The Proxy Advisory Duopoly

A challenge for institutional investors who realize that they must exert pressure for improved governance and for active investors who must push for improved performance is that to do so, they must, among other things, review numerous proxy statements each year and consider the various shareholder votes required. Few companies—especially outside of the Big Three—have the resources to do so. Therefore, many have outsourced their research to and follow recommendations from proxy advisory firms.

"[ISS and Glass Lewis] have created models of what they think good governance looks like," writes Jim Woodrum, clinical professor at the Kellogg School of Management at Northwestern University. "And both use various algorithms to determine whether a given company is deserving of a 'yes' vote on Say on Pay, and whether individual board members should be supported."[45]

"The most interesting thing about these firms," Woodrum continues, "is that their business model requires them to change their guidelines on a regular basis. After all, if they had a straightforward set of rules and all companies adopted them, there would then be no need for ISS or Glass Lewis to exist. As a result, both firms tend to move the goalposts on a regular basis, and this results in that most popular boardroom conversation: 'What does ISS think about that?'"[46]

ISS was founded in 1985 and controls over 60 percent of the governance advisory business. *Institutional Investor* profiled the firm in 2018, calling it "The Mysterious Private Company Controlling Corporate America: How Eight Men inside a Maryland Office Park Decide the Fate of the Country's Greatest Companies" in the article's headline.[47] "That ISS has become the kingmaker in proxy contests between billionaire hedge fund activists and their multi-billion-dollar corporate prey," writes *Institutional Investor*, "is even more astonishing given that ISS itself is worth less than $1 billion and started out as a back-office support system, helping shareholders cast their ballots on what are typically mundane matters of corporate governance. Says one former ISS executive who now works at a hedge fund: 'ISS sort of stumbled into this powerful role.'"[48]

ISS, majority owned by Deutsche Börse Group, has 3,200 employees, serves approximately 4,200 institutional clients, and produces some 50,000 proxy analyses in 100 markets. Glass Lewis was founded in 2003 and controls most of the rest of the advisory market. The company was sold in March 2021 by the Ontario Teachers' Pension Plan, one of the largest pension systems in Canada, and Alberta Investment Management Corporation to the private equity firm Peloton Capital Management and Stephen Smith, a Canadian financial services entrepreneur.

There are three other proxy advisory firms worth mentioning as well—Egan-Jones Proxy Services, founded in 2002 and a subsidiary of a credit rating agency; Segal Marco Advisors, an investment consulting firm founded in 2017; and ProxyVote Plus, which was started in 2002—but their combined influence is small, as together they have just 3 percent of the proxy advisory market.[49]

The influence of ISS and Glass Lewis, in particular, has grown significantly since the 2007–9 financial crisis, as Enron and similar scandals prompted changes in shareholder voting, including the SEC's introduction of a shareholder vote on executive pay as a result of Dodd-Frank.[50]

Opinions are very much split about the value of ISS and Glass Lewis as well as the potential dangers of having so much power concentrated in the two companies. Elson has "great respect" for them: "They offer a neutral view on corporate governance based on neutral factors, and they call it like they see it. As outsiders looking into a company, based on objective factors, making a decision one way or the other, I respect them a lot. I've been a big fan of theirs for years." As an attorney for activists, Steve Wolosky of Olshan appreciates their value: "Clearly, they make it easier, in a sense that institutions have to vote, so all mutual funds have to vote. It helps quite a bit if you can get ISS or Glass Lewis to support you as an activist. Your chances of running a successful contest are greatly enhanced. It's next to impossible for an activist to win a proxy contest if both ISS and Glass Lewis aren't on board."

However, the *Wall Street Journal* has been critical of the proxy advisory business, with the editorial board writing in 2023 that "Glass Lewis says it provides 'active ownership engagement' to institutional investors 'to collectively influence your companies, ensuring the highest standards of transparency and best practices in ESG are maintained.' [But] shareholder activists also pay Glass Lewis to boost their campaigns. It's hard to believe its activist clients don't influence the firm's recommendations."[51] In January 2023, Elon Musk wrote on Twitter (now X), "Far too much power is concentrated in the hands of 'shareholder services' companies like ISS and Glass Lewis, because so much of the market is passive/index funds, which outsource shareholder voting decisions to them. ISS and Glass Lewis effectively control the stock market."[52]

David Larcker and Brian Tayan of the Stanford Graduate School of Business, along with James R. Copland of the Manhattan Institute, argue that it is particularly concerning that ISS's and Glass Lewis's recommendations are not back-tested to see whether following them leads to better performance. "Neither ISS nor Glass Lewis discloses whether its voting guidelines or historical voting recommendations have been tested to ensure that they are associated with positive future corporate performance, in terms of operating results or stock price returns," the authors write. "Without comprehensive evidence it is difficult to know whether their voting guidelines are consistent with increased shareholder or stakeholder value."[53]

Ultan has seen them become more important: "ISS is always hesitant to present themselves as any sort of decision-maker. They're just putting out their opinion and it's up to their clientele. They like to downplay it, but they have a certain agenda and objective." Of course, as he reminded me, "with votes now publicly disclosed, institutions have to really have a foundation for their voting decisions. Not to mention that with the emergence of environmental and social concerns, from political contributions and lobbying to climate change, to diversity, to human rights, reproductive health care, guns, conflicts in foreign lands, portfolio managers themselves don't necessarily have that knowledge or interest. This has ended up empowering ISS and Glass Lewis because how better to rationalize a certain vote than to say there's an independent third party that's telling us how we should vote?"

Paterson agrees: "A lot gets outsourced in practical terms to ISS, and ISS has become extraordinarily influential, particularly as regards governance-related topics." And while the Big Three can and do hire their own teams to do the research, few others do. In part, it is an economic issue, but even more importantly, ISS and Glass Lewis provide the third-party validation these companies value.

According to one study, "95 percent of institutional investors vote in favor of a company's 'say on pay' proposal when ISS recommends a favorable vote while only 68 percent vote in favor when ISS is opposed (a difference of 27 percent). Similarly, equity plan proposals receive 17 percent more votes in favor; uncontested director elections receive 18 percent more votes in favor; and proxy contests 73 percent more votes in favor when ISS also supports a measure."[54]

Jay Clayton, former chair of the SEC, "sought to rein in" ISS and Glass Lewis by changing the rules to permit lawsuits against them in case they made misleading statements and requiring them to disclose any conflicts of interest. "ISS sued to block the rule," writes the *Wall Street Journal*, "but why oppose the rules if it is as transparent as it claims? . . . The duopolists want to impose onerous reporting burdens on public companies, ranging from climate to racial equity, while avoiding accountability and disclosure themselves."[55]

Jamie Dimon has also been critical of proxy advisory firms, writing in the 2023 JPMorganChase Annual Report,

> While data and recommendations may form pieces of the information mosaic, [asset managers'] votes should ultimately be based on an independent application of their own voting guidelines and policies. To the extent they use recommendations from proxy advisors in their decision-making processes, they should disclose that they do so and should be satisfied that the information upon which they are relying is accurate and relevant. However, many companies would argue that this information is frequently not balanced, not representative of the full view and not accurate.
>
> Some have argued that it's too hard and too expensive to review the large number of proxies and proxy proposals. This is both lazy and wrong. If issues are important to a company, they should be important to the shareholder—for the most part, only a handful of proposals are important to companies. . . . By the end of 2024, J.P. Morgan Asset Management generally will have eliminated third-party proxy advisor voting recommendations from its internally developed voting systems. Additionally, the firm will work with third-party proxy voting advisors to remove their voting recommendations from research reports they provide to J.P. Morgan Asset Management by the 2025 proxy season.[56]

Many have expressed concerns about the conflicts that the proxy advisory firms have by reviewing governance policies and recommending how to vote for the same companies to whom they offer and sometimes provide consulting services. Elson agrees: "I do think their consulting is problematic, because it gives you the impression of a pay to play, not that it necessarily occurs, but it's certainly that impression, and I've always been worried about that part of the business."

There is also concern that the proxy advisory firms are essentially making policy without third-party comments or authorization. Attorney

Neil Whoriskey—a partner at Milbank and formerly a partner at Cleary Gottlieb and co-chair of the firm's M&A group and Corporate Advisory practice—has been critical of ISS and Glass Lewis, writing that they have created a "new civil code," "arrogat[ing] to themselves the power to make law . . . ruling over decisions on board composition, director qualifications, term limits, majority voting standards, executive compensation, capital structure, poison pills, staggered boards, the advisability of mergers, spin-offs and recapitalizations, and, increasingly, ESG policies. . . . The vote of [their] clients is often decisive and the implications of the votes—especially when considered in the aggregate—have far-reaching consequences for the operation and performance of US public corporations." He continues, "There is considerable evidence that the proxy advisory firms often get the wrong answer." For example, he points to the firms' stance against staggered boards, discussed earlier, as an example of where they have bowed to the will of activists: "The proxy advisors continue to persist in enforcing their thorough-going opposition to classified boards, even after numerous empirical studies have shown this position to be value destructive."[57]

I spoke with Whoriskey, and while reiterating his criticism of the proxy advisory firms, he also explained that on big issues such as a contested director election or a sale of the company, the major institutions do their own research. "I think the bigger places, in deals that are close, they'll read ISS, but they do their own evaluation," he said. "A big deal getting approved, the portfolio managers are involved in it."

However, regardless of how one feels about ISS and Glass Lewis, the reality is that they are—and will almost certainly continue to be—highly influential. After all, according to a 2023 *Wall Street Journal* article, "175 asset managers, controlling more than $5 trillion in assets, voted with ISS more than 95% of the time."[58] Boards and management teams must keep the major governance advisory firms' policies and recommendations at the forefront of their thinking.

Governance Considerations

Talking to institutional investors—and understanding their concerns—is critical. Certainly, it can help keep a board aware of new issues that interest major investors. In recent years, ESG topics have become something that investors want companies to address and discuss. In today's world, that list has to include artificial intelligence as well. For example, over 40 percent of S&P 500 companies have discussed artificial intelligence in their most recent annual reports, according to Bloomberg.[59]

Mike Allen, of the Delaware law firm Richards Layton & Finger, agrees and walked me through his thinking on the importance of institutional investors: "It's very important for companies to have a sense of who the large holders are in their stock and what sort of voting patterns they have. Certain institutional investors vote as they see fit and may have their own policies and guidelines, and some follow whatever ISS recommends. Having a good handle on who your institutions are and what their voting policies are, if any, provides a lot of information. We always think it is better for companies to have some measure of active engagement with their large institutional stockholders."

Given the importance of institutional investors and the increasingly broad scope of their concerns and influence, here are six key actions for every board to consider regarding this critical constituency:

1. Stay abreast of the institutional investors with significant holdings in your company and especially any changes in that mix: Who is buying, and who is selling? Also, be aware of what price they paid compared to the recent stock price. Pay particular attention to any institutions that are known to act in concert with activists.
2. Understand your major institutions' policies on significant issues, along with the policies and recommendations from ISS and Glass Lewis. Then note any differences between the large institutions and the proxy advisory firms as well as where your company may not be consistent with these mandates.
3. Establish a cadence of communication with the major institutions, including how often, what the topics will be, and who will attend.
4. The senior management team—particularly the CEO, CFO, and head of investor relations—should meet regularly with the major institutional investors to discuss performance, strategy, and other issues. Use these meetings and any other forums to proactively communicate why your company has made the choices it has on any potentially contentious points in advance of any friction. Forums can range from additional public disclosures, to conversations at investor meetings, to formally scheduled in-person meetings with specific agendas.
5. The board leader, often accompanied by the CEO, should seek to meet at least once per year with these same major investors and provide

another point of contact for them to express any concerns or points of view. These conversations often focus primarily on governance.
6. Engage directly with ISS and Glass Lewis periodically too. You want to fully understand any of their concerns prior to any shareholder votes that may be difficult. This can include a worse-than-expected result of a Say-on-Pay vote or a contested vote on director elections given the involvement of an activist.

Paterson makes the point that while indexing and large institutional investors continue to grow, this creates opportunities for smaller institutions: "Index funds are influential, but actually driving things are sometimes the smaller shareholders, because they are often the ones who have the appetite to be vocal in the moment." His comment is a good reminder that directors should listen to and try to address the concerns of all shareholders, not just the largest ones.

As discussed, shareholders elect directors to oversee management teams and companies for these owners. Institutional investors matter, and every director should be thinking carefully about how a company communicates with its usually largest and most influential investors. It should not take a threat, and certainly not a desire for a certain shareholder vote, to meet with and listen to your institutional shareholders.

Chapter 9
Distressed Companies and Financial Restructurings

It is fair to say that no company wants to embark on a financial restructuring, the process by which a struggling company generally attempts to reduce its debt and perhaps other liabilities (such as above-market leases, a major litigation judgment, liabilities stemming from asbestos or other causes, etc.) and increase liquidity. In this chapter, I will discuss in-court and out-of-court restructurings, which each have their own particular issues, and the governance topics that arise. Of course, operations-enhancing efforts may well take place at the same time, such as reducing costs and renegotiating contracts. The unpredictability and constantly changing nature of industries, businesses, and capital markets that boards and management teams face mean that many companies do end up in financial jeopardy and need to take steps to resolve it or restructure.

I have been involved as an independent director in some 30 restructuring situations, ranging from a small automotive supplier, Techniplas; to the iconic retailers Toys"R"Us and Bed Bath & Beyond; to the global oncology care provider GenesisCare. There are numerous governance and management challenges in these situations, from retaining and incentivizing management and employees to negotiating with lenders, and in the case of an in-court restructuring, there are additional challenges, such as satisfying the court's numerous information requests and gaining court approval for major actions, having sufficient liquidity for what is often a long process, and getting to an agreed-upon plan and new capital structure to gain the debtholder votes and court approval necessary to emerge from a Chapter 11 reorganization under the bankruptcy code.

It is very possible—and, indeed, it is the objective—to emerge from a restructuring as a stronger company and to go on to create value for the shareholders. We start with a historical perspective on restructuring and its remarkable growth over the past approximately 50 years. A director's responsibilities can change during a restructuring, and this chapter will explain how a director needs to approach these new challenges and help oversee the company through what will almost certainly be one of its most difficult times.

The History of Restructuring

The history of restructuring can be traced back to the end of the nineteenth century. As Professor David A. Skeel of the University of Pennsylvania writes, "If the early history of flexible, reorganization-based corporate bankruptcy could be distilled to a single word, that word would be 'railroads.'"[1] It is the railroad failures of the late 1800s that led to the idea that managers could be left in place to operate during times of financial distress and reorganize companies as opposed to simply allowing them to be sold off piecemeal without the chance to recover.

There was no bankruptcy law when the railroads began to struggle, roughly 100 years into the life of the nation, and there was a question as to whether Congress was lawfully allowed to intervene. As Skeel writes, there were "serious doubts as to whether Congress could regulate the bankruptcy of corporations, given that the states regulated all other aspects of a corporation's existence."[2] At the same time, the interstate nature of the railroad business made it very difficult for individual state legislatures to help.

Skeel explains that this challenge—keeping the railroads from failing through government intervention—paved the way for corporate restructurings. The principal interest groups, "not just the managers of railroads," Skeel writes, "but shareholders, creditors, investment bankers, and railroad lawyers . . . were squarely in favor of reorganizing rather than liquidating the railroads."[3]

And so they did. Managers worked to take the patchwork of debt and negotiate terms with the creditors for a reorganization. It was not necessarily a cooperative effort—many creditors complained that the railroads were squeezing them out of fair compensation—but despite hundreds of railroads entering receivership between the 1870s and the start of World War I, the trains continued to run.[4] While not an unmitigated success—railroads that entered receivership later failed at a rate more than twice as high as those that did not, and the process did not end up resolving financial problems in the same way as companies are able to do today[5]—what happened in the railroad industry did serve to set up a corporate restructuring system that remained in place for decades and is often termed "equity receivership."[6]

In an equity receivership, the court appoints an individual to take control of a company in order to keep it functioning and at the same time seeks to satisfy the needs of the creditors. When it came to the railroads, these equity receiverships largely ended up keeping control in the hands of the existing managers. While courts had the authority, and even the obligation, to appoint a neutral party as the receiver, judges would often appoint officers of the insolvent railroad instead, and these officers would in many cases "sell" the railroad to the existing bondholders.[7] "For example," writes the Economic History Association, "in the Wabash receivership of 1886 . . . the debt exchange resulted in the creation of a new railroad with the assets of the old. Often the transformation was simply a matter of changing 'Railway' to 'Railroad' in the name of the corporation."[8]

The Bankruptcy Act of 1898 codified this equity receivership system for companies beyond the railroads, creating a debtor-friendly regime that could help protect companies from creditors.[9] As Mark A. Perelman of the Yale School of Management summarizes, the 1898 act reversed previous laws that had "allowed creditors to initiate involuntary [bankruptcy] procedures against farmers and laborers . . . [and] focused on rehabilitating debtors with limited judicial review of discharges."[10]

It may be that this went too far. The US Supreme Court decided, in a series of cases in the 1920s, that the railroads had actually been a special case and that manager-led reorganizations, while not limited to that industry alone, needed to be evaluated carefully. "In *Harkin v. Brundage*," Skeel writes, "the Court suggested that it would not simply rubberstamp [these debt exchange arrangements]. The Court was still more explicit in *Shapiro v. Wilgus*, where it indicated that these techniques passed muster in railroad cases only because railroads were 'public service corporation[s].'"[11]

Congress took notice, and President Franklin Roosevelt's New Deal—while generally more focused on legislation to help the poor and unemployed and restore the US economy in the midst of the Great Depression—included a revision to the 1898 legislation that moved some control away from managers. The Chandler Act of 1938 ended the equity receivership system and gave significant power to independent, court-appointed bankruptcy trustees.[12]

In 1978, with creditors frustrated by a rising number of filings, Congress passed the comprehensive Bankruptcy Reform Act. But the bankruptcy bar, according to Todd J. Zywicki of the George Mason University School of Law, "seized the reins of the reform effort . . . [and] both personal and business bankruptcy laws were made more lax rather than strict."[13] The act "brought Wall Street lawyers and banks back into bankruptcy practice by increasing fees, increasing prestige, and further weakening public oversight of the process . . . reinvigorat[ing] professional control of bankruptcy proceedings and professional influence in Congress."[14] It marked the beginning of our modern, professional-led system, and reorganizations became "a business and strategic decision rather than a last resort."[15]

"The 1978 act was a big deal," says Jamie Sprayregen, a prominent bankruptcy attorney who founded Kirkland & Ellis's Restructuring group in 1990 and played a key role in helping build it into the market leader before retiring last year and is now a vice chair of Hilco Global, which provides a variety of financial services. "The four biggest things the 1978 act did were create the automatic stay so that creditors couldn't keep seeking payment on debts, keep the debtor in possession of the company, allow for debtor-in-possession financing, and significantly, establish market rate compensation for professionals. Before that, the big firms wouldn't get involved because they couldn't get market rates."

"Before 1978," Sprayregen summarizes, "trustees got appointed automatically. That meant that management and boards would wait until a company was on death's door—because who wants to put themselves out of a job? Now management got to stay, and the board got to stay, and they could get financing from their traditional banks and use whatever counsel they wanted."

The debtor-in-possession system was chosen not because it was necessarily perfect but because, as Sprayregen puts it, "it was the least worst. It was a compromise to let the management who brought the problems stay in control, but it was thought to be better than bringing in a new leader like the bankruptcy trustee. But because of discomfort with the debtor-in-possession system, all kinds of extrastatutory elements grew up around it, like chief restructuring officers and independent directors and all the professionals now consulted as part of the process."

It has been said that the first modern restructurings can be traced back to the garment district of New York City, where many small businesses were established and grew but often then struggled too. Eventually, thanks to the features of the 1978 act described earlier, more and more distressed companies saw the benefits of a bankruptcy reorganization.

At first, companies often turned to accounting firms for advisory help. Why accountants? Sprayregen explains, "The SEC commissioner back in the late 1930s was [future Supreme Court Justice] William O. Douglas. His administration put out a scathing report on how railroad organizations worked and changed laws to make it virtually impossible for the big investment banks to be involved in railroad reorganizations, at least until things were changed in 2005. In effect, if you underwrote the security, then you couldn't be the banker—so that knocked out most of the investment banks, which led to accounting firms taking the lead on bankruptcies because they weren't conflicted."

Bob Manzo, a very early player in restructuring who began his career as an accountant, working as an auditor in the early 1980s for Arthur Andersen, the Big Eight accounting firm (back when there were eight; now we have the Big Four), took me through the early contemporary history of restructuring as he saw it.

At the time he started his career, business owners went to their accounting firms when they were in financial distress. Some of the accountants who specialized in this area started to see the potential of the business and went out on their own. Manzo followed a similar trajectory. He moved from accounting to consulting, eventually starting a boutique advisory firm in 1990, Policano & Manzo, which was sold a decade later to FTI Consulting.

Manzo explained that two of the pioneers in advising on restructurings were Frank Zolfo, who left Touche Ross (now Deloitte), a major accounting firm, to start his own firm, and Art Newman, who eventually started the restructuring practice at Blackstone (which is now part of the investment banking firm PJT). Newman went from being an accountant to a commercial banker to an investment banker and ended up working on the restructuring of General Motors and many other large companies.[16]

For years, restructuring was seen as a "low-quality" business by the major law firms—largely because pre-1978, they could not charge market rates for the work. These top firms would pass business to small boutiques that generally worked on either the debtor (company) side or the creditor (lender) side. Weil was one of the first big law firms to embrace bankruptcy as a major source of business. Harvey Miller joined Weil in 1969 as the firm's 14th partner. He created the bankruptcy group at the firm and ran it for 33 years before leaving to join the investment bank Greenhill.[17] He returned to Weil less than five years later, in time to take on the 2008 Lehman Brothers bankruptcy filing. Over the course of his career, Miller worked on smaller retail bankruptcies before moving on to what his biography called "nearly every landmark bankruptcy case," including General

Motors, American Airlines, Texaco, WorldCom, Enron, Eastern Airlines, and more.[18] He passed away in 2015. Once Weil established its restructuring practice, many of its "Big Law" competitors followed.

Firms such as Manzo's worked alongside the lawyers. They were earlier called "turnaround firms" and today are often known as financial advisors (as opposed to investment bankers), at first helping banks improve companies by, say, putting new executives in place and now generally helping management provide the extensive financial information required by investors and courts as well as assisting with operating improvements. One of the first and largest is Alvarez & Marsal. AlixPartners and FTI are among the other major financial advisors in restructurings.

Given the conflict rules as explained earlier, there were few investment bankers involved early in the growth of advising distressed companies until the rules changed. One of the first, in the early 1980s, was David Supino at Lazard. I remember him walking the shabby halls of Lazard's offices at One Rockefeller Plaza in New York City and having a growing presence in an emerging business that seemed countercyclical to the M&A business—an attractive proposition. Wilbur Ross—later the Secretary of Commerce under President Donald Trump—developed the restructuring practice at the investment bank Rothschild in the 1980s. David Ying at Donaldson, Lufkin & Jenrette and Art Newman played major roles in investment banks joining the coterie of restructuring advisors.

Brian Fox, a managing director at Alvarez & Marsal, told me quite simply, "Restructuring was not seen as an attractive business until many realized how profitable it is."

As corporations continued to grow bigger and bigger through the 1980s—largely thanks to the growth of M&A discussed in chapter 6—financial restructurings became part of the landscape in a way they never had before. Part of this was due to the development of high-yield or junk bonds and the explosion in private equity deals that created the potential for more restructurings. In fact, a record number of bankruptcies were filed in the 1980s and early 1990s—a rise "well over 100 percent" in the decade that followed the passage of the 1978 act[19]—including prominent corporations such as Federated Department Stores, Eastern Airlines, Greyhound, and Texaco.[20]

It took time for the various constituencies to realize the potential benefits of bankruptcy. As Sprayregen explains, "It took some number of years for people to believe the new code really meant what it said and that we weren't still dealing with the system of the old days. We needed the judges who used to be referees to accept the fact that the system had changed. The sophistication of the capital markets grew. People started accepting the bankruptcy system."

As the 1980s proceeded, the current ecosystem of advisors—law firms focused on the legal aspects of the process, investment banks focused on capital structures and capital raising, and consulting firms focused on information requirements and operational improvements—took shape.[21]

Michael Milken's development of high-yield bonds opened the door to alternative forms of financing and much greater amounts of debt for a given company. Capital structures grew far more complex. Previously, companies and banks (borrowers and lenders, respectively) were generally reluctant to be aggressive and adversarial. Vendors and banks often used to comprise the entirety of the capital structure of a company, and there were typically expectations of modest returns. These parties were often patient and could manage through a down cycle.

However, banks then moved from predominantly lenders to underwriters who did not hold substantial portions of the debt. James B. (Jimmy) Lee—with his hard-charging style and omnipresent suspenders—was initially at Chemical Bank (today JPMorganChase). He is credited with creating the syndicated bank loan in the late 1980s. This is a structure where banks underwrite a loan for fees before selling most or even all of the credit to investment firms and other parties.

Then private debt funds entered the market. In the wake of the 2007–9 financial crisis, when regulated banks were forced to retrench, this new capital source became much larger, growing to nearly $500 billion in 2020.[22] Marc Lipschultz is the co-CEO of Blue Owl Capital, a private capital firm with some $235 billion under management, and formerly the global head of energy and infrastructure at KKR. "Using private lenders was a nonidea until the last 10 years and probably even the last five for big companies and big sponsors [private equity firms]. But the private debt market has grown substantially because it works," he told me. "If you can innovate a solution that actually meets a need for the market and meets a need for investors, like any product, financial services or otherwise, that's what innovation's about." Lipschultz continues:

> The banks made a business decision to not be actual lenders to these companies. It opened up a very significant reason we exist, which is

that as long-term users of capital, our clients like to know who they're dealing with. Private credit is just the corollary to private equity, where in a world in which the bank is no longer your lender, if you don't really know who your lender is on a given day, you've lost that continuity and focus. I believe that the banks' shift over decades out of being an actual lender to instead be an intermediary—which is a perfectly rational business choice on their part—created the opportunity for [private] lenders to step in and help people who value a long-term partnership. We provide for those who value the predictability and the privacy and the partnership, or "the three Ps."

At the same time, these firms are very focused on good governance at the companies to which they lend. "We're the ones that bear the downside," Lipschultz explains, "since our business is either get paid back or lose capital. We can do lots of diligence, but then there's also what happens after we lend. Governance matters a lot to us."

Direct lending funds have proven to be an attractive, fast-growing alternative to syndicated bank loans due to their efficiency, flexibility, and certainty of execution. It is estimated that the private credit market now exceeds approximately $1.5 trillion and could increase to $2.8 trillion by 2028.[23] Banks and investment firms have become interested in branching out into this business, too, as it has grown in prominence.

For example, in September 2024, Citi and Apollo announced an agreement to form a $25 billion private credit lending program. Previously, Wells Fargo and Centerbridge had set up a similar, if smaller, partnership.[24] In addition, in late 2024 BlackRock announced the acquisition of HPS, a major player in private credit with assets of almost $150 billion, for $12 billion.[25]

These newer debtholders or creditors are often not as patient as traditional banks were in the past, as extended time frames lower their returns and tie up capital. An active secondary market where debt is purchased by distressed debt hedge funds also grew substantially around the time of the Great Recession.

These changes have combined to make corporate financial structures much more complex than in the past, with nonbanks providing as much as 90 percent of newly issued debt capital, up from less than 30 percent in 1994.[26] They have also increased the push toward restructurings.

Barry Ridings retired from the investment bank Lazard in 2014 as a managing director and vice chair after a prominent career stretching almost 40 years in the bankruptcy advisory business. Ridings credits the rise in Chapter 11 cases to the fact that "capital structures have gotten so complicated, and creditors are very difficult."

Add in a softening economy, and restructurings have exploded. For example, energy companies had generally earned tremendous profits through the energy crisis of the 1970s, but as oil prices fell, the industry crashed. In other sectors, the growth in information and communications technology meant that many companies had grown too fast and taken on too much debt. Deregulation of the airline, oil and gas, financial services, and broadcasting industries meant more and more troubled businesses. And with the dramatic increase in e-commerce, the store-based retail industry has gone through traumatic changes.

Two Broad Categories of Restructurings

In the most general terms, a restructuring can proceed either out of court through negotiations with lenders or in court under the bankruptcy code. The out-of-court effort is a nonjudicial process where a financially troubled company and its significant creditors reach an agreement on adjusting the company's obligations. This requires creditors to ultimately be willing to work with the company and to have confidence that the company can go forward on sound financial footing and repay its restructured loans. The advantages are that an out-of-court restructuring can typically be accomplished much more quickly than an in-court process, therefore reducing the time that management is less focused on its business, and at a far lower cost by avoiding greater professional fees, potential litigation, and other costs. The reality is that an out-of-court restructuring can be more likely to succeed in cases where creditors believe that the debtor has (1) a leverage and/or liquidity problem but beneath that struggle is a quality business and/or (2) an alternative—a bankruptcy filing—that will be worse for creditors.

Steve Zelin, a partner and global head of the Restructuring and Special Situations group at PJT Partners, one of the leading investment banking firms for restructurings, believes that the out-of-court process is generally far preferable to its alternative. "It works well when regular markets fail to provide sufficient liquidity and new sources of capital can help a company restructure and avoid a Chapter 11," he said. "The out-of-court process provides more options and flexibility and is faster and less expensive than going to court."

Robert Drain was a bankruptcy judge in the Southern District of New York for 20 years, overseeing some of the country's largest cases, including the Purdue Pharma bankruptcy. In fact, from 2016 to 2023, 10 cases with at least $1 billion of debt were brought before him, the third largest number of such cases in the country.[27] He is now of counsel at Skadden. He said to me, "I would always recommend an out-of-court restructuring if at all possible. In-court proceedings are traumatic for a company. They're very expensive. Things happen beyond your control at times. In the nonbankruptcy, or workout, context, you threaten to go to court, and knowing how that might play out really determines how the entire situation will get resolved."

There are numerous tools available in an out-of-court restructuring. Examples include waivers for a certain period of time, such as permitting a company to remain in violation of a covenant in exchange for a fee. There can also be amendments to credit agreements, such as extending the maturity of a debt security, perhaps in return for a higher interest rate and maybe a small pay down of principal—again along with a fee, of course. There can be debt-for-debt exchanges, where lenders exchange existing debt for new debt. Changing the interest from cash to paid in kind (or PIK), where interest is paid in additional debt securities, and/or extending the maturity, perhaps in return for a higher coupon, are two examples of adjustments that creditors may find acceptable and that also take near-term pressure off the company. There can be a new equity raise, whether by existing creditors swapping debt for equity or new cash raised by selling equity to creditors and/or other parties. Of course, one possible path in an out-of-court restructuring is selling certain assets or business units or even the entire company.

Today, there is a lot of talk about "liability management exercises" (LMEs) or liability management transactions, where new or existing debtholders work with the borrower to provide liquidity without going to court. While there is no specific definition of these deals that have become much more frequent, Josh Sussberg, a partner in the Restructuring practice group and member of the executive committee at the law firm Kirkland & Ellis, told me simply that "these have been going on forever."

"These exercises are financial," he explained, "from the standpoint that you're not affecting operational change. You're merely utilizing capacity that you have under your credit agreements to enhance liquidity and maybe extend indebtedness. It doesn't solve an underlying business issue, but it certainly can get a company the time it needs to potentially grow out of whatever issues it's facing and avoid an in-court bankruptcy."

One remarkably successful example of an out-of-court restructuring is the case of Apple, which was "90 days from going bankrupt" in 1997, according to cofounder Steve Jobs.[28] Jobs discontinued the company's Newton (handheld digital assistant) division,[29] which had cost Apple $100 million in development, and negotiated a $150 million investment from Microsoft with an assurance from Bill Gates that his company would continue to support the Macintosh with its Microsoft Office suite of products for at least five years.[30] Apple went on to become, at times, the most valuable company in the world.[31]

As another example, Manzo told me that Related Companies—led by Stephen Ross, the prominent real estate developer—was highly distressed in the early 1990s. However, the banks that had loaned him money did not want him to file for bankruptcy. They believed that an out-of-court restructuring would preserve more value, worked with him, and today, Related is an enormous real estate company and the largest landlord in New York City, and Ross is a billionaire whose name graces the University of Michigan business school and who owns the Miami Dolphins football team.

A more recent example, from 2023, is the case of Wheels Up, one of the largest private aviation companies in the world. I was a consultant to the company's board during its out-of-court restructuring. Then Chief Legal Officer Laura Heltebran explains, "I led the team that prepared us for a potential in-court restructuring while simultaneously partnering with our CFO/interim CEO to work toward an out-of-court option. We worked quickly to source capital, keeping the board well informed and positioning it to consider and approve the most attractive offer fast, all while keeping our larger team focused on operating the company."

Wheels Up received a new $500 million credit facility led by Delta Airlines—Delta and the other lenders also gained control of the company. The turnaround plan included a deeper strategic partnership with Delta, which was previously an investor. George Mattson, a longtime Delta board member, was appointed as the new CEO. "Wheels Up's private aviation offerings serve as a crucial complement to and an extension of Delta's premium leisure and corporate travel offerings," Mattson told me. "And Wheels Up is benefiting tremendously from Delta's operational capability and commercial reach."

The problem, of course, is that not every company goes on to be a success after an out-of-court restructuring. According to Moody's, more than one in six out-of-court restructurings are followed by an in-court bankruptcy filing within three years.[32] A major disadvantage of out-of-court processes is a lack of a "fresh start." While certain problems—perhaps near-term liquidity as one—can be mitigated, such as by reducing an interest rate for a few quarters and/or postponing an amortization payment, there is no legal ability, as there is in a Chapter 11 in-court restructuring (as we will discuss next), to have an automatic stay to create time for a more comprehensive solution or to ultimately have a court approve a fresh start with a completely new capital structure, with perhaps burdensome contracts and other liabilities extinguished too.[33]

In addition, when there are a large number of creditors with different viewpoints, the issues are usually more complex and a fulsome restructuring is often necessary. Ridings explains that it depends on whether you have holdouts and how you can deal with them: "In an out-of-court, you can't bind the dissidents, so you have to get them to agree—if you can."

When court becomes unavoidable, there are a number of options. There is, for example, a Chapter 7 liquidation, allowing a business to be turned over to a bankruptcy trustee for an orderly sale of the assets, where creditors are paid from whatever pool of money becomes available. In a Chapter 7 situation, no further debts exist when the liquidation is complete, and while the owners are typically left with nothing once creditors are paid, neither are they personally liable for the shortfall. Chapter 7 carries with it the enormous downside that the company no longer exists in the end and is shut down. There were 7,631 Chapter 7 business filings in the 12 months that ended September 30, 2022, though these were largely small businesses.[34]

Most large companies going through bankruptcy will file instead for a Chapter 11 reorganization.[35] In this process, all creditors and equity holders are involved in a public, court-supervised procedure. Chapter 11 is seen by most as a debtor-friendly system, with tools such as the automatic stay, the ability to reject contracts, and voting rules that permit plans to be imposed without 100 percent approval. The principle underlying all of this is that if a company is worth more as an operating concern than by being liquidated, the system should allow it to restructure and continue.[36]

In Chapter 11, the debtor or company continues to operate, run by management as a debtor-in-possession, and can negotiate a "plan of reorganization," ultimately a court-approved restructuring. Given the automatic stay, creditors are generally barred from taking action against the debtor or its assets during a Chapter 11.

The mechanics of a Chapter 11 case can be complex. The process starts with the filing of a petition with the bankruptcy court, usually a voluntary petition filed by the debtor but sometimes an involuntary petition filed by a certain number of creditors that must follow various rules. This petition includes, among other things, an explanation of what led to the filing and information about the debtor's assets and liabilities, current income and expenditures, and contracts and leases.[37]

An early question is in which state the company should file. There are often many choices. The law allows for filing where a company is incorporated, in its principal place of business, in the location of its principal assets, or where any of its affiliates has a current bankruptcy case pending.[38]

At this point, the debtor becomes a debtor-in-possession, a status held until a plan of reorganization is approved by the court, the case is dismissed or converted to Chapter 7, or a trustee is appointed to manage the company instead of the debtor. Actions by the debtor-in-possession or the company that are outside the ordinary course of business require bankruptcy court approval after notice to the parties in interest, with the opportunity for a court hearing. Of course, court approval takes some of the decision-making away from the board and management.

The automatic stay goes into effect immediately. It stops creditors from pursuing judgments, collection activities, foreclosures, or repossessions of property from the debtor, accomplishing two aims: first, keeping the debtor in the best possible position to continue to operate the business, and second, putting all creditors on a level playing field, preventing one or some from seizing assets at the expense of others.[39] The automatic stay gives the debtor time to negotiate with creditors and hopefully find a productive, comprehensive solution.

Another critical piece of a Chapter 11 case is the "avoiding powers" that the debtor-in-possession holds. For example, transfers of money or property made within a window, generally 90 days before filing, can be canceled if doing so will serve the creditors at large, and transfers to insiders (relatives, partners, directors, officers, and the like) from up to one year in the past can be canceled as well.[40] In addition, a fraudulent transfer made within two years of a bankruptcy filing can be unwound. A fraudulent transfer is when a debtor either transfers property with the intent to hurt creditors or makes a transfer for less than "reasonably equivalent value" and, at the time of such transfer, was insolvent or met other related tests. It is complex and difficult to show that a fraudulent transfer took place.

Debtors have 120 days to file a plan of reorganization, a period that may be extended to as long as 18 months before creditors are then allowed to file competing plans. A plan of reorganization details the different classes of claims and how they will be handled by the debtor. It must be voted on by creditors who are set to receive less than the full value of their claims—but it does not need full approval from creditors. Rather, it requires the approval of two-thirds by dollar amount and one-half in number of the holders of any impaired tranche of debt who vote.[41]

Thanks largely to prenegotiated filings, even as the number of restructurings has increased, the time from filing to confirmation had fallen from a median of 457 days in 2000 to 103 days in 2020.[42] According to the *Annual Review of Financial Economics*, "Of 1,184 Chapter 11 filings through June 2022 by companies with at least $100 million in assets, pre-arranged or pre-packaged bankruptcies—largely agreed to with creditors prior to filing in court—accounted for 26% of the filings between 1980 and 2009 versus 54% of filings in 2010 and later."[43]

These arrangements have made the process easier and faster. Hybrids between the out-of-court and in-court processes, a prearranged filing means that a general deal has been struck between the debtor and creditors, while a prepackaged bankruptcy means that a deal has been struck and the debtor has the votes to approve a plan of reorganization. In other words, the company enters Chapter 11 with a plan almost in place in the case of a prearranged bankruptcy or approved in the case of a prepackaged bankruptcy. This avoids a lengthy court process but still allows companies to use the beneficial features of a Chapter 11 bankruptcy filing.

It is typical for a distressed company to hire legal advisors, and often investment banking and financial advisors, to help prepare for and navigate a restructuring. As the Department of Justice guidelines state, the employment of "attorneys, accountants, financial advisors, turnaround specialists, and other professionals" is authorized by the bankruptcy code.[44]

Board members and CEOs, even highly experienced ones, often have little knowledge of the restructuring process until their companies go through it. I talked to Dave Brandon, who, among other senior leadership roles, was the CEO of Toys"R"Us, where he was hired in a troubled situation and the company soon filed for a Chapter 11 bankruptcy. I was an independent director of a major subsidiary of Toys"R"Us during this process. "I'd been a turnaround guy to some extent," Brandon told me, "but never to a point where liquidation or bankruptcy was ever a consideration, and I naively knew it was going to be messy, and I knew we were going to have to restructure, but I never imagined that it would take the shape of a public filing and I didn't have that experience. You start to learn more about the risks and liabilities, the complexities of these intercompany loans and transfers. It was pretty clear to me why we needed to bring on these experienced professionals to help guide us."

Sussberg summarizes well the role of advisors in the process: "The investment bank is there to really help lead a transaction, whatever that transaction may look like—finding financing, running a sale process and then trying to orchestrate a stand-alone restructuring. The financial advisors are there to help supplement management and help with day-to-day cash flow, forecasting, reporting requirements, gathering of information, and really being the financial go-between with all the other parties. And then the lawyers are there to facilitate all those parties being able to implement the various financial, operational, and overall restructuring perspectives and helping to deal with all the various constituents."

Of course, there are downsides to a Chapter 11 proceeding. The business may not be able to recover. At a minimum, public knowledge that a company is in Chapter 11 can cause customers, employees, and other constituents to look elsewhere if there are other options available to them—though Jared Ellias, the Scott C. Collins Professor of Law at Harvard Law School, has disputed this notion regarding employees. Ellias, who explained to me that he "does research at the intersection of law and economics" with a focus on bankruptcy, found, when studying the relevant data, that employees know when things are not going well and leave regardless of a bankruptcy filing. "The departures after a bankruptcy filing are probably best understood as a continuation of pre-existing trends," he writes, "[and] after bankruptcy, Chapter 11 companies that reorganize look just like everybody else—they don't lose workers at significantly higher rates than others in their industry." He argues that bankruptcy, in fact, stabilizes losses.[45]

Implications for the Fiduciary Responsibilities of Directors

Directors are, of course, charged with oversight of companies on behalf of the shareholders or stakeholders. This oversight obligation continues in an out-of-court or in-court restructuring. Sussberg counsels,

> As a director one of the ways you satisfy your duty of care is by relying upon your advisors. That's not to say that directors shouldn't

push back and challenge advice and question what's happening. They absolutely should; that's the best process. After all, your decisions don't always have to be the right decisions. But if you follow the right process and you rely on advice and actually look and spend time on the metrics and understand everything that's going into this, you don't have to be right at the end of the day. You just have to make the decision in the appropriate way.

It has sometimes been assumed that a major implication for directors when a company is in financial distress is that when the company is solvent, directors have a fiduciary responsibility only to shareholders, whereas when the company is near or "in the zone of" insolvency, directors are responsible to creditors. This is not the case. Directors owe fiduciary duties solely to the corporation and its stockholders, not creditors directly, even as the corporation approaches insolvency or in fact becomes insolvent.[46]

In *North American Catholic Educational Programming Foundation Inc. v. Gheewalla*, the Delaware Supreme Court found that "when a solvent corporation is navigating in the zone of insolvency, the focus for Delaware directors does not change: directors must continue to discharge their fiduciary duties to the corporation and its shareholders by exercising their business judgment in the best interests of the corporation for the benefit of its shareholder owners."[47]

Scott Greenberg is Gibson, Dunn & Crutcher's global chair of Business Restructuring and Reorganization and a member of the firm's executive committee. He has a particular focus on advising creditors in restructurings. Previously, he was a partner at Jones Day, where he was co-head of the Jones Day Business Restructuring & Reorganization practice. He simplified directors' obligations in a conversation with me: "It's pretty easy: directors should try to maximize value to stakeholders, and that value will be distributed given the waterfall of priorities. Certainly, in a distressed situation, directors should have a heightened sense of the implications of their actions."

This does not mean that creditors have no recourse if they feel the company has wronged them. If a corporation becomes insolvent, creditors become the residual stakeholders in the company. As such, they have standing to bring derivative—as opposed to direct—claims against directors who breach their fiduciary duties.[48] A derivative suit is one filed on behalf of the corporation, while a direct action would be one filed on the creditors' own behalf. Since there are no fiduciary duties owed directly to the creditors, they can only file on behalf of the company.

There is a question, in many cases, about whether or not a company is insolvent. An investment banking or financial advisory firm can do a solvency analysis. This generally includes a balance sheet test, or valuing all assets and liabilities at current market value and seeing if total assets exceed total liabilities, and a cash flow or liquidity test that seeks to determine whether the company should be able to meet its liabilities as they come due.[49]

In addition to solvency work, an investment banking firm may be called on to provide additional valuation work for the board and company, including a valuation of collateral and whether the collateral's value is adequately protected during the case as well as a valuation of the business to help determine the ultimate distribution of value to various tranches in the capital structure—analyses that are important for directors to understand and consider carefully when making key decisions.

It is important to remember that directors should retain the protection of the business judgment rule whether the company is solvent or insolvent. As discussed earlier, as long as directors satisfy the duties of care and loyalty, they can expect to be insulated from liability for actions taken in good faith under the belief that they are acting in the company's best interest. The Delaware Court of Chancery wrote in *Quadrant v. Vertin* that directors are not liable for "continuing to operate [an] insolvent entity in the good faith belief that they may achieve profitability, even if their decisions ultimately lead to greater losses for creditors."[50] Of course, it is prudent for directors of distressed companies, including those about to file for an in-court restructuring, to confirm that there is an appropriate amount of D&O insurance provided by creditworthy parties.

The Importance of Independent Directors

In a distressed situation, independent directors are often put in place at a holding company and/or various subsidiaries to help avoid conflicts of interest as the company makes financial decisions that may benefit one creditor over another or address the interests of an investment firm owner, create a good record of corporate governance, and preserve the business judgment rule standard. In addition, most corporate directors do not have restructuring experience, and there can be value in one or more independent directors who understand the process and can help the board and management. This can be the case even when a Chapter 11 filing is uncertain.

Judge Drain sees tremendous value in independent directors as long as they fulfill their duties as fiduciaries and do not act in the interest of a particular constituent responsible for their appointment: "They've been there before. They know they can come up to speed very quickly."

In the fall of 2022, as one example, the vaping company Juul Labs added two restructuring experts to its board as the company searched for a financial rescue. The company told the *Wall Street Journal*, "[The independent directors'] broad experience with companies exploring strategic options will help determine what path is best for our company."[51] By January 2024, the company had not filed for bankruptcy and had raised $1.27 billion in new capital. In late 2023, "WeWork reshuffled its board after the resignation of three directors who disagreed with its governance and strategy," reported the *Wall Street Journal*, "replacing them with corporate bankruptcy experts as it cast doubt on its ability to survive turmoil in the office-building market. . . . Independent directors carry weight in bankruptcy court, where judges tend to defer to their conclusions about how to restructure businesses fairly."[52]

Judge Drain believes that "independent directors with relevant experience can help the rest of the board through the process and take some of the burden away from the rest of the board and from management so that the business can continue to run smoothly. They can also coordinate communication and oversee the advisors in a way that can help with the process."

Judge Shelley Chapman is senior counsel in the Business Reorganization and Restructuring Department and chair of the Alternative Dispute Resolution practice group at Willkie, where she previously served as a partner from 2001 to 2010. Prior to rejoining Willkie in 2022, she was a US bankruptcy judge for the Southern District of New York for 12 years. Among other cases, she oversaw the Lehman Brothers bankruptcy case, the largest bankruptcy case in history. I testified in front of her at some length in the Sabine Oil & Gas Chapter 11 case as an independent director of Sabine. In that case, the creditors' committee sought the right or "standing" to prosecute various claims on behalf of the company that the Sabine board had evaluated and decided not to pursue. Judge Chapman found for the company and against the creditors on all claims, and it was nice of her to say in her opinion that "Mr. Foster's testimony revealed a competent grasp of the multiple and complicated potential claims at issue."

"It's a very big challenge and responsibility to be a director of a distressed company," she told me. Ellias agrees with Judges Drain and Chapman: "Putting an independent expert on your board prebankruptcy to help guide the process has become a norm already, but I think it will become a universal norm over the next couple of years in the same way as how well-advised companies file for bankruptcy with a financing and key employee incentive plan for senior management already in place."

I should note that Professor Ellias prefers the term "bankruptcy director" to "independent director." He explains that he "finds the independent director term confusing, because normally we think of independent directors as fearless advocates for the interests of shareholders, whereas bankruptcy directors often hold themselves out as objective experts who are just trying to do the right thing." This is a good point.

At the same time, there has been some recent questioning of independent directors in restructurings. In fact, I initially contacted Professor Ellias because I disagreed with a paper that he wrote, along with Ehud Kamar and Kobi Kastiel of Tel Aviv University, which argued that "proponents [of independent or bankruptcy directors] tout their experience and ability to expedite the reorganization and thus protect the firm's viability and its employees' jobs. Opponents argue that they suffer from conflicts of interest that harm creditors."[53] This piece was read with real interest by many in the restructuring ecosystem—including me.

In this paper, Ellias and his colleagues reported that they found that the recovery rate for unsecured creditors is, on average, approximately 20 percent lower when there is a bankruptcy director. They also found reason to suspect a proshareholder bias, in that shareholders (often private equity firms) usually appoint these directors without consulting creditors, and the ecosystem is relatively small, with the same directors being appointed again and again. They identify the "lure of future engagements" as a potential conflict for these directors.

As an experienced independent director in restructurings, I did not put much credence in this study and disagree with the "lure of future engagements" accusation. There are numerous reasons why creditors may recover more or less, and these are certainly beyond the control of the independent directors at the parent company and any subsidiaries. There are usually just one or two independent directors at these companies, not a majority. Therefore, a study that seeks to evaluate independent directors at least in part on creditor recoveries makes little sense to me.

Professor Ellias spoke with me at length. He clarified that his findings on a lower recovery with a bankruptcy director did not mean "that there's some causal relationship between the director and creditor recoveries." More likely, "bankruptcy directors are there for the more difficult situations, and I think that's what you see when finding that creditor recoveries are relatively lower. These directors are basically expert trauma surgeons brought in when the patient is particularly wounded."

As far as the "lure of engagement" and the implication that independent directors are not highly ethical, which is not my experience and an assertion I find unfair, Ellias clarified that as well:

> The question we were asking is what perverse incentives might warp independent director decisions. It's not to say that every independent director's decision-making is warped by those incentives but rather, what are the things that we need to think about guarding against? We don't assume that everybody's always going to do the right thing. Corporate law doesn't make that assumption; corporate law believes that you need to have guardrails in place. The repeat player dynamic is not distinct to independent directors in Chapter 11. Bankruptcy lawyers, bankruptcy judges, all of Chapter 11 is a world of repeat players, and in many ways, that's very healthy. We have disclosure rules more generally, but because the [bankruptcy] code doesn't contemplate this bankruptcy director role, there are no ethical conflict rules here, and that's something that I think judges need to consider.

That is a fair point.

Of course, the "lure of engagement" exists in many situations outside of bankruptcy. For example, an investment banker may be accused of encouraging an unattractive transaction to earn a contingent or success fee from a client, and a director of a public company may be accused of approving high compensation for a CEO to encourage that the director is continually reappointed to the board.

"I think the courts," adds Judge Drain, "even before that article came out, have wised up to that concern and are focusing on the positions that the independent directors are taking as opposed to their identity. You set the tone with those directors and tell them, look, this is what we expect here. We are not going to be able to run this case if you come in with anything other than a charge to get the best deal, given all the factors that you have to take into account."

The reality is that there are certainly some professionals in various contexts who do not do their jobs well, but as discussed throughout this book, governance has improved very substantially over time. In addition, as in any business, various constituencies, from shareholders to company advisors to creditors and others, learn who the most effective independent directors are. I have often been recommended by attorneys and creditors but always appointed by the company or debtor. Finally, I have only been involved in restructurings for multiple companies owned by the same private equity firm three times.

Among the key issues that an independent director usually addresses in a restructuring is whether the estate has a colorable or potentially successful legal claim against one or more parties that would be a potential asset of the bankruptcy estate and whether various nondebtor third parties should be released from any potential liability after emergence. An investigation is usually done by an independent law firm overseen by one or more independent directors.

In the GenesisCare bankruptcy, where I was the sole independent director and thus only member of the special committee as well as chair of the parent company, I oversaw a detailed, monthslong investigation by special counsel. After extensive work and deliberations, the special committee recommended, and the company agreed, not to grant certain former officers and directors releases from potential liability under the reorganization plan.

Releases also made the news in February 2024 in a case in which the Boy Scouts had reached a $2.5 billion settlement with more than 82,000 victims regarding decades of claims of sex abuse. The settlement was halted after 144 claimants appealed, insisting that the settlement should not bar future claims against organizations that worked with the Boy Scouts, including churches, local Boy Scouts councils, and insurers that provided the organization coverage.[54]

Many believe that while some releases may seem distasteful, they can add real value. "I think that if someone's making a meaningful and substantial contribution to help facilitate a reorganization," says Sussberg, "that otherwise would not be available but for the protection of a release, you have to consider it under those circumstances and those facts because it means maybe someone gets a recovery or maybe someone doesn't."

In the case of Purdue Pharma, the maker of the much-maligned pain medication Oxycontin that filed for bankruptcy in 2019, thousands of lawsuits against the company were settled in a 2022 agreement in exchange for more than $10 billion (including up to $6 billion directly from the Sackler family—which had previously controlled the company and withdrawn as much as $11 billion from it over the years[55]) to be spent on opioid treatment and prevention and for the Sackler family to be released, or exempt, from civil lawsuits.[56] At issue is whether, in a bankruptcy restructuring, third-party nondebtors such as the Sacklers, who have denied any wrongdoing, can be protected from future civil suits brought by other third parties (as opposed to the estate) as part of a Chapter 11 plan of reorganization. The argument against this hinges on the bankruptcy system overreaching by allowing individuals to be released from liability from third parties and not just companies being released from obligations that may be owed to third parties. With $40 trillion in lawsuits currently pending against Purdue Pharma and the Sacklers, victims worry that acceptance of the settlement will preclude a potentially larger recovery.[57] Supporters of the settlement say that the alternative is years of unproductive litigation.[58]

This case reached the Supreme Court and received an enormous amount of press coverage. "There's huge implications for all of corporate bankruptcy [with the Purdue Pharma case]," University of Chicago law professor Anthony J. Casey told the *New York Times* prior to the ruling. "I think this is probably the most important bankruptcy case before the court in 30, maybe 40 years."[59]

In June 2024, the Supreme Court ruled, in a 5–4 decision, that the Sacklers could not in fact be shielded from lawsuits as part of the settlement. This may endanger the settlement—and quite possibly a timely recovery for victims—as well as affect other cases that have relied on similar liability shields.[60] "The Sacklers have not filed for bankruptcy and have not placed virtually all their assets on the table for distribution to creditors, yet they seek what essentially amounts to a discharge," writes Justice Neil Gorsuch in the majority opinion. "They hope to win a judicial order releasing pending claims against them brought by opioid victims. They seek an injunction 'permanently and forever' foreclosing similar suits in the future. And they seek all this without the consent of those affected. The question we face thus boils down to whether a court in bankruptcy may effectively extend to nondebtors the benefits of a Chapter 11 discharge usually reserved for debtors. . . . Nothing in present law authorizes the Sackler discharge."[61]

Writing for the dissenting four judges, including Chief Justice John Roberts, Justice Brett Kavanaugh stated, "Today's decision is wrong on the law and devastating for more than 100,000 opioid victims and their families. The Court's decision rewrites the text of the U.S. Bankruptcy Code and restricts the long-established authority of bankruptcy courts to fashion fair and equitable relief for mass-tort victims."[62] Nonetheless, our country's highest court ruled on this key issue in many bankruptcies.

On March 18, 2025, Purdue Pharma filed a new $7.4 billion plan of reorganization. Creditors can opt in to support releases for the Sacklers and thus collect a settlement payment from the family, or they can choose to opt out of the settlement and retain the ability to take legal action against the family. The Sacklers will contribute up to $1 billion more to this reorganization plan than they would have contributed to the plan proposed previously. The company hopes to emerge from bankruptcy in summer 2025.[63]

In general, there is still a lack of clarity on how third-party releases will be handled. While it is clear that nonconsensual third-party releases are generally not allowed, there is a continuing debate on what constitutes "consent" to grant a third-party release that will not run afoul of the Supreme Court's ruling. When addressing consent, most judges before and after the Purdue Pharma case have permitted a so-called opt-out release construct as long as creditors have a genuine opportunity to exercise their opt-out right. Under this construct, a creditor that votes on a plan and returns a ballot but does not check a box to opt out of a release can be said to have approved releases of third parties. On the other hand, some judges have required an "opt-in" construct that requires an affirmative action by creditors to agree to a release, such as checking a box on their ballots to opt into releases of third parties.

Related to releases but less contentious are exculpations that eliminate liability for participants in the bankruptcy process during a Chapter 11 case as opposed to behavior before a bankruptcy case. Judge Drain notes, "I think exculpations should be fairly routine, particularly if it's a case where there's been an active group of creditors and transactions have been approved by the court."

Restructurings are a critical part of some companies' life cycles, and it is important for board members to understand the major issues involved in these proceedings. Ridings warns of repeat bankruptcies if companies do not get it right: "It's a challenge for the board to get the best capital structure when you get out of the restructuring, whether an in-court or out-of-court, because so many times we see companies file more than once."

Adds Judge Chapman, "Many times you'll look at a set of projections and you'll look at what happened. And you'll ask, 'What in the world were they thinking?' You look for reasonable explanations because you assume good faith and hard work, but it's important to present the downside case too."

Postreorganization governance is critical as well. As a judge, Drain was often "stunned by the fact that parties would put so much work into getting the plan confirmed and then very little work and thinking about corporate governance thereafter. They're so focused on getting out that they don't think of the obvious next step."

In many ways, restructurings can provide enormous value to the US economy. "We're good at transparency," says Judge Chapman. "We're good at due process. Overall, it's a very good system."

"I think the thesis behind the bankruptcy code is that there's more value in a company alive than dead," adds Sussberg. "And we've seen that time and time again. When companies liquidate, there are fewer jobs, there's less commerce, and there's less of an ability for people to be able to collect what they potentially lost over time. There are many, many companies, some of the biggest companies in the world, that have reorganized in Chapter 11 for various reasons and continue to operate and continue to produce value and provide service to millions and millions and millions of people. And so I think the bankruptcy code works."

Chapter 10
Environmental, Social, and Governance Issues

As first mentioned in chapter 2, it was 1970 when economist Milton Friedman wrote that the only responsibility of business is to increase profits. And yet any director, executive, or investor over the past 30-plus years would be remiss to ignore the rise—and perhaps the fall, or at least the waning if you look at the most recent trends—of ESG and how concerns over the environment (E) and issues of social concern (S) and corporate governance (G) have become a major part of conversations in boardrooms, at investor conferences, and in related forums.

The ESG issues investors have paid the most attention to have evolved over recent years—from human rights to climate change and issues of diversity, including racial justice—but at the same time, the premise of ESG has evolved as well. Thirty years ago, ESG was driven by the idea that companies should care about matters beyond profits. Now proponents of the ESG movement make the case that caring about these issues, and acting in ways that demonstrate that concern, in fact leads to greater profitability and that improving performance on ESG topics is not just a public good but can be a competitive advantage.

And yet there are others who say we have gone too far and that ESG not only is impossible to measure objectively—with different measures generating contradictory lists of top-performing companies—but pulls boards and management away from their ultimate responsibility to deliver profits for shareholders.

In this chapter, I will trace the rise of ESG and the recent backlash against it and then discuss the broader issue of shareholder versus stakeholder capitalism and the implications for directors today: Should they seek to maximize shareholder or broader stakeholder value?

The Rise of ESG

The ESG movement grew out of the broader push toward corporate social responsibility that began in the 1970s—a time of social reform more generally—when the US government started to regulate commerce in socially mindful ways that it never had before, establishing the Environmental Protection Agency, the Consumer Product Safety Commission, the Occupational Safety and Health Administration, and other similar organizations.[1] Corporations were expected to look at their impacts more broadly than just through the lens of shareholders alone but also at how their behaviors were affecting all stakeholders (employees, customers, communities, etc.).

The Reagan administration in the 1980s moved the focus back to corporate self-regulation, as government mandates were disfavored politically, but industrial catastrophes such as the Union Carbide plant rupture in India that killed thousands and, around the same time, a move to ban US investment in South Africa driven by concerns about apartheid caused investors to insist that corporations be more responsible and not just focused on profitability.[2]

The momentum that resulted in today's ESG movement began to build. In 1990, the first socially responsible investment index was launched by MSCI, a stand-alone public company that was originally Morgan Stanley Capital International before it was separated in 2009.[3] In 1992, the United Nations Environment Program issued the Statement of Commitment by Financial Institutions on Sustainable Development. Major banks, including Deutsche Bank, HSBC, NatWest, Royal Bank of Canada, and Westpac signed onto a set of commitments, including "recommend[ing] that financial institutions develop and publish a statement of their sustainability policy and periodically report on the steps they have taken to promote the integration of environmental and social considerations into their operations."[4]

In 1994, consultant and thought leader John Elkington coined the term "Triple Bottom Line," a sustainability framework that "examines a company's social, environment, and economic impact," the precursor to ESG.[5] The ESG terminology was unveiled in a United Nations (UN) report in 2004 titled "Who Cares Wins." The report, a joint initiative among some of the world's largest financial institutions, including Credit Suisse, Deutsche Bank, Goldman Sachs, Morgan Stanley, UBS, and more—18 financial institutions from nine countries, with total assets under management exceeding $6 trillion—encouraged analysts to use ESG factors in their research, financial institutions to integrate them into their investment processes, investors to reward ESG behaviors, and companies to "[implement] environmental, social and corporate governance principles and policies and . . . prioritise environmental, social and governance issues accordingly."[6]

Following that report, in 2006 the UN issued Principles for Responsible Investment, asking signatories to "incorporate ESG issues into investment analysis and decision-making processes."[7] While these efforts were notable, the next step was to shift from principles to practice and figure out how to effectively measure and track companies' ESG efforts so that it could be determined whether commitments that were made were actually implemented.

Over the next decade, more companies began reporting on their ESG-related activity, more ESG-focused investment funds were launched, and the idea that ESG issues could not be ignored became more accepted.

As mentioned in chapter 8, BlackRock, founded in 1988 by a group led by Larry Fink, is the largest asset manager in the world. Fink's annual letters to the business community were at first largely focused on governance issues, but in more recent years, they have made broader recommendations about the importance of looking beyond financial performance, including on environmental (such as climate change) and social issues.[8] This shift began in many ways in 2018, when Fink's annual letter stated that companies must fulfill a broader purpose than just strong financial performance:

> To prosper over time, every company must not only deliver financial performance, but also show how it makes a positive contribution to society. Companies must benefit all of their stakeholders, including shareholders, employees, customers, and the communities in which they operate. Without a sense of purpose, no company, either public or private, can achieve its full potential. It will ultimately lose the license to operate from key stakeholders. It will succumb to short-term pressures to distribute earnings, and, in the process, sacrifice investments in employee development, innovation, and capital expenditures that are necessary for long-term growth.[9]

The *New York Times* heralded Fink's 2018 letter as a "watershed moment on Wall Street, one that raises all sorts of questions about the very nature of capitalism. . . . For the world's largest investor to say [this] aloud—and declare that he plans to hold companies accountable—is a bracing example of the evolution of corporate America."[10]

Pressure had built for companies to address ESG concerns, particularly climate change issues, and the question of whether companies should serve just shareholders or broader stakeholders began to be raised more often.

Eighteen months later, the Business Roundtable, a nonprofit association of the CEOs of many of the largest companies in the world, with a board that includes Tim Cook of Apple, Jamie Dimon of JPMorganChase, and Mary Barra of General Motors, issued a 2019 Statement on the Purpose of a Corporation "signed by 181 CEOs who commit to lead their companies for the benefit of all stakeholders—customers, employees, suppliers, communities and shareholders,"[11] overturning 22 years in which the organization and its members had declared that a company's principal purpose was maximizing shareholder returns. The new statement said that "companies should serve not only their shareholders, but also deliver value to their customers, invest in employees, deal fairly with suppliers and support the communities in which they operate."[12] "While each of our individual companies serves its own corporate purpose," the statement continued, "we share a fundamental commitment to all of our stakeholders."[13]

This perhaps marked the moment when ESG moved to the forefront of corporate consciousness. By 2020, 88 percent of publicly traded companies had ESG initiatives in place.[14] And as of 2023, more than three-quarters of S&P 500 companies incorporated ESG metrics into their executive compensation plans, up from less than two-thirds just two years earlier.[15]

In 2021, a survey by Coller Capital found that 47 percent of private equity investors believed that a robust ESG policy would improve long-term returns. "The fact that half of all private equity investors think ESG investing will in itself boost their portfolio returns should be a wake-up call to anyone who still thinks ESG is a 'nice to have' or a PR tool," said Jeremy Coller, the founder of Coller Capital.[16]

In December 2022, Deloitte, one of the "Big Four" accounting firms with approximately 450,000 employees worldwide, published a survey of companies and their ESG disclosures, finding that corporations "are starting to see the strategic benefits that can be realized through enhanced ESG governance, controls, and disclosure."[17] Deloitte's survey revealed that ESG efforts percolated throughout most companies, with a broad range of anticipated benefits. Nearly all companies (99 percent) expressed a "willingness to invest in new technologies and tools in order to be prepared to meet stakeholder expectations."[18] Among the expected business outcomes from enhanced ESG reporting were talent attraction and retention, increased efficiencies and returns on investments, enhanced trust with stakeholders, premium pricing of products, brand/reputation enhancement, and reduced risk.[19]

To that end, former Caterpillar CEO Doug Oberhelman told me, "a company won't survive very long without paying attention to the environment, paying attention to its governance, and worrying about how it is perceived socially." Major shareholders were increasingly insisting on attention to ESG issues, while advocacy groups were more often attacking companies that they thought were not addressing these issues appropriately. Employees and even customers were increasingly vocal in their expectations about what constitutes good corporate behavior.

This attention to ESG efforts can be seen from examining companies and also looking at investor trends. Which ESG-related issues are relevant for any particular company vary. Kristy Balsanek, the global co-chair, Environmental, Social and Governance (ESG), and a partner at the law firm DLA Piper, told me that "every company's concerns are different, because each company needs to assess what is material to them based on stakeholder expectations, as well as what their management and strategy is, who their employees are, and what they're looking to achieve. The governance piece is often overlooked, but that's really key to ensuring that there is effective oversight, responsibility, and awareness throughout the entire enterprise."

Regarding investors and investments, as of 2023, there were over 14,000 ESG investment funds holding more than $7 trillion in assets.[20] More broadly, data shows that there was more than $30 trillion invested in ESG assets as of 2022, though that was down from $35 trillion two years earlier.[21]

The three prongs of ESG—environment, social, and governance—each cover very different issues, and each component is worth looking at in more detail.

Environment

The environmental piece of ESG concerns the impact of a company on the planet and the issues companies should address to help maintain a sustainable world where they can operate effectively and efficiently.

Environmental issues were the first in the ESG triumvirate to reach a tipping point in the public consciousness. Senator Gaylord Nelson organized the initial Earth Day in 1970, with 10 percent of the US population (an estimated 20 million people) attending Earth Day–related events.[22] The Environmental Protection Agency was formed later that same year.[23]

According to the Sustainability Accounting Standards Board (SASB), a nonprofit organization founded in 2011, the most relevant environmental issues today are greenhouse gas emissions, air quality, energy management, water and wastewater management, waste and hazardous materials management, and ecological impacts.[24]

While many companies have taken these issues quite seriously for years, *Harvard Business Review* wrote in 2023 that even the "so-called 'hard to abate' sectors like cement, steel, and aluminum . . . are starting to turn the ship," citing, for example, partnerships to develop low- or no-carbon manufacturing technologies.[25]

There has been particular attention paid to environmental disclosures, as the European Union (EU) has mandated certain disclosures on climate risks, pollution, biodiversity, and more,[26] and California has become the first US state to mandate similar disclosures—on climate-related risks and pollution across supply and value chains—for companies with annual revenues in excess of $500 million (for climate-related financial risks) and $1 billion (for greenhouse gas emissions) beginning in 2026.[27]

"There's a shift now in disclosure and reporting from voluntary frameworks to mandatory requirements," explains Balsanek, "and a lot of that is being driven by the EU companies that are multijurisdictional [that] are now required to report, and in the US, California is really leading the way, but other states have efforts in the pipeline as well."

The SEC announced its required disclosures in March 2024 to go into effect starting in fiscal year 2025, whereby public companies must disclose their greenhouse gas emissions. However, these rules were put on pause soon after being announced, as multiple industry groups challenged them and numerous state attorneys general sued the SEC on the grounds that it had gone beyond its statutory authority.[28]

Even if enacted, the new rules would still fall well short of the original SEC proposal that would have had companies reporting not just their direct emissions but certain indirect ones as well. These are known as "Scope 3" emissions, and their inclusion in the initial March 2022 plan was hotly contested by companies claiming that the reporting would be overly burdensome. Scope 3 disclosures are not in the final SEC requirements.

Scope 1, 2, and 3 emissions, to briefly explain, are fairly straightforward: Scope 1 emissions are from sources a company owns or controls (i.e., fuel burned in a building's furnace); Scope 2 emissions are generated indirectly by a company's purchases (i.e., buying electricity for its facilities); and Scope 3 emissions are those that emerge somewhere in the company's value chain that happen due to the company's activities but not from sources owned or controlled by the business (e.g., business travel).[29]

The sustainability nonprofit Ceres has advocated for mandatory disclosures for years. "Without clear and comparable climate disclosures from companies," the organization writes, "investors cannot evaluate climate risks for individual holdings or make plans to address the systemic risks of climate change across their portfolios and the real economy.... Making climate risk disclosures part of required financial filings will dramatically improve the quality of data for investors."[30]

On the other side, organizations such as the US Chamber of Commerce argue that mandatory disclosure is expensive and unworkable and may be unnecessarily broad and potentially confusing to investors if the information is not in fact material to a company's financial success. There is a clause in the new SEC rule that limits Scope 2 disclosures only to what is considered material.[31] "In the proposed climate disclosure rule," the Chamber of Commerce writes, "the SEC's own estimate [found] that the proposed disclosures from this one rule would be two-and-a-half times more expensive than all SEC disclosures companies currently make, combined, raising the total cost burden associated with its related forms from a total of $3.9 billion to $10.2 billion."[32] Pushback such as this led to the weakened final rules.

Interestingly, it is not clear that mandatory disclosures will increase the amount of information that companies provide. "I think there's going to be a decrease," Balsanek predicts, "because for so long under a voluntary framework, everyone has been throwing out as much information as possible. But once you get into a mandatory framework, companies are going to have to be very careful and rigorous and perhaps offer less information overall." Of course, information mandated by the SEC and provided in SEC filings should be of higher quality.

Social

The social component of ESG generally centers around a company's impact on employees, customers, suppliers, and communities. SASB tracks a number of social metrics: human rights and community relations, customer privacy, data security, access and affordability, product quality and safety, customer welfare, selling practices and product labeling, human capital, labor practices, employee health and safety, and employee engagement, as well as diversity, equity, and inclusion (DEI).[33] A 2021 BNP Paribas global study on ESG found that 51 percent of the 356 institutional investors surveyed felt that the social pillar of ESG is the most challenging to analyze because of the difficulty in obtaining data and the lack of standard metrics.[34]

DEI, in particular, has been a tremendous focus of the *S* in ESG. When discussing the nominating and governance committee in chapter 4, I touched on the issue of diversity at the board level, California's 2018 law (since struck down) requiring boards to have a certain number of female directors, and large institutional investors announcing expectations that boards should increase diversity. In chapter 11, I will discuss board diversity in more detail, and in chapter 12, I will talk about diversity in the context of a CEO search, but of course, diversity efforts must extend far beyond the board and CEO.

For some time, most large public company boards and management teams, as well as the leadership at numerous other companies and organizations, have been increasingly focused on improving the diversity of their workforces, growing the pipeline of diverse senior executive candidates, and trying to ensure comparable pay for comparable jobs at every level regardless of sex, race, age, and other factors.

Paula Sneed has spent much of her career thinking about these issues. "There has been a long-standing corporate governance focus on both board gender and racial diversity. However, there has not been as much focus on C-suite diversity," she told me. "Boardroom diversity is visible because you see pictures in proxies. In short, progress in boardroom diversity has been limited, and progress in C-suite diversity has been slow, disappointing, and frustrating."

And yet sometimes concerns about diversity and improving statistics on this topic can encourage trying to meet quotas rather than thinking more broadly. As Mario Carbone told me, "I want the absolute best, and I don't care who you are or where you came from." By broadening the search for any new hire and seeking diversity of candidates, the expectation is to increase diversity naturally.

As raised in chapter 4, the current administration and Congress are overturning various diversity efforts quickly. Further steps by the White House and Congress to discourage or forbid DEI initiatives are expected. There have already been meaningful reactions. For example, ISS announced on February 11, 2025, that "for shareholder meeting reports published on or after February 25th, ISS will no longer consider the gender and racial and/or ethnic diversity of a company's board when making vote recommendations with respect to the election or re-election of directors at U.S. companies."[35] In addition, some companies, from JetBlue to KKR, have included DEI as a "risk factor" in their SEC filings. Comments have included concerns about legal, reputation, hiring, retention, investment, and capital-raising risks if differing expectations among varied stakeholders are not managed effectively.

While the SEC does not currently mandate disclosures about social issues, including diversity, this may be coming. "We added disclosures around management discussion and analysis [of financial results] some 40 to 50 years ago," Gary Gensler, then chair of the SEC, said in 2023. "We added disclosures around the environment in the 1970s; we added disclosures around executive compensation, and so forth. What does that mean for the 2020s? There are tens of trillions of dollars of assets under management and investors are looking to companies to disclose information about climate risks and about cyber risk. Building upon work from predecessors in this job, we're also looking at workforce or what one might call 'human capital' disclosures. . . . There is a benefit to some standardization, to get to consistency, comparability and decision usefulness."[36] However, the political environment has changed substantially.

Governance

The governance pillar of ESG relates to general corporate governance, business ethics, risk management, and compliance issues.[37] A well-governed company is one where the board lives up to its duties, after all. The rise of ESG has meant increased attention on governance matters such as board diversity, corporate defense mechanisms, executive pay, term limits, and retirement ages.

ISS's global governance principles center on four ideas: accountability, stewardship, independence, and transparency. ISS believes that boards should be accountable to shareholders through regular board elections and by responding to investor input. It advocates for shareholders needing a simple majority vote to change governance provisions or approve transactions. It believes companies should exceed regulations and general industry standards around ESG. It thinks boards should be independent, with an independent leader and sufficiently independent committees. And it argues for enough transparency for shareholders to make informed voting decisions.[38] Additionally, its proxy voting guidelines support taking steps to mitigate climate-related risks, decrease the use of poison pills, and reduce problematic non-performance-based executive pay programs, among other issues.[39]

The UN's Principles for Responsible Investment focus on a number of key governance issues: tax fairness, responsible political engagement, cybersecurity, executive pay, corporate purpose, anticorruption, whistleblowing, and director nominations.[40] The World Economic Forum advocates for a similar list, adding the ideas of transparency and fair competitive practices.[41]

One of the governance issues that boards today must think about is how to oversee ESG issues. This is an area that many companies are still grappling with, and there is a wide range of approaches that different boards and management teams have taken.

ESG oversight can be handled at the board level, of course. While there has not traditionally been a board committee devoted to ESG, there sometimes is such a committee, and companies are increasingly adding this responsibility to the nominating and governance committee and even using a new name for this committee, such as the governance and sustainability committee at Lear.

Another good option is to split the ESG efforts among the three major committees, such as with the audit committee taking responsibility for cybersecurity, ethics, and compliance; the compensation committee dealing with human capital management and DEI issues; and the governance committee (perhaps renamed the governance and sustainability committee) overseeing governance, safety, and environmental issues.

At the management level, Balsanek insists that it is important for companies to have cross-functional ESG oversight to provide that coordinated, effective actions are being taken: "It's about making sure it's being managed on a day-to-day basis too. You need an ESG committee at the executive level and then ESG champions or points of contact within the different teams."

Many companies, including some I am involved with, handle ESG at the management level this way: the environmental prong is handled by an ESG-specific team, social issues are handled by the human resources group, and governance is under the purview of the general counsel's office. The ESG team acts as a coordinator too: it keeps up with legislation, compliance, and risk management requirements; responds to customer and consumer requests; drives the annual sustainability report (more about this report later); and monitors peers and ratings. This group also works with the business units to push the entire company in a more sustainable direction.

Deloitte's December 2022 survey found that, at the management level, ESG efforts are being led at companies most commonly by a chief sustainability officer (42 percent), CFO (37 percent), or chief strategy officer (29 percent).[42] As far as board-level oversight, 55 percent of the 300 companies surveyed put at least some responsibility for ESG with an ESG/sustainability committee, 39 percent with the compensation committee, 37 percent with the nominating and governance committee, 30 percent with the full board, and 30 percent with the audit committee.[43] (These numbers add to more than 100 percent because of companies assigning responsibilities to multiple committees.)

For boards in all cases, no matter how directors choose to address ESG responsibilities—whether by oversight at the board level; dividing up the E, S, and G among existing committees; adding ESG to one existing committee; or creating a new ESG committee—having ESG at the top of mind has been an important shift.

The Challenges of Measurement and Reporting

One of the biggest challenges when it comes to ESG has been how to measure it. This is an issue that may be addressed to some extent by the SEC if and when it mandates certain disclosures, but the issue is broader. There are two separate concerns at play. One is what metrics are critical to measure commitments and progress—of which there is often little agreement. Brian Tayan of Stanford University, for instance, has found low correlations between different ESG ratings providers.[44] But perhaps the larger concern is the utility of the metrics. In that same report, Tayan finds that "ESG ratings have low associations with environmental and social outcomes."[45]

These issues exist despite the fact that the sustainability metrics industry has exploded. Sustainability ratings have grown from ad hoc, manual reports into a big business, with a number of organizations attempting to create metrics that they hope will be widely adopted. In 2023, Ethan Rouen of Harvard Business School, Kunal Sachdeva of Rice University, and Aaron Yoon of Northwestern University published a paper explaining that ESG reports have become "among the fastest growing voluntary disclosures in history."[46] From virtually no reporting at the start of the 21st century, reports have become "nearly ubiquitous," and yet there is no standardization and a notable lack of auditing.[47]

It has been very challenging to figure out what to measure, how to measure it, and whether, even at the highest level, a company is "good" or "bad" in terms of ESG. As the *Wall Street Journal* wrote in August 2023, "Tesla could be a poster child for the confusion surrounding ESG ratings. Should the carmaker have a high ESG score because it makes electric vehicles, a low one because of some of its labor practices and autopilot risks or a middling one that averages things out? Different ratings companies give different answers and therein lies the problem: Many investors look to ESG scores as an easy way to compare firms based on their environmental, social and governance practices, but so far they have largely failed to deliver that."[48]

SASB has been behind much of the movement toward figuring out what ESG outcomes matter—in terms of stakeholder relevance—for which companies and how to measure them. At the core of its work is the idea of financial materiality: which factors are critical for companies in specific industries and actually drive economic gains. For instance, air quality and emissions are material factors for companies in the transportation industry but may not be for companies in health care.[49]

Yet SASB is just one of a number of organizations creating and advocating for different sets of metrics that often do not align with each other. *Harvard Business Review* writes that there are "at least seven well-known sustainability reporting frameworks and standards available, each one backed by credible organizations with reputable individuals on their Board."[50] These include SASB along with the Carbon Disclosure Project, Climate Disclosure Standards Board, Global Reporting Initiative, International Integrated Reporting Council, Taskforce on Climate Related Financial Disclosures (TCFD), and World Economic Forum International Business Council.[51] Because of the EU and California legislation and pending SEC rules, the TCFD metrics—which those three bodies are all looking to—have become very important.

Despite the lack of consistency and a clear link to outcomes, interest in and demand for ESG reporting has continued to grow. According to 2023 research from McKinsey, over 95 percent of S&P 500 companies now issue a sustainability report.[52] These documents have become ubiquitous, yet there are no defined standards for them. A sustainability report describes the ESG impacts of a company's activities and often discusses ESG risks and how they are being managed. More than anything, it is a communication tool used by companies to describe their ESG positions, accomplishments, and commitments.

The consulting and advisory firm Teneo analyzed 200 sustainability reports from S&P 500 companies in 2022, finding that the length ranged from 11 pages to 273 pages, with an average of 77 pages; half of the reports referred to the idea that a "formal materiality assessment was conducted to help determine ESG priorities"; and just over half indicated that at least some data in the report had been externally assured or verified.[53]

It is unclear who is reading these reports and what impact they are having. Data has shown that as many as 89 percent of investors consider ESG issues in their investing choices, but it is not clear what this means in practice and what resources investors are consulting in making their ESG-related judgments.[54]

The Backlash against ESG

Perhaps as recently as 2022, it would have been hard to make the case that the focus on ESG was on anything but an upward trajectory. This is despite the fact that it has been hard to find conclusive evidence that ESG efforts deliver alpha or excess investment returns.[55] Indeed, the *Financial Times* reported in 2021 on Felix Goltz of the investment service Scientific Beta and his findings: "'The claims of positive [ESG] alpha in popular industry publications are not valid because the analysis underlying these claims is flawed,' with analytical errors 'enabling the documenting of [ESG] outperformance where in reality there is none.'"[56]

Yet in 2023, ESG seemed to stall. This is in part because of political pressure from the right, with, for example, Florida governor Ron DeSantis signing legislation to "protect" his state from ESG, banning state officials from investing public money toward ESG goals, and stopping ESG bond sales.[57] Along similar lines, the Tennessee state attorney general, Jonathan Skrmetti, sued BlackRock, accusing the firm of violating consumer protection laws by prioritizing ESG concerns over investment returns without fully informing investors. "For years . . . BlackRock has misled consumers about the scope and effects of its widespread ESG activity," read the complaint.[58] Blackrock has rejected these allegations.[59]

In a mid-2023 report, Leah Malone and Emily Holland of the law firm Simpson Thacher & Bartlett wrote, "More than one-third of states have passed anti-ESG laws in 2023, most ESG-related shareholder proposals failed to garner majority support, new lawsuits have been filed challenging companies' ESG-related activities and decisions, and some companies seem to be distancing themselves from the term 'ESG' itself."[60]

In addition, investors pulled more than $13 billion from ESG funds in 2023, just less than 5 percent of the $323 billion in total ESG assets, according to Morningstar.[61]

The saga of Exxon and the activist hedge fund Engine No. 1 illustrates in some ways the rise and waning of ESG. In 2021, Exxon was pushed to take more action to combat climate change by Engine No. 1, and the hedge fund won three board seats at the company, including Oberhelman's.

Three years later, in 2024, sensing that the mood had changed, Exxon accused some activists of "advancing environmental agendas that the oil major says do little to help the company's economic performance or create shareholder value," according to the *New York Times*.[62] Exxon, in fact, sued certain investors to keep their climate proposals off the shareholder ballot, "arguing that U.S. securities law allows the company to toss petitions that 'deal with matters relating to the company's ordinary business operations.'"[63] The lawsuit was dismissed after the proposals were withdrawn. Mark van Baal of the climate-focused nonprofit organization Follow This, one of the "activists" that Exxon sued, said, "If allowed to continue, this case could have had a detrimental effect on shareholder proposals focused on climate."[64]

In any event, it is clear that broad support for ESG has decreased. Even BlackRock's Fink has been backing away from his enthusiasm about ESG, or at least his enthusiasm over the name, saying at the Aspen Ideas Festival in 2023 that he is no longer using the term *ESG* because it has been politically "weaponized," and he was "ashamed" to be involved in a debate over it.[65]

Hedge fund manager Boaz Weinstein of Saba Capital Management has attacked BlackRock for ignoring its ESG-related governance recommendations in the running of its funds, arguing that the staggered boards at its funds and the limited voting rights of some shareholders go against what the company preaches. "After clearly defining the E.S.G. standards it demands as a shareholder and professing to set the bar for the industry, one would expect BlackRock to hold itself to an even higher standard," Weinstein told the *New York Times*'s DealBook. "But it turns out, it does the complete opposite when it comes to its own funds."[66]

In February 2024, JPMorganChase and State Street left the investor group Climate Action 100+, and BlackRock scaled back its support, "weaken[ing] the climate group's plan to use shareholder influence to step up pressure on polluting companies to decarbonise," according to the *Financial Times*.[67] On the other hand, in March 2024, JPMorganChase agreed to begin disclosing the ratio of its clean energy to fossil fuel financing to help investors better understand its commitment to climate efforts.[68]

Of course, with the 2024 election of Donald Trump as president and a Republican Congress, ESG issues may well continue to retreat. For example, Trump has gone so far as to say that climate change is a hoax.[69]

At the same time, it may be at least partially the case that some of the backlash against ESG is overstated, and companies (and investors) are still committed to various goals but moving away from the perhaps-now-stigmatized ESG acronym.

"I think companies may move on from using the term ESG because of how politicized it has become," says Balsanek, "but I don't think the underlying concerns are going away. I think companies recognize that doing well in terms of environment, social, and governance actually creates long-term value, which is the goal in the end." Balsanek introduced me to the term *greenhushing*, in which there is less discussion publicly but perhaps just as much attention privately—and just as much ultimate impact.

Directors and ESG

The sustainability nonprofit Ceres makes the case that board oversight of ESG should involve risk identification, assessment, and mitigation, as well as determining what measures to take in order to support long-term sustainability.[70] Boards need to identify which issues are material for their companies and see that their actions are in line with generating long-term shareholder value.

"The impact of ESG efforts is realized over a much longer time than the typical investment horizon of one to three years," Muir Paterson of Citi told me. "So a lot of investors may typically underweight ESG relative to more traditional factors, but it's very important not to ignore it." For example, a commitment of company resources and capital to increase the use of renewable energy undoubtedly has a financial payback of longer than the five years over which capital expenditures are often evaluated. In addition, while reducing a company's use of fossil fuels may well be good for society, it is unclear how to measure whether employees will be more excited to work for such a company and whether investors will reward companies for these efforts. Paterson adds, "Maximizing value should focus not only on the near-term returns but also on the long-term risks. You need to optimize value for the sustainable risk profile that you as a company want to operate under, and that you think you can sell to enough investors credibly, in order to get the capital to execute." In other words, a company that pollutes the environment is hurting, and may well help ruin, the market in which it is trying to grow.

Shareholders versus Stakeholders

The debate over ESG speaks to the broader issue of who a company should serve—just the shareholders who invest in the company's stock or the broader stakeholders—and whether the role of a corporation is merely to make as much money as possible or to make profits and also positively impact the world.

According to the law firm Skadden, the broader term *stakeholder* officially refers to "certain non-stockholder constituencies named in anti-takeover 'constituency statutes' adopted by over 30 states starting in the early 1980s that a board was permitted to consider as potentially having interests in a company; these included the aforementioned employees, customers, suppliers and communities."[71] Each group has different demands and concerns.[72]

Ultimately, the critical question for directors is to whom they are responsible. There can be a moral debate, but the law is fairly clear. Mike Allen of the Delaware law firm Richards Layton & Finger says that when it comes to the shareholder versus stakeholder debate, "the simple language [the law] for a Delaware corporation is that you should be focused on shareholder value. However, that doesn't mean you can't consider other constituencies, like employees and customers and the community, to the extent that it is consistent with your fiduciary duty to the company stockholders." Allen went on to explain, "For example, most public companies do charitable work that clearly is not directly for the benefit of stockholders, but ask if there is ultimately a benefit to the stockholders by being a good corporate citizen and enhancing the brand. There is often a pathway to get there clearly within the law."

Daniel Slifkin of Cravath has a similar point of view: "A competent board could easily say that to maximize value for the long run, I shouldn't be pumping pollutants into the water supply and harming my employees or exposing myself to massive liabilities in the future. I should instead be building parks for my employees, because they'll want to work here. They'll want to work harder. When Paul O'Neill became the chair of Alcoa, he focused on safety at work, insisting there could be no fatalities at any of the company's facilities. By focusing on that, he really energized the workforce."

The Delaware Court of Chancery clarified these issues in April 2024, when it threw out a case brought by an activist investor against Meta that argued that directors should manage companies based on broad societal impact.[73] Vice Chancellor J. Travis Laster declared in no uncertain terms that Delaware law requires fiduciary duties to a company's shareholders and not to a larger set of investors and stakeholders across society.[74] Thus, boards need to be thinking along those same lines when making their decisions.

Just as critical as the board's decisions are the way the board communicates its decisions. Steve Lipin of Gladstone Place believes that communication is a key to ESG success. "Thirty to 40 years ago," he told me, "if you looked at corporate messaging, it was mostly shareholder driven. Now the aperture has widened, and companies are communicating much more about their mission, the benefits that they bring to communities, and the social good."

As Harvard Business School professor George Serafeim wrote in his 2022 book, *Purpose and Profit: How Business Can Lift Up the World*, it becomes a positive feedback loop where the more a company can make investors realize the benefits of ESG, the more they will demand increased ESG efforts, and the more these steps will pay off in the investment marketplace.[75]

While some see a company's pursuit of goals other than pure financial profit as a distraction, many question the assumption that stakeholder capitalism sacrifices economic returns, particularly in the long run. After all, a society destroyed by climate change, inequality, corruption, and the other ESG agenda items will likely lead to the destruction of tremendous amounts of economic value for shareholders. The best path to profits, some would argue, including Serafeim, is to help build a better society.[76]

Alex Edmans, professor of finance at London Business School, and Bruce Bolger, founder of the Enterprise Engagement Alliance, have written that the idea of stakeholder capitalism needs more clarity. Even some ESG proponents view it incorrectly, they argue, assuming that "the value that a company creates [is] a fixed pie, and stakeholder capitalism redistributes the pie from shareholders ('them') to stakeholders ('us') . . . [meaning] their recommendations involve overturning shareholder primacy—putting workers on boards, restricting shareholders' rights, and requiring companies to have a legally binding social purpose."[77]

But that is not necessarily the way to look at it. "The pie is not fixed," they insist. "Stakeholder capitalism involves growing the pie, creating value for both shareholders and stakeholders. . . . For example, the '100 Best Companies to Work For' delivered stock returns that beat their peers by 2.3–3.8% per year over a 28-year period. Investing in workers doesn't sacrifice profits; it enhances profits in the long term."[78]

Marty Lipton has advocated for something he and his firm call "The New Paradigm," or a relationship between corporations and their stakeholders as one of collaboration and cooperation around the common goal of creating sustainable long-term value.[79] "This is what corporate governance is all about," Lipton told me. "The board has the authority and the responsibility of setting the purpose of the corporation and how to achieve that purpose, and the only way you can deal with all the stakeholders effectively and properly is to use business judgment to decide. It's no different than the board deciding the amount of indebtedness a company is going to incur."

Oberhelman reaches a similar conclusion from a slightly different perspective: "The shareholders own the company, and your first loyalty as a board member is to the shareholders. But if you're successful with your shareholders, you'll have funds to afford all the other things that you have to get done. So for a CEO to ever say we don't take care of all of our stakeholders is absolutely wrong."

There are different views on this important topic. Harvard Law School professor Lucian Bebchuk—Lipton's foe in much of his work on behalf of companies trying to defeat activists as discussed in chapter 7—argues the other side. He has called stakeholder commitments by major corporations largely "illusory."[80] By this he means that even if companies are making promises that go beyond economic results, the amount of effort and money being put behind achieving them is insignificant.

The shareholder versus stakeholder question is an issue boards have had to consider much more in recent years than ever before, and governance has been affected in significant ways. More broadly, in my time serving on boards, few elements have changed the role as much as the rise of ESG issues and now the uncertainty around them. And the issue of how you address ESG topics while focusing on long-term shareholder value is among the most important considerations that boards currently face.

Section IV
What Can Directors Do to Promote Long-Term Success?

Chapter 11
New Directors: Recruiting, Diversity, and Onboarding

Who a board should recruit—and how the board and management should onboard new directors to have them add value as quickly as possible—is a critical issue, made even more important these days by the bright spotlight on directors. As we turn now to the final section of this book, focused on practical issues that directors should understand and address thoroughly, this chapter will discuss a high-quality process for recruiting directors, diversity in the boardroom, and an effective onboarding program.

Recruiting New Directors

Replacing or adding a new board member is a time- and labor-intensive undertaking. The nominating and governance committee usually leads the effort. However, this is a critical board decision. Therefore, I believe that each director should be kept well informed and participate in this important effort, including interviewing any final candidates. This process requires a substantial commitment from all sitting directors.

Ted Dysart, managing director at the executive search firm Russell Reynolds Associates, told me, "Go slow to go fast. Get alignment. Understand clarity around what you're looking for."

The recruiting process should start with determining the skills that the current board lacks or that should be enhanced. Every board should have a current skills matrix that includes the attributes and competencies of existing directors. Often it is just a simple spreadsheet; one example is to have the names of the directors in the far-left column and a list of characteristics and skills across the top. Characteristics may include age, board tenure, gender, other diversity considerations, number of boards served on at present and in total, and committee assignments, including as chair, at present and in total. Skills may include experience in the particular industry and in various functions (operations, finance, legal, technology, cybersecurity, ESG, human capital, etc.), international experience, and any other specific skills the board may want, such as restructuring experience. Some boards assign numerical scores to the various metrics. I have seen situations where, for example, a "3" indicates some experience in a particular area, a "2" indicates substantial experience, and a "1" means extensive experience. While some may posit that a well-informed board knows the makeup of its directors, a skills matrix memorializes it and keeps it current, much like even an experienced pilot should still have a checklist to follow when flying an aircraft.

By reviewing and updating the skills matrix regularly—usually annually and when there is a board seat opening—a board can determine what skills or characteristics the current directors have and consider which ones may be needed. This tool is also a good way to plan for directors who may be nearing any term limit or approaching retirement age. For example, I was a director of a company that had just named a new CEO. He was a very accomplished executive but had never run a public company. Our board had no directors at the time who were active executives at public companies. We realized this would be something potentially helpful, and so we soon added the CEO of a public company to our board. In another situation, I was on the board of a company with a growing business unit that had substantial technology in an industry where change was happening very quickly. At the time, the company had neither a director with significant technology experience nor a chief technology officer. We soon added both.

Anna Catalano, who served in various leadership roles at energy producers BP and Amoco from 1979 until her retirement in 2003 and who has been on some 15 corporate boards since then, sees functional expertise—such as in information technology and human resources—as usually an important skill set for a board. That said, she cautions that directors should not be siloed in their areas of functional expertise. "Everyone you recruit should be recruited to be a full director, with the same job and liability, not head of a particular function," she told me. I wholeheartedly agree.

Indeed, none of this is to say that a skills matrix should always be the primary driver of the recruitment process. And remember that directors oversee the business, and executives manage it, so one or more directors certainly should not and cannot make up for management lacking the necessary skills. A superb director with deep experience still has perhaps just 10 days on-site and maybe 200 hours per year devoted to the company. A strong team working on an important issue every day with a reasonable budget—and good board oversight—is the recipe for success.

I believe it is important to balance the desire for specific knowledge and experience with a consideration of the "best athletes"—people who, for broad reasons and chemistry but not necessarily a specific skill set, would likely make superb directors. And even if it is clear to the board that particular knowledge is needed, it is critical that the candidates have broad business acumen and are a good cultural fit with the board and management team.

Fred Lynch, former president and CEO of Masonite, looks at this important topic broadly and thoughtfully: "I think what makes an effective board is having a diversity of opinions and diverse backgrounds. You need to have board members that are intellectually curious and see themselves as there for a purpose. They want to make the company better. They want to make management better. They really want to make a difference."

Ron Lumbra, partner at the executive search firm Heidrick & Struggles, told me that in his experience, "the very best directors bring wisdom, judgment, and first-class decision-making. But they also have to do it in a way that will build cohesion. They can't just be the smartest guy in the room. They have to be trusted by their fellow directors and have relationships with their fellow directors. They build that trust by being someone who is able to listen, exchange openly, and process what other directors bring to the table."

The current company and board are very important when looking for a new director. You need to understand both—well. It is important to consider the company's strategy: Are any particular skills and experiences needed to help provide effective oversight and guidance? How does the board function now? Does it need more of a particular perspective? Chemistry is a crucial consideration that will never be accurately captured in a skills matrix. A board filled with strong personalities may not be the right one for a quiet, introverted director—but that same director might thrive on a board given to long discussions. Dysart commented, "It's a question of how good a fit a person is within the existing group dynamic and whether the goal is to change the dynamic or keep it relatively static. It comes down to how well you understand how a person has behaved historically to get a sense of how they're going to behave in your boardroom."

Doug Oberhelman, former CEO of Caterpillar, believes that current or former CEOs bring a lot of useful experience to boards. "I have found over the years that when active CEOs are on boards, the tendency for them is to want to help," he says. "I always felt that when I was on an outside board, listening to the CEO, I knew exactly the level of detail that they wanted from me as a board member, because I was a CEO too."

Lumbra explains that directors sometimes need to have a certain stature to be effective. "Take a company like Exxon or JPMorgan," he told me. "You may be a smart person, but if you haven't had the career success that many of their directors have, you're just not going to be taken seriously, and as a result you won't be effective."

Dysart adds that an important and, in my experience, sometimes overlooked point is that a big part of the process should be identifying not just great candidates but great candidates who are appropriate for the company and its strategy when the vacancy needs to be filled. "There are directors who fit for a company as it is approaching insolvency or coming out of bankruptcy," he told me, "and there are directors who are a better fit for a company that's on a growth trajectory. Those skill sets are not necessarily the same."

In talking to the more than 75 people I interviewed for this book and having interacted with hundreds of directors as an investment banker and corporate director, what comes up again and again in conversations about what makes a good director, more than industry or functional expertise, are two basic characteristics: the ability to listen and the ability to work effectively in a group.

Dysart summarizes: "You need an element of courage and the ability to manage by influence. The best directors ask questions in a way that elicits certain behavior over time from management teams or even their colleagues on the board."

Finding the Right People

It is important to find directors who have both the skills and the personal attributes to make a positive impact. Jerry Rosenfeld is a vice chair of investment banking at Lazard and a professor, distinguished scholar, and codirector of the Leadership Program on Law and Business at the New York University School of Law. He explains, "Director selection these days is a very thorough process. In proxy statements, companies are mandated to include a description of each director's skills. Each director must have a reason for being on the board."

A search for a new director should be process based—although this process can be different depending on the needs of the organization. For boards looking to recruit value-added directors, soft skills (such as the ability to communicate well) are just as important as hard skills (such as industry or functional knowledge).

The search usually starts with a so-called specification or "spec," a detailed document that may be as long as 10 pages describing the company, including its industry, business, and competitive position, as well as the experience and traits sought in a new director and the dates of the next few years' board meetings (so that no time is wasted if candidates have material conflicts). Candidates are then contacted, and interviews are held. Unlike with executives, where you may interview as many as 10 or more candidates for an open slot and decide afterward who to extend an offer to, it is typical to interview director candidates in the order in which you believe that you prefer them and try to limit the number of candidates that you reject.

Sometimes, sitting directors source new directors from their own networks and tools such as LinkedIn. Often, search firms are used to help source and evaluate candidates. Of course, the sitting directors ultimately decide who to add to their group. A high-quality search firm committed to the project can leverage its deep network, research capabilities, and judgment to be very helpful.

An interesting discussion concerns director independence. It used to be the case that several senior executives of a company would be on the board. Today, it is almost always just the CEO. Howard Ungerleider retired from Dow as president and CFO and is now at the private equity firm CD&R. He told me that Dow, similar to many companies, "used to have the CEO, the CFO, and the head of manufacturing on the board—nine independent directors and three management directors. I think the experience of the executives would end up helping us, providing better information to the other directors."

"I would still have the vast majority of the directors be independent," he added, "but having at least two if not three people with some experience from inside the company would yield a better governance outcome because if you think about it today, if the CEO wants to control the narrative, he or she can, making sure the rest of the management team rarely speaks to the board and limiting the amount of shared information." Dysart agrees: "One of the downsides of Sarbanes-Oxley is that we started to value independence over all else."

And yet independence has become the rule. Under NYSE and NASDAQ rules, independent directors must comprise the majority of a public company's board[1]—but most go much further. The push for increased independence, combined with the push for diversity, has led to a decline in the number of nonindependent directors outside of the CEO. The average S&P 500 board had just 1.6 nonindependent directors in 2023, with the CEO the only nonindependent director on 65 percent of S&P 500 boards, an 8 percent increase over the past decade.[2] The search firm Korn Ferry has written that "boards have become more strategic about filling vacant seats with [independent] directors from specialized fields that align with business objectives," leaving less room for members of the management team.[3]

My view is that rethinking the current expectation that the CEO should usually be the only member of management on the board would be valuable. To me, there is, for example, a real difference between, say, a CFO and a senior operating executive who participate for much of the time in the board meetings and a CFO and a senior operating executive who are director colleagues, entitled to all board materials and to participate in all board deliberations and votes.

Finding an effective mix of directors is critical, because the consequences are significant. Suboptimal board members can harm an organization, and good board members can add real value. Ultimately, at the end of the recruiting process, an offer is made, and the onboarding process begins. But before we move to that discussion, it is important to spend some time looking at board diversity, a very significant issue today.

Board Diversity

As discussed in chapter 4 and chapter 10, board diversity is a topic of much discussion by various constituencies today. In the board context, diversity is often used to refer to diverse viewpoints and backgrounds. However, the focus in recent years has largely been on increasing the number of women on boards and, to a somewhat lesser extent, ethnic and other underrepresented groups. There was pressure for some time from different parties for more diverse directors. But that pressure has been reduced, and there are many loud voices, including from our nation's capital, for substantially less effort on diversity generally. It is unclear where the boardroom is going when it comes to the issue of diverse directors. As discussed earlier but to reiterate, California's 2018 law requiring boards to have at least two or three female directors by 2022 depending on board size was struck down as unconstitutional. In addition, BlackRock had urged 30 percent diversity on all boards, with at least two women and one director from an underrepresented group, and had indicated that it would vote against nominating and governance committee members if a company did not explain its approach to diversity on the board.[4] However, BlackRock has no board diversity statements in its 2025 proxy voting guidelines. I suspect that where we land on this issue will vary from industry to industry and company to company.

The former treasurer of the state of California, Kathleen Brown, is a partner at the professional services firm Manatt and was previously at Goldman Sachs and Bank of America as well as the Democratic nominee for governor of California. She also serves on a number of boards. Brown urges consideration of age diversity in addition to gender and ethnic diversity: "I think that there is tremendous value in having diverse-age work groups, and we don't often think about that. But consider the wisdom that older board members may bring, the knowledge that they have, the patience, and the experience that any particular crisis will pass. Matched with the energy, the enthusiasm, and the innovative risk-taking of the younger generation, the combination can be really powerful. I think multigenerational teams are the new new thing."

I had not thought of age diversity until Brown mentioned it to me. Laura Carstensen is the Fairleigh S. Dickinson Jr. Professor in Public Policy at Stanford University and founding director of the Stanford Center on Longevity. Her research on aging has been funded by the National Institute on Aging for more than 30 years. Professor Carstensen supports the notion of age diversity as an important board consideration. She explained to me,

> For most of human evolution, life was so short that the population of the planet was just filled with young people. Today, we have roughly as many 5-year-olds as 65-year-olds. We have a 60-year span of birth times now represented in the workforce, and different generations are bringing different skills with them. Older people have lots of knowledge and expertise. They're more emotionally stable, more prosocial, and perhaps more interested in helping other colleagues. Younger workers are working on their own, ambitious, and fast. When you put those kinds of skills together, the mix should be something quite interesting. To the extent that people know more, they're more valuable, and they can contribute more. For roles based in knowledge, like serving on a board, productivity evidence looks like it only goes up.

Also of note is that former Connecticut state senator and corporate director Ted Kennedy Jr. has been pushing boards to consider disability as a diversity characteristic as well. Kennedy, who lost a leg from cancer at age 12, says, "The business case of disability inclusion is very strong. . . . The challenges disabled people face make them expert problem-solvers. People with disabilities experience the need to adapt, analyze and overcome situations all day long . . . [and] bring an added perspective to Boards that leads to better decision-making."[5] Of 485 companies surveyed in a 2023 report, only 7 percent had a director with a disability on their board.[6]

Admiral Mike Mullen has long been a champion of diversity: "I think we all need to remember that from a bottom-line standpoint, a diverse leadership team produces results, and so it's a great thing."

Indeed, there is McKinsey research from 2023 that shows a 39 percent increased chance of outperformance for companies in the top 25 percent of ethnic and gender diversity as compared to those in the bottom 25 percent. "Our latest analysis shows that companies with greater diversity on their Boards of directors are more likely to outperform financially. . . . Companies in the top quartile for Board-gender diversity are 27 percent more likely to outperform financially than those in the bottom quartile. Similarly, companies in the top quartile for ethnically diverse Boards are 13 percent more likely to outperform than those in the bottom quartile," McKinsey writes in its 2023 report, *Diversity Matters Even More: The Case for Holistic Impact*.[7]

On the other hand, the research is not uniformly positive. The Wharton School of the University of Pennsylvania professor Katherine Klein has found more inconsistent results: "Rigorous, peer-reviewed studies suggest that companies do not perform better when they have women on the board. Nor do they perform worse. Depending on which meta-analysis you read, Board gender diversity either has a very weak relationship with board performance or no relationship at all."[8] Looking at over 100 studies, she finds "no evidence available to suggest that the addition, or presence, of women on the board actually causes a change in company performance . . . [and thus] no business case for—or against—appointing women to corporate boards. Women should be appointed to boards for reasons of gender equality, but not because gender diversity on boards leads to improvements in company performance."[9] Her explanation? "It's not clear that male and female board members differ all that much in their values, experiences, and knowledge."[10]

Nevertheless, beyond the research, practitioners see the value of diversity. "There are really valid reasons to have this diversity," Lumbra told me. "Say a third of your workforce is Hispanic or Black or 75 percent of your customers are women. It is probably good for you to have that view in your boardroom."

Among new directors, there has been significantly more diversity in recent years than there had been previously. In 2023, 67 percent of new S&P 500 director appointments were filled by diverse candidates (46 percent women and 36 percent underrepresented minorities, with 15 percent of new directors falling into both of those categories), a small drop from 72 percent in 2022 and 2021 but up from 50 percent and 38 percent in 2018 and 2013, respectively.[11] However, because the average board tenure is nearly eight years, diversity statistics move somewhat slowly. Thirty-three percent of S&P 500 directors are female (an 83 percent increase compared to 2013), and 24 percent are underrepresented minorities.[12] As of 2022, all S&P 500 boards had at least one woman director, and 98 percent had more than one (compared to 61 percent in 2012).[13] Four percent of S&P 500 directors self-identify as LGBTQ+.[14]

As mentioned in chapter 4, the summer of 2020—and the murder of George Floyd—was a turning point for contemporary board diversity issues.[15] ISS and Glass Lewis followed by mandating diversity requirements. For example, in its 2023 recommendations, ISS expected at least one female board member and at least one racially/ethnically diverse director at Russell 3000 and S&P 1500 companies.[16] However, it does not continue that approach in 2025.[17]

NASDAQ has been pushing for more disclosure from listed companies about diversity on boards. In December 2023, new rules finally went into effect—after two years of unsuccessful court challenges—requiring companies to have either a woman, underrepresented minority, or LGBTQ+ board member, or information present in their proxy statements or on their websites explaining why they do not.[18] These requirements were to increase over the next few years, depending on the size of the company and the NASDAQ market tier on which it is listed, ultimately requiring multiple diverse directors.[19] However, in December 2024, the US Circuit Court of Appeals rejected the NASDAQ's diversity efforts by finding that the SEC made a mistake in approving its related rules. There may be an appeal to the Supreme Court.[20]

The NYSE, on the other hand, has opted for what it calls a "market-driven" approach and does not have specific disclosure requirements.[21]

It is important to note that some pools from which many directors are chosen still lack substantial diversity, which can make recruiting diverse directors challenging. For example, looking at the 674 unique companies in either the S&P 500 or Fortune 500 in 2023 (there are many companies on both lists, so eliminating the duplicates results in a total list of 674), just 9 percent of sitting CEOs and 19 percent of CFOs were women, with 13 percent of CEOs and 13 percent of CFOs being racially or ethnically diverse.[22] These numbers lag behind board diversity levels and certainly need to be addressed.

"Board diversity exceeds C-level diversity, and it exceeds it because it's much more measurable, and it's incredibly visible," Lumbra says. Paula Sneed, an experienced director and a Black woman herself, offered me an additional perspective, particularly about the need for boards to become more visible to young women and minorities so those groups can even know that serving on a board is an option. "In 1990, I read a *Fortune* article about women on US corporate boards. The numbers were staggeringly low, less than 11 percent. The number of women of color on boards was well under 1 percent. That gave me something to aspire to. I joined my first board in 1995," Sneed told me. "Now the number of women and Black, Brown, and Asian directors is much higher, because of two things: greater diversity in senior levels of corporations and greater knowledge about board opportunities among diverse men and women."

Dysart agrees that the pipeline needs to be expanded:

If we're going to move the needle significantly on diversity, we need to see more diversity in the CEO and CFO suite. If you look at the diversity of the executive suite, it tends to be in roles that aren't about the profit and loss statements and not the places that typically lead to the CEO job: general counsel, human resources, compliance, internal audit. We need to change that. I find it ironic that we had good success in the last decade of diversifying boardrooms in a meaningful way, but you look at those same companies, and in their executive suites they're no more diverse than their fellow companies that don't have diverse boards.

Sandra Horbach has worked on these issues extensively at Carlyle. "I generally think companies want to bring diverse perspectives into the boardroom," she says. "But I also believe that diversity is not just racial or gender-based; it's diversity of experience as well."

However, Lumbra, who has testified in front of the US House Committee on Financial Services on diversity in the boardroom and who, aside from his role recruiting directors, is himself the chair of the University of Vermont Board of Trustees (the third African American board chair in that board's history), adds a caution: "Companies need the right to run their businesses as they see fit. There are of course always going to be great reasons to have diversity, but if a party asks for 30 percent women, what if you have 25 percent? What if you're in a business that simply has very few women in general—the chemical sector, for example. Does 30 percent really make sense in that business? Along the same lines, why shouldn't it be 75 percent in the fashion industry?"

At the same time, there has been a backlash over quotas and diversity needs to fit within the larger mandate of directors who are effective. "As important as diversity is," Brown told me, "it can't be the only thing. You've got to look at other factors and make sure you have the right person for the job, because the worst thing is when a director doesn't work out and it's a diverse candidate."

"Directors see the value in Board diversity but feel the issue has become politicized," writes PwC in its 2023 corporate directors survey. "While most directors agree that diversity brings unique perspectives and enhances Board performance, more than half believe that diversity efforts are driven by political correctness; about one-third suggest that diversity efforts put less-qualified candidates on the board."[23]

The PwC data shows a drop in the percentage of male directors who believe gender diversity on boards is important, from 90 percent in 2016 to 73 percent in 2023.[24] The percentage of male directors who believe that board diversity improves board performance also fell from 85 percent in 2019 to what the study calls a "record-low" 76 percent in 2023.[25] Indeed, the Heidrick & Struggles Board Monitor shows board diversity trends beginning to decline in 2022. "Surprisingly, in 2022, the share of seats going to first-time directors, women, and directors from diverse ethnicities dropped . . . while there was an increase in the share of seats going to directors with CEO, CFO, and prior public company board experience and directors over the age of 60," the report states.[26]

This trend generally tracks society at large, with the Supreme Court's 2023 ruling ending race-based considerations in college admissions bleeding into concerns over diversity goals in the corporate world. As the *New York Times* wrote in January 2024, "While polling indicates that most Americans believe it's good for companies to focus on diversity, equity and inclusion, there's a wide partisan divide: In a Pew survey last year, 78 percent of workers who identified as Democrats agreed with this sentiment, while just 30 percent of Republican workers thought the same."[27]

There is certainly tension from multiple directions. While the Supreme Court's ruling does not affect corporate initiatives regarding diversity, equity, and inclusion (DEI)—working to reduce bias in hiring and promotion, making special efforts to reach out to diverse candidates, facilitating mentorship programs, and the like—scrutiny has increased. Specifically, companies need to be sure they are not instituting racial quotas and crossing the line into illegality. We have also discussed the growing political pushback on diversity and concern from various groups over broader DEI initiatives.

However, as long as corporate efforts to increase diversity are linked to business outcomes, they should be protected. A 2023 case against Starbucks brought by a group challenging its DEI policies was dismissed by a federal District Court in Washington, affirming the right of boards to pursue programs they believe are in the company's best interests.[28] Chief Judge Stanley A. Bastian wrote, "Whether DEI and ESG initiatives are good for addressing long simmering inequalities in American society is up for the political branches to decide. If Plaintiff remains so concerned with Starbucks' DEI and ESG initiatives and programs, the American version of capitalism allows them to freely reallocate their capital elsewhere."[29]

At the same time, as one example of some current sentiments, PwC dropped certain of its diversity targets in early 2024.[30] The firm ended race-based eligibility criteria for a student internship program and backed away from a pledge to use minority-owned suppliers for 40 percent of its procurement spending.[31] Goldman Sachs and JPMorganChase similarly removed ethnic and gender criteria for some of their fellowship programs.[32] More recently, Google, Meta, and other companies have eliminated mandates and goals to increase their employee populations from underrepresented groups. In addition, companies are increasingly striking text such as "diversity, equity, and inclusion" from their public documents.

Perspectives on a diverse board, executive suite, and workforce are constantly evolving and should be considered by every director not only when a board vacancy arises but also more broadly in every organization.

Orientation and Onboarding

Once a candidate has accepted an invitation to join a board, the nominating and governance committee is usually tasked with the orientation and onboarding process for the new director. These two terms refer to different activities. Orientation is an initial welcome, while onboarding is the longer-term process that allows the director to get situated and make a valuable impact as quickly as possible.

Joining a board can be overwhelming for anyone who is not adequately prepared. Board members play complex, important roles: they are expected to help make key decisions on the oversight of the CEO, strategy, financial reporting, and other important topics. A 2023 survey found that 34 percent of public company boards do not even have a formalized onboarding process.[33] While alarming, this may in fact be an improvement over the recent past; a 2017 study by Heidrick & Struggles found almost half of respondents noting that their boards did not have a defined onboarding experience—and that 20 percent of new board members did not even meet with the CEO.[34]

To properly onboard new directors, the process should have a number of steps, with an orientation as only the start. The orientation might simply include telephone calls from the board chair and CEO welcoming their new colleague as well as providing an organized electronic or hard copy file of business, financial, and other information.

While some companies have new directors attend a webinar to formally start the onboarding process, I prefer at least one full-day orientation session. Ideally in person, this should cover, among other things, the culture of the organization, a deep dive into each of the business units, an overview of financial results and projections, a review of key company metrics, and a discussion of governance issues. It is also useful for a new director to visit company locations, whether manufacturing facilities, distribution centers, stores, restaurants, or otherwise.

At Lear, the Fortune 500 global automotive supplier where I am a director, orientation involves a meeting with the CEO's staff to welcome the new director to the board. As part of the broader onboarding process, the new director receives a welcome message from the general counsel that includes access to the website that we use for historical and current board materials and information such as strategy and budget information, the minutes of board meetings, committee meeting materials, the company's corporate governance documents, SEC filings, and other detailed nonpublic information. In particular, the new director is guided to the most recent strategy, long-range plan, and budget presentations. Access to the broader management team and a tour of one or more company manufacturing facilities are provided too. Finally, membership is arranged in the NACD, and subscriptions are set up for *Agenda*, the weekly *Financial Times* publication on governance, and *Automotive News*.

It can also be good for incoming directors to attend a board meeting before their first official one. Without the pressure to participate, this can help new directors gain insight into how meetings are run and how issues are resolved. It can also help them start to build relationships with their new colleagues. Another useful element is to have new directors attend each committee meeting for the first year before assigning them to one or more committees. This way they understand what each committee does and where they might fit in best. Just as Admiral Mullen lauded the benefits of the audit committee earlier, Steve Girsky, CEO and a director of Nikola as well as a former senior executive and board member at General Motors, told me something similar, saying that "you learn a lot about a company from the audit committee."

Some companies have new director mentoring programs, where a new board member is assigned a director "buddy" who is available to answer questions and offer advice on issues and protocols. As Lumbra explains, "The worst thing that happens for a board that has made progress together over a long period of time is that a new person comes in and raises an issue that's already been litigated and settled for five years. But how would they have known that unless they had a board mentor saying, 'Interesting point but we dealt with that, it's behind us, and I'll brief you later'?"

If individuals are unsure of the role they play on the board, it can slow down and even derail the work the board is trying to accomplish. Taking the time to build a defined and effective new director onboarding process can increase the quality of interactions with fellow board members and allow the newest members to get up to speed with the inner workings of the organization and their role more quickly, improving the efficacy of the entire board. It is something many companies shortchange, and they should not.

It is also important for new directors not to just rely on the company's onboarding process but to supplement it on their own by finding out as much as they can about the company and how they can best add value. Gregg Polle, vice chair of M&A at Bank of America, suggests that a new director should quickly try to establish a good rapport with the CEO and, if there is a separate head of the board, that person too. Over time, relationships with the entire board and senior management team are, of course, crucial.

New Directors: Recruiting, Diversity, and Onboarding 213

Oberhelman believes the onboarding process should be much more substantial than it currently is: "I would do half a day on governance material, another day with lower management, finance, engineering, manufacturing, and IT, maybe an hour each at a high level, just so when a topic comes up, you're not ignorant, and you're prepared to make a decision or support an idea."

Catalano makes a good point: "Employees get a job description. Directors should too [but they do not]."

I believe continuing education for directors has become critical as the scope of issues considered by the board has expanded. It can be particularly useful to have education on evolving topics such as cybersecurity, climate risks, and artificial intelligence. Education can be provided at board meetings and perhaps between committee meetings and a board dinner on day one. Some boards also pay for directors to attend director education classes and conferences. I subscribe to several governance newsletters and have attended and spoken at governance conferences held by organizations such as the NACD and Corporate Board Member as well as attended executive education programs on governance at Harvard Business School and the University of California, Berkeley Law School. There is always something to learn, and interacting with director colleagues can be very valuable.

The final piece of any onboarding discussion concerns how new directors should act as they adjust to the role, and in posing that question to many directors, there was a common theme: listen before you speak.

Doug Benham, former CEO of Arby's and an experienced director, said, "The mistake that I think people make sometimes is they come on and try to prove their worth right away without really understanding situations. You need to sit back, listen, learn the business, and learn the personality of the board."

As Steve Key, who was CFO of Textron and Conagra and has been a director of various companies, recounted to me, "[I transitioned] from an executive position, where I was in charge and expected to make decisions, to the role of director, where guiding the executives to make the right decision is of paramount import. And that was a tough transition for me. Eventually, I adopted the Socratic method of being a director: ask questions that cause thinking and rethinking to move in the right direction."

Charles Elson of the University of Delaware builds on that: "Every director who tries to make a splash in their first meeting ends up being incredibly disappointing. What you say in your first meeting often proves to be wrong." I could not agree more.

Chapter 12
The Chief Executive Officer

The CEO is usually the highest-ranking executive at a company, reporting to the board and typically on the board. The senior operating executives (such as a president, a COO, and business unit leaders) and senior staff executives (such as the CFO and general counsel) report to the CEO. There may also be a president; if the CEO does not have the president title too and there is a separate president, that is typically the second-highest-ranking position. The roles and responsibilities of a separate CEO and president can vary based on a company's size, needs, and other factors. However, the CEO usually is responsible for the overall strategy and direction of the company and is its public face. The president, similar to a COO, may well be responsible for day-to-day operations. A smaller private company or organization that needs less organizational structure, given fewer demands on management and no public shareholders or disclosure requirements, may not have a CEO, and a president can be the senior leader.

Therefore, the CEO is, of course, critical to any company. The board spends much of its time working with as well as evaluating and compensating the CEO and managing the succession process, including the selection of a new CEO when appropriate. CEO succession is quite possibly the most important task of a corporate board. Howard Ungerleider, retired president and CFO of Dow, told me that "the single most important thing a board does is hire or fire the CEO." And while we looked in chapter 5 at the differences between the job of CEO and that of the board's chair—and the complexities regarding whether the two roles should be held by the same individual—there is much more worth discussing about the CEO, from key characteristics of strong CEOs to succession planning, the recruitment process, board and CEO interactions, and how a board can determine when it is time to make a CEO change.

The Role and Characteristics of a Great CEO

The CEO is the day-to-day leader of a company, but a successful CEO is much more than that. Excelling as CEO requires tremendous breadth, including developing and executing a value-added corporate strategy, building a strong leadership team, making effective decisions about how to allocate capital, communicating effectively with the entire range of stakeholders, helping determine a successor, and signing off on internal controls and financial statements.[1]

In *Harvard Business Review*, A. G. Lafley, the former CEO of Procter & Gamble, described a CEO as having a four-pronged set of responsibilities: defining the outcomes and constituents that matter most, deciding what businesses a company is in and what businesses it is not in, balancing present and future, and shaping an organization's values and standards.[2]

When it comes to CEOs, executive recruiter Peter Crist of Crist Kolder Associates told me, "First and foremost, the person must be an operator [with operator not limited to business unit leaders but, for instance, the CFO as well]. Second, the CEO needs to be an empathetic leader. Third, energy and a tireless passion for what they're doing."

Jed York, principal owner and CEO of the San Francisco 49ers, explains, "I think the CEO's role is simple to describe and not necessarily simple to execute. You have to make sure that you can define the key problems that your organization faces and the challenges that you need to overcome—and figure out the right people to put in place to help execute. If I'm the expert in the room among a bunch of other people, I put the wrong team together. As a CEO, ultimately, you have to make the decisions that people can't make on their own."

Uniquely, it is lonely in the CEO role. Directors have colleagues and other C-level executives have a team of peers, but the CEO is the only executive at his or her level, with ultimate authority, responsibility, and accountability. He or she manages the C-level and reports to the board. As Mark Manoff, who spent 39 years at EY, including in various leadership roles, told me, "It's hard for a CEO to go to even their most senior executives inside and talk about issues." For example, "if you can create that relationship where there's mutuality and trust and a CEO wants to look to the lead [audit] partner, like the accountant from a big accounting firm, and can trust their independent view, then that's a really good thing."

While the job is rewarding, it is also very difficult. Howard Heckes served as the CEO of Masonite, where I was a director and chair of the audit committee for about 15 years from 2009 to 2024, leading the company through a major price increase and substantially increased margins before the nearly $4 billion sale of the company to Owens Corning. Heckes had previously run the Architectural Coatings portfolio, with some $2.5 billion in annual revenue, at Valspar, a leading paint company that was sold to Sherwin-Williams. His experience and success at Valspar informed his actions and accomplishments at Masonite:

> The first thing I thought about [when approached by a recruiter about the CEO job] was what we could do to win. When I took over the Industrial Coatings business, paint was exactly like it was 100 years ago. We did consumer research and found that there were two reasons that people—DIYers—don't paint more often: the first reason is it's a pain and the second reason is that they have no idea what the room is going to look like after it's painted, so they just leave it the way it is. We attacked that with a "love your color" guarantee, where if you don't love your color, [you can] return it to the store and we will give you a free new paint color. That was just one example of changing an old category.

Heckes drew a parallel to when he was approached about the CEO position at Masonite: "It was the same with doors. So I was pretty enthusiastic about what I thought could be an opportunity to really make a difference in the category. I wanted us to quickly do some research to better understand our customers and the opportunities. And on my third day on the job, I toured our largest manufacturing facility and realized that with our capacity and technology, we were not being paid fair value for our products." Heckes changed his initial focus, and by day three, he was already starting to design what ended up being a 25 percent price increase that changed Masonite and, in many ways, the industry. He had also met with and started to evaluate the executive team that he inherited to try, among other things, to convince the internal candidates for his job to stay on.

Just in that story, Heckes demonstrates thoughtful strategic thinking, the ability to seize an unexpected opportunity, and strong leadership—three critical areas for any CEO. Being an effective CEO is a balancing act.

The characteristics of strong CEOs have been studied repeatedly. McKinsey has written that "great CEOs are bold," explaining that between one-third and one-half of new CEOs fail within their first 18 months, and so prompt action is key.[3] A study of 2,600 leaders by Elena Botelho and Kim Powell of the leadership consulting firm ghSMART found that successful CEOs show quick decisiveness, engage with an eye toward impact, are relentlessly reliable, and can adapt boldly to changing situations.[4]

I spoke with a number of leaders about how they view the CEO role; the elements they emphasized were somewhat different but complementary. CEO recruiter Jim Citrin of Spencer Stuart advises, "It's all about thought leadership and people leadership. You can be the greatest people leader in the world, but if you don't know where to take a company or an organization, then it's kind of meaningless. At the same time, you can be the most brilliant thought leader in the world, but if you can't rally people to get behind you and deliver results, you won't succeed. No one can do it alone."

Admiral Mullen sees the core skills of a CEO as hardly different from the skills of a leader in the military: "Leaders are leaders. You have to be comfortable with change, and leading change, since the world is changing at such a rapid pace."

For Ron Klain, the key elements of leadership are empathy and vision. "People who can engage their teams on a personal level are effective leaders," he told me. "They lead by having a vision and getting the organization to buy into it."

Mario Carbone of Major Food Group describes a great leader as someone who is "willing to do anything you're currently doing . . . imbuing confidence in the team because they know you could take over if needed." He sees good CEOs as students and teachers at once, always learning but also passing along their skills to the next layer of managers coming up behind them.

Having worked with hundreds of CEOs as an investment banker, corporate director, and private equity investor, I would summarize what makes a great CEO as someone with a thoughtful vision who can lead a team to deliver the desired results, doing so with integrity and thoughtfulness and being able to address the many unexpected issues that will arise, all while working in a transparent and cooperative way with the board, senior management, shareholders, and broader stakeholders.

Finding that superb leader—who has the desired qualities and is a good fit for the company at the time—is not often easy and, in an ideal world, should start well before the vacancy arises. This is why planning CEO succession is a critical responsibility for an effective board.

Succession Planning

Before—often years before—a successful CEO recruitment process begins, a board should be thinking about the current CEO and his or her transition out of the role. After all, in many ways a board's most important job is the selection, oversight, evaluation, and compensation of the company's most senior executive: the CEO. Therefore, CEO succession should always be a focus for an engaged board.

Two succession processes that were managed especially well—which Jim Citrin recommended to me for this book—were at Mastercard and Cisco. Both involved boards and exiting CEOs who were committed to a succession process and spent years planning and preparing.

In fact, even though Mastercard transitioned its CEO in February 2020 from Ajay Banga, who held the position starting in 2010, to Michael Miebach, the seeds of that change were planted prior to Banga being hired. "Before Ajay even had the job," according to an article Banga and former Mastercard board chair Richard Haythornthwaite wrote for *Harvard Business Review*, "we [the board] were imagining his replacement."[5]

The Mastercard transition to Banga had been the product of an external search, but the board wanted to be sure it had appropriate internal candidates the next time. Up front, Banga set out to serve for a decade, and a plan followed from there. "We [the board] cast a wide net, considering more than 40 internal employees and a handful of standout externals before selecting our finalists," Banga and Haythornthwaite wrote. "We committed to inclusivity in decision-making, asking the entire Board to participate. We insisted on solving for tomorrow's problems, not today's, in clarifying what type of new leader we needed. We focused on developing and retaining all our current and future stars—not just filling the top job. Finally, we pledged to keep our minds open and our personal opinions to ourselves until the last moment, while also discouraging early preferences and groupthink from the directors."[6]

Five years into Banga's tenure, the board had identified 42 executives to receive personalized leadership training and exposure to the board, including board-level mentors and making presentations to the directors. The board also worked with Banga to understand the skills he believed would be needed for his successor to thrive and to define the job description: the specification, or "spec," for the next CEO. Working with a major search firm, Egon Zehnder, external candidates were compared with internal candidates. With years of meetings, discussions, and open communication behind them, the board felt well equipped to make an informed choice when the time came, unanimously selecting Miebach.[7] This is an example of a very well-considered and -executed CEO succession process.

The story was similar at Cisco in 2015, when Chuck Robbins replaced the company's longtime CEO, John Chambers, who had led Cisco since 1995 and oversaw annual revenue growth from less than $2 billion to almost $50 billion and a stock price that increased from around $2 per share to more than $20. The board had regular conversations about succession, making clear that it was happy with Chambers's leadership but still mindful of the need to look ahead.[8] The board, with the help of Citrin and Spencer Stuart, established a "spec" and performed a series of 360-degree evaluations of certain internal talent to help consider who best matched the needs of the role after Chambers. From there, the board chose a very limited number of internal candidates with whom all directors, not just the board members on the nominating and governance committee, had a series of one-on-one interviews.[9]

The top candidates were then asked to write memoranda describing their vision of Cisco's future and present their visions to the board. Chambers was deliberately not part of this process so that the rest of the board would not be swayed by his views. Again, and as it should be, the decision was unanimous, and when Robbins was announced, the stock price remained stable, a sign that the public supported the decision.[10]

Starting the process so far in advance makes sense because of the importance of the CEO position. Charles Elson explains, "You always should have people lined up who you think could move into the top roles quickly in the event of illness, death, or someone leaving in a dramatic situation—getting poached, say—and you also want to know who is being groomed for the future."

Crist has seen how hard these conversations can be: "Too many boards shy away from talking about succession, and don't have it on the agenda. It has to be a topic item all the time, with a cadence that is known to the board. Too many boards only see the CEO and CFO, and occasionally someone gets to make a presentation. A board has to see layer one and layer two of leadership. The board has to think about the next three- to five-year cycle."

Indeed, Admiral Mullen told me, "The hardest job I've ever had as a senior leader was getting the right person in the right job at the right time. Picking the right successor is the most important job the board has."

Heckes and Masonite is an example of a CEO succession process in which I was involved. We had been pleased with Fred Lynch, who had been CEO for nearly 10 years. "He was very intentional about believing that a CEO often becomes less effective after 10 years and that his expiration date was coming up," remembers Bob Byrne, Masonite's independent board chair, although issues with the company's manufacturing led Lynch to stay on a little longer to lead the company's return to operational excellence.

Masonite had grown dramatically from some $40 million in EBITDA when it emerged from a Chapter 11 bankruptcy reorganization in 2009 to around $275 million in EBITDA for 2018. The company had an approximately 30 percent market share and one slightly larger competitor, Jeld-Wen, but pricing was not as disciplined as you might expect with this oligopoly structure, and margins were relatively low. Wholesalers and distributors captured some margin at the expense of Masonite and Jeld-Wen, with the "big box" customers (Home Depot and Lowe's) proving challenging. Volume growth had been limited.

The board, including Lynch, believed that there was one internal candidate and perhaps a second. However, the board decided to be thorough and run a full search. Lynch told me, "Your job as CEO is to make sure you have a viable internal candidate. I also believe that it makes sense to conduct a full search, to make sure you have the best option out there. Of course, the CEO is going to be biased for their internal candidate."

I felt that Masonite was at a strategic crossroads and probably needed a new CEO from outside the company who really understood the "voice of the customer" and could enhance our marketing. It seemed that a few directors wanted a new perspective and an external candidate, while some preferred an internal candidate who was well known, and others were not sure.

As we launched the Masonite search process, Byrne remembers, "We first decided that we should have an ad hoc committee—a search committee—with the chairs of our audit, compensation, and nomination and governance committees on it to lead the process. We wanted broad input and perspective on everything from selecting the search firm through the vetting of candidates. We agreed that any director was welcome to attend any of the ad hoc committee meetings to make it inclusive."

I served on the ad hoc committee. I was also part of a so-called CEO succession committee at another company where the nonexecutive chair led the appointment of members that he thought would be most appropriate. The nominating and governance committee often leads the CEO succession and recruitment effort, and I have seen that too. Importantly, regardless of what committee spearheads this important process, all board members should be invited to the committee meetings and should be highly engaged in CEO succession and the recruitment of a CEO.

The Masonite ad hoc committee decided to retain a search firm and, after presentations from several major firms and substantial discussions, selected Spencer Stuart. The search firm suggested dividing the process into six phases it would assist with; the board agreed:

1. Building alignment within the board regarding the requirements
2. Evaluating the members of the leadership team to identify internal candidates
3. Identifying external candidates
4. Helping the board with its deliberations
5. Guiding the transition once the decision is made
6. Helping the CEO with plans for the first 100 days

One of the most important things Byrne remembers about the process is that we required weekly updates to move the effort along and a broad group of candidates, not just available ones or those who simply seemed strong. The Spencer Stuart team evaluated internal and external candidates with interviews, references, psychological testing, and comparisons to market data that it had developed over time. It also helped reconcile input from the directors, all of whom had different perspectives and, sometimes, different views.

After every director interviewed a number of candidates in one location over a long but productive day, we invited our finalists to each present to the board their strategic vision for the company. "We wanted to see how well they understood the company," Byrne said, "how well they listened to the directors and how they assessed the opportunities. We wanted to hear about competitive threats to the extent that they knew them and the potential pitfalls, to understand their risk tolerance and to know how enthusiastic they were for driving change, or if they were going to play it conservatively with more of the same."

Ultimately, the unanimous consensus was for change and an enhanced focus on the customer, and as you now know, we selected Howard Heckes.

"I suspect that every CEO would like as part of their legacy to be identifying and grooming their successor," explains Byrne, "and while Fred felt like he did that, he understood that this was a director prerogative, and he really made Howard feel welcome." Strong leaders put their opinions aside and act in the way that best serves the company, even if they are walking away.

CEO succession is only getting more important in today's rapidly changing business environment. In 2023, there was an increased rate of turnover.[11] According to the Challenger, Gray & Christmas (Challenger) CEO Turnover Report, through November 2024 almost 2,000 CEOs had announced their departures that year for various reasons, the highest annual number since Challenger started reporting on CEO changes in 2002.[12] The average tenure for Fortune 500 CEOs is just seven years.[13]

Of course, while many CEO transitions are planned—86 percent of S&P 1500 successions were planned in 2023, a number similar to previous years—some are not, and all boards need to have systems in place to evaluate CEOs and know when it may be time to make a change.[14]

All of that said, succession planning is important and should lead to a good result, but the key is to identify and recruit a superb replacement. Filling the role successfully comes down to understanding what you are looking for and then putting an effective process in place to hire that person.

Recruiting and Hiring an Effective CEO

As seen in the Masonite discussion, the recruitment of a new CEO usually starts with a committee: sometimes the nominating and governance committee and perhaps a special committee. The first step is often to decide whether or not to use an executive search firm. It is typical to do so. Five executive search firms, wrote Matthieu Favas in *The Economist* in 2020, dominate the industry: Spencer Stuart, Heidrick & Struggles, Russell Reynolds Associates, Egon Zehnder, and Korn Ferry.[15] An estimated 80 to 90 percent of Fortune 250 companies use firms such as these for CEO succession, even when the successful candidate may well be an internal one.[16] Favas writes, "Recruiters can be crucial in helping build consensus when, as is so often the case, Boards are split. It is as diplomats that the best headhunters earn their keep."[17]

Once a search firm is hired, the committee (and board) works with the firm to put together the specification with the desired attributes for the role. These include the skills and capabilities sought in the next leader as well as personal characteristics and leadership style.

And yet while the "spec" is crucial, flexibility is necessary as well. To that end, "the spec is really important as the cornerstone of the process," says Citrin, "but I've seen searches go awry and bad outcomes result when a board takes that spec too literally. You can set the criteria too precisely and then solve for those criteria too perfectly. But the criteria might be wrong. Don't become a prisoner to the spec." He adds that a rigorous analysis is critical: "Look at the organizations that have done the best job at doing what you're trying to do and look at the individuals who currently or formerly led those results. At the same time, be open-minded to creative and out-of-the-box ideas, even ones that don't seem as logical, because many of the highest-performing CEOs I've found were not the most obvious or the most logical; for instance, Mark Thompson coming in from the BBC to become the CEO of the *New York Times* or Hubert Joly coming from outside retail to save Best Buy and turn the company around."

A key question when considering potential candidates is internal versus external: Do you want someone already in the company or someone new from outside? In recent years, inside candidates have dominated. According to Spencer Stuart data, 68 percent of new CEOs in S&P 1500 companies were internal hires in 2023, down from 72 percent in 2022 but still quite significant.[18] These insiders, however, do include a small number of candidates who might better be termed insider-outsiders: those who were recruited from outside into other roles and promoted to CEO within 18 months.

Data suggests that an internal candidate is less risky, particularly during a crisis such as the COVID-19 pandemic.[19] This is logical, because a current company executive should already know the company and understand the culture. At the same time, conventional thinking is that an external hire can be more of a change agent: this leader typically comes with a fresher approach. Academic studies on whether internal or external hires drive more shareholder value are not conclusive; they do show that companies doing well are more likely to go with internal candidates.[20]

Aside from the biases that may advantage or disadvantage an internal or external candidate, it is important to remember that just because an executive was successful in one situation does not mean that he or she will be successful in another one. It is critical to examine why the executive was impactful and whether that skill set and style will likely transfer to the new role.

While the media has thoroughly covered Bob Iger and Howard Schultz returning to Disney and Starbucks, respectively, as "boomerang" CEOs retaking their old CEO positions, there have, in fact, been only 22 boomerang CEOs in the S&P 500 since 2010, and they do not tend to do as well the second time around.[21] On the other hand, CEOs who come from the board—6 percent in recent years—have driven stronger results than CEOs hired from the inside or outside.[22] But there is a very limited number of directors who have become CEOs.

Clem Johnson, president of the executive search firm Crist Kolder, with whom I worked on a CFO search for Masonite, says, "Given the extent to which the CFO role has elevated in strategic importance and expanded in scope, in many organizations, this person is the natural number two."[23] However, I have heard many board members say that a CFO "has not run anything," having not had overall responsibility for a "P&L" (profit and loss statement) or led a business unit. Importantly, a high-quality CFO is a key part of senior management; well versed in the company's strategy, business, and financial performance; and along with the CEO, the primary interface with investors. Remember that the CEO, while ultimately responsible for the business, does not run it: as we have discussed, the CEO has a diverse portfolio of responsibilities, including interfacing with the board and shareholders, leading the management team, driving the development and execution of the strategy, and, with the CFO, attesting to the internal controls and financial statements.

I have been a director of Lear, a Fortune 500 automotive supplier, for some time. Matt Simoncini, the former CFO, was CEO from 2011 to 2018 and was very successful, leading tremendous growth in shareholder value. Today, Ray Scott is the CEO. He previously ran both of the company's business units and has positioned Lear as one of the most attractive companies in a large, important industry. Two very successful CEOs with very different backgrounds for different times at the company.

In terms of previous positions, 57 percent of new S&P 1500 CEOs were promoted from a COO or president role in 2023, and just 5 percent rose directly from the CFO role, a number I find surprisingly low (that same figure was 15 percent in 2022, also low in my view).[24] Another 5 percent of new CEOs in 2023 were what Spencer Stuart calls "leapfrog" leaders who came from somewhere below the second layer of management.[25] Additionally, 82 percent of new CEOs in the S&P 1500 were serving in their first public company CEO role.[26]

Naren Gursahaney has been through CEO recruiting processes as a candidate, CEO, and director. "Beyond the search firm–provided references," Naren told me, "it was valuable to test our own networks of people who knew the candidate. Those informal references were perhaps more valuable, because I was getting feedback from somebody I knew and trusted would be candid."

Ron Lumbra has a different perspective: "Directors are human beings, and they're sometimes too easily swayed by people in their own networks. A single positive or negative comment from someone they know may take a candidate and swing him or her to become either a must-have or someone they won't even talk to. I see really good people overlooked, because one person happened to hear something from someone in their network."

Some believe that perhaps no feedback is more important than that of exiting CEOs. They have had the job and know what it entails. However, they may well have an understandable bias for internal candidates, as Lynch admitted. "A CEO who is a board member," says Steve Sterrett, the former CFO of Simon Property and an experienced director, "has every right to participate in the search. But while he deserves a seat at the table because he's a director, he doesn't deserve an outsized seat." Of course, the CEO is moving on and is often leaving the board too; the board going forward has to live with the new CEO.

It is a huge undertaking to recruit and hire a new CEO—which is why most companies hope for stability in the position. "It's very stressful for everybody," says Ungerleider. "By the time they make the choice, everybody wants to exhale and not worry about it for a while—but that's actually the worst thing that can happen. It really does take a good lead director or chair or committee head to quickly force the dialogue both on CEO performance as well as on the next CEO succession."

Interacting with and Evaluating CEOs

It is very important, as Chief Justice Strine believes, for a CEO to be "strong and secure." "And that CEO," he continues, "should want a strong board and strong subordinates. You want a culture where everyone is willing to hear different points of view." Daniel Slifkin of Cravath adds, "Boards fall short when the directors are too deferential to the CEO, too afraid to jump in and say something that goes against the CEO's plan."

In fact, as Steve Key, the former CFO of Textron and Conagra who has been a director of a number of companies, says, "Great cultures are normally a by-product of great leadership." In other words, culture emanates from the top or with the CEO (and the board).

The board leader, whether the chair or the lead independent director if the CEO is also the chair, is the primary interface between the board and the CEO, but all directors should have a strong relationship and interact regularly with the CEO. A CEO looking to maximize the value of the board should contact directors as needed to draw on their particular areas of expertise—whether financial, operational, or otherwise. It is a best practice, in any case, for the CEO to touch base one-on-one with every director a few times each year.

Heckes found it very useful to sit on the board of another public company while he was the Masonite CEO to see how it felt from the director's side and be more effective with his board. What he experienced about the content and timing of materials sent to the board and how different directors engaged was valuable. "I was told by a lot of different people that one of the things all new CEOs underestimate is what it takes to manage the board," he told me, "and I'd say that's definitely true. We had nine different very successful executives in very different walks of life. Everybody kind of had their own idea about what their role was, and everybody had their own amount of time that they were willing to allot. One-on-one calls were really helpful to figure out what everyone needed."

The board, of course, has to evaluate the CEO. There is usually an annual evaluation, often with the assistance of the compensation consultant, for yearly compensation decisions on salary, bonus, and equity. The CEO should set a series of objectives on a yearly basis, with input and ultimate approval from the compensation committee and then the full board. Some of these should be quantitative and some qualitative. At the end of the year, the CEO should perform a self-evaluation against the objectives. The directors should also complete a CEO evaluation form with a variety of questions and space for additional comments. Topics might include strategy, leadership, executive team, succession planning, financial results, risk, ESG, investor communications, and board interactions. Then the compensation committee and full board should review the CEO's evaluation and the board's evaluations before having the board leader and perhaps the compensation committee chair meet with the CEO to discuss the evaluations and compensation as well as consider objectives for the following year.

As a practical matter, the board's evaluation of the CEO should be continuous. Experienced director Anna Catalano says, "I find that with technology disruptions happening as quickly as they are these days, I worry the tenure for some CEOs will be shortened because they will not be current."

Determining when a CEO's tenure has run its course is a tremendous challenge for boards—and yet it is perhaps their single biggest responsibility. "When you lose confidence in a leader," Admiral Mullen told me, "they're done. And if you're that leader in whom confidence has been lost, it's time for you to step aside."

"There's no single signal," adds Citrin. "Boards obviously develop a sense. Sometimes there are signals from the team when the CEO loses credibility. Sometimes the CEO isn't facing reality or is super defensive about their performance and not really addressing problems—and that's a signal in itself."

"It's easy to remove a CEO when the enterprise is not doing well," says Crist. "But if that's not the case, there's all this gray area: you've been in the chair long enough, it's time to change, we're going to lose our great succession candidate inside if you don't start giving signals."

According to Elson, boards know when a CEO has been there too long: when the air of excitement around the CEO starts to go away. "They find it hard to innovate. It becomes routine to them."

"By the time I left Masonite," adds Lynch, "I was the longest-tenured person on the leadership team. If you're the longest-tenured C-level executive, it's time for you to go. I had started to find that I was getting impatient with the decisions."

A new CEO, once in place, has to perform immediately. There is hardly a grace period these days, even if there might have been one in the past. Citrin explains,

> It used to be the case that there was a pretty good honeymoon period, and CEOs had the opportunity to develop a strategy. Investors don't give new CEOs time anymore, and even internal stakeholders are pushing. They want to know right at the time of the announcement: Who is this person? Why this person? What is the new CEO going to do? A big mistake is when CEOs don't move fast enough to form their team and set their strategic vision. Another mistake is overpromising and underdelivering. If you look at great CEOs, they lay out exactly where they want to go, and quarter after quarter after quarter they explain how they're getting there. Investors start to see that credibility and reward them.

A straightforward transition process should put the board and CEO on a path to a very positive relationship. In any event, the relationship, in all cases, needs to be strong in order for the CEO to succeed, even as it is also the case that the board does have the power to make a change.

Every board on which I have served has spent tremendous energy trying to make sure it had the right CEO at the right time, built and maintained a strong relationship with the CEO, and managed the succession process as well as the recruitment and onboarding efforts for the next CEO. It is not easy. In good times, these topics can sometimes fade into the background. But they should not.

Chapter 13
Risks and Crises

Given that a board's role is to oversee management on behalf of the shareholder owners, the consideration of risk—and a thoughtful, dynamic plan to mitigate risk and react to any crisis—is very important. Earlier in the book, I discussed the failures at Blue Bell and Boeing, where courts held directors liable for falling short in their attempts to manage risk. In this chapter, I will take a closer look at risks and crises from a board's perspective: What should directors do to understand and oversee a risk mitigation plan as well as oversee the development and execution of a crisis response plan?

Risk Management

When I think about the difference between risks and crises, I consider risks problems that can generally be anticipated so plans can be put in place to lessen them, whereas crises are unexpected and thus it is difficult to be prepared to address them. In other words, for known risks, a board and management team should manage them, but for unexpected crises, the only option is to have a general crisis response plan ready.

While internal audit standards require an annual risk assessment to help develop the internal audit plan, I believe that all companies should perform a comprehensive risk assessment at least annually, including interviews with a wide range of personnel, often leveraging work done by the internal audit team, if there is one. To focus attention on the most critical risks, the survey should identify the top risks, perhaps limited to 10, and assign a risk owner to each to see that these are constantly monitored and managed as well as to create accountability or provide that someone is in charge of mitigation. Efforts to mitigate should be determined, executed, evaluated, and updated regularly.

Howard Ungerleider walked me through the risk management process when he was at Dow: "We had a very robust enterprise risk management process which was constantly in motion. Every year, we would put together a three-by-three grid. On one axis was the likelihood of an event happening. On the other axis was the impact if that event were to happen. Depending on where a risk was in the matrix—high impact and high risk, for example—we would have a deep discussion at a board level, and there would be a subject matter expert or experts assigned to it and ultimately accountable for a plan." Ungerleider continued:

> Then we would discuss mitigation. Here's what would likely be the impact, and here's what we're doing about it to make sure that we could stay in front of the issue. The high-impact risks were managed at a board level, the medium-impact risks were handled by the management team, and the low-probability or low-impact risks either weren't proactively managed or we had a reactive plan when those risks emerged. But we were constantly reassessing, once or twice a year, challenging ourselves based on where the world was and asking if we had the right risks. We would also bring in outside experts to challenge us and poke holes in the plan—which was really meaningful.

To oversee risks and a crisis plan, a board might adopt a risk committee or assign this responsibility to the audit committee. A board should give risk and crisis management high priority to communicate an important "tone at the top" or show that the board sees these efforts as critical. As Charles Elson explains, "This is all a part of ordinary business today. You have to keep very alert to the business and alert to risk. That's why you have risk thermometers."

Risks are constantly evolving, and a board needs to recognize potential disruptions and stresses, whether from the economy, capital markets, geopolitical conflicts, climate change, supply chain pressures, customer issues, and more. Some experts think of risks as being in three buckets: operational risks (damage to physical structures, for instance), financial risks (lack of liquidity, for example), and strategic risks (poor business decisions for one).[1] Having plans in place for all three types of risks is important.

Current Risk Areas of Note
Cybersecurity
In talking to experienced directors, there is a lot of concern about fast-growing, potentially very serious cybersecurity risks. Cybersecurity refers

to the protection of systems and data from digital attacks, which are often aimed at stealing sensitive information, causing business interruption, and extorting money.[2] The global cost of cybercrime in 2022 was estimated at more than $8 trillion.[3] Business email compromise attacks alone, where bad actors gained access to email systems and either demanded and received payments or attained sensitive information, resulted in $55 billion in losses between 2013 and 2023.[4]

The largest hack of 2023 was the MOVEit incident, which affected more than 62 million people.[5] MOVEit, a third-party file transfer tool, is used by many large private and government organizations to move sensitive data. Attackers were able to take advantage of a security vulnerability and steal personal information.

Cybersecurity is a fundamental business risk. Data breaches can have significant stakes for directors, as illustrated by a 2019 settlement involving Yahoo! The former officers and directors of Yahoo! agreed to pay $29 million (ultimately covered by insurance) to settle a case where they were accused of breaching their fiduciary duties after three billion user accounts were compromised in a series of cyberattacks between 2013 and 2016.[6] However, the defendants denied any wrongdoing.[7]

Companies should focus not on a cybersecurity strategy but rather on a business strategy with appropriate cybersecurity protections, including personnel, tools, and plans to protect against cybercrime and react quickly and effectively to any cybersecurity breaches. In addition, "near misses," or successfully thwarted efforts to hack into systems, should be reviewed in detail—as all near misses related to safety ought to be.

Given the magnitude of cybersecurity risk, including the prevalence of "bad actors" and the harm to businesses that they can inflict, as well as directors' obligations to oversee this important risk, cybersecurity is an important topic for all directors to understand.

"I think the cyber area is a huge crisis that any of us can face these days," Doug Benham told me. From manufacturing to services companies and in virtually all industries, a cyberattack can literally shut down operations.

As Ron Klain explains, "The attackers are ahead of the defenders, and I don't think there's a company in America that's truly prepared to have its systems knocked offline. How often are the records backed up, and how long would it take to restore those backups and turn your company's operations back on?"

One of the worst problems Klain had to deal with in his first few months as Chief of Staff to President Biden was a cyberattack on Colonial Pipeline in May 2021. The company, responsible for delivery of almost half of the fuel for the East Coast of the US with over 5,000 miles of pipeline from Texas to New Jersey, was attacked by hackers, affecting billing and payment systems and causing a five-day disruption.[8] I met Jen Easterly, the director of the US Cybersecurity & Infrastructure Security Agency (CISA), during a series of cybersecurity training sessions for directors organized by the NACD at the White House and United States Secret Service Training Center last year. She writes, "A ransomware attack on Colonial Pipeline captured headlines around the world with pictures of snaking lines of cars at gas stations across the eastern seaboard and panicked Americans filling bags with fuel, fearful of not being able to get to work or get their kids to school."[9] Ultimately, Colonial Pipeline paid a $4.4 million ransom, only part of which was recovered.[10]

A related risk is that a "bad actor" can break into a company's social media accounts and post offensive information that hurts the company's reputation and alienates customers.

Climate Change

Climate change is a quickly evolving risk with which we are all familiar. The threat of "climate change" first made the front page of the *New York Times* in 1981.[11] It has become a major, perhaps existential threat. *An Inconvenient Truth*, the book by Vice President Al Gore that later became an Academy Award–winning documentary film, brought international attention to climate change and global warming, and Gore shared the 2007 Nobel Peace Prize for his efforts.

The World Economic Forum writes, "Climate change is visibly disrupting business. It is driving unprecedented physical impacts, such as rising sea levels and increased frequency of extreme weather events. At the same time, policy and technology changes that seek to limit warming and reduce the associated physical impacts can also cause disruption to business."[12]

"Unlike other forces that might impact specific sectors or regions, climate change presents universal challenges and opportunities," writes Professor George Serafeim of Harvard Business School.[13] "Its effects unfold over longer time horizons, introducing a business planning challenge. This necessitates a rethinking of traditional business models and strategies and demands resilience, adaptability, and foresight . . . [with] considerable risks to current business models, supply chains, and operational strategies."[14]

With President Donald Trump back in office and Republicans in control of Congress, various efforts to address climate change are being rolled back, such as the US withdrawing from the Paris Agreement under the United Nations Framework Convention on Climate Change and an executive order that, among other things, discourages regulatory and financial advantages for electric vehicles. Nonetheless, many boards and management teams continue to address climate change in the same way they seek to evaluate and minimize other risks. Of course, some companies (such as those in the oil and gas industry) will be more impacted than, say, a retailer (but a retailer's supply chain, for example, can certainly be impacted by climate change). Do not minimize this risk just because it is complex and uncertain and sometimes seems to be in the distant future.[15] As Mark Carney, then governor of the Bank of England, said in 2015, "Once climate change becomes a defining issue for financial stability, it may already be too late."[16]

Geopolitical Risk

When it comes to geopolitical risk, the COVID-19 pandemic illustrated clearly and tragically that there are issues beyond a company's control that can seriously damage businesses. More recently, the conflicts in Ukraine and Israel have become relevant for boards in a number of ways, such as with impacts on supply chains, the appropriateness of operating in Russia, and whether to take positions on major global issues. Geopolitical risks are those that affect a company but are outside the legal jurisdiction of where the company is headquartered.

The International Institute for Management Development has identified nearly 30 corporate risks related to geopolitical instability, including closed transportation or trade routes, damaged infrastructure, global energy supplies, rising tariffs, and workforce disruptions.[17] These are all important areas to address with plans to minimize their negative impacts on businesses should they arise.

I spoke with the former two-term governor of Indiana and two-term US senator from Indiana, Evan Bayh, who is currently a senior advisor to Apollo and an experienced corporate director: "Even companies you wouldn't expect have geopolitical risks. I'm on the board of a hotel chain, and we have 100 hotels around the United States—what kind of geopolitical risk do they have? Probably 15 percent of the business is in the Northern California area, and because of the souring of relations between China and the United States, there are a lot fewer Chinese visitors coming to visit—and it's actually materially affecting the business."

I asked Senator Bayh how companies should attack geopolitical risks:

> The first step is to evaluate the vulnerability of the company. It might be a second- or third-order effect instead of a direct effect, but it's there for everyone. First, you get educated, and only then do you need to decide what, if anything, you can do about it and whether it's worth the cost or not.
>
> The last thing to keep in mind is that in assessing geopolitical risk, you have to get outside your own culture and your own framework for decision-making, because sometimes there are irrational actors out there who will do things that will affect your business, and you think they'll never do those things, but they're just looking at the world from a completely different perspective.

We live in a very global world. Even as many US companies "reshore" or bring back supply chains, manufacturing, and other aspects of business to America, most major companies have international operations. Geopolitical risks are complex and threatening. Boards must be aware of them and oversee effective, ongoing efforts by management to identify, update, and manage them.

Artificial Intelligence

Artificial intelligence (AI), according to IBM, is "technology that enables computers and machines to simulate human intelligence and problem-solving capabilities."[18] The release of ChatGPT and other generative AI tools has allowed the technology to make inroads in business to a much greater extent than previously. AI-powered chatbots are now used in many enterprises[19] in such areas as content production, marketing, inventory management, product recommendations, customer relationship management, customer service, financial forecasting, fraud detection, cybersecurity and fraud management, digital personal assistants, and more.[20]

Remarkable and, in fact, unbelievable as it sounds, a survey of hundreds of CEOs by the consulting firm AND Digital found that 43 percent of them believed that AI could replace their positions.[21] Whatever your view on this finding, it gives you a sense of AI's enormous opportunities—and risks.

I do not know where AI technology will lead, but I do know that human oversight and judgment will be critical at every turn. I hope that directors and senior management teams will be cautious and thoughtful as AI becomes more and more integrated into decision-making and the products and services that companies create and provide.

Social Media

Social media refers to a range of technology platforms that allow ideas and information to be shared widely—among the public and between companies and the public. Popular platforms are always changing but include Facebook, Instagram, Snapchat, TikTok, YouTube, X (formerly Twitter), and others. It has been estimated that approximately 60 percent of the world's population uses social media.[22]

While social media can be hugely beneficial to companies looking to disseminate information and grow their relationships with customers, it can also pose major risks. Bud Light, as one example, was criticized in 2023 after a social media promotion with a transgender influencer, Dylan Mulvaney, led to boycotts and criticism from both sides of the political aisle.[23] Bud Light sales in the month following the promotion fell by 26 percent.[24] "In the aftermath of the Bud Light controversy, many consumer brand marketers have become acutely aware of the potential pitfalls of taking stances on controversial social issues and fearful of experiencing a similar backlash and the accompanying financial and reputational costs," writes *Harvard Business Review*.[25]

It is incumbent on every director to have a basic understanding of social media, including how any company on whose board a director sits uses it to communicate internally and externally as well as the opportunities and risks with social media for the particular company. While social media will likely play a larger role with a branded consumer company than, say, a manufacturing business, social media creates opportunities, positive and negative, for all companies. It is a fast-changing area that needs to be understood and addressed by all directors.

Whether the risks are long-standing or evolving, once the board oversees the determination of the company's major risks and a plan to mitigate them, it has to be aware of how to comply with the related SEC requirements for risk disclosures.

SEC Requirements and "Material" Risks

I discussed earlier the back-and-forth regarding the SEC's climate disclosure requirements, which remain unresolved at the time of writing, but climate is by no means the only topic on which the SEC has considered or implemented required risk disclosures. In 2023, the SEC adopted rules requiring disclosure of material cybersecurity incidents (on Form 8-K) as well as the disclosure of cybersecurity risk management, strategy, and governance in a company's annual report.[26] The disclosures must include a description of how the board oversees and management acts with regard to cybersecurity threats as well as any processes in place and consultants or third parties who have been engaged.[27]

This requirement builds on the broader 2020 risk disclosure rules that require companies to disclose all "material" risks, or those that reasonable investors would deem important. Previously, companies were required only to disclose their "most significant" risks.[28] The SEC also requires companies to include a summary if the disclosures exceed 15 pages and to use relevant headings to make the disclosures clearer.[29]

In 2023, research by Deloitte and the University of Southern California Marshall School of Business Peter Arkley Institute for Risk Management found that S&P 500 companies disclose an average of 32 risks in their annual reports, on average 13.5 pages in length.[30] In reviewing S&P 500 company disclosures in 2021, the year after the broader requirements were implemented, researchers from Deloitte and the institute found a wide range of risks disclosed, including recruitment and retention of talent, cybersecurity, stock price volatility, litigation, regulatory investigations, disasters, accounting changes, tax law changes, access to capital, financial reporting, and more.[31] When it came to climate change–related risks, companies pointed to potential risks from physical damage to corporate assets, customer disruptions, higher costs, changes in demand, and regulatory and legal concerns. With human capital, companies discussed various people risks, such as labor relations and collective bargaining issues.[32]

Comments from the SEC regularly offer guidance on additional risks that companies should pay attention to in their disclosures. In 2022, for instance, the SEC suggested disclosures, where necessary, regarding the impact of inflation as well as the Russia/Ukraine war.[33] Artificial intelligence, cryptocurrency, and data privacy laws are other current issues that may present significant risks and should perhaps be disclosed.[34]

A company's major risks can be determined by thoughtful interviews of management, employees, and board members and perhaps the use of outside consultants as well. Then a plan can be put in place to monitor and try to reduce these risks. On the other hand, a crisis is a major problem that arises suddenly and unexpectedly.

Crisis Management

A crisis typically falls into one of these general categories: business, financial, physical assets, cybersecurity, natural disasters, or geopolitical. While a crisis is generally unanticipated and the board and management may well find themselves at least somewhat unprepared, senior management should have in place a list of key responders for a crisis (both internal executives and external advisors) and a general crisis response plan ready to be implemented. As a fiduciary for shareholders, a board should oversee the preparation and any updating of the crisis response plan as well as oversee the response to a crisis.

A detailed crisis management plan should have the following characteristics:

1. The plan should be developed by management, approved by the board, and put "on the shelf" in case of a sudden crisis.
2. The plan should contain a broad framework suitable for addressing an unexpected challenge while providing flexibility for an organization to adapt to a particular situation. Among other things, this should include a list of who should be contacted under what circumstances, from senior management to directors, and what advisors will be used, such as information technology experts and specialists in cybersecurity.
3. The plan should note clear roles and responsibilities for executives and employees at different levels of the company, empower the most appropriate personnel to take the most effective steps, and provide a matrix to escalate concerns and decisions as required.
4. Communications plans should be incorporated, perhaps including templates for messaging to different stakeholders.
5. The plan should be rehearsed on a regular basis to address value-threatening, company-threatening, and life-threatening situations.

Strategies are more effective if executives and key employees stress-test them in advance. Planning should be thorough and led by someone senior or a committee of senior executives. You cannot anticipate every crisis, so the plan may well have to be modified in real time as a crisis reveals itself. Even with a plan in place, management, overseen by the board, must be proactive in carrying out the steps necessary to manage the crisis.

For instance, a product recall requires both a sizable logistics commitment and a communications strategy and other efforts to help protect a company's reputation. A fire at a major manufacturing facility would demand supply chain changes and efforts to preserve customer relationships.

The death of the CEO, a major natural disaster, or another pandemic can be particularly challenging. Boards should not be involved in day-to-day operational issues. However, during a crisis, a board should be kept well informed and sign off on any major decisions.

At Lear, where I am on the board, we have specific plans, depending on the type of issue, that indicate, for example, when a crisis needs to be escalated to the C-level as well as when we need to engage external partners, notify insurance partners, and bring something to the board. Having an entire organization know the critical thresholds for seeking help is important to keep things from growing out of control.

Chancellor Andre Bouchard, formerly of the Delaware Court of Chancery, sums it up well: "Have a specific reporting system. You can't just ignore it."

"I think most companies are too reliant on outside consultants," Klain adds. "They hire a cybersecurity consultant who writes a cybersecurity plan, and they put it on a shelf in the facility. They check a box on a checklist: we hired a great consultant. But the consultant's not the person you're going to call [first] when there's a crisis. You need to make sure the people inside the company who are going to be there are fully engaged."

Steve Girsky, who lived through the crisis at Nikola described in the next section, points to the need for experienced directors during a crisis even more than during stable times: "Having a group of independent directors is valuable. Having some crisis experience on the board, or experience with a difficult situation, is even better. You want people who are comfortable with discomfort."

The Crisis at the Automotive Technology Company Nikola

Inaccurate disclosures by a company, particularly by its chair and/or CEO, can cause a crisis. That was the case with Nikola, an electric and hydrogen-powered heavy truck maker for which I served as an expert witness in an arbitration where, in late 2023, the company was awarded over $165 million in damages from its founder and former executive chair, Trevor Milton.[35]

Nikola had been founded by Milton in 2014 as a maker of hydrogen-powered glider trucks, claiming to revolutionize the electric vehicle industry by replacing the need for nickel batteries with hydrogen gas, an unlimited resource. The company released the "Nikola One" freight truck prototype in 2016, stoking enormous excitement, and used its purported technology to develop plans for personal watercraft vehicles and off-road utility vehicles as well.[36] Nikola went public on June 4, 2020, and days later, its market capitalization was nearly $30 billion, more than Ford Motor Company at the time.

Just a few months later, on September 10, 2020, Hindenburg Research, a firm then focused on activist short selling in situations where it contends that it has uncovered fraud and corporate malfeasance, published a report containing a number of allegations about Nikola—not all of which turned out to be accurate—including that Nikola was "an intricate fraud built on dozens of lies."[37] (Nate Anderson, Hindenburg's founder, announced earlier this year that he was shutting the firm, citing the stress of this work.[38])

Hindenburg's report alleged the following, among other things:

- "In the face of growing skepticism over the functionality of its truck, Nikola staged a video called 'Nikola One in Motion' which showed the semi-truck cruising on a road at a high rate of speed. Our investigation of the site and text messages from a former employee reveal that the video was an elaborate ruse—Nikola had the truck towed to the top of a hill on a remote stretch of road and simply filmed it rolling down the hill."
- "Nikola announced it would revolutionize the battery industry . . . [but] the technology was vaporware."
- "Nikola [secretly] had an electricity cable snaked up from underneath the stage into [a] truck in order to falsely claim the Nikola One's electrical systems fully functioned."[39]

Within two weeks, Milton announced his resignation from Nikola, and Girsky became chair. Girsky was later named CEO in August 2023. He had combined the special-purpose acquisition company (SPAC) that he led, VectoIQ Acquisition Corporation, with Nikola. Girsky was previously a well-known automotive analyst at Morgan Stanley, a private equity investor at Centerbridge, and ultimately, a vice chair at General Motors. "We were not prepared for the crisis," Girsky told me. "I was the new guy. You join a board, and you try to feel your way around, understand the culture . . . and then by the third board meeting, we were in crisis."

Girsky quickly acted to stabilize the situation: "We hired a major law firm, and we told them to do an independent investigation. The firm reached out to the SEC and said we're going to proactively report this, and the SEC said they were already investigating. We told Milton we couldn't work with him anymore. We did the investigation, the results came out, and we went on from there. We tried to get the facts as quickly as we could." According to Girsky,

> Transparency has been really important. You need to be out there, presenting the facts as you know them, not crawling into your shell. Building back trust doesn't happen overnight. Communication is important—to investors, the public, customers, suppliers, employees. You need to have a consistent message, and the message can change as the facts change. Over time, things you thought were true may not be true, but if you understand you're not going to win back your investors overnight, you can lay the groundwork and keep the organization focused. We had to manage the external and then manage the internal, even when so much was going on.

This was not the first crisis in which Girsky played a major role. At General Motors, he helped navigate the company through its bankruptcy filing in 2009. "When you're dealing with a big consumer products company and all of a sudden you hire bankruptcy advisors, it becomes a self-fulfilling prophecy," he explained to me. "GM's going bankrupt? I'm not going to buy their cars. It creates a vicious cycle. You need to manage the business and try to not panic people, but you also need to be prepared."

After Milton resigned from the company, Nikola initiated an arbitration proceeding against him for breach of fiduciary duty, and in November 2023, a three-member panel of arbitrators found that Milton violated his fiduciary duties of loyalty and good faith to Nikola and found him liable to Nikola for over $165 million in damages to compensate the company for, among other things, a $125 million fine that Nikola had earlier agreed to pay the SEC in a settlement.[40] In December 2023, in a separate criminal case, Milton was sentenced to four years in prison.[41] He is currently free on bond as he appeals the decision and has continued to be difficult for Nikola and Girsky. After the more than $165 million award, "Milton quickly turned into the company's No. 1 antagonist," wrote the *Wall Street Journal* in May 2024. "Two years in a row, he refused to vote his shares to allow the company to raise capital, which would have diluted his stake, contributing to repeated postponements of shareholder meetings."[42]

By mid-2024, Nikola had produced more than 80 hydrogen-powered electric trucks, wholesaling 75 to dealers, as it continued to try to recover from the crisis.[43] However, in late January 2025, the stock had tumbled to less than $1 per share and a market capitalization of just $75 million. Then in mid-February of 2025, Nikola filed for bankruptcy and expects to sell its assets and wind down the company.[44] In late March 2025, President Donald Trump pardoned Milton.

Lessons in the Aftermath of Crises: COVID-19 and Boeing

A lot was written about crisis management during and now after the unexpected COVID-19 global pandemic. Looking back, the pandemic did offer an unexpected opportunity to think beyond what had generally been true for most businesses, such as the requirement for numerous workers to be in an office. Boards and management teams learned to function during the pandemic without usually being able to have in-person meetings.

"It's much harder for directors to do their jobs virtually," Charles Elson said in 2021, pointing to side meetings and body language as two important things lost when meetings turned remote.[45] Of course, even in the midst of COVID-19, many people, from factory workers to doctors and nurses, continued to do their jobs as and where they always had. I am a strong believer that the vast majority of people should spend most of their "office time" in the company's offices interacting and collaborating with colleagues.

I wrote a piece in *CFO* during the pandemic, noting that COVID reminded us that "responses to crisis-related challenges should be scalable and account for all parts of a business, including operations, IT, and supply chain. An experienced board should pass on prior crisis management experiences and stay well informed about issues, from employee safety to liquidity to financial performance to compliance . . . [especially] in a stressful environment."[46]

It is notable that only 37 percent of respondents in a 2020 survey of 693 public company directors believed their boards had a strong understanding of the crisis management plans at their companies.[47] This certainly demonstrates a need for more attention to this important topic.

We can learn additional crisis management lessons from how events unfolded at Boeing with its string of safety debacles. In a 2023 report by the Federal Aviation Administration (FAA), compiled after the agency reviewed thousands of pages of Boeing documents, conducted multiple surveys and over 250 interviews, and hosted meetings at various locations with Boeing employees, recommendations were issued for how Boeing should act in the future. These recommendations can provide lessons for companies more broadly.

Regarding safety culture, the FAA recommended that Boeing conduct safety surveys and ensure the results are received and acted on by leadership as well as create a reporting mechanism that is well known, well tracked, transparent, and free of any potential concerns for retaliatory measures.[48] The FAA also recommended that policies and procedures be propagated throughout the organization and that metrics be specific and applied appropriately.[49] In addition, the FAA suggested that an interdisciplinary team be put in place to manage and oversee safety risks and the implementation of the recommendations in the report.[50]

These ideas can be incorporated into every company's risk mitigation and crisis management plans: make sure the appropriate people understand the plans, feel secure that they can report concerns without repercussion, and can make appropriate changes as necessary.

Risks are always present, and crises will inevitably happen, but it is incumbent on boards and management teams to have plans in place and consistently revisit plans to minimize risks and have a general plan to react to crises.

Chapter 14
Keeping a Board Fresh and Sharp

"Sometimes people join a board thinking that they're there for life," former chair, two-time CEO, and experienced director Naren Gursahaney told me, "but you have to contribute every day." There may well be additional benefits from the experience and expertise that directors bring as their knowledge and insights about the company increase over time. However, a board seat, as with a CEO position or any executive or employee role, should not be a tenured position. Each director should consistently add value. In addition, new perspectives and new points of view can be helpful, especially as a company changes and the desired attributes for board members change.

The reality is that some board members sometimes do need to be replaced. Jane Stevenson, vice chair of Board & CEO services at Korn Ferry and global leader of the firm's CEO Succession practice, and Anthony Goodman, senior client partner at Korn Ferry and head of the firm's Board Effectiveness practice, have written about this issue: "If there's one issue management and boards can agree on, it's the need to replace certain directors who are unable to deal effectively with today's hyper-evolving business world. . . . Nine out of ten C-suite executives believe at least one director on their board should be replaced . . . [and] 48% [of directors themselves] also think one or more of their board counterparts should be removed, most often citing performance issues as the reason."[1]

To that end, while just 6 percent of S&P 500 company boards have term limits, nearly 70 percent have retirement ages as of 2022.[2] But these blunt instruments are not the only tools available to keep boards fresh and sharp. While this chapter will look at term limits and retirement ages, I will also explain a mechanism discussed less often: individual director evaluations. While board evaluations are required by the NYSE and NASDAQ, many boards conduct performance reviews of the board as a whole and its committees, not necessarily each board member. Individual evaluations are often viewed as potentially disruptive or even opening a company up to litigation risk. I believe these concerns are overstated and that individual director evaluations should be a part of a comprehensive plan to help a board be consistently effective. I also will introduce the idea of director licensing to increase the public's confidence in directors who, after all, have the critical role of overseeing management on behalf of the owners or shareholders.

In my numerous discussions with a wide range of experienced, accomplished people for this book, perhaps no set of topics inspired as wide a variety of perspectives as the ones in this chapter. I hope to offer a fair and balanced view on term limits, retirement ages, and individual director evaluations as well as introduce the idea of director licensing.

Term Limits

There are increasing conversations about and more support from various governance organizations for term limits of generally about 10 years for directors of publicly traded companies. The idea is to refresh boards and adjust for an organization's changing needs and director skill sets.

We are very familiar with the idea of term limits in US politics. The president is limited to two four-year terms, and 37 states have term limits for their governors. Seventeen state legislatures have term limits, though there are no term limits for members of the US Congress. Despite widespread public support for term limits—in a June 2023 Pew Research survey, 87 percent of respondents favored limiting the number of terms for members of Congress[3]—research often finds them failing to result in the outcomes that supporters advocate. Rather, term limits have been shown to increase party polarization[4] and reduce economic growth.[5]

The corporate world is, of course, very different from the political world, and it would be shortsighted to assume that research findings in politics hold true for companies. But, for example, the large audit, tax, and advisory services firm Grant Thornton argues that term limits for corporate directors are necessary to promote diversity, keep a board's skill sets current, and provide a respectful way to remove ineffective board members.[6]

At the same time, there is no reason to wait for directors to reach a term limit if they are ineffective or disruptive. It undermines the board's ability to be the most effective overseer of the company and is unfair to the shareholders to whom the board is responsible. However, for boards that fail to make sufficient efforts to diversify and remove ineffective directors, term limits are a way to accomplish these goals.

But the price of term limits may be a loss of organizational knowledge and valuable board members who still have much to contribute as well as the need to spend more time recruiting and onboarding new board members and the risk that new directors will not be as effective as the ones they replace. Experienced directors bring "institutional memory" and years of experience with a company's history, management, competitive position, mission, and values.

Research in the *North American Journal of Economics and Finance* has shown that "long-tenured directors are better monitors and advisors because experience and skills accumulate over time . . . [and] have greater reputation concerns, and therefore are more committed to their fiduciary duties to shareholders."[7] Additional research looking at S&P 1500 companies from 1998 to 2013 found that independent directors with extended tenures had a higher level of commitment, and their presence was correlated with lower CEO pay, higher CEO turnover-performance sensitivity, a smaller likelihood of the company intentionally misreporting earnings, and a higher quality of acquisitions.[8]

Neither ISS nor Glass Lewis has strict policies regarding term limits, but Glass Lewis wants term limits applied without waivers where they exist and will encourage voting against the nominating and governance committee chair if term limits (or age limits) have been waived for two or more consecutive years.[9] Internationally, there is more of a movement toward limiting the years of board service than there has been in the US. In the UK, as one example, after nine years, a director is no longer considered independent.[10]

There is a range of opinions on this issue. Gursahaney told me, "It's really important to have that history of where the company came from and what it is today. Directors need to know what mistakes have been made along the way. I wouldn't want a whole board of people who have 20-plus years of experience, but I'm not a fan of term limits just for the sake of term limits as long as you have a good mix of new board members and those who've been around for a while."

Ted Dysart of Russell Reynolds Associates raises an analytical perspective on this sometimes emotional issue. "It can depend on the industry," he says. "I was talking to someone at an oil company who pointed out that a 10-year term limit when you're making $20 billion [investment] bets that play out over 50 years is a pretty short period and means you won't have any directors around who know why you spent $20 billion 14 years ago."

Chief Justice Strine argues the other side of this topic. "Rigidity is not my thing, but I think it strains the concept of independence when somebody's hitting a tenure of 10 years, or even 8 years. You get comfortable with each other, and especially if it's the same management team, you lose freshness and distinctness. And if you have term limits but make exceptions, then you create incentives for people to do the wrong thing. If you're running an institution, the institution has to be larger than the person."

Steve Girsky believes the addition of new energy outweighs the loss of expertise. "I'm a big fan of term limits," he told me. "You want to keep getting new energy on a board, and you want to make sure they maintain independence from management. I don't know what the right number is, but maybe it's seven years. You need a year to learn about the company, and then some time to add value."

Ed Hockaday, the former CEO of Hallmark, has suggested the idea of terms that can be renewed. This way, you force a discussion of a director's effectiveness and make their continued service contingent on some sort of evaluation.[11] This, to me, is an argument not for term limits but for individual director evaluations, which I address later in this chapter.

I believe that committed, high-quality directors do not get stale over time but instead should become more effective. Once a director understands a sector and a company in detail and has gained real credibility with the management team and the other directors, that director is often more insightful on company-specific issues and more able to thoughtfully consider out-of-the-box ideas.

In my opinion, while term limits should be examined, there are other more effective ways to refresh a board. Many companies rely on director retirement ages to do just that, although this is not an ideal solution either.

Retirement Ages

Surveys find broad public support for mandatory retirement ages in government, with 74 percent of Americans in the June 2023 Pew Research survey supporting an age limit for Supreme Court justices.[12]

In the corporate world, there are some industries where mandatory retirement ages are quite common. Partners in the "Big Four" accounting firms have mandatory retirement ages of around 60. Some companies have age limits in place for CEOs, but there are examples of boards making exceptions to these policies. For example, in 2022, Target ended its mandatory retirement age of 65 in order to extend the tenure of its 63-year-old CEO, Brian Cornell, by three years.[13] Caterpillar did the same in order to retain CEO Jim Umpleby.[14] The average age of outgoing S&P 1500 CEOs in 2023 was 61.6.[15]

The prevalence of a retirement age requirement for board members has declined slightly, and the retirement age has often increased a little. From 2018 to 2022, the percentage of S&P 500 companies with mandatory retirement based on age fell from 70 percent to 67 percent, and of the companies with a mandatory retirement age, the most common age rose from 72 to 75.[16]

For Howard Ungerleider, the problem with a mandatory retirement age as the mechanism for refreshment is that "it almost tells boards not to pick the 45-year-old, because you don't want them on the board for 30 years." This is a problem because the perspectives of younger directors can be hugely valuable. Girsky, who is a strong supporter of term limits, says, "Telling someone to walk off the board because they're 72 is a little strange to me. I could be president of the United States, but I can't be on a public board?" After all, as 1-800-FLOWERS's Jim McCann pointed out to me, "If Warren Buffett was available and interested in being on your board, would you really turn him down because he's too old?"

On the other hand, Gursahaney thinks the age limit can be useful in shaping directors' expectations of their tenure: "I like it because in some ways it takes away some of those hard discussions that you need to have and makes it easier from a planning perspective."

I believe that experienced directors can be effective beyond the typical retirement age and well into their 70s. Longer life expectancy and easy access to information can help keep directors current on industry trends even if they are no longer working full time. However, I do think that some directors can become dated if their only connection to the business world is a few boards on which they sit. I believe this is another reason to evaluate individual director performance. I have also reluctantly come to the view that, at some point, a retirement age is only logical, and a retirement age of 75 is generally prudent.

At the same time, Laura Carstensen offers a unique idea that I think is worth considering: "What about another category for board members—alumni members who can still be tapped when useful, maybe even brought in for some meetings, kept on in some capacity so the company can still benefit?"

If the goal—as it should be—is to improve the quality of directors and boards, a retirement age, similar to a term limit, is not the most timely or effective way to refresh a board. Boards should not have to wait to replace directors if they do not perform well. Unfortunately, a recent survey conducted by PwC, a "Big Four" accounting firm, found that 48 percent of directors would replace at least one director, and 58 percent of investors do not trust boards of companies in which they invest to remove underperforming directors.[17] It is not fair to the shareholders, other board members, or management to retain an ineffective director.

Individual Director Evaluations

Since 2009, the NYSE has required boards of listed companies to evaluate themselves annually, but there are no guidelines for how such evaluations should be made.[18] The NYSE does require disclosure of the evaluations.[19] According to the "Annual State of Board Evaluations in the U.S. 2024" published by Korn Ferry and Gibson Dunn, 98 percent of S&P 500 companies report information on their board evaluations in their proxy statements—but just 50 percent conduct individual director evaluations.[20] Even for those companies that do evaluate directors, it is unclear how robust these evaluations are.[21] Many companies rely on written questionnaires or electronic surveys that can be very long and provide a limited opportunity for written input.[22] In one survey, as reported by NYSE Governance Services, just 36 percent of directors felt their most recent board evaluation was "very effective," with some directors reporting that the process was "all form, no substance," board members were "not candid," and there was no follow-through.[23] Christopher Drewry of the law firm Latham & Watkins has seen a lack of accountability in the evaluation process: "The seriousness with which evaluations have often been taken leaves some room for improvement. I think boards sometimes ignore the benefit of a good evaluation process."

The reality is that even if intentions are good, effective evaluations can be difficult to perform. Directors may not fully recognize the value of each other's contributions, especially if some directors are more or less inclined to speak up at board meetings as opposed to contributing in other ways, perhaps through back channels to the chair or management. Determining the appropriate criteria for evaluations is challenging, especially as different directors contribute in different ways at different times. Knowing evaluations will be made public, even in summary form, may deter some qualified individuals from taking seats on boards.

However, an effective annual review process for individual directors, just as companies have for management teams, is really the only way to determine whether directors are performing well. Many boards do not go this route despite recommendations from ISS, Glass Lewis, and large institutional investors.[24] Indeed, ISS suggests "individual director evaluations, conducted annually."[25]

Best practices in this area should involve interviews of individual directors concerning each of their fellow directors by the chair, lead independent director, chair of the nominating and governance committee, or a third party such as an outside attorney or one of various governance advisory firms that offers board evaluation services. Assessments should include consideration of each director's attendance, preparation, skill sets, and chemistry with other board members and management, as well as specific board contributions. This should be a thoughtful annual exercise.

Of course, there is no reason to embarrass anyone. I have been involved in a number of situations with a poorly performing director who no longer had the board's support. In all cases, the director was distracting the board and not making a substantial contribution. In general, the distractions included leaving the boardroom for substantial periods of time for non-board business, asking numerous detailed questions that were not relevant as well as demanding an excessive amount of information, and being strident on various topics such as appropriate leverage, and almost unwilling to consider other points of view. In one case, the director had a "change in responsibilities" or retired from his executive position. In such a situation, it is typically a requirement that you submit your resignation as a board member, but the board usually does not accept your resignation. In this case, we did accept it. In the other cases, the chair asked the directors not to run for reelection, and they agreed.

Particularly given the move toward annual elections for every director, it is very difficult for shareholders to make informed choices if there is no evaluation process—and if the results of the process are not made public. Of course, the directors are evaluating themselves. However, there is no apparent alternative.

Many fear that revealing the results of individual director evaluations will make people uncomfortable and harm working relationships. Charles Elson worries that directors may take their personal grudges out on each other rather than evaluating their peers fairly. He told me that "individual evaluations are difficult. They're easier said than done and can sometimes be used as a sword against a difficult director rather than a poor director. They can end up providing cover to remove a director who really is quite valuable but who has perhaps become irritating because they ask the tough questions." Along similar lines, Chancellor Bouchard fears that rigorous evaluations can affect board chemistry and create a "corrosive culture of telling on other directors, cutting against what is typically an amicable culture in a boardroom."

There is also concern that documenting a director's shortcomings could open the company up to litigation. However, I have never heard of litigation as a result of an individual director evaluation. More importantly, I asked Andy Rossman, of the litigation law firm Quinn Emanuel, about this. He said, "I haven't seen litigation as a result of an individual director evaluation. You can expect that whatever records you create are going to be examined. So you know, just be careful. But the process of evaluating directors, I think it's important."

Mike Allen of the Delaware law firm Richards Layton & Finger agrees: "I think boards need to be thoughtful about how individual director evaluations are presented and what they look like, because there is at least some risk that they could get turned over in a theoretical discovery proceeding—though I admit I have not seen this happen in practice."

While there are a number of reasonable concerns about individual director evaluations, I believe that none of them is sufficient for boards to fail to evaluate members of the body elected by the shareholders to oversee the company. Members of senior management are evaluated at least annually. Concerns and criticisms raised can create issues among senior management. However, that does not mean that evaluations should be paused or canceled. Issues must be addressed.

Gursahaney says, "I do think it's a good practice, but it's not universally done because it's tough for people to be hard on their peers, even when they ought to be. I think most boards end up tolerating poor performance for way too long. We're all here only as long as we're relevant. If you're not adding value anymore, you shouldn't be on the board."

"If you ask every board member to rank their fellow directors," adds Dysart, "the same two people would be at the bottom of everyone's list."

It does not have to be an adversarial process, offers Anna Catalano.

Looking at each director's performance every year clearly seems to me to be a more effective, more timely way to manage board refreshment than term limits or retirement ages, although I admit that others I respect feel differently. I just believe that there is no reason to have to wait until a term limit or retirement age to deal with an ineffective director.

Director Licensing

Underpinning potential concerns about directors staying in their positions too long or not being effective is whether every director is in fact qualified and current for the job. To address this, I have advocated for a director licensing requirement.

Many occupations require licenses to show competence. Accountants, investment bankers, physicians, private investigators, security guards, and massage therapists are among those who must earn a license to hold their positions. While licensees are not necessarily excellent at what they do, a license does confirm that someone has fulfilled certain requirements determined by a reputable authority.

And yet the people who govern corporate America do not need any particular training or license in order to serve. Most directors have been successful and are arguably well qualified. And I share many people's frustration with bureaucracy and excessive regulations. However, I believe it would increase confidence in corporate boards to require licenses for directors of publicly traded companies in the US.

Obtaining a license for a profession generally requires a certain amount of experience and the passing of a written examination. For example, to become a licensed certified public accountant, state requirements generally include a bachelor's degree with 150 hours of education and a specific number of hours in accounting and business that vary by state; the passing of a 16-hour, four-section uniform certified public accountant examination; and at least one year of accounting experience, along with continuing education requirements to renew the license.

Similarly, the Series 7 has historically been the basic license for securities professionals, with an examination including sections on customer issues, securities markets, economic and financial issues, and portfolio analysis. All registered individuals also have to complete periodic computer-based training focused on compliance, regulations, ethics, and sales practices.

A license for directors of public companies could follow a similar pattern. Because effective directors can come from so many backgrounds, an appropriate education requirement is difficult to define. However, capable directors must be thoughtful and mature. Therefore, an age and experience requirement is a possibility: perhaps a director ought to be at least 35 years of age with 10 years of full-time work experience. A test could include sections on the major topics presented in this book, including legal standards, basic accounting and finance principles, and ethics, including rules regarding conflicts. Continuing education, while pursued by many directors, should also be required, as standards change, and directors ought to be required to stay current on the business and governance environment.

The NACD offers a Directorship Certification.[26] Harvard Business School and Stanford Business School offer corporate director programs as do many other schools and organizations. While the NACD has over 24,000 director members and is highly regarded, and Harvard and Stanford business schools are generally the most highly ranked business schools, none of these institutions is a legal or regulatory body, and so their programs, while perhaps a model for a national license, are not currently serving that function.[27]

Peter Crist, for one, likes the idea of a license administered by an independent agency. "I would find that interesting," he told me.

Though every company and every industry is different, there is common ground and questions all directors should be able to address. As Chief Justice Strine explained, "A core set of questions every director should have to answer if they're going to serve effectively include: How does this company make money? Are we making a profit? Who are the key executives helping us make a profit? Who are the people to whom we're selling our products or services, and how are they affected by what we do?"

A license that confirms that directors have solid backgrounds and a grounding in key issues could help increase confidence in corporate governance.

Chapter 15
Looking Forward and Recommendations

To achieve good governance, I strongly believe that you have to understand first how boards have functioned in the past and then understand the guideposts for how they can be effective today. This is why I structured the book as I did. We first went briefly through the history of corporate governance. Then we went into more detail about the contemporary history of transactions (M&A, LBOs, activism, and restructurings), the growth of the institutional investor, and the advent of ESG. Finally, with that foundation and perspective, we covered at length the topics I believe are most critical for boards to be effective today, including recruiting and onboarding new directors, managing the relationship with the CEO, navigating risks and crises, and keeping a board fresh and adding value.

I hope this has left you with a robust appreciation of how much governance has improved over the past decades, how complex and dynamic the field is, and the opportunities to make boards stronger stewards of shareholder interests.

No matter the challenges that a board faces, following a set of well-informed principles and guidelines can put every director and board in the strongest position to make the most effective decisions to maximize long-term shareholder value. Excellent corporate governance is the board's responsibility and happens one director at a time.

To summarize, here are my 10 recommendations for each director to contribute to "good governance."

1. Understand Board Culture and Chemistry

It is important for all directors to understand how they can make the most impact as well as to consider whether a board is optimized for openness to ideas from all of its members and functioning in a way that promotes strong oversight and value maximization.

It can be hard to find your way when you first join a board, because the culture and dynamics of every board are different. "Part of it is chemistry,"

Andy Rossman says. "Directors need to be able to get along and have a respectful and vigorous dialogue. This point is often overlooked, but having directors aligned in economic interests is important. You want directors motivated to elevate the share price as much as possible."

While all of my "10 steps" should contribute to a value-enhancing strategy, you have to understand and work within the culture to be impactful. "The analogy I like to draw," says Chief Justice Strine, "is comparing public company directors to university trustees. We understand that those are people who care deeply about the institution. Public company directors need to as well. The board—and management—need to care enough to put the company above themselves."

A simple but important example is to be proud of every company on whose board you serve—or do not be a director of that company. I am a longtime director of Lear, which is a leader in automotive seats among other products. I only own cars with Lear seats.

2. Evaluate the CEO, Corporate Strategy, and Capital Allocation

Two of the most important responsibilities of a board are (1) hiring, evaluating, compensating, and sometimes replacing the CEO and (2) challenging and ultimately approving corporate strategy and capital allocation.

By definition, the CEO is the most important executive in the company, and the board is responsible for having an excellent CEO in place. Directors must interact effectively with the most senior executive, evaluate and compensate him or her, put a succession plan and process in place, and hire a successor when necessary.

"It's really hard to be an effective board if you don't have a fundamentally sound business strategy and sense of the industry," says Chief Justice Strine. To that end, directors need to spend significant time and energy learning about the company and its industry and diving deeply into strategy. A well-considered corporate strategy that is approved by the board and then executed well by management is the linchpin of a successful company.

A capital strategy, usually referred to as capital allocation, is also critical. This generally refers to the use of a company's free cash flow for capital expenditures, debt reduction, acquisitions, and returns of capital to shareholders through dividends and/or stock repurchases. A thoughtful approach to recommendations by management on these topics is also crucial to a company's success.

3. Oversee, Do Not Manage

Directors must remember that they are there to advise and oversee, not dig into the details or be involved in day-to-day operations. Directors should oversee the CEO, not act in any way as a CEO, and should advise on strategy and capital allocation, not try to determine strategy and capital allocation. This is a critical principle for any quality director.

I have been involved in a number of situations where directors consistently crossed the line from oversight to management—by asking too many questions, wading into the weeds beyond what was appropriate for a board member, and distracting the board from its core oversight responsibilities—and were asked not to stand for reelection.

It is also worth noting that while it is good for those with particular functional knowledge on subjects such as information technology, supply chain, and financing to participate a little more in those topics, all directors should be accomplished people with informed views on most subjects. Even a director who is an expert in a particular area is not in charge of that area. A director oversees it in conjunction with board colleagues.

4. Be Engaged and Informed

Even beyond the CEO and strategy issues discussed earlier, a good director is engaged in all major issues and works hard to be as well informed as possible. Intellectual curiosity and a desire to help solve problems, as well as to coach people to improve, are important traits you must possess. As is a commitment to prepare diligently. Read and digest all board materials in advance of any meetings. Learn as much about the company as you can.

"I went into every board position trying to learn as much as I could about the business," says Paula Sneed, "just like I would approach my work on a day-to-day basis."

"Be prepared," adds Sandra Horbach. "Do your homework. It's important to listen and maintain an open mind as things are being discussed."

5. Be Respectful and Inclusive

Expect and require all directors to be respectful of each other and maintain a tone that invites discussion and debate rather than shutting down voices that may not be as loud. Listen, try to ask questions first, and offer your views later.

"No one should be trying to prove anything," adds Pete Stavros. "The best advice I could have heard when I first joined a board is to relax, learn, contribute when it makes sense, and don't force it. I see it all the time in boardrooms, people not genuinely listening and trying to contribute but instead trying to kind of demonstrate they're smart, and that's not helpful."

Listening, however, does not mean hanging back and letting others dominate. "What prevents a board from being effective," Chancellor Bouchard told me, "is that no one can be shy on a board. You have to speak up. Nobody likes people who are obnoxious. But you have to express a point of view. You can't be a wallflower or a 'yes' person, because that's never going to be helpful."

6. Recognize That Strong Board Leadership Is Critical

Respectful and respected leadership is important to maximize the effectiveness of any group. A board is no exception. The leader needs to be trustworthy, create good chemistry, and insist that everyone is heard. The best leaders are committed to seeking unanimity on decisions and bringing people who may disagree to a place where they feel understood and know that their points of view have been considered.

Key for a leader is also understanding that the role is not just to defer to management but to push back when necessary and provide an independent voice and perspective. "Don't assume what you're being told is accurate," says Chancellor Bouchard. "You do need to have a strong leader who can stand up to a CEO who may in some cases try to drive the board in a certain direction. Leaders need to be able to resist that kind of pressure while still maintaining a productive and useful relationship."

7. Have Effective Committees, but the Entire Board Should Approve Major Decisions

This is a point that can be overlooked. You should, of course, have in place at least the three major committees and any additional committees that may help the board do its work effectively and efficiently. However, the entire board should be briefed on all committee work and approve any proposed major committee decisions.

When it comes to committee chairs, they should be well versed in the committees' work and well-regarded leaders—and the board leader, with input from the committees and the broader board, should coordinate the selection of committee chairs. Typically, a director should be an effective, well-regarded member of a particular committee before being appointed the chair.

8. Add Value-Added, Diverse Directors as Needed

It is important to keep the skills matrix current and be aware of any particular needs that the board has. At the same time, be open to "best athletes," because the most effective directors are usually knowledgeable about numerous issues and not just one narrow area. As you consider candidates for open board seats, think about their experience, knowledge, and perceived chemistry with the rest of the board and management.

While the nominating and governance committee will typically run the search for a new director, all directors, including the CEO, should meet any finalists, and there should be unanimous agreement on any candidate who is offered a board seat. Have in place a prompt orientation and detailed onboarding process so that new directors can get up to speed as quickly as possible and begin to add value soon after their appointment.

9. Directors Must Remain Current

Encourage board members to stay current with governance, business, financial, and other relevant topics.

Board education is valuable and can be provided by the company, sometimes in the "dead time" between the end of committee meetings on day one and a board dinner, often along with management, during or after dinner, or even during the regular board meeting. Also, directors should take advantage of continued learning opportunities in various forums, such as outside conferences and education programs. Directors should be reimbursed for these important efforts, and particularly useful experiences should be recommended to all directors.

10. Keep the Board Fresh

A corporate directorship should not be a tenured position. A board, its committees, and in my opinion, individual directors, should be evaluated in detail annually. As discussed, there are different views on term limits, retirement ages, and individual director evaluations. But what is most important is that every member of the board should at all times be fully capable of overseeing management and the company on behalf of the shareholders.

While it is unpleasant to ask a director to step down or not run for reelection at the next annual meeting, it must be done when necessary. After all, the CEO and other members of management are constantly evaluated and at risk of losing their jobs for lack of good performance; directors should be too.

*

I have been asked many times, "How do I become a corporate director?" There is no one answer. However, there is always a need for a diverse group of successful people with a wide range of backgrounds and skill sets to help oversee companies.

Start by thinking through how you would describe your experience and knowledge succinctly as well as why you would make a good director. What in your past shows that you work well in a group? What committee(s) could you contribute to and why? Of course, stay current with governance issues by, for example, joining the NACD and attending governance conferences and governance education programs.

More tactically, approach your contacts in the broad business community, including executives, investors, executive search professionals, attorneys, investment bankers, accountants, and others, to express your interest. Look for a board seat as you would look for any job.

*

Taken together, these recommendations—and, indeed, an understanding of the topics explored throughout this book—can hopefully set up any director, and any board, for success. Corporate governance, as I have reiterated again and again, has grown stronger over the past generations—but it remains an area that can continue to improve. All directors should continually strengthen their commitment to good governance by delivering oversight with care and loyalty to every company they serve and be informed, thoughtful advocates for shareholders and broader stakeholders.

Acknowledgments

Leadership of organizations, and particularly of businesses, has interested me ever since I can remember. I became a director of two small public companies more than two decades ago, and shortly thereafter, the first of three New York State governors appointed me as a trustee of the New York Power Authority, the state utility. And then I joined the Masonite board in 2009. From those beginnings to today, I have always been excited about the challenges of being a director and excited to be in a boardroom.

Writing this book has been an engaging process of trying to distill a career's worth of experiences into a guide that I hope will benefit others. I am grateful to the hundreds of directors and hundreds of executives who have been and continue to be my colleagues, clients, and in many cases, friends. You never stop learning from experienced people trying to help maximize value for shareholders and stakeholders.

I interviewed more than 75 people for this book, most of whom you "met" in these pages. I trust you agree with me that the book was very much enhanced by the many people who shared their perspectives. My thanks to all of them, many of whom I have known for years, some who are newer contacts, and others who were introduced to me for this book; many of them were or have become friends. They are all listed in the appendix.

For some time, I had a pretty clear idea of the structure and content of a book on corporate governance that I wanted to write. In fact, I had drafted and revised a table of contents and summary over a few years. However, it was a "cold call" from Mike Dubes that got the project started. Thank you, Mike. Along the way, I was fortunate to connect with Madeleine Morel, who introduced me to Jeremy Blachman. Then this book became a reality. Jeremy has been an incredible partner in every aspect of this "playbook": convincing me to modify the initial table of contents, doing remarkable research, turning more than a few ideas and opinions into more readable prose, helping manage the numerous interviews, fielding requests and emails from me at all hours, and guiding me through the publishing process. He has been supportive and responsive, and this book would not exist without him. I hope to do another one together. I suppose that thanks is also due to American Airlines and Delta Airlines. For all the frustrations with commercial air travel, my time in the air is among my most productive; many pages of this book were written and edited in the sky.

To a rookie such as me, the publishing process initially appeared opaque and slow. But then I met Mark Fretz at Radius, and it was almost literally a breath of fresh air. Thank you to Mark, Julia Sloan, and others at Radius. The editing by Tyler Loveless at Open Boat certainly improved the text, and I hope that you like the cover design by Pete Garceau as much as I do. Danny Constantino, Jennifer Boeree, and the team at Scribe were a pleasure to work with and superb in the production of the book. Andrew Amine made me look as good as I can in the book jacket photograph. Finally, Kathleen Schmidt developed and helped execute a thoughtful marketing plan. Lacy Kirkland and Jane Wesman have provided valuable input on this important topic too. A special thank you to my daughter, Rebekah, who taught me how social media works and has created a strong presence for the book in a medium that is still new to me.

I have worked for and with many people over the years who have contributed mightily to my knowledge and this book and have been important more broadly in my life. It all really started for me with Steve Golub, Jerry Rosenfeld, Josh Gotbaum, and Jamie Kempner in the late 1980s at Lazard. Jerry remains a particularly valued mentor and friend. In recent years, I am grateful for the assistance of numerous people who have helped in various ways with this book. At the risk of missing some, thanks to Tim Bernlohr, Kathleen Brown, Marcel Bucsescu, Anna Catalano, Rick Chesley, John Church, John Federici, Jim Glerum, Andrew Gordon, Daniel Gross, Brad Halverson, Chad Hudnut, Rob Kindler, Matt Rhodes-Kropf, Steve Reisman, Marc Roitman, Steve Rosenblum, Mike Rossi, Paul Schnell, Fran Scricco, Steve Serajeddini, Steve Silver, Greg Smith, Rob Steele, Charles Tauber, Elina Tetelbaum, Scott Ullem, Harry van Dyke, Cathy Ward, Andreas Weller, and Jake Wood.

I started Current Capital Partners in 2008—it was well in motion before the Great Recession—to be a boutique advisory and merchant banking firm focused on M&A and restructuring advisory work as well as capital raising; corporate management services, or sitting on boards and doing expert witness work in corporate litigation; and private equity investing. We have a terrific core team: Connor Donovan and Justin Levine, two fast-rising bankers who are truly partners; Matt Grayson, who does what young bankers do and more; and Greg Hartley, our operating partner who adds a unique perspective to our advisory teams. They keep me energized.

I want to remember too many business colleagues and friends who are no longer with us. My close friend whom I miss dearly, Jim Risher, was, among other positions, the CEO of Exide Electronics. He trusted me as his primary banker when I was just a vice president at Lazard, and the company was hit with a hostile takeover at a 100 percent premium to its then stock price from a corporate buyer—we fought the attack off and sold the company to a "white knight" at a higher price. Jim also showed me that you can be a successful executive as well as a "good guy" with a big heart. I still picture that sad, warm day in North Carolina when he was buried far too soon. George Lorch taught me that you can literally make just a few thoughtful comments at a two-day board meeting and have the largest impact. I miss Ed Arditte, Steve Gerard, and Bill Oesterle too.

Most importantly, thanks to Roni, Rebekah, Jack—and Winston. Roni, you will smile when I recount yet again that sweltering Atlanta day when I saw this adorable girl across the room, asked her to dinner, looked in my wallet when the bill came, and saw neither a credit card nor enough cash. I never imagined that the next 40-plus years would be as special and fun as they have been. To many more. We realized, of course, when Rebekah arrived, followed by Jack, that there is nothing as special as a wonderful family—so much love and joy. It is all about tomorrow to me. With your kindness, determination, and accomplishments, Rebekah and Jack, even at this time of many uncertainties, I am optimistic about the future. And Winston, our youngest family member: Who knew that a 20-pound canine with just a two-month gestation period could be such good company and bring so much happiness?

Jonathan F. Foster
April 28, 2025
New York City

Appendix

Interviews

Thank you to everyone who shared their time, experience, and opinions with me in interviews:

Mike Allen, Director and Chair of the Corporate Advisory Group; Vice Chair of the Corporate Department, Richards Layton & Finger

Kristy Balsanek, Partner and Global Co-chair of Environmental, Social, and Governance, DLA Piper

Senator Evan Bayh, Senior Advisor, Apollo Global Management; former two-term governor of and two-term US Senator from Indiana

Doug Benham, former President and Chief Executive Officer, Arby's Restaurant Group

Larry Berg, Senior Partner, 26North; Co-managing Owner, Los Angeles Football Club; former Senior Partner, Apollo Global Management

Chancellor Andre Bouchard, Partner in the Litigation Department, Paul, Weiss, Rifkind, Wharton & Garrison; former Chancellor of the Delaware Court of Chancery

David Brandon, Chair, former Executive Chair, and former Chief Executive Officer, Domino's Pizza; Executive Advisor to KKR; former Chief Executive Officer, Toys"R"Us; former Director of Athletics, University of Michigan; former President and Chief Executive Officer, Valassis

Kathleen Brown, Partner, Government and Regulatory, Manatt, Phelps & Phillips; former Chair of Midwest Investment Banking, Goldman Sachs; former Democratic Nominee for Governor of California; former Treasurer of California

Robert Byrne, former Chair, Masonite International; Founder and former President, Power Pro-Tech Services

Mario Carbone, Managing Partner, Major Food Group

Laura Carstensen, Professor of Psychology and Health Policy and the Fairleigh S. Dickinson Jr. Professor in Public Policy, Stanford University; Director, Stanford Center on Longevity

John Casesa, Senior Managing Director, Guggenheim Securities; former Group Vice President, Global Strategy, Ford Motor Company

Anna Catalano, Active Director and former executive, BP and Amoco

Judge Shelley Chapman, Senior Counsel in the Restructuring Department and Chair of the Alternative Dispute Resolution practice, Willkie Farr & Gallagher; former US Bankruptcy Judge for the Southern District of New York

Jim Citrin, Leader of Chief Executive Officer Practice; Co-leader of Board Practice; Member of Board, Spencer Stuart

Peter Crist, Founder, Crist Associates; Vice Chair, Korn Ferry; Founder, Crist Partners; former Co-head of North America and Member of Executive Committee, Russell Reynolds Associates

Judge Robert Drain, Of Counsel, Corporate Restructuring, Skadden, Arps, Slate, Meagher & Flom; former US Bankruptcy Judge for the Southern District of New York

Christopher Drewry, Partner and Global Co-chair of Shareholder Activism & Takeover Defense Practice, Latham & Watkins

Ted Dysart, Managing Director, Russell Reynolds Associates

John Dyson, Chair, Millbrook Capital Management; former Chair, New York Power Authority; former Deputy Mayor of the City of New York

Lawrence Elbaum, Co-head of Shareholder Activism Practice and Partner in Mergers and Acquisitions Group, Sullivan & Cromwell

Jared Ellias, Scott C. Collins Professor of Law, Harvard Law School

Len Elmore, Senior Lecturer, Columbia University; former Prosecutor, Kings County (Brooklyn); former player in the National Basketball Association

Charles Elson, Founding Director, Weinberg Center for Corporate Governance and retired Woolard Chair in Corporate Governance at University of Delaware

Brian Fox, Managing Director, Alvarez & Marsal North American Commercial Restructuring Practice

Steven Gartner, Retired Chair Emeritus, Willkie Farr & Gallagher

Steve Girsky, President and Chief Executive Officer, Nikola Corporation; former Managing Partner, VectoIQ; former Senior Vice Chair and President of Europe, General Motors; former President, Centerbridge Industrial Partners; former Managing Director and Senior Analyst, Morgan Stanley Global Automotive and Auto Parts Research Team

Scott Greenberg, Partner, Global Chair of Business Restructuring and Reorganization Practice Group and Member of Executive Committee, Gibson, Dunn & Crutcher; former Partner and Co-head of Business Restructuring & Reorganization Practice, Jones Day

Naren Gursahaney, former Interim Chief Executive Officer, Servicemaster; former President and Chief Executive Officer, ADT; former President, Tyco Engineered Products and Services; former President, GE Medical Systems Asia

Howard Heckes, former President and Chief Executive Officer, Masonite International; former Executive Vice President and President Global Coatings, Valspar

Laura Heltebran, former Chief Legal Officer, WheelsUp; former Senior Vice President and Deputy General Counsel, Hilton Worldwide; former Senior Vice President and Deputy General Counsel, Hewlett Packard Enterprise

Brook Hinchman, Managing Director and Head of North America, Oaktree Global Opportunities Strategy

Sandra Horbach, Partner and Chair of Americas Corporate Private Equity and former Co-head of Americas Corporate Private Equity, Carlyle; former Partner, Forstmann Little

Ken Jacobs, Senior Chair and Senior Advisor to the Board and former Chair and Chief Executive Officer, Lazard

Steve Key, former Executive Vice President and Chief Financial Officer, Textron and ConAgra; former Managing Partner of the New York office, Ernst & Young

Rob Kindler, Partner and Global Chair of Mergers and Acquisitions Group, Paul, Weiss, Rifkin, Wharton & Garrison; former Vice Chair, Global Head of Mergers and Acquisitions and Member of Management Committee, Morgan Stanley; former Global Head of Mergers and Acquisitions, JPMorganChase; former Partner, Cravath, Swaine & Moore

Ron Klain, Chief Legal Officer, Airbnb; 30th White House Chief of Staff to President Joe Biden; Chief of Staff to Vice President Joe Biden; Chief of Staff to Vice President Al Gore; Chief of Staff and Counselor to the US Attorney General; former Partner and National Practice Group Chair, O'Melveny & Myers; General Counsel, Revolution

Ele Klein, Partner, Co-chair of the Mergers and Acquisitions and Securities Group, Co-chair of the Global Shareholder Activism Group, and Member of Executive Committee, Schulte Roth & Zabel

Rich Klein, Senior Managing Director, Hilco Corporate Finance

Gregg Lemkau, Co–Chief Executive Officer, BDT & MSD; former Co-head of Investment Banking and Member of Management Committee, Goldman Sachs

Steve Lipin, Founder and Chief Executive Officer, Gladstone Place Partners; former US Senior Partner, Brunswick Group; former Finance Editor, the *Wall Street Journal*

Marc Lipschultz, Co–Chief Executive Officer, Blue Owl Capital; former Global Head of Energy and Infrastructure and Member of Management Committee, KKR

Marty Lipton, Founding Partner, Wachtell, Lipton, Rosen & Katz

Ron Lumbra, Partner and Member of Chief Executive Officer and Board of Directors Practice and former Managing Partner of the Americas region and Centers of Excellence, Heidrick & Struggles

Fred Lynch, Operating Partner, AEA Middle Market Private Equity; former President and Chief Executive Officer, Masonite International

Mark Manoff, Operating Partner, MidOcean Partners; former Vice Chair Markets, Member of Executive Board and Operating Committee, and Founder of the Center for Board Matters, Ernst & Young

Bob Manzo, Senior Managing Director (retired), FTI Consulting; Co-founder, Policano & Manzo

Gary Matt, Vice President of Corporate Development, Thermo Fisher; former Managing Director, Barclays

George Mattson, Chief Executive Officer, Wheels Up; former Partner and Co-head of Global Industrials Group, Goldman Sachs

Jim McCann, Founder, Chair, and Chief Executive Officer, 1-800-FLOWERS.COM

Peter McCausland, Founder, Chair, and Chief Executive Officer (retired), Airgas

Admiral Mike Mullen, 17th Chair of the US Joint Chiefs of Staff for Presidents George W. Bush and Barack Obama; 28th Chief of Naval Operations

Daniel Neff, Partner, Member of the Executive Committee, and former Co-chair, Wachtell, Lipton, Rosen & Katz

Doug Oberhelman, Executive Chair (retired) and former Chair and Chief Executive Officer, Caterpillar

Muir Paterson, Head of Strategic Advisory Solutions, Citi; former Chief Operating Officer of Mergers and Acquisitions Advisory Group,

Goldman Sachs; former Director of Corporate Governance, Wellington Management; Co-founder of Special Situations Group, Institutional Shareholders Services (ISS)

Gregg Polle, Vice Chair of Mergers and Acquisitions, Bank of America

Dr. Jonathan Rich, Advisor, Apollo Global Management; Chair and Chief Executive Officer (retired), Lumileds; Chair and Chief Executive Officer (retired), Berry Global

Barry Ridings, Vice Chair of US Investment Banking (retired), Lazard

Jerry Rosenfeld, Senior Advisor to the Chief Executive Officer and Vice Chair of US Investment Banking, Lazard; Professor of Practice and Distinguished Scholar in Residence, Co-director of Leadership Program on Law and Business, and Faculty Director, Institute for Executive Education, New York University School of Law

Andy Rossman, Managing Partner of New York office and Chair of Mergers and Acquisitions Litigation, Quinn Emanuel Urquhart and Sullivan

Jim Rubright, Chief Executive Officer (retired), Rock-Tenn

Robert Seminara, Partner, Head of Europe, and Member of Leadership Team, Apollo Global Management

Daniel Slifkin, Partner and former Head of Litigation, Cravath, Swaine & Moore

Paula Sneed, Executive Vice President, Global Marketing Resources and Initiatives (retired), Kraft Foods

Jamie Sprayregen, Vice Chair, Hilco Global; Partner, Founder, and Head of the Restructuring Group and Member of the Management Committee (retired), Kirkland & Ellis; former Co-head of Restructuring Group, Goldman Sachs

Pete Stavros, Co-head of Global Private Equity, KKR; Founder and Chair, Ownership Works

Steve Sterrett, Chair, Berry Global; Lead Trustee, Equity Apartments; former Senior Executive Vice President and Chief Financial Officer, Simon Property Group

Chief Justice Leo E. Strine Jr., Of Counsel in Corporate Department, Wachtell, Lipton, Rosen & Katz; Michael L. Wachter Distinguished Fellow in Law and Policy, University of Pennsylvania Carey Law School; Senior Fellow, Harvard Program on Corporate Governance; former Chief Justice, Delaware Supreme Court; former Chancellor and Vice Chancellor, Delaware Court of Chancery

Josh Sussberg, Partner in Restructuring Group and Member of Executive Committee, Kirkland & Ellis

Matt Turner, President, Pearl Meyer Executive Compensation

Beth Daley Ullem, Founder and President, Quality and Safety First

Bill Ultan, Managing Director, Member of Corporate Governance Consulting Group and Member of Senior Leadership Team, Sodali

Howard Ungerleider, Operating Advisor, Clayton, Dubilier & Rice Funds; President, Chief Financial Officer, and Member of Senior Executive Committee (retired), Dow

Neil Whoriskey, Partner and Member of Corporate Group, Milbank; former Partner, Co-chair of Mergers & Acquisitions Practice, and Co-chair of Corporate Governance Practice, Cleary Gottlieb Steen & Hamilton

David Wise, Vice Chair of Rewards, ESG Partner, and Member of North American Leadership, Korn Ferry

Steve Wolosky, Chair Emeritus of Shareholder Activism Practice, Olshan Frome Wolosky

Jed York, Principal Owner and Chief Executive Officer, San Francisco 49ers

Steve Zelin, Partner, Global Head of the Restructuring and Special Situations Group, and Member of Management Committee, PJT Partners

Notes

Chapter 2: How We Got to Now

1. Brian R. Cheffins, "The History of Corporate Governance" (ECGI Working Paper Series in Law, working paper no. 184/2012, January 2012), https://www.ecgi.global/sites/default/files/working_papers/documents/SSRN-id1975404.pdf.
2. Adam Smith quoted in Harwell Wells, "The Birth of Corporate Governance," Assistant Professor of Law, Temple University Beasley School of Law, https://digitalcommons.law.seattleu.edu/cgi/viewcontent.cgi?article=1017&context=sulr.
3. Wells.
4. Wells.
5. John Morris, "Corporate Governance in America: A Brief History," *Strategic Management*, 2nd ed., https://open.oregonstate.education/strategicmanagement/chapter/2-corporate-governance-in-america-a-brief-history/.
6. A. A. Sommer Jr., "The Impact of the SEC on Corporate Governance," *Law and Contemporary Problems* 41, no. 3, https://scholarship.law.duke.edu/cgi/viewcontent.cgi?article=3525&context=lcp.
7. Dan Byrne, "What Is the History of Corporate Governance?," Corporate Governance Institute, https://www.thecorporategovernanceinstitute.com/insights/lexicon/why-does-corporate-governance-matter-a-look-back-at-history/.
8. Stanley Vance, *The Corporate Director: A Critical Evaluation* (Homewood, IL: Dow Jones-Irwin, 1968).
9. Myles L. Mace, *Directors: Myth and Reality* (Boston: Harvard Business School Press, 1971), 206.
10. "Goldberg Is Off Board," *New York Times*, October 19, 1972, https://www.nytimes.com/1972/10/19/archives/goldberg-is-off-board.html.
11. "Goldberg Is Off Board."
12. Morris, "Corporate Governance."

13 Sommer, "Impact of the SEC."
14 Cheffins, "History of Corporate Governance."
15 Staff Report of the Securities and Exchange Commission to the Special Subcommittee on Investigations, *The Financial Collapse of the Penn Central Company* (Washington, DC: US Government Printing Office, August 1972), https://www.sechistorical.org/collection/papers/1970/1972_0803_CollapsePenn_1.pdf.
16 Cheffins, "History of Corporate Governance."
17 Cheffins.
18 Cheffins.
19 Cheffins.
20 Mary Ann Cloyd, "Shareholder Activism: Who, What, When, and How?," Harvard Law School Forum on Corporate Governance, April 7, 2015, https://corpgov.law.harvard.edu/2015/04/07/shareholder-activism-who-what-when-and-how/.
21 Milton Friedman, "A Friedman Doctrine—the Social Responsibility of Business Is to Increase Its Profits," *New York Times*, September 13, 1970, https://www.nytimes.com/1970/09/13/archives/a-friedman-doctrine-the-social-responsibility-of-business-is-to.html.
22 Friedman.
23 Edwin Chan, "Icahn Takes Another $500 Million Bite Out of Apple," Reuters, January 23, 2014, https://www.reuters.com/article/business/icahn-takes-another-500-million-bite-out-of-apple-idUSBREA0L1EE/.
24 Bengt Holmstrom and Steven N. Kaplan, "Corporate Governance and Merger Activity in the US: Making Sense of the 1980s and 1990s" (NBER working paper no. 8220, April 2001), https://www.nber.org/system/files/working_papers/w8220/w8220.pdf.

Chapter 3: The Core of the Corporate Directors' Role

1 *In re Smurfit-Stone Container Corp. S'Holder Litig.*, C.A. No. 6164-VCP (Del. Ch. May 20, 2011, revised May 24, 2011) (Parsons, V.C.).
2 *In re Smurfit-Stone.*
3 *In re Smurfit-Stone.*
4 Mark Basch, "Smurfit Kappa, WestRock Agree to Merger," *Jacksonville Daily Record*, September 12, 2023, https://www.jaxdailyrecord.com/news/2023/sep/12/smurfit-kappa-westrock-agree-to-merger/.

5   "Boeing in Fortune Rankings," *Fortune*, n.d., https://fortune.com/company/boeing/fortune500/.

6   *In re The Boeing Company Derivative Litigation*, Consol., C.A. No. 2019-0907-MTZ (Del. Ch. Sept. 7, 2021).

7   *In re Boeing*.

8   David Shepardson, "Boeing Directors Agree to $237.5 Million Settlement over 737 MAX Safety Oversight," Reuters, November 6, 2021, sec. Transactional, https://www.reuters.com/legal/transactional/boeing-directors-agree-2375-million-settlement-over-max-safety-oversight-2021-11-05/.

9   Lila MacLellan, "Boeing's Board Faces Scrutiny Yet Again: 'It's a Bad Board, and It Has Been a Bad Board for a Long Time,'" Yahoo! Finance, January 16, 2024, https://finance.yahoo.com/news/boeing-board-faces-scrutiny-yet-124500373.html.

10   Nate Freeman, "How Chef Mario Carbone Built the Most Celebrity-Studded Restaurant on Earth," *Vanity Fair*, August 10, 2022, https://www.vanityfair.com/style/2022/08/how-chef-mario-carbone-built-the-most-celebrity-studded-restaurant-on-earth.

11   "The Role of the Board of Directors in Enron's Collapse," *Hearing before the Permanent Subcommittee of Investigations of the Committee on Governmental Affairs, US Senate*, 107th Cong., 2nd session, Senate Hearing 107-511, May 7, 2002, https://www.govinfo.gov/content/pkg/CHRG-107shrg80300/html/CHRG-107shrg80300.htm.

12   Julian Velasco, "How Many Fiduciary Duties Are There in Corporate Law?," *Southern California Law Review* 83 (2009–10): 1231, https://scholarship.law.nd.edu/law_faculty_scholarship/590.

13   *Smith v. Van Gorkom*, 488 A.2d 858 (Del. 1985).

14   *Smith v. Van Gorkom*.

15   *Smith v. Van Gorkom*.

16   *Guth v. Loft Inc.*, 5 A.2d 503 (Del. 1939).

17   *Guth v. Loft*.

18   *Guth v. Loft*.

19   Velasco, "How Many Fiduciary Duties."

20   Allison L. Land and Peter D. Luneau, "Indemnification Considerations for Directors and Officers of Delaware Entities," Skadden, February 9, 2021, https://www.skadden.com/insights/publications/2021/02/indemnification-considerations.

21. Deborah A. DeMott, "Limiting Directors' Liability," *Washington University Law Quarterly* 66 (1988): 295–323.
22. Jef Feeley, Dana Hull, and Bloomberg, "Elon Musk's $56 Billion Pay Pact Was Killed by Lawyers Who Are Now Seeking 29 Million Tesla Shares to Cover Legal Fees," *Fortune*, March 2, 2024, https://fortune.com/2024/03/02/lawyers-seek-tesla-shares-for-legal-fees-in-elon-musk-pay-case/amp/.
23. Lewis S. Black Jr., *Why Corporations Choose Delaware* (New York: CSC, 1999), https://corpfiles.delaware.gov/pdfs/whycorporations_english.pdf; Pádraig Floyd, "Delaware's Corporate Law Primacy Is Under Attack," Agenda, February 12, 2024, https://www.agendaweek.com/c/4420274/573764/delaware_corporate_primacy_under_attack.
24. Black, *Why Corporations*.
25. Black.
26. "In Memory of William T. Allen," Wachtell, Lipton, Rosen & Katz, n.d., https://www.wlrk.com/william-t-allen/.
27. Jeff Montgomery, "Delaware Mourns the Chancellor Who 'Saved Corporate Law,'" Law360, October 16, 2019, https://www.law360.com/articles/1209272.
28. Jack B. Jacobs, "To Bill Allen: A Final Tribute," *CLS Blue Sky Blog*, October 17, 2019, https://clsbluesky.law.columbia.edu/2019/10/17/to-bill-allen-a-final-tribute/.
29. Jill E. Fisch, "The Peculiar Role of the Delaware Courts in the Competition for Corporate Charters," *SSRN Electronic Journal* 68, no. 4 (May 2000).
30. Fisch.
31. Mike Leonard and Jennifer Kay, "Match.com Spin Case Revived in Major Ruling on Insider Deals," Bloomberg Law, April 4, 2024, https://news.bloomberglaw.com/esg/match-com-spinoff-case-revived-in-major-ruling-on-insider-deals.
32. Matthew P. Salerno et al., "Delaware Court of Chancery Invalidates Common Provisions in Stockholder Agreements," Cleary Gottlieb Steen & Hamilton, March 4, 2024, https://www.clearymawatch.com/2024/03/delaware-court-of-chancery-invalidates-common-provisions-in-stockholder-agreements/.
33. Erin Mulvaney and Theo Francis, "Battle over Shareholder Pacts Strains Delaware's Business Courts," *Wall Street Journal*, July 14, 2024, https://www.wsj.com/business/shareholder-agreements-delaware-corporate-law-b083e768.

34 Nicholas O'Keefe and Douglass D. Lightfoot, "Delaware Enacts Controversial Market Practice Amendments to Its General Corporation Law," Foley, July 18, 2024, https://www.foley.com/insights/publications/2024/07/delaware-market-practice-amendments-general-corporation-law/.

35 O'Keefe and Lightfoot.

36 Tom Hals, "Delaware Lawmakers Approve Corporate Bill That Critics Call Giveaway to Billionaires," Reuters, March 25, 2025, https://www.reuters.com/world/us/delaware-lawmakers-vote-corporate-bill-critics-call-giveaway-billionaires-2025-03-25/?campaign_id=4&emc=edit_dk_20250326&instance_id=150976&nl=dealbook&regi_id=86437969&segment_id=194419&user_id=4992626c025f3a0d7f3ba740551d7534.

37 Pádraig Floyd, "Delaware's Corporate Law Primacy Is Under Attack," Agenda, February 12, 2024, https://www.agendaweek.com/c/4420274/573764/delaware_corporate_primacy_under_attack.

38 Jef Feeley and Matthew Bultman, "TripAdvisor Can Reincorporate in Nevada, Delaware Judge Says," Bloomberg Law, February 20, 2024, https://news.bloomberglaw.com/litigation/tripadvisor-can-reincorporate-in-nevada-delaware-judge-says.

39 John C. Coffee Jr., "Cleary Gottlieb Discusses Delaware Decision on Conversion of Company into Nevada Corporation," March 4, 2024, https://clsbluesky.law.columbia.edu/2024/03/04/cleary-gottlieb-discusses-delaware-decision-on-conversion-of-company-into-nevada-corporation/.

40 Gregory B. Maffei, et al. v. Dennis Palkon, et al. C.A. No. 2023-0449-JTL (Del. Ch. February 4, 2025).

41 Mike Ives, "SpaceX Is Now Incorporated in Texas, Elon Musk Says," New York Times, February 15, 2024, https://www.nytimes.com/2024/02/15/business/spacex-delaware-texas.html.

42 Elon Musk (@elonmusk), "SpaceX has moved its state of incorporation from Delaware to Texas!," X (formerly Twitter), February 14, 2024, 7:27 p.m, https://twitter.com/elonmusk/status/1757924482885583112.

43 "Delaware versus Nevada: What Are the Critical Distinctions in Nevada Corporate and LLC Law?," CSC Blog, May 26, 2021, https://blog.cscglobal.com/nevada-corporate-and-llc-law/.

44 "Delaware versus Nevada."

45 Adam S. Parker, "Does the State of Incorporation Matter?" Trivariate Research, August 29, 2024, https://trivariateresearch.com/does-the-state-of-incorporation-matter/.

46. Lori McMillan, "The Business Judgment Rule as an Immunity Doctrine," *William & Mary Business Law Review* 4 (2013), https://scholarship.law.wm.edu/wmblr/vol4/iss2/5.
47. *In re Citigroup Inc. Shareholder Derivative Litigation*, 964 A.2d 106, 126 (Del. Ch. 2009).
48. McMillan, "Business Judgment Rule."
49. McMillan.
50. *Marchand v. Barnhill*, 212 A.3d 805 (Del. 2019).
51. *Marchand v. Barnhill*.
52. *Marchand v. Barnhill*.
53. *Marchand v. Barnhill*.
54. *In re Caremark Intern. Inc. Derivative Litigation*, 698 A.2d 959 (1996).
55. *Stone v. Ritter*, 911 A.2d 362, 369 (Del. 2006) (citing In re Caremark Int'l Inc. Derivative Litig., 698A.2d 959, 971 (Del. Ch. 1996)).
56. *Marchand v. Barnhill*, 212 A.3d 805 (Del. 2019).
57. *Marchand v. Barnhill*.
58. *In re The Boeing Co. Derivative Litig.*, C.A. No. 2019-0907-MTZ (Del. Ch. Sept. 7, 2021).
59. *In re Boeing*.
60. Shepardson, "Boeing Directors Agree."
61. Shepardson.
62. Michael Hiltzik, "Column: Was Any Board Worse Than Boeing's in 2019?," *Los Angeles Times*, January 4, 2020, https://www.latimes.com/business/story/2020-01-03/boeing-board-bad-management.
63. Lila MacLellan, "Boeing's Board Is Also to Blame for Its Latest Scandal," *Fortune*, January 16, 2024, https://fortune.com/2024/01/16/boeing-board-plane-737-max-crash/.
64. Niraj Chokshi, "Boeing Names New C.E.O. as It Looks to Recover from Safety Crisis," *New York Times*, July 31, 2024, https://www.nytimes.com/2024/07/31/business/boeing-kelly-ortberg-ceo.html.
65. *Kahn v. Lynch Communication Systems*, 638 A.2d 1110 (Del. 1994).
66. *Weinberger v. UOP, Inc.*, 457 A.2d 701 (1983).
67. *Weinberger v. UOP*.
68. *In re Oracle Corporation Derivative Litigation*, C.A. No. 2017-0337-SG (Del. Ch. May 12, 2023).
69. *In re Oracle*.
70. *In re Oracle*.

71 Adam M. Grant, *Think Again: The Power of Knowing What You Don't Know* (New York, New York: Viking, 2021).
72 Chris O'Connor, "Ch. 4: Think Again by Adam Grant," BookTalk.org, August 6, 2021, https://www.booktalk.org/ch-4-think-again-by-adam-grant-t32678.html.

Chapter 4: The Three Major Board Committees

1 Brenda S. Birkett, "Recent History of Corporate Audit Committees," *Accounting Historians Journal* 13, no. 2 (1986), https://egrove.olemiss.edu/aah_journal/vol13/iss2/9.
2 Michael Chatfield and Richard Vangermeersch, "History of Accounting: An International Encyclopedia," *Individual and Corporate Publications* 168 (1996), https://egrove.olemiss.edu/acct_corp/168.
3 Chatfield and Vangermeersch.
4 "Requirements for Public Company Boards," Weil, January 3, 2022, https://www.weil.com/-/media/files/pdfs/2022/january/requirements_for_public_company_boards_including_ipo_transition_rules.pdf.
5 "Requirements."
6 Jamie Smith, "How Committees Are Evolving to Meet Changing Oversight Needs," EY, October 17, 2022, https://www.ey.com/en_us/board-matters/how-committees-are-evolving-to-meet-changing-oversight-needs.
7 Lindsay Frost, "New Board Committees Flourish as Disruption Piles Up," Agenda, January 2, 2024, https://www.agendaweek.com/c/4366244/566444/board_committees_flourish_disruption_piles.
8 Birkett, "Recent History."
9 Birkett.
10 Birkett.
11 Michael W. Peregrine and Charles W. Elson, "The Important Legacy of the Sarbanes Oxley Act," Harvard Law School Forum on Corporate Governance, August 30, 2022, https://corpgov.law.harvard.edu/2022/08/30/the-important-legacy-of-the-sarbanes-oxley-act/.
12 Sarbanes-Oxley Act, P.L. No. 107–204, 116 Stat. 745 (2002).
13 Peregrine and Elson, "Important Legacy."
14 "Requirements for Public Company Boards," Weil, August 2023, https://governance.weil.com/wp-content/uploads/2023/08/PCAG-Chart-of-Board-Requirements-August-2023.pdf.
15 Sarbanes-Oxley Act.

16. 2021 U.S. Spencer Stuart Board Index.
17. 2021 U.S. Spencer Stuart Board Index.
18. Peregrine and Elson, "Important Legacy."
19. "AS 3101: The Auditor's Report on an Audit of Financial Statements When the Auditor Expresses an Unqualified Opinion," PCAOB, n.d., https://pcaobus.org/oversight/standards/auditing-standards/details/AS3101.
20. Peregrine and Elson, "Important Legacy."
21. Scott Parker, "Four Reasons All Private Companies Need a SOX Compliance Program," AuditBoard, October 14, 2020, https://www.auditboard.com/blog/4-reasons-private-companies-need-sox-compliance-programs/.
22. "SOX Compliance amid Rising Costs, Labor Shortages and Other Post-Pandemic Challenges," Protiviti, June 2022, https://www.protiviti.com/sites/default/files/2022-06/2022-sox-compliance-survey-protiviti.pdf.
23. NACD Future of the American Board: Audit Committee Blueprint.
24. 2021 U.S. Spencer Stuart Board Index.
25. "Requirements for Public Company Boards," Weil, January 3, 2022, https://www.weil.com/-/media/files/pdfs/2022/january/requirements_for_public_company_boards_including_ipo_transition_rules.pdf.
26. Harvard Law School Forum on Corporate Governance, Compensation Committee Guide 2020, https://corpgov.law.harvard.edu/2020/03/19/compensation-committee-guide-2020.
27. Harvard Law School Forum on Corporate Governance, Compensation Committee Guide 2020.
28. Theresa Tovar, Robert Newbury, and Don Delves, "The Compensation Committee Role in Human Capital Management Is Growing," WTW, November 17, 2022, https://www.wtwco.com/en-us/insights/2022/11/compensation-committee-role-in-human-capital-management-is-growing.
29. "NYSE Listed Company Manual Section 303A Corporate Governance Standards Frequently Asked Questions," NYSE, July 28, 2021, https://www.nyse.com/publicdocs/nyse/regulation/nyse/FAQ_NYSE_Listed_Company_Manual_Section_303A_7_28_2021.pdf; "Benefits Blast: Key Implementation Steps for Listed Companies as Deadline for Adopting Clawback Policies Rapidly Approaches," Winston & Strawn blog, August 16, 2023, https://www.winston.com/

en/blogs-and-podcasts/benefits-blast/key-implementation-steps-for-listed-companies-as-deadline-for-adopting-clawback-policies-rapidly-approaches.

30 Kevin F. Hallock, "The Relationship between Company Size and CEO Pay," Workspan, February 2011, https://archive.ilr.cornell.edu/sites/default/files/workspan/02-11-Research-for-the-real-world_0.pdf.

31 Tom Taulli, "Restricted Stock Grants Are Increasingly Popular. What Advisors Need to Know," *Barron's*, September 21, 2022, https://www.barrons.com/advisor/articles/rsus-popular-options-advisors-51663776779.

32 2021 U.S. Spencer Stuart Board Index.

33 Josh Bivens and Jori Kandra, "CEO Pay Has Skyrocketed 1,460% since 1978: CEOs Were Paid 399 Times as Much as a Typical Worker in 2021," Economic Policy Institute, October 4, 2022, https://www.epi.org/publication/ceo-pay-in-2021/.

34 Ownership Works, https://ownershipworks.org/.

35 Miriam Gottfried, "Blackstone to Grant Equity to Most Employees in Future U.S. Buyouts," *Wall Street Journal*, May 21, 2024, https://www.wsj.com/finance/blackstone-to-grant-equity-to-most-employees-in-future-u-s-buyouts-3c5fed45.

36 Sharon Terlep, "Boeing to Tie More of Employees' Incentive Pay to Safety," *Wall Street Journal*, March 8, 2024, https://www.wsj.com/business/boeing-to-tie-more-of-employees-pay-to-safety-15c27813.

37 Terlep.

38 "Compensation Committee Guide 2020," Harvard Law School Forum on Corporate Governance, 2020, https://corpgov.law.harvard.edu/2020/03/19/compensation-committee-guide-2020.

39 "Compensation Committee Guide 2020."

40 "Streamline Your Professional Services Workflow," SP Global, n.d., https://www.spglobal.com/market-intelligence/en/solutions/products/sp-capital-iq-pro.

41 "Compensation Committee Guide," Wachtell, Lipton, Rosen & Katz, January 2022, https://www.wlrk.com/webdocs/wlrknew/ClientMemos/WLRK/WLRK.27957.22.pdf.

42 *In re Walt Disney Derivative Litigation*, 907 A 2d 693 (2005).

43 *In re Walt Disney*.

44 *In re Walt Disney*.

45 Laura M. Holson, "Ruling Upholds Disney's Payment in Firing of Ovitz," *New York Times*, August 10, 2005, https://www.nytimes.com/2005/08/10/business/media/ruling-upholds-disneys-payment-in-firing-of-ovitz.html.

46 Kara Nuzback, "Chandler Looks Back on Career as Chancellor," *Cape Gazette*, June 14, 2011, https://www.capegazette.com/article/chandler-looks-back-career-chancellor/12027.

47 "The Tesla Executive Compensation Ruling: What Directors Need to Know," Pearl Meyer, February 2024, https://pearlmeyer.com/insights-and-research/client-alert/tesla-executive-compensation-ruling-what-directors-need-know.

48 "Tesla Executive."

49 "Tesla Executive."

50 Jason Karaian and Jack Ewing, "Musk's Tesla Pay Package Got Big Margin in Shareholder Vote," *New York Times*, June 14, 2024, https://www.nytimes.com/2024/06/14/business/tesla-elon-musk-pay-vote-stock.html.

51 Associated Press, "Elon Musk Wins Back His $44.9 Billion Tesla Pay Package in Shareholder Vote," NPR, June 14, 2024, https://www.npr.org/2024/06/14/g-s1-4359/elon-musk-tesla-pay-package-shareholder-vote.

52 *Richard J. Tornetta v. Elon Musk, Robyn M. Denholm, Antonio J. Gracias, James Murdoch, Linda Johnson Rice, Brad W. Buss, and Ira Ehrenpreis*, C.A. No. 2018-0408-KSJM, December 2, 2024, https://courts.delaware.gov/Opinions/Download.aspx?id=372420.

53 Jill E. Fisch, Darius Palia, and Steven Davidoff Solomon, "Is Say on Pay All about Pay? The Impact of Firm Performance," *Faculty Scholarship at Penn Carey Law* 1931 (2018).

54 Ryan Colucci, "Say on Pay: 10-Year Landscape and 2021 Expectations," Compensation Advisory Partners, March 8, 2021, https://www.capartners.com/cap-thinking/say-on-pay-10-year-landscape-and-2021-expectations/.

55 Fisch, Palia, and Solomon, "Is Say on Pay All about Pay?"

56 Fisch, Palia, and Solomon.

57 Dade Hayes, "Netflix Shareholders Nix Executive Compensation Plan by Nearly 3-to-1 Margin in Non-binding Vote—Update," Deadline, June 6, 2023, https://deadline.com/2023/06/netflix-shareholder-meeting-wga-strike-executive-compensation-1235398208/.

58 Hayes.

59 "The Effects of Say on Pay Failures," Equilar blog, October 3, 2019, https://www.equilar.com/blogs/428-the-effects-of-say-on-pay-failures.html.
60 "Effects of Say on Pay."
61 Mark Gurman and Bloomberg, "Apple's Tim Cook Takes a Rare CEO Pay Cut after Pushback. But He'll Still Earn a Fortune," *Fortune*, January 13, 2023, https://fortune.com/2023/01/12/apple-tim-cook-compensation-ceo-pay-cut-investors-base-salary-stock-awards-2023/.
62 "SEC Adopts Rule for Pay Ratio Disclosure," SEC press release, August 5, 2015, https://www.sec.gov/news/press-release/2015-160.
63 Benjamin Sombi, "CEO Pay Ratio: What You Need to Know," Human Capital Hub, May 16, 2024, https://www.thehumancapitalhub.com/articles/ceo-pay-ratio-what-you-need-to-know.
64 NACD Future of the American Board: Compensation Committee Blueprint.
65 NACD Future of the American Board: Compensation Committee Blueprint.
66 "Charter of the Compensation and Human Capital Committee of the Board of Directors," Levi Strauss & Co., December 7, 2021, https://s23.q4cdn.com/172692177/files/doc_downloads/gov/2021/Compensation-and-Human-Capital-Committee-Charter_Final-12.pdf.
67 Ani Huang and Richard R. Floersch, "The Expanded Role of the Compensation Committee," Harvard Law School Forum on Corporate Governance, August 3, 2022, https://corpgov.law.harvard.edu/2022/08/03/the-expanded-role-of-the-compensation-committee/.
68 Vicki L. Bogan, Ekaterina Potemkina, and Scott E. Yonker, "What Drives Racial Diversity on U.S. Corporate Boards?," Harvard Law School Forum on Corporate Governance, January 17, 2022, https://corpgov.law.harvard.edu/2022/01/17/what-drives-racial-diversity-on-u-s-corporate-boards/.
69 Peter Eavis, "Corporate Board Diversity Increased in 2021. Some Ask What Took So Long," *New York Times*, January 3, 2022, https://www.nytimes.com/2022/01/03/business/corporate-board-diversity.html.
70 Crist Kolder Associates, Volatility Report, Summer 2024, https://static1.squarespace.com/static/62164a05607c3e5978f251ec/t/66bf839ebdc1163280315f1d/1723827103979/Crist+Kolder+2024+Volatility+Report+Summer.pdf.

71 Crist Kolder Associates.
72 Jody Godoy, "California Law Requiring Women on Company Boards Struck Down," Reuters, May 17, 2022, https://www.reuters.com/legal/legalindustry/california-law-requiring-women-company-boards-struck-down-2022-05-16/.
73 Billy Nauman, "State Street to Insist Companies Disclose Diversity Data," Financial Times, January 10, 2021, https://www.ft.com/content/2e512c76-4733-4821-8425-136ab9b98426.
74 Institutional Shareholder Services, "France Pushes Forward on Gender Diversity within French Corporate Management Bodies via the Rixain Act," ISS Insights, October 3, 2022, https://insights.issgovernance.com/posts/france-pushes-forward-on-gender-diversity-within-french-corporate-management-bodies-via-the-rixain-act/.
75 Kerry E. Berchem et al., "ISS, Glass Lewis and BlackRock Issue 2025 Voting Guidelines," Akin Gump Strauss Hauer & Feld LLP, n.d., https://www.akingump.com/en/insights/alerts/iss-glass-lewis-and-blackrock-issue-2025-voting-guidelines.
76 Emma Hinchliffe, "Women CEOs Run 10.4% of Fortune 500 Companies. A Quarter of the 52 Leaders Became CEO in the Last Year," Fortune, June 5, 2023, https://fortune.com/2023/06/05/fortune-500-companies-2023-women-10-percent/.
77 Kim Elsesser, "JetBlue Will Be the First Major U.S. Airline with a Female CEO," Forbes, January 9, 2024, https://www.forbes.com/sites/kimelsesser/2024/01/09/jetblue-will-be-the-first-major-us-airline-with-a-female-ceo.
78 "Sustainability Action Report: Survey Findings on ESG Disclosure and Preparedness," Deloitte, December 2022, https://www2.deloitte.com/content/dam/Deloitte/us/Documents/audit/us-survey-findings-on-esg-disclosure-and-preparedness.pdf.

Chapter 5: Board Leadership

1 Stanislav Shekshnia, "How to Be a Good Board Chair," Harvard Business Review, January 20, 2021, https://hbr.org/2018/03/how-to-be-a-good-board-chair.
2 "2022 U.S. Spencer Stuart Board Index," Spencer Stuart, 2002, https://www.spencerstuart.com/-/media/2022/october/ssbi2022/2022_us_spencerstuart_board_index_final.pdf.

3 "2023 CEO Transitions," Spencer Stuart, January 2024, https://www.spencerstuart.com/research-and-insight/2023-ceo-transitions.
4 "2023 CEO Transitions."
5 Peter R. Gleason and Sue Cole, "SEC Climate Comment Letter," NACD, n.d., https://www.nacdonline.org/files/PDF/NACD-%20Board%20Leadership-%20Chairman,%20CEO,%20and%20Lead%20Director.pdf.
6 Amcor, "Amcor and Berry to Combine in an All-Stock Transaction, Creating a Global Leader in Consumer and Healthcare Packaging Solutions," PR Newswire, November 19, 2024, https://www.prnewswire.com/news-releases/amcor-and-berry-to-combine-in-an-all-stock-transaction-creating-a-global-leader-in-consumer-and-healthcare-packaging-solutions-302309723.html.
7 Steve Gelsi, "Morgan Stanley's James Gorman Stepping Down as Executive Chair by Year-End," Morningstar, May 23, 2024, https://www.morningstar.com/news/marketwatch/20240523401/morgan-stanleys-james-gorman-stepping-down-as-executive-chair-by-year-end.
8 Amelia Lucas, "Former Starbucks CEO Howard Schultz Steps Down from Coffee Chain's Board," CNBC, September 14, 2023, https://www.cnbc.com/2023/09/13/former-starbucks-ceo-howard-schultz-to-step-down-from-board.html.
9 Heather Haddon, "Howard Schultz Is Back-Seat Driving Starbucks. That's a Problem for His Successor," *Wall Street Journal*, May 9, 2024, https://www.wsj.com/business/hospitality/howard-schultz-is-back-seat-driving-starbucks-thats-a-problem-for-his-successor-225cd0d9.
10 Haddon.
11 Andrew Ross Sorkin et al., "Starbucks Replaces Chief Executive after Activist Investor Campaigns," *New York Times*, August 13, 2024, https://www.nytimes.com/2024/08/13/business/dealbook/starbucks-ceo-out-laxman-narasimhan.html.
12 Martin Lipton and Jay W. Lorsch, "A Modest Proposal for Improved Corporate Governance," *Business Lawyer* 48, no. 12 (November 1992): 59–77.
13 Gleason and Cole, "SEC Climate Comment Letter."
14 Thuy-Nga T. Vo, "To Be or Not to Be Both CEO and Board Chair," Faculty Scholarship, paper 184 (2010), http://open.mitchellhamline.edu/facsch/184.

15. "About the Center," Columbia Law School Ira M. Millstein Center, n.d., https://millstein.law.columbia.edu/content/about-center.
16. "Corporate Governance Legend Ira M. Millstein Dies at 97," Weil, Gotshal & Manges LLP, March 14, 2024, https://www.weil.com/articles/corporate-governance-legend-ira-m-millstein-dies-at-97; Sam Roberts, "Ira M. Millstein, Corporate Lawyer with Public Impact, Dies at 97," *New York Times*, March 14, 2024, https://www.nytimes.com/2024/03/14/nyregion/ira-millstein-dead.html?smid=em-share.
17. "Chairing the Board: The Case for Independent Leadership in Corporate North America," Millstein Center for Corporate Governance and Performance, 2009, https://scholarship.law.columbia.edu/global_markets_corporate_ownership/34.
18. "Chairing the Board."
19. "Requirements for Public Company Boards," Weil, January 3, 2022, https://www.weil.com/-/media/files/pdfs/2022/january/requirements_for_public_company_boards_including_ipo_transition_rules.pdf.
20. Vo, "To Be or Not to Be."
21. David DiMolfetta, "Facebook Faces Renewed Push to Split CEO, Chairman Roles amid Controversies," S&P Global Market Intelligence, October 14, 2021, https://www.spglobal.com/marketintelligence/en/news-insights/latest-news-headlines/facebook-faces-renewed-push-to-split-ceo-chairman-roles-amid-controversies-66913978.
22. Emily Glazer, "Shareholders Press Facebook for Governance Changes," *Wall Street Journal*, December 13, 2021, https://www.wsj.com/articles/shareholders-press-facebook-for-governance-changes-11639404002.
23. Glazer.
24. DiMolfetta, "Facebook Faces Renewed Push."
25. Noor Al-Sibai, "Many Facebook Shareholders Wish They Could Fire Mark Zuckerberg," Futurism, November 1, 2022, https://futurism.com/the-byte/facebook-shareholders-mark-zuckerberg-control.
26. Wachtell, Lipton, Rosen & Katz, "Nominating and Corporate Governance Committee Guide 2023."
27. Wachtell, Lipton, Rosen & Katz.

28 Joseph Mandato and William Devine, "Why the CEO Shouldn't Also Be the Board Chair," *Harvard Business Review*, March 4, 2020, https://hbr.org/2020/03/why-the-ceo-shouldnt-also-be-the-board-chair.

29 Leslie Josephs, "It's Not Just Boeing. More Companies Are Splitting CEO and Chairman Roles," CNBC, November 5, 2019, https://www.cnbc.com/2019/11/05/its-not-just-boeing-more-companies-are-splitting-ceo-and-chairman-roles.html.

30 Mandato and Devine, "Why the CEO."

31 Mandato and Devine.

32 Andrew Tangel, Sharon Terlep, and Alison Sider, "Airline CEOs Seek Meeting with Boeing Directors to Address Production Problems," *Wall Street Journal*, March 21, 2024, https://www.wsj.com/business/airlines/airline-ceos-seek-meeting-with-boeing-directors-to-address-production-problems-cb12e6d4?.

33 Mandato and Devine, "Why the CEO."

34 Wachtell, Lipton, Rosen & Katz, "Nominating and Corporate Governance Committee Guide 2023."

35 "United States Proxy Voting Guidelines Benchmark Policy Recommendations," ISS, January 9, 2025, https://www.issgovernance.com/file/policy/active/americas/US-Voting-Guidelines.pdf.

36 "In-Depth: Independent Board Chairman," Glass Lewis, March 2016, https://www.sec.gov/Archives/edgar/data/1048286/000119312522081138/d235712ddef14a.htm.

37 "The Role of the Board, Chairman and Non-executive Directors—the UK Corporate Governance Code," Pinsent Masons, January 2, 2010, https://www.pinsentmasons.com/out-law/guides/the-role-of-the-board-chairman-and-non-executive-directors--the-uk-corporate-governance-code.

38 Millstein Center for Corporate Governance and Performance, "Chairing the Board: The Case for Independent Leadership in Corporate North America," 2009.

39 Millstein Center for Corporate Governance and Performance.

40 Millstein Center for Corporate Governance and Performance.

41 "Corporate Governance," OECD, n.d., https://www.oecd.org/corporate/OECD-Corporate-Governance-Factbook.pdf.

42 Ryan Krause and Matthew Semadeni, "Apprentice, Departure, and Demotion: An Examination of the Three Types of CEO–Board

Chair Separation," *Academy of Management Journal* 56, no. 3 (2013): 805–26, http://dx.doi.org/10.5465/amj.2011.0121.

43 Jamie Dimon, "Chairman and CEO Letter to Shareholders: Annual Report 2023," JPMorganChase, April 8, 2024, https://reports.jpmorganchase.com/investor-relations/2023/ar-ceo-letters.htm.

44 David F. Larcker and Brian Tayan, "Chairman and CEO: The Controversy over Board Leadership Structure," Stanford Closer Look Series, June 24, 2016, https://www.gsb.stanford.edu/sites/default/files/publication-pdf/cgri-closer-look-58-independent-chair.pdf.

45 Matteo Tonello, "Separation of Chair and CEO Roles," Harvard Law School Forum on Corporate Governance, September 1, 2011, https://corpgov.law.harvard.edu/2011/09/01/separation-of-chair-and-ceo-roles/.

46 Tonello.

47 Dennis Carey, Ram Charan, Joseph E. Griesedieck, and Michael Useem, "Choosing a New Board Leader: Eight Questions," Knowledge at Wharton, March 7, 2023, https://knowledge.wharton.upenn.edu/article/choosing-a-new-board-leader-eight-questions/.

48 Larcker and Tayan, "Chairman and CEO."

49 Larcker and Tayan.

50 Michael Blanding, featuring Hubert Joly, "Best Buy: How Human Connection Saved a Failing Retailer," Harvard Business School, May 4, 2021, https://www.library.hbs.edu/working-knowledge/best-buy-how-human-connection-saved-a-failing-retailer.

51 Larcker and Tayan, "Chairman and CEO."

52 Mackenzie Weinger, "Dimon Keeps CEO, Chairman Titles," Politico, May 15, 2012, https://www.politico.com/story/2012/05/dimon-keeps-ceo-chairman-titles-076323.

53 Donal Griffin, "Stripping Dimon of Chairman Title Is 'Nuts,' Langone Says," Bloomberg, April 26, 2013, https://www.bloomberg.com/news/articles/2013-04-26/stripping-dimon-of-chairman-title-is-nuts-langone-says.

Chapter 6: Mergers, Acquisitions, and Sales of Companies

1 "Shareholder Litigation Involving Acquisitions of Public Companies," Cornerstone Research, 2019, https://www.cornerstone.com/

wp-content/uploads/2021/12/Shareholder-Litigation-Involving-Acquisitions-of-Public-Companies-2018.pdf.

2. Elizabeth Clark and Courtney Quirós, "The Last of Us: Mergers and Acquisitions Lawsuits in Decline," American Bar Association, May 30, 2023, https://www.americanbar.org/groups/litigation/resources/newsletters/class-actions-derivative-suits/last-us-mergers-acquisitions-lawsuits-decline/; "Securities Class Action Filings: 2023 Midyear Assessment," Cornerstone Research, 2023, https://www.cornerstone.com/wp-content/uploads/2023/07/Securities-Class-Action-Filings-2023-Midyear-Assessment.pdf.

3. Marina Martynova and Luc Renneboog, "A Century of Corporate Takeovers: What Have We Learned and Where Do We Stand?," ECGI, https://www.ecgi.global/sites/default/files/working_papers/documents/SSRN-id820984.pdf.

4. Martynova and Renneboog.

5. Emily Liner, "What's behind the All-Time High in M&A?," Harvard Law School Forum on Corporate Governance, March 16, 2016, https://corpgov.law.harvard.edu/2016/03/16/whats-behind-the-all-time-high-in-ma/.

6. Liner.

7. Sangjun Cho and Chune Young Chung, "Review of the Literature on Merger Waves," *Journal of Risk and Financial Management* 15, no. 10 (2022): 432, https://www.mdpi.com/1911-8074/15/10/432.

8. "United States—M&A Statistics," IMAA—Institute for Mergers, Acquisitions, and Alliances, December 20, 2024, https://imaa-institute.org/mergers-and-acquisitions-statistics/united-states-ma-statistics/.

9. "United States—M&A Statistics."

10. Berkeley Lovelace Jr., "Steve Case to AT&T: Learn from My AOL-Time Warner Failures," CNBC, June 13, 2018, https://www.cnbc.com/2018/06/13/steve-case-to-att-learn-from-my-aol-time-warner-failures.html.

11. Bruce Nelan, "Felix Rohatyn, Wall Street Wizard Who Helped Save NYC From Bankruptcy, Dies at 91," *Washington Post*, December 14, 2019, https://www.washingtonpost.com/local/obituaries/felix-rohatyn-wall-street-wizard-who-helped-save-nyc-from-bankruptcy-dies-at-91/2019/12/14/41f880fe-1ebe-11ea-87f7-f2e91143c60d_story.html.

12 Sewell Chan, "Felix G. Rohatyn, Financier Who Piloted New York's Rescue, Dies at 91," *New York Times*, December 23, 2019, https://www.nytimes.com/2019/12/14/nyregion/felix-rohatyn-dead.html.
13 *Smith v. Van Gorkom*, 488 A.2d 858 (Del. 1985).
14 *Smith v. Van Gorkom*.
15 *Smith v. Van Gorkom*.
16 *Smith v. Van Gorkom*.
17 *Smith v. Van Gorkom*.
18 *Smith v. Van Gorkom*.
19 *Smith v. Van Gorkom*.
20 *Smith v. Van Gorkom*.
21 *Smith v. Van Gorkom*.
22 *Smith v. Van Gorkom*.
23 *Smith v. Van Gorkom*.
24 Stephen A. Radin, "The Director's Duty of Care Three Years after Smith v. Van Gorkom," *Hastings Law Journal* 39 (1988), https://repository.uchastings.edu/hastings_law_journal/vol39/iss3/9.
25 Radin.
26 Radin.
27 Bernard S. Sharfman, "The Enduring Legacy of Smith v. Van Gorkom," *Delaware Journal of Corporate Law* 33, no. 2 (2008): 287–309, October 7, 2008, https://ssrn.com/abstract=1059962.
28 Sharfman.
29 Radin, "Director's Duty of Care."
30 John A. Humbach, "Director Liability for Corporate Crimes: Lawyers as Safe Haven?," *New York Law School Law Review* 55 (2010), http://digitalcommons.pace.edu/lawfaculty/650/.
31 Jacob Bernstein, "The Debt King," *New York Times*, January 11, 2022, https://www.nytimes.com/2022/01/07/style/ron-perelman.html; Tom Maloney, "Ron Perelman's Empire Loses Crown Jewel as Revlon Goes Bankrupt," Bloomberg, June 17, 2022, https://www.bloomberg.com/news/articles/2022-06-17/ron-perelman-s-empire-loses-crown-jewel-as-revlon-goes-bankrupt?embedded-checkout=true; Carlie Porterfield, "Collector Ron Perelman Sold $963m Worth of Art to Pay Off Debt," The Art Newspaper—International Art News and Events, May 22, 2024, https://www.theartnewspaper.com/2024/05/22/collector-ron-perelman-sold-963m-worth-of-art-to-pay-off-debt.

32 Bernstein, "Debt King."
33 Bernstein.
34 *Revlon, Inc. v. MacAndrews & Forbes Holdings*, 506 A.2d 173 (1986).
35 Julian Velasco, "Just Do It: An Antidote to the Poison Pill," *Emory Law Journal* 52 (2003), https://scholarship.law.nd.edu/law_faculty_scholarship/103.
36 Kris Frieswick, "Poison Pill Popping," *CFO*, October 15, 2001, https://www.cfo.com/news/poison-pill-popping/682610/.
37 Guhan Subramanian, "A New Era for Raiders," *Harvard Business Review*, November 2010, https://hbr.org/2010/11/a-new-era-for-raiders.
38 Charles M. Nathan, "Triggering a Poison Pill," Harvard Law School Forum on Corporate Governance, April 11, 2009, https://corpgov.law.harvard.edu/2009/04/11/triggering-a-poison-pill/.
39 Scott J. Davis, "Delaware Supreme Court Upholds Poison Pill in Versata," Harvard Law School Forum on Corporate Governance, October 19, 2010, https://corpgov.law.harvard.edu/2010/10/19/delaware-supreme-court-upholds-poison-pill-in-versata/.
40 Subramanian, "New Era for Raiders."
41 "Corporate America's Medicine against Coronavirus," Deal Point Data, March 20, 2020, https://www.dealpointdata.com/res/dpd_coronavirus_corp_america_03202020.pdf.
42 Shira Ovide, "Marty Lipton: Why I Invented the Poison Pill," *Wall Street Journal*, December 29, 2010, https://www.wsj.com/articles/BL-DLB-30356.
43 Zachary Gubler, "What's the Deal with Revlon?," *Indiana Law Journal* 96, no. 2 (2021), https://www.repository.law.indiana.edu/ilj/vol96/iss2/3.
44 Gubler.
45 Robert J. Cole, "High-Stakes Drama at Revlon," *New York Times*, November 11, 1985, https://www.nytimes.com/1985/11/11/business/high-stakes-drama-at-revlon.html.
46 Cole.
47 Sujeet Indap, "Revlon to Leave Bankruptcy without Longtime Owner Ron Perelman," *Financial Times*, April 3, 2023, https://www.ft.com/content/2b54fb24-d6ba-4114-94ec-db40e485a037.
48 Clark W. Furlow, "Reflections on the Revlon Doctrine," *University of Pennsylvania Journal of Business Law* 11 (2009), https://scholarship.law.upenn.edu/jbl/vol11/iss3/1.

49 "Takeover Law and Practice," Wachtell, Lipton, Rosen & Katz, 2022, https://www.wlrk.com/webdocs/wlrknew/ClientMemos/WLRK/WLRK.28044.22.pdf.
50 "Takeover Law and Practice."
51 Gubler, "What's the Deal with Revlon?"
52 "Takeover Law and Practice."
53 *Moran v. Household Intern., Inc.*, 500 A.2d 1346 (Del. 1985).
54 Leslie Picker, "Why Airgas Was Finally Sold, for $10 Billion Instead of $5 Billion," *New York Times*, September 5, 2016, https://www.nytimes.com/2016/09/06/business/dealbook/why-airgas-was-finally-sold-for-10-billion-instead-of-5-billion.html.
55 Bob Fernandez, "Newest Purchase by Airgas Is a Packaged-Gas Business," *Philadelphia Inquirer*, April 3, 2007, https://www.inquirer.com/philly/business/20070403_Newest_purchase_by_Airgas_is_a_packaged-gas_business.html.
56 Picker, "Why Airgas."
57 Potter Anderson & Corroon LLP, "Air Products and Chemicals, Inc. V. Airgas, Inc," Lexology, March 3, 2011, https://www.lexology.com/library/detail.aspx?g=9b54dff2-5701-4d30-8d19-ca7526ef348c.
58 David Carnevali and Anirban Sen, "PGT Rebuffs Latest $2.2 Bln Bid from Koch-Backed Miter Brands—Sources," Yahoo Finance, December 13, 2023, https://finance.yahoo.com/news/pgt-rebuffs-latest-2-2-171106212.html.
59 *Corwin v. KKR Financial Holdings LLC*, 125 A.3d 304.
60 *Corwin v. KKR*.
61 Oderah Nwaeze, "The Corporate Guide: Stockholders Demanding Corporate Records? What You Should Know," JD Supra, January 21, 2022, https://www.jdsupra.com/legalnews/the-corporate-guide-stockholders-4897031/.
62 *Lavin v. West Corporation*, C.A. No. 2017-0547-JRS (Del. Ch. December 29, 2017).
63 *Lavin v. West Corporation*.
64 Brent J. Horton, "Terra Incognita: Applying the Entire Fairness Standard of Review to Benefit Corporations," *University of Pennsylvania Journal of Business Law* 22, no. 4 (2020), https://scholarship.law.upenn.edu/cgi/viewcontent.cgi?article=1611&context=jbl.
65 Horton.

66 *Gottlieb v. Heyden Chemical Corporation*, 33 Del. Ch. 177 (Del. 1952) 91 A.2d 57.
67 *Weinberger v. UOP, Inc.*, 457 A.2d 701 (Del. 1983)
68 Horton, "Terra Incognita."
69 "Takeover Law and Practice."
70 *In re MFW Shareholders Litigation*, Court of Chancery of the State of Delaware, May 29, 2013, 67 A.3d 496 (Del. Ch. 2013)
71 "Takeover Law and Practice."
72 Emily Sanders Hopkins, "Charles Dyson: Financier, Philanthropist," *Ezra Magazine* 3, no. 1 (Fall 2010), https://ezramagazine.cornell.edu/FALL10/worthsupporting1.html.
73 Daniel Gross and Forbes Magazine, *Forbes Greatest Business Stories of All Time* (New York: John Wiley, 1996).
74 Arleen Jacobius, "KKR Reports $601 Billion in AUM, up 16% Year-over-Year, with Flagships Now Minority of Fundraising," Pensions & Investments, August 1, 2024, https://www.pionline.com/money-managers/kkr-reports-601-billion-aum-16-year-over-year-flagships-now-minority-fundraising; "KKR Private Equity," KKR, 2025, https://www.kkr.com/invest/private-equity.
75 Leslie M. Smith, "Private Equity's Growing Role in M&A Has Clear Benefits," Dentons, August 7, 2023, https://www.dentons.com/en/insights/articles/2023/august/7/private-equitys-growing-role-in-m-and-a-has-clear-benefits.
76 Ellen Carr, "The New LBO Market: It's Gone Private," *Financial Times*, February 24, 2023, https://www.ft.com/content/0758d47f-ed50-47b5-bea1-20946271bc6a.
77 Kate Briquelet, "Leon Black Finally Opens Up about His Pal Jeffrey Epstein," Daily Beast, September 19, 2024, https://www.thedailybeast.com/leon-black-finally-opens-up-about-his-pal-jeffrey-epstein/.
78 John Plender, "Private Equity Faces a Reckoning," *Financial Times*, November 11, 2023, https://www.ft.com/content/b27e7a59-d319-4f84-bf4a-a3659efd725b.
79 "The Truth Revealed: Private Markets Beats Public Markets—Even after Fees," Hamilton Lane, May 18, 2023, https://www.hamiltonlane.com/en-us/insight/truths-revealed/private-beats-public.
80 Plender, "Private Equity."
81 Andrew R. Brownstein, Benjamin M. Roth, and Elina Tetelbaum, "Use of Special Committees in Conflict Transactions," Harvard

Law School Forum on Corporate Governance, September 23, 2019, https://corpgov.law.harvard.edu/2019/09/23/use-of-special-committees-in-conflict-transactions/.
82 Peter Howson, *Due Diligence: The Critical Stage in Mergers & Acquisitions* (London: Routledge, 2017).
83 Patrick A. Gaughan *Mergers, Acquisitions, and Corporate Restructurings*, 4th ed. (Hoboken: John Wiley & Sons, 2007).
84 Joshua Rosenbaum and Joshua Pearl, *Investment Banking: Valuation, Leveraged Buyouts, and Mergers & Acquisitions* (Hoboken: Wiley, 2013).
85 John C. Coates IV, "M&A Contracts: Purposes, Types, Regulation, and Patterns of Practice" (ECGI Working Paper Series in Law, working paper no. 292/2015, May 2015), https://www.ecgi.global/sites/default/files/working_papers/documents/SSRN-id2593866.pdf.
86 Alexandra Reed Lajoux, *The Art of M&A*, 5th ed. (New York: McGraw Hill, 2019).
87 Steve Kaplan, "Forget What You've Read: Most Mergers Create Value," *Chicago Booth Review*, May 21, 2016, https://www.chicagobooth.edu/review/forget-what-youve-read-most-mergers-create-value.
88 Kaplan.
89 Marc Goedhart, Tim Koller, and David Wessels, "The Six Types of Successful Acquisitions," McKinsey & Company, May 10, 2017, https://www.mckinsey.com/capabilities/strategy-and-corporate-finance/our-insights/the-six-types-of-successful-acquisitions.
90 Andrew Ross Sorkin et al., "Jamie Dimon Issues an Economic Warning," *New York Times*, April 8, 2024, https://www.nytimes.com/2024/04/08/business/dealbook/jamie-dimon-economy-inflation-letter.html.
91 Sorkin et al.

Chapter 7: The Rising Influence of Activist Investors

1 Emma Sjöström, "Shareholder Activism for Corporate Social Responsibility: What Do We Know?," Wiley Online Library, June 13, 2008, https://onlinelibrary.wiley.com/doi/abs/10.1002/sd.361.
2 David Kostin and Jenny Ma, "Shareholder Activism: What Investors Seek, Which Companies Are Targeted, and How Stocks Perform," Harvard Law School Forum on Corporate Governance, May 30, 2023, https://corpgov.law.harvard.edu/2023/05/30/shareholder

-activism-what-investors-seek-which-companies-are-targeted-and-how-stocks-perform/.
3 Kostin and Ma.
4 Steve Klemash and David Hunker, "What Boards Need to Know about Shareholder Activism," Harvard Law School Forum on Corporate Governance, April 3, 2021, https://corpgov.law.harvard.edu/2021/04/03/what-boards-need-to-know-about-shareholder-activism/.
5 Adam Kommel, Arun Verma, and Ken Kohn, "Bloomberg Activism Screening Model," Harvard Law School Forum on Corporate Governance, February 20, 2021, https://corpgov.law.harvard.edu/2021/02/20/bloomberg-activism-screening-model.
6 Svea Herbst-Bayliss, "Activist Hedge Fund Marcato Capital to Shut Down after Drop in Assets," Reuters, December 22, 2019, https://www.reuters.com/article/us-hedgefunds-marcato/activist-hedge-fund-marcato-capital-to-shut-down-after-drop-in-assets-idUSKBN1YQ0LW.
7 "Corrected-Update 2-Lear Settles with Activist Investors, to Boost Buybacks," Reuters, April 1, 2013, https://www.reuters.com/article/lear-marcato/corrected-update-2-lear-settles-with-activist-investors-to-boost-buybacks-idUSL3N0CO1QU20130401.
8 Jeff Bennett and David Benoit, "Activist Investor Urges Auto Parts Maker Lear to Split Up," *Wall Street Journal*, February 3, 2015, https://www.wsj.com/articles/activist-investor-urges-auto-parts-maker-lear-to-split-up-1423000727.
9 Nathan Bomey, "Lear Makes Move after Activist Investor's Maneuver," *Detroit Free Press*, February 17, 2015, https://www.freep.com/story/money/cars/2015/02/17/lear-share-buyback-dividend-mick-mcguire/23542259/.
10 Jeff Gramm, "The Activist Playbook Is Nearly 90 Years Old—and the First Chapter Was Written by Warren Buffett's Mentor," Business Insider, June 16, 2016, https://www.businessinsider.com/benjamin-graham-was-the-first-shareholder-activist-2016-6.
11 Walter Frick, "The Case for Activist Investors," *Harvard Business Review*, March 2016, https://hbr.org/2016/03/the-case-for-activist-investors.
12 Frick.
13 Frick.

14 Douglas Martin, "John J. Gilbert Is Dead at 88; Gadfly at Corporate Meetings," *New York Times*, July 17, 2002, https://www.nytimes.com/2002/07/17/business/john-j-gilbert-is-dead-at-88-gadfly-at-corporate-meetings.html.

15 Douglas.

16 J. Robert Brown, "Corporate Governance, Shareholder Proposals, and Engagement between Managers and Owners," *Denver Law Review Forum* 94, no. 36 (2017), https://digitalcommons.du.edu/cgi/viewcontent.cgi?article=1071&context=dlrforum.

17 Stuart L. Gillian and Laura T. Starks, "Corporate Governance Proposals and Shareholder Activism: The Role of Institutional Investors," *Journal of Financial Economics* 275 (2000).

18 "Unlocking Value: The Role of Activist Alternative Investment Managers," Simmons & Simmons, 2014.

19 "Unlocking Value."

20 Svea Herbst-Bayliss, "Activist Investors Enjoy Strong Rebound in '23, Gird for More Proxy Fights," Reuters, January 16, 2024, https://www.reuters.com/business/finance/activist-investors-enjoy-strong-rebound-23-gird-more-proxy-fights-2024-01-16/.

21 Malcolm McKenzie, "Activist Campaigns Outperform the Market When Targeting Operational Transformation," Alvarez & Marsal, October 8, 2020, https://www.alvarezandmarsal.com/insights/uk-activist-targets-outperform-despite-covid-19.

22 Mary Ann Deignan, Rich Thomas, and Kathryn Night, "Do Activists Beat the Market?," Harvard Law School Forum on Corporate Governance, August 1, 2023, https://corpgov.law.harvard.edu/2023/08/01/do-activists-beat-the-market/.

23 Deignan, Thomas, and Night.

24 Andrew Kutscher and Douglas Saper, "Enhancing Value or Stifling Innovation: Examining the Effects of Shareholder Activism and Its Impact on American Capitalism," Brown University, May 4, 2018, https://entrepreneurship.brown.edu/wp-content/uploads/2019/01/Kutscher-and-Saper_Final-Shareholder-Activism-Essay.pdf; Paolo Confino, "Satya Nadella's Triumphant Tenure Hits a New Peak as Microsoft Tops $3 Trillion in Market Value—Its Stock Is up 1,006% since He Took Over," *Fortune*, January 24, 2024, https://fortune.com/2024/01/24/microsoft-3-trillion-market-capitalization-ceo-satya-nadella-apple-rivalry/.

25 Nicole Norfleet, "It's Over: Ackman Sells His Target Shares," *Minnesota Star Tribune*, May 17, 2011, https://www.startribune.com/it-s-over-ackman-sells-his-target-shares/121994259/.
26 Joe Nocera, "Investor Exits and Leaves Puzzlement," *New York Times*, May 29, 2009, https://www.nytimes.com/2009/05/30/business/30nocera.html.
27 "Carl Icahn: The Icahn Lift Documentary with 60 Minutes," Investing Principle, December 18, 2018, https://www.youtube.com/watch?v=02xY5M8v5jo.
28 iBillionaire Capital, "Carl Icahn's History with Netflix," Medium, July 1, 2015, https://medium.com/ibillionaire/carl-icahns-history-with-netflix-3c7e25a9ce6e.
29 Nathan Bomey, "Carl Icahn Failed to Disclose Stock Collateral, SEC Charges," Axios, August 19, 2024, https://www.axios.com/2024/08/19/carl-icahn-stock-sec-charges-settlement; Niket Nishant, "Carl Icahn's Firm Cuts Dividend in Half after Short-Seller Attack, Shares Slump," Reuters, August 4, 2023, https://www.reuters.com/business/finance/carl-icahns-investment-firm-cuts-dividend-months-after-hindenburg-report-2023-08-04/.
30 Christiaan Hetzner, "Hedge Fund Billionaire Bill Ackman Goes for the Jugular with His Archrival Carl Icahn on the Ropes, Comparing His Firm to the Infamous Implosion of Archegos," Yahoo Finance, May 25, 2023, https://finance.yahoo.com/news/hedge-fund-billionaire-bill-ackman-132557971.html.
31 Yvan Allaire and François Dauphin, "A 'Successful' Case of Activism at the Canadian Pacific Railway: Lessons in Corporate Governance," Harvard Law School Forum on Corporate Governance, December 23, 2016, https://corpgov.law.harvard.edu/2016/12/23/a-successful-case-of-activism-at-the-canadian-pacific-railway-lessons-in-corporate-governance/.
32 Zaw Thiha Tun, "Bill Ackman's Greatest Hits and Misses," Investopedia, June 25, 2019, https://www.investopedia.com/articles/investing/032216/bill-ackmans-greatest-hits-and-misses.asp.
33 William D. Cohan, "Starboard Value's Jeff Smith: The Investor CEOs Fear Most," *Fortune*, December 3, 2014, https://fortune.com/2014/12/03/starboard-capitals-jeff-smith-activist-investor-darden-restaurants/.
34 Emily Stewart, "Peltz Says He's No Activist; Discovers Power of Cheeseburger," The Deal, June 8, 2016, https://thedealnewsroom

.tumblr.com/post/145609711857/peltz-says-hes-no-activist-discovers-power-of.
35 Siddharth Cavale, "Nelson Peltz Revives Campaign to Split up PepsiCo," Reuters, February 20, 2014, https://www.reuters.com/article/us-peltz-pepsico-idUSBREA1J0B720140220.
36 Leslie Picker, "Billionaire Investor Nelson Peltz Sells Stake in PepsiCo," *New York Times*, May 14, 2016, https://www.nytimes.com/2016/05/14/business/dealbook/billionaire-investor-nelson-peltz-sells-stake-in-pepsico.html.
37 Michelle Celarier, "SEC Tightens 13D Disclosure Rules—and Throws Swaps into the Mix," *Institutional Investor*, October 11, 2023, https://www.institutionalinvestor.com/article/2cb1rsku6c8u09zfxo5q8/culture/sec-tightens-13d-disclosure-rules-and-throws-swaps-into-the-mix.
38 Andrew Ackerman, "SEC Rule Change Could Ease Path for Activist Investors to Gain Seats on Corporate Boards," *Wall Street Journal*, November 17, 2021, https://www.wsj.com/articles/sec-corporate-board-universal-ballot-11637164553.
39 "5 Trends in Shareholder Activism That Have Emerged in 2023," Barclays, July 19, 2023, https://www.cib.barclays/our-insights/5-trends-in-shareholder-activism-that-have-emerged-in-2023.html.
40 "Shareholder Activism Update: Early Look at 2023 Trends," Lazard, April 18, 2023, https://www.lazard.com/research-insights/shareholder-activism-update-early-look-at-2023-trends.
41 Jody Foldesy, Gregory Rice, and Simon Weinstein, "To Defeat an Activist Investor, Think Like One," BCG Global, April 28, 2021, https://www.bcg.com/publications/2021/strategies-for-managing-activist-investors.
42 Deignan, Thomas, and Night, "Do Activists Beat the Market?"
43 "2019 Annual Activism Survey: Active Managers and Activism," SquareWell Partners, 2019, https://squarewell-partners.com/wp-content/uploads/2018/07/2019-SquareWell-Survey-Active-Managers-and-Activism-1.pdf.
44 David Benoit, "Activism's Long Road from Corporate Raiding to Banner Year," *Wall Street Journal*, December 26, 2015, https://www.wsj.com/articles/activisms-long-road-from-corporate-raiding-to-banner-year-1451070910.

45 "Annual Review of Shareholder Activism 2023," Lazard, January 8, 2024, https://www.lazard.com/research-insights/annual-review-of-shareholder-activism-2023/.

46 Andrew Baker, David F. Larcker, Brian Tayan, and Derek Zaba, "The Evolving Battlefronts of Shareholder Activism" (Rock Center for Corporate Governance at Stanford University working paper, March 6, 2023), https://ssrn.com/abstract=4380801.

47 Michael J. De La Merced, "Disney Gains Support from ValueAct Capital as Nelson Peltz Challenges Board," *New York Times*, January 3, 2024, https://www.nytimes.com/2024/01/03/business/dealbook/disney-valueact-nelson-peltz.html.

48 Lauren Thomas, "The Priciest Shareholder Fight Ever Is Headed to Disney's Boardroom," *Wall Street Journal*, February 11, 2024, https://www.wsj.com/business/deals/disney-investors-stock-shareholders-2bb7382d.

49 "Berry Global Announces Appointment of Three New Directors and Forms Capital Allocation Committee," Business Wire, November 23, 2022, https://www.businesswire.com/news/home/20221122005901/en/Berry-Global-Announces-Appointment-of-Three-New-Directors-and-Forms-Capital-Allocation-Committee.

50 Alexandra Stevenson, "Activist Hedge Fund Starboard Succeeds in Replacing Darden Board," *New York Times*, October 10, 2014, https://archive.nytimes.com/dealbook.nytimes.com/2014/10/10/activist-hedge-fund-starboard-succeeds-in-replacing-darden-board/.

51 Stevenson.

52 Stevenson.

53 Joseph Guinto, "Who Wrecked J.C. Penney?" D Magazine, October 16, 2013, https://www.dmagazine.com/publications/d-ceo/2013/november/who-wrecked-jc-penney/.

54 "An Investor Calls," *Economist*, February 5, 2015, https://www.economist.com/briefing/2015/02/05/an-investor-calls.

55 David Benoit and Vipal Monga, "Are Activist Investors Helping or Undermining American Companies?," *Wall Street Journal*, October 5, 2015, https://www.wsj.com/articles/activist-investors-helping-or-hindering-1444067712.

56 Kevin Helliker, "Europe Courts Marty Lipton," Brunswick, March 7, 2018, https://www.brunswickgroup.com/marty-lipton-lawyer-i7277/.

57 Leo E. Strine Jr., "Who Bleeds When the Wolves Bite? A Flesh-and-Blood Perspective on Hedge Fund Activism and Our Strange Corporate Governance System," *Yale Law Journal* 126, no. 6 (2017), https://www.yalelawjournal.org/feature/who-bleeds-when-the-wolves-bite-a-flesh-and-blood-perspective-on-hedge-fund-activism-and-our-strange-corporate-governance-system.

58 Program on Corporate Governance, Harvard Law School, February 2025, https://pcg.law.harvard.edu.

59 "Why Activists Are So Active, and What to Do Now," Corporate Board Member e-newsletter, September 29, 2023.

60 "SRP Media Releases," Shareholder Rights Project at Harvard Law School, n.d., http://www.srp.law.harvard.edu/communications.shtml.

61 "Corporate Governance and Staggered Boards: Trends and Analysis," Star Equity Fund, n.d., https://www.sec.gov/Archives/edgar/data/1600422/000092189522001556/ex995to13da109271001_051022.pdf.

62 Lynn S. Paine and Will Hurwitz, "Brief Note on Staggered Boards," Faculty & Research, Harvard Business School, December 2022, https://www.hbs.edu/faculty/Pages/item.aspx?num=63294.

63 "Proposal to Repeal Classified Board," Shareholder Rights Project at Harvard Law School, n.d., http://www.srp.law.harvard.edu/Template-Proposal.pdf.

64 Lucian A. Bebchuk, John C. Coates, and Guhan Subramanian, "The Powerful Antitakeover Force of Staggered Boards: Theory, Evidence, and Policy," *Stanford Law Review* 54 (2002): 887–951, https://ssrn.com/abstract=304388.

65 Ryan Derousseau, "Why 'Staggered' Boards Are Paying off for Stock Investors," *Fortune*, April 30, 2019, https://fortune.com/2019/04/30/staggered-boards-stock-investors/.

66 Yakov Amihud, Markus Schmid, and Steven D. Solomon, "Settling the Staggered Board Debate," *University of Pennsylvania Law Review* 166 (2018), https://scholarship.law.upenn.edu/penn_law_review/vol166/iss6/3.

67 Lyuba Goltser, Kaitlin Descovich, Bianca Lazar, and Julie Rong, "Governance and Securities Alert," Weil, 2023, https://www.weil.com/-/media/files/pdfs/2022/december/alert_2023_iss_and_gl_voting_policy_updates.pdf.

68 Rosa A. Testani et al., "Proxy Advisory Firms Issue 2023 Voting Guidelines," Akin Gump Strauss Hauer & Feld LLP, February 6, 2023, https://www.akingump.com/en/insights/alerts/proxy-advisory-firms-issue-2023-voting-guidelines.

69 "2022 Policy Guidelines," Glass Lewis, 2022, https://resources.glasslewis.com/hubfs/2023%20Guidelines/2023%20United%20States%20Benchmark%20Policy%20Guidelines.pdf.

70 Emiliano M. Catan and Marcel Kahan, "The Never-Ending Quest for Shareholder Rights: Special Meetings and Written Consent," *Boston University Law Review* 99, no. 3 (2019): 743–86, https://www.bu.edu/bulawreview/files/2019/06/CATAN-KAHAN.pdf.

71 "Delaware Courts Provide Guidance on Advance Notice Bylaws," Paul, Weiss, February 5, 2024, https://www.paulweiss.com/practices/transactional/mergers-acquisitions/publications/delaware-courts-provide-guidance-on-advance-notice-bylaws?id=50152.

72 Catan and Kahan, "Never-Ending Quest."

Chapter 8: The Growing Impact of Institutional Investors

1 Simon Glossner, Pedro Matos, Stefano Ramelli, and Alexander F. Wagner, "Do Institutional Investors Stabilize Equity Markets in Crisis Periods? Evidence from COVID-19," Swiss Finance Institute Research Paper No. 20-56, European Corporate Governance Institute—Finance Working Paper No. 688/2020, February 20, 2024, https://ssrn.com/abstract=3655271.

2 John Coates, *The Problem of Twelve: When a Few Financial Institutions Control Everything* (New York: Columbia Global Reports, 2023).

3 Coates.

4 Claire Donnelly and Meghna Chakrabarti, "Are Index Funds Getting Too Powerful?," *On Point*, WBUR.Org, August 7, 2023, https://www.wbur.org/onpoint/2023/08/07/how-index-funds-are-shaping-corporations-and-the-american-economy.

5 Coates, *Problem of Twelve*.

6 Jonathan Lewellen and Katharina Lewellen, "Institutional Investors and Corporate Governance: The Incentive to Increase Value," Tuck School of Business at Dartmouth, May 2018, https://faculty.tuck.dartmouth.edu/images/uploads/faculty/katharina-lewellen/Institutional_incentives_5_2018.pdf.

7   Lewellen and Lewellen.
8   Lucian A. Bebchuk, Alma Cohen, and Scott Hirst, "The Agency Problems of Institutional Investors," *Journal of Economic Perspectives* 31, no. 3 (Summer 2017), https://pubs.aeaweb.org/doi/pdfplus/10.1257/jep.31.3.89.
9   Bebchuk, Cohen, and Hirst.
10 Bebchuk, Cohen, and Hirst.
11 Matt Krantz, "One Investor Is the Largest Owner of Two-Thirds of U.S. Companies," Investor's Business Daily, August 15, 2022, https://www.investors.com/etfs-and-funds/sectors/sp500-one-investor-is-the-largest-owner-of-two-thirds-of-u-s-companies/.
12 "Private Pension Plan Bulletin Historical Tables and Graphs, 1975–2022," US Department of Labor, Employee Benefits Security Administration, September 2024, https://www.dol.gov/sites/dolgov/files/ebsa/researchers/statistics/retirement-bulletins/private-pension-plan-bulletin-historical-tables-and-graphs.pdf.
13 "L.120.B State and Local Government Employee Retirement Funds: Defined Benefit Plans," Financial Accounts Guide, Board of Governors of the Federal Reserve System, n.d., https://www.federalreserve.gov/apps/fof/DisplayTable.aspx?t=l.120.b.
14 Stuart Gillan and Laura Starks, "Corporate Governance Proposals and Shareholder Activism: The Role of Institutional Investors," *Journal of Financial Economics*, 57 (2000), https://mx.nthu.edu.tw/~jtyang/Teaching/Corporate_Governance/Papers/Gillan,%20Stark%202000.pdf.
15 Paul N. Watkins and Kathleen Barceleau, "The 30-Year History of Diluting ERISAu2019s Fiduciary Duty," *Federalist Society* 25 (January 16, 2024), https://fedsoc.org/fedsoc-review/the-30-year-history-of-diluting-erisa-s-fiduciary-duty.
16 Kurt N. Schacht and Karina Karakulova, "The Department of Labor Carpet Bombs Investor Protection," Blue Sky Blog, September 29, 2020, https://clsbluesky.law.columbia.edu/2020/09/29/the-department-of-labor-carpet-bombs-investor-protection/.
17 "The Deals Decade: Rise of Institutional Investors," Securities and Exchange Commission Historical Society, the Center for Audit Quality Gallery on Corporate Governance, n.d., https://www.sechistorical.org/museum/galleries/caq/caq04b_rise_of_institutional_investors.php.

18 "Deals Decade."
19 "Deals Decade."
20 Editorial Board, "Cracking the Proxy Advisory Duopoly," *Wall Street Journal*, July 12, 2023, https://www.wsj.com/articles/proxy-advisory-firms-glass-lewis-institutional-shareholder-services-esg-investing-761e044f; Ike Brannon, "Diminishing the Power of Proxy Advisory Firms," Capital Policy Analytics, n.d., https://www.sec.gov/comments/s7-22-19/s72219-6702944-206071.pdf.
21 Coates, *Problem of Twelve*.
22 Coates.
23 "Vanguard Announces the Passing of Founder John C. Bogle," Vanguard, press release, January 16, 2019, https://corporate.vanguard.com/content/corporatesite/us/en/corp/who-we-are/pressroom/Press-Release-Vanguard-Announces-Passing-Of-Founder-Jack-Bogle-011619.html.
24 Knowledge at Wharton Staff, "Farewell, John Bogle: A Tribute to the Father of Indexing," Knowledge at Wharton, January 17, 2019, https://knowledge.wharton.upenn.edu/article/farewell-john-bogle-tribute-father-indexing/.
25 Warren Buffett, "Words of Praise: Warren Buffett on Jack Bogle," A Simple Model, July 7, 2022, https://www.asimplemodel.com/bips/bip-feed/words-of-praise-warren-buffett-on-jack-bogle.
26 Coates, *Problem of Twelve*.
27 Caleb Griffin, "Margins: Estimating the Influence of the Big Three on Shareholder Proposals," *SMU Law Review* 73, no. 3 (2020), https://scholar.smu.edu/smulr/vol73/iss3/6.
28 Griffin.
29 Griffin.
30 Caleb Griffin, "We Three Kings: Disintermediating Voting at the Index Fund Giants," *Maryland Law Review* 79 (2020), https://ssrn.com/abstract=3365222.
31 Griffin, "Margins."
32 Griffin.
33 John C. Bogle, "Bogle Sounds a Warning on Index Funds," *Wall Street Journal*, November 29, 2018, https://www.wsj.com/articles/bogle-sounds-a-warning-on-index-funds-1543504551.
34 Farhad Manjoo, "What BlackRock, Vanguard and State Street Are Doing to the Economy," *New York Times*, May 12, 2022, https://www

.nytimes.com/2022/05/12/opinion/vanguard-power-blackrock-state-street.html.
35 Andrea Pawliczek, Ashley Nicole Skinner, and Laura Wellman, "A New Take on Voice: The Influence of BlackRock's 'Dear CEO' Letters," SSRN, January 2021, https://ssrn.com/abstract=3763042.
36 Pawliczek, Skinner, and Wellman.
37 "Meet Our Company," State Street, n.d., https://www.statestreet.com/us/en/asset-manager/about/our-story.
38 Jeremy W. Peters, "State Street to Acquire Investors Financial for $4.5 Billion," *New York Times*, February 6, 2007, https://www.nytimes.com/2007/02/06/business/06street.html.
39 "BlackRock 2004 Global Voting Spotlight," BlackRock Investment Stewardship, 2024, https://www.blackrock.com/corporate/literature/publication/2024-investment-stewardship-voting-spotlight.pdf.
40 "BlackRock 2004 Global Voting Spotlight."
41 "Investment Stewardship: 2023 Annual Report," Vanguard, 2024, https://corporate.vanguard.com/content/dam/corp/advocate/investment-stewardship/pdf/policies-and-reports/investment_stewardship_2023_annual_report.pdf.
42 "Asset Stewardship Report," State Street, n.d., https://www.ssga.com/us/en/institutional/ic/insights/asset-stewardship-report.
43 Lindsey Stewart, "How BlackRock, State Street, and Vanguard Cast Their ESG Proxy Votes," Morningstar, June 12, 2023, https://www.morningstar.com/sustainable-investing/how-blackrock-state-street-vanguard-cast-their-esg-proxy-votes.
44 "BlackRock Continues Expansion of Voting Choice to Retail Investors," Wachtell Memo, February 20, 2024.
45 Jim Woodrum, "How Can Boards Coexist with ISS and Glass Lewis?," Northwestern Kellogg, n.d., https://www.kellogg.northwestern.edu/executive-education/the-kellogg-experience/thought-leadership/iss-glass-lewis.aspx.
46 Woodrum.
47 Michelle Celarier, "The Mysterious Private Company Controlling Corporate America: How Eight Men inside a Maryland Office Park Decide the Fate of the Country's Greatest Companies," *Institutional Investor*, January 29, 2018, https://www.institutionalinvestor.com/article/2bsxtm9a2dyhr8r96cbnk/culture/the-mysterious-private-company-controlling-corporate-america.

48 Celarier.
49 David Larcker, Brian Tayan, and James R. Copland, "The Big Thumb on the Scale: An Overview of the Proxy Advisory Industry," Harvard Law School Forum on Corporate Governance, Manhattan institute, June 14, 2018, https://corpgov.law.harvard.edu/2018/06/14/the-big-thumb-on-the-scale-an-overview-of-the-proxy-advisory-industry/.
50 James R. Copland, David F. Larcker, and Brian Tayan, "Proxy Advisory Firms: Empirical Evidence and the Case for Reform," Manhattan Institute, n.d., https://media4.manhattan-institute.org/sites/default/files/R-JC-0518-v2.pdf.
51 "WSJ Editorial Board: Cracking the Proxy Advisory Duopoly," press release, House Committee on Financial Services, July 13, 2023, https://financialservices.house.gov/news/documentsingle.aspx?DocumentID=408911.
52 Musk quoted in Luc Olinga, "Elon Musk Accuses Two Influential Firms of Controlling the Stock Market," TheStreet, January 24, 2023, https://www.thestreet.com/technology/elon-musk-accuses-two-influential-firms-of-controlling-the-stock-market.
53 Larcker, Tayan, and Copland, "Big Thumb on the Scale."
54 Larcker, Tayan, and Copland.
55 Editorial Board, "Cracking the Proxy Advisory Duopoly."
56 Jamie Dimon, "Chairman and CEO Letter to Shareholders: Annual Report 2023," JPMorganChase, April 8, 2024, https://reports.jpmorganchase.com/investor-relations/2023/ar-ceo-letters.htm.
57 Neil Whoriskey, "The New Civil Code: ISS and Glass Lewis as Lawmakers," CLS Blue Sky Blog, July 28, 2020, https://clsbluesky.law.columbia.edu/2020/07/28/cleary-gottlieb-discusses-the-new-civil-code-of-iss-and-glass-lewis/.
58 Editorial Board, "Cracking the Proxy Advisory Duopoly."
59 Matthew Bultman, "AI Disclosures to SEC Jump as Agency Warns of Misleading Claims," Bloomberg Law, February 8, 2024, https://news.bloomberglaw.com/securities-law/ai-disclosures-to-sec-jump-as-agency-warns-of-misleading-claims.

Chapter 9: Distressed Companies and Financial Restructurings

1. David A. Skeel Jr., "An Evolutionary Theory of Corporate Law and Corporate Bankruptcy," *All Faculty Scholarship* 1300 (1998), https://scholarship.law.upenn.edu/faculty_scholarship/1300.
2. Skeel.
3. Skeel.
4. Stephen J. Lubben, "Railroad Receiverships and Modern Bankruptcy Theory," *Cornell Law Review* 89 (2004): 1420, https://scholarship.law.cornell.edu/clr/vol89/iss6/2.
5. Lubben, 1420.
6. Skeel, "Evolutionary Theory."
7. "Bankruptcy Law in the United States," Economic History Association, 2023, https://eh.net/encyclopedia/bankruptcy-law-in-the-united-states/.
8. "Bankruptcy Law in the United States."
9. Stephen J. Lubben, "Railroad Receiverships and Modern Bankruptcy Theory," *Cornell Law Review* 89, no. 6 (September 2004), https://scholarship.law.cornell.edu/cgi/viewcontent.cgi?article=2971&context=clr.
10. Mark A. Perelman, "A Bankruptcy History of Manias & Panics," Timeless Investor, n.d., https://www.timelessinvestor.com/wp-content/uploads/2020/06/SSRN-id3554155.pdf.
11. Skeel, "Evolutionary Theory."
12. Vincent L. Leibell Jr., "The Chandler Act—Its Effect upon the Law of Bankruptcy," *Fordham Law Review* 9 (1940), https://ir.lawnet.fordham.edu/flr/vol9/iss3/5.
13. Todd J. Zywicki, "The Past, Present, and Future of Bankruptcy Law in America," *Michigan Law Review* 101 (2003), https://repository.law.umich.edu/mlr/vol101/iss6/28.
14. Zywicki.
15. Zywicki.
16. Shira Ovide, "Art Newman, Founder of Blackstone's Restructuring Group, Dies," *Wall Street Journal*, December 16, 2010, https://www.wsj.com/articles/BL-DLB-29933.
17. "In Memoriam: Harvey R. Miller '59, Bankruptcy Law Pioneer, Devoted Alumnus, Respected Teacher," Columbia Law School, April 27, 2015,

https://www.law.columbia.edu/news/archive/memoriam-harvey-r-miller-59-bankruptcy-law-pioneer-devoted-alumnus-respected-teacher.

18 "In Memoriam: Harvey R. Miller (1933–2015)," Weil Restructuring, April 27, 2015, https://restructuring.weil.com/news/in-memoriam-harvey-r-miller-1933-2015/.

19 William J. Boyes and Roger L. Faith, "Some Effects of the Bankruptcy Reform Act of 1978," *Journal of Law & Economics* 29, no. 1 (1986): 139–49, https://www.jstor.org/stable/725405.

20 "Is The Latest Corporate Bankruptcy Strategy a Death Knell for Pensions?," Knowledge at Wharton, October 6, 2004, https://knowledge.wharton.upenn.edu/article/is-the-latest-corporate-bankruptcy-strategy-a-death-knell-for-pensions/.

21 "Certified Insolvency & Restructuring Advisor—CIRA," AIRA, n.d., https://www.aira.org/cira.

22 Patrick Drury Byrne et al., "Private Debt: A Lesser-Known Corner of Finance Finds the Spotlight," S&P Global, October 12, 2021, https://www.spglobal.com/en/research-insights/featured/special-editorial/private-debt.

23 "Understanding Private Credit," Morgan Stanley, n.d., https://www.morganstanley.com/ideas/private-credit-outlook-considerations.

24 "Citi and Apollo Announce $25 Billion Private Credit, Direct Lending Program," Citigroup press release, September 26, 2024, https://www.citigroup.com/global/news/press-release/2024/citi-and-apollo-announce-25-billion-private-credit-direct-lending-program.

25 "BlackRock to Acquire HPS Investment Partners to Deliver Integrated Solutions Across Public and Private Markets," Business Wire, December 3, 2024, https://www.businesswire.com/news/home/20241203219893/en/BlackRock-to-Acquire-HPS-Investment-Partners-to-Deliver-Integrated-Solutions-Across-Public-and-Private-Markets/.

26 Edith Hotchkiss, Karin S. Thorburn, and Wei Wang, "The Changing Face of Chapter 11 Bankruptcy: Insights from Recent Trends and Research," *Annual Review of Financial Economics* 15, no. 1 (November 1, 2023): 351–67, https://www.annualreviews.org/doi/full/10.1146/annurev-financial-100521-103241.

27 Alexander Gladstone, Andrew Scurria, and Akiko Matsuda, "This Judge Made Houston the Top Bankruptcy Court. Then He Helped His

Girlfriend Cash In," *Wall Street Journal*, June 19, 2024, https://www.wsj.com/finance/bankruptcy-court-houston-jones-freeman-dbba77e9.

28 Zee M. Kane, "Steve Jobs: Apple Was 90 Days from Going Bankrupt," TNW, June 2, 2010, https://thenextweb.com/news/steve-jobs-90-days.

29 Alyson Shontell, "The Amazing Story of How Steve Jobs Took Apple from Near Bankruptcy to Billions in 13 Years," Business Insider, January 19, 2011, https://www.businessinsider.com/how-steve-jobs-took-apple-from-near-bankruptcy-to-billions-in-13-years-2011-1#1997-partnering-with-the-enemy-microsoft-1.

30 Nick Whigham, "The Forgotten Microsoft Deal That Saved Apple from Bankruptcy," New Zealand Herald, August 4, 2020, https://www.nzherald.co.nz/business/the-forgotten-microsoft-deal-that-saved-apple-from-bankruptcy/QU3F4C5YHUQM5LAZSQ2JBF7DZQ/.

31 Lyle Daly, "The Largest Companies by Market Cap in January 2025," Motley Fool, January 6, 2025, https://www.fool.com/research/largest-companies-by-market-cap/.

32 Jason Roderick Donaldson, Edward R. Morrison, Giorgia Piacentino, and Xiaobo Yu, "Restructuring vs. Bankruptcy," Center for Law & Economic Studies, Columbia University, October 2, 2020, https://law-economic-studies.law.columbia.edu/sites/default/files/content/Morrison%20Donaldson%20Piacentino%20Yu%20-%20Restructuring%20vs%20Bankruptcy_BlueSky%20(rcvd%202020%2010%2002).pdf.

33 Kevin M. Lippman and Julian P. Vasek, "Workout Tactics and Other Strategies to Avoid Chapter 11 Bankruptcy," paper presented at the 37th Annual Jay L. Westbrook Bankruptcy Conference, November 15–16, 2018, Austin, Texas, https://www.munsch.com/portalresource/lookup/wosid/cp-base-4-20104/overrideFile.name=/Lippman_Vasek_Westbrook%20Paper%20-%20Bankruptcy%20Alternatives%20(final).pdf.

34 Sarah George, "Small Business Bankruptcies on the Rise," Yahoo Finance, December 7, 2023, https://finance.yahoo.com/news/small-business-bankruptcies-rise-190510936.html.

35 "Bankruptcy: What Happens When Public Companies Go Bankrupt," SEC, February 2, 2009, https://www.sec.gov/reportspubs/investor-publications/investorpubsbankrupt.

36 Hotchkiss, Thorburn, and Wang, "Changing Face of Chapter 11."

37 "Chapter 11—Bankruptcy Basics," United States Courts, n.d., https://www.uscourts.gov/services-forms/bankruptcy/bankruptcy-basics/chapter-11-bankruptcy-basics.
38 Lawrence V. Gelber and Erik Schneider, "Location, Location, Location—How to Choose a Bankruptcy Venue," DailyDAC, December 8, 2022, https://www.dailydac.com/where-to-file-bankruptcy/.
39 John D. Ayer, Michael Bernstein, and Jonathan Friedland, "Chapter 11 '101': An Overview of the Automatic Stay," American Bankruptcy Institute Journal, n.d., https://www.kirkland.com/siteFiles/kirkexp/publications/2430/Document1/Friedland%20-%20An%20Overview%20of%20the%20Automatic%20Stay.pdf.
40 "Chapter 11—Bankruptcy Basics."
41 Mike Harmon, "A Primer on Restructuring Your Company's Finances," *Harvard Business Review*, June 9, 2020, https://hbr.org/2020/06/a-primer-on-restructuring-your-companys-finances.
42 Hotchkiss, Thorburn, and Wang, "Changing Face of Chapter 11."
43 Hotchkiss, Thorburn, and Wang.
44 "Retention and Compensation of Professionals in Bankruptcy," Department of Justice, December 4, 2019, https://www.justice.gov/ust/Prof_Comp.
45 Rachel Reed, "Does Filing for Bankruptcy Make Employees Flee?," Harvard Law Today, September 20, 2023, https://hls.harvard.edu/today/does-filing-for-bankruptcy-make-employees-flee/.
46 Daniel Gal et al., "How Directors Can Manage the UK Supreme Court's 'Balancing Exercise' in Difficult Times," Skadden Insights, December 13, 2022, https://www.skadden.com/insights/publications/2022/12/2023-insights/a-possible-recession/how-directors-can-manage.
47 *North American Catholic Educational Programming Foundation, Inc. v. Gheewalla* (Del. Supr. 2007), https://casetext.com/case/nacepf-v-gheewalla.
48 Gal et al., "How Directors Can Manage."
49 Brad Eric Scheler, Gary L. Kaplan, and Jennifer L. Rodburg, "Director Fiduciary Duty in Insolvency," Harvard Law School Forum on Corporate Governance, April 15, 2020, https://corpgov.law.harvard.edu/2020/04/15/director-fiduciary-duty-in-insolvency/.
50 Scheler, Kaplan, and Rodburg.
51 Andrew Scurria and Jennifer Maloney, "Juul Adds Two Restructuring Experts to Its Board," *Wall Street Journal*, October 7, 2022, https://

www.wsj.com/articles/juul-adds-two-restructuring-experts-to-its-board-11665168669?st=14bg1vzd0f8end5&reflink=article_email_share.

52 Alexander Gladstone, Akiko Matsuda, and Konrad Putzier, "WeWork Taps Directors with Bankruptcy Chops after Board Resignations," *Wall Street Journal*, August 9, 2023, https://www.wsj.com/articles/wework-taps-directors-with-bankruptcy-chops-after-board-resignations-254aaca4.

53 Jared Ellias, Ehud Kamar, and Kobi Kastiel, "The Rise of Bankruptcy Directors," Harvard Law School Forum on Corporate Governance, February 14, 2022, https://corpgov.law.harvard.edu/2022/02/14/the-rise-of-bankruptcy-directors/.

54 Dietrich Knauth, "US Supreme Court's Alito Pauses Boy Scouts $2.46 Billion Abuse Settlement," Reuters, February 16, 2024, https://www.reuters.com/legal/us-supreme-courts-alito-temporarily-halts-boy-scouts-246-bln-abuse-settlement-2024-02-16/.

55 "Attorney General Formella Announces up to $6 Billion National Settlement with Purdue Pharma and Sacklers; New Hampshire to Receive $46 Million If Agreement Approved," New Hampshire Department of Justice, press release, March 3, 2022, https://www.doj.nh.gov/news/2022/20220303-settlement-purdue-pharma-sacklers.htm.

56 Abbie VanSickle, "At Core of Purdue Pharma Case: Who Can Get Immunity in Settlements?," *New York Times*, December 3, 2023, https://www.nytimes.com/2023/12/03/us/politics/oxycontin-supreme-court-purdue-sacklers.html.

57 Amy Howe, "Court Conflicted over Purdue Pharma Bankruptcy Plan That Shields Sacklers from Liability," SCOTUSblog, December 4, 2023, https://www.scotusblog.com/2023/12/purdue-bankruptcy-sacklers/#.

58 VanSickle, "At Core of Purdue."

59 VanSickle.

60 Abbie VanSickle, "Supreme Court Jeopardizes Purdue Pharma Deal, Rejecting Protections for Sacklers," *New York Times*, June 27, 2024, https://www.nytimes.com/2024/06/27/us/supreme-court-opioid-settlement.html.

61 *Harrington, United States Trustee, Region 2 v. Purdue Pharma L. P. et al.*, Certiorari to the United States Court of Appeals for the Second Circuit,

No. 23–124. Argued December 4, 2023—Decided June 27, 2024, https://www.supremecourt.gov/opinions/23pdf/23-124_8nk0.pdf.
62 *Harrington v. Purdue Pharma.*
63 "Purdue Pharma L. P. Files New Plan of Reorganization Providing for More Than $7.4 Billion in Creditor Distributions," Purdue Pharma, March 18, 2025, https://www.purduepharma.com/news/2025/03/18/purdue-pharma-l-p-files-new-plan-of-reorganization-providing-for-more-than-7-4-billion-in-creditor-distributions/.

Chapter 10: Environmental, Social, and Governance Issues

1 Minzhi (Luna) Wang, "Environmental, Social, and Corporate Governance: A History of ESG Standardization from 1970s to the Present," undergraduate senior thesis, Department of History, Columbia University, April 5, 2023, https://sites.asit.columbia.edu/historydept/wp-content/uploads/sites/29/2023/05/Wang-Luna_thesis.pdf.
2 Wang.
3 "Explore 30 Years of ESG," MSCI, n.d., https://www.msci.com/esg/30-years-of-esg.
4 "UNEP Statement of Commitment by Financial Institutions (FI) on Sustainable Development," UN Environment Programme, 1992, https://wedocs.unep.org/handle/20.500.11822/42662.
5 John Elkington, "25 Years Ago I Coined the Phrase 'Triple Bottom Line.' Here's Why It's Time to Rethink It.," *Harvard Business Review*, June 25, 2018, https://hbr.org/2018/06/25-years-ago-i-coined-the-phrase-triple-bottom-line-heres-why-im-giving-up-on-it.
6 Sandra Maria Barroca Silveira, "O Audiovisual como Recurso para Resgate Reputacional: A Teoria da Reparação da Imagem e o Discurso de Renovação na Comunicação ESG em Cenário Pós-crise," Programa de Pós-graduação em Comunicação Social—Interações Midiatizadas, Pontifícia Universidade Católica de Minas Gerais, 2022, note 28, https://bib.pucminas.br/teses/ComunicacaoSocial_SandraMariaBarrocaSilveira_30103_Textocompleto.pdf.
7 "What Are the Principles for Responsible Investment?," PRI, August 6, 2024, https://www.unpri.org/about-us/what-are-the-principles-for-responsible-investment.
8 Andrea Pawliczek, Ashley Nicole Skinner, and Laura Wellman, "A New Take on Voice: The Influence of BlackRock's 'Dear CEO' Letters," SSRN, January 2021, https://ssrn.com/abstract=3763042.

9. Larry Fink, "Larry Fink's Annual Letter to CEOs: A Sense of Purpose," BlackRock, 2018, https://aips.online/wp-content/uploads/2018/04/Larry-Fink-letter-to-CEOs-2018-BlackRock.pdf.
10. Andrew Ross Sorkin, "BlackRock's Message: Contribute to Society, or Risk Losing Our Support," *New York Times*, January 15, 2018, https://www.nytimes.com/2018/01/15/business/dealbook/blackrock-laurence-fink-letter.html.
11. "Business Roundtable Redefines the Purpose of a Corporation to Promote 'an Economy That Serves All Americans,'" Business Roundtable, August 19, 2019, https://www.businessroundtable.org/business-roundtable-redefines-the-purpose-of-a-corporation-to-promote-an-economy-that-serves-all-americans.
12. "One Year Later: Purpose of a Corporation," Business Roundtable, n.d., https://purpose.businessroundtable.org/.
13. "Business Roundtable Redefines."
14. "Global Survey Finds Businesses Increasing ESG Commitments, Spending," NAVEX, February 23, 2021, https://www.navex.com/blog/article/environmental-social-governance-esg-global-survey-findings/.
15. "Maximizing the Benefits of ESG Performance Metrics in Executive Incentive Plans," The Conference Board, December 20, 2023, https://www.conference-board.org/publications/ESG-performance-metrics-in-executive-compensation-plans.
16. Connor Lott, "Coller Capital's PE Barometer Shows ESG Conviction, Regulatory & Tax Fears," AlixPartners, June 16, 2021, https://insights.alixpartners.com/post/102h0j3/coller-capitals-pe-barometer-shows-esg-conviction-regulatory-tax-fears.
17. "Sustainability Action Report: Survey Findings on ESG Disclosure and Preparedness," Deloitte, December 2022, https://www2.deloitte.com/content/dam/Deloitte/us/Documents/audit/us-survey-findings-on-esg-disclosure-and-preparedness.pdf.
18. "Sustainability Action Report."
19. "Sustainability Action Report."
20. Nakul Nair, "ESG Funds: What Makes for Good Performance?," Bloomberg Professional Services, August 8, 2023, https://www.bloomberg.com/professional/blog/esg-funds-what-makes-for-good-performance/.
21. Alastair Marsh, "Global ESG Assets Fell to $30.3 Trillion from $35 Trillion Amid US Pullback," Bloomberg, November 28, 2023,

https://www.bloomberg.com/news/articles/2023-11-29/global-esg-market-shrinks-after-sizable-drop-in-us.

22 "Marking over 50 Years of Earth Day and Sustainability," Press Release, G&A Institute, n.d., https://www.ga-institute.com/nc/news/newsletter/press-release/article/marking-over-50-years-of-earth-day-and-sustainability-focused-mutual-funds.html.

23 "Marking over 50 Years."

24 "Materiality Finder," Sustainability Accounting Standards Board, n.d., https://sasb.org/standards/materiality-finder/.

25 Andrew Winston, "2023: A Strange, Tumultuous Year in Sustainability," *Harvard Business Review*, December 28, 2023, https://hbr.org/2023/12/2023-a-strange-tumultuous-year-in-sustainability.

26 Avery Ellfeldt, "U.S. Companies Scramble Ahead of EU Climate Disclosure Rules," E&E News by POLITICO, October 17, 2023, https://www.eenews.net/articles/us-companies-scramble-ahead-of-eu-climate-disclosure-rules/.

27 Loyti Cheng, David A. Zilberberg and Emily Roberts, "California Enacts Major Climate-Related Disclosure Laws," Harvard Law School Forum on Corporate Governance, October 22, 2023, https://corpgov.law.harvard.edu/2023/10/22/california-enacts-major-climate-related-disclosure-laws/.

28 Hiroko Tabuchi, "Court Temporarily Halts S.E.C.'s New Climate Rules," *New York Times*, March 15, 2024, https://www.nytimes.com/2024/03/15/climate/sec-climate-rules-lawsuit.html.

29 "Scope 3 Emissions," Yale Sustainability, n.d., https://sustainability.yale.edu/priorities-progress/climate-action/greenhouse-gas-emissions/scope-3-emissions; "What Are Scope 1, 2 and 3 Carbon Emissions?," National Grid Group, July 1, 2024, https://www.nationalgrid.com/stories/energy-explained/what-are-scope-1-2-3-carbon-emissions.

30 Kirsten Spalding, "For Investors with Net Zero Commitments, the SEC's Proposed Mandatory Climate Disclosure Rule Is Crucial," Ceres, April 8, 2022, https://www.ceres.org/news-center/blog/investors-net-zero-commitments-secs-proposed-mandatory-climate-disclosure-rule.

31 Evan Williams, "The Chamber Fights Back against Counterproductive Corporate Disclosure Requirements," US Chamber of Commerce, January 30, 2024, https://www.uschamber.com/finance/

corporate-governance/effective-material-corporate-disclosure-is-the-cornerstone-of-u-s-capital-markets.
32. Williams.
33. "Materiality Finder."
34. "The ESG Global Survey 2021," BNP Paribas, September 2021, https://www.theia.org/sites/default/files/2021-09/The%20ESG%20Global%20Survey%202021.pdf.
35. Institutional Shareholder Services, "Statement Regarding Consideration of Diversity Factors in U.S. Director Election Assessments," ISS Insights, February 11, 2025, https://insights.issgovernance.com/posts/statement-regarding-consideration-of-diversity-factors-in-u-s-director-election-assessments/.
36. Lloyd M. Johnson Jr., "A Mission For Inclusion: In Conversation with Gary Gensler," SEC, n.d., https://www.sec.gov/sec-stories/mission-inclusion-conversation-gary-gensler.
37. "Materiality Finder."
38. "ISS Global Voting Principles," ISS, February 8, 2021, https://www.issgovernance.com/policy-gateway/iss-global-voting-principles/.
39. Rosa A. Testani et al., "Proxy Advisory Firms Issue 2023 Voting Guidelines," Akin Gump Strauss Hauer & Feld LLP, February 6, 2023, https://www.akingump.com/en/insights/alerts/proxy-advisory-firms-issue-2023-voting-guidelines.
40. "Environmental, Social and Governance (ESG) Issues," PRI, n.d., https://www.unpri.org/sustainability-issues/environmental-social-and-governance-issues.
41. "Defining the 'G' in ESG: Governance Factors at the Heart of Sustainable Business," World Economic Forum, June 2022, https://www3.weforum.org/docs/WEF_Defining_the_G_in_ESG_2022.pdf.
42. "Sustainability Action Report."
43. "Sustainability Action Report."
44. Brian Tayan, "ESG Ratings: A Compass without Direction," Harvard Law School Forum on Corporate Governance, August 24, 2022, https://corpgov.law.harvard.edu/2022/08/24/esg-ratings-a-compass-without-direction/.
45. Tayan.
46. Ethan Rouen, Kunal Sachdeva, and Aaron Yoon, "The Evolution of ESG Reports and the Role of Voluntary Standards," Harvard Law School Forum on Corporate Governance, November 21, 2022,

https://corpgov.law.harvard.edu/2022/11/21/the-evolution-of-esg-reports-and-the-role-of-voluntary-standards/.

47 Ethan Rouen, Kunal Sachdeva, and Aaron Yoon, "Sustainability Meets Substance: Evaluating ESG Reports in the Context of 10-Ks and Firm Performance," SSRN, March 15, 2024, https://ssrn.com/abstract=4227934.

48 Rochelle Toplensky and Florence Lo/Reuters, "Why ESG Ratings Are All Over the Map," *Wall Street Journal*, August 17, https://www.wsj.com/finance/investing/esg-ratings-f569f60e.

49 "Figure 22. The SASB Materiality Map—Sector Level," ResearchGate, n.d., https://www.researchgate.net/figure/The-SASB-Materiality-Map-Sector-level_fig10_337195912.

50 Tim Rogmans and Karim El-Jisr, "Designing Your Company's Sustainability Report," *Harvard Business Review*, January 14, 2022, https://hbr.org/2022/01/designing-your-companys-sustainability-report.

51 Rogmans and El-Jisr.

52 Jay Gelb et al., "Investors Want to Hear from Companies about the Value of Sustainability," McKinsey & Company, September 15, 2023, https://www.mckinsey.com/capabilities/strategy-and-corporate-finance/our-insights/investors-want-to-hear-from-companies-about-the-value-of-sustainability.

53 "What's ESG Got to Do with It? The Current State of U.S. Sustainability Reporting," Teneo Insights, Fall 2022, https://www.teneo.com/app/uploads/2022/09/2022-State-of-US-Sustainability-Report.pdf.

54 Brian Baker, "ESG Investing Statistics 2023," Bankrate, January 31, 2023, https://www.bankrate.com/investing/esg-investing-statistics.

55 Michael E. Porter, Mark Kramer, and George Serafeim, "Where ESG Fails," *Institutional Investor*, October 16, 2019, https://www.institutionalinvestor.com/article/2bswdin8nvg922puxdzwg/opinion/where-esg-fails.

56 Steve Johnson, "ESG Outperformance Narrative 'Is Flawed', New Research Shows," *Financial Times*, May 3, 2021, https://www.ft.com/content/be140b1b-2249-4dd9-859c-3f8f12ce6036.

57 Isla Binnie and Ross Kerber, "DeSantis Signs Sweeping Anti-ESG Legislation in Florida," Reuters, May 3, 2023, https://www.reuters.com/business/sustainable-business/desantis-signs-sweeping-anti-esg-legislation-florida-2023-05-02/.

58 Thomas Catenacci, "Tennessee Sues BlackRock in First-of-Its-Kind ESG Lawsuit," Fox Business, December 18, 2023, https://www.foxbusiness.com/politics/tennessee-sues-blackrock-first-of-its-kind-esg-lawsuit.

59 Qwenton Briggs, "'ESG Evasion' & the Anti-ESG Campaign: Tennessee's Call for Clarity and Consumer Protection against BlackRock, Inc., the World's Largest Asset Manager," *Kentucky Law Journal* 112, March 5, 2024, https://www.kentuckylawjournal.org/blog/esg-evasion-the-anti-esg-campaign-tennessees-call-for-clarity-and-consumer-protection-against-blackrock-inc-the-worlds-largest-asset-manager.

60 Leah Malone and Emily Holland, "ESG in Mid-2023: Making Sense of the Moment," Harvard Law School Forum on Corporate Governance, August 31, 2023, https://corpgov.law.harvard.edu/2023/08/31/esg-in-mid-2023-making-sense-of-the-moment/.

61 J. Edward Moreno, "Exxon Sues to Prevent Climate Proposal from Getting a Shareholder Vote," *New York Times*, January 22, 2024, https://www.nytimes.com/2024/01/22/business/exxon-climate-change-lawsuit.html; "U.S. Sustainable Funds Landscape 2024 in Review," Morningstar, n.d., https://www.morningstar.com/lp/sustainable-funds-landscape-report.

62 Andrew Ross Sorkin et al., "After New Hampshire, Business Braces for a Trump Nomination," *New York Times*, January 24, 2024, https://www.nytimes.com/2024/01/24/business/dealbook/trump-nomination-business.html.

63 Moreno, "Exxon Sues."

64 Clara Hudson, "Exxon Case Dismissal Leaves Path for More Suits to Toss ESG Bids," Bloomberg Law, June 20, 2024, https://news.bloomberglaw.com/esg/exxon-case-dismissal-leaves-path-for-more-suits-to-toss-esg-bids.

65 John Frank, "Larry Fink 'Ashamed' to Be Part of ESG Political Debate," Axios, June 25, 2023, https://www.axios.com/2023/06/26/larry-fink-ashamed-esg-weaponized-desantis.

66 Andrew Ross Sorkin et al., "Is Tucker Carlson Too Hot for Twitter to Handle?," *New York Times*, May 10, 2023, https://www.nytimes.com/2023/05/10/business/dealbook/tucker-carlson-elon-musk-twitter.html.

67 Brooke Masters and Patrick Temple-West, "JPMorgan and State Street Quit Climate Group as BlackRock Scales Back," *Financial*

Times, February 15, 2024, https://www.ft.com/content/3ce06a6f-f0e3-4f70-a078-82a6c265ddc2.

68 Amanda Gerut, "Jamie Dimon Takes a Stand by Signing JPMorgan up as the First Big Bank to Reveal a Key Clean Energy Metric to Investors," Yahoo Finance, March 4, 2024, https://finance.yahoo.com/news/jamie-dimon-takes-stand-signing-010243726.html.

69 Mark Joyella, "On Fox, Donald Trump Calls Climate Change a 'Hoax': 'In the 1920's They Were Talking about Global Freezing,'" *Forbes*, March 23, 2022, https://www.forbes.com/sites/markjoyella/2022/03/21/on-fox-donald-trump-calls-climate-change-a-hoax-in-the-1920s-they-were-talking-about-global-freezing/.

70 "Running the Risk: How Corporate Boards Can Oversee Environmental, Social and Governance (ESG) Issues," Ceres, November 20, 2019, https://www.ceres.org/resources/reports/running-risk-how-corporate-boards-can-oversee-environmental-social-and-governance.

71 "Stockholders versus Stakeholders—Cutting the Gordian Knot," Skadden, August 5, 2020, https://www.skadden.com/-/media/files/publications/2020/08/stockholders-versus-stakeholders--cutting-the-gord.pdf.

72 CFI Team, "Stakeholder," Corporate Finance Institute, 2023, https://corporatefinanceinstitute.com/resources/accounting/stakeholder/.

73 Dorothy Atkins, "Chancery Tosses Meta Activist Investor Suit over Social Ills," Law360, April 30, 2024, https://www.law360.com/delaware/articles/1831409.

74 Atkins.

75 George Serafeim, *Purpose and Profit: How Business Can Lift Up the World* (New York: HarperCollins Leadership, 2022).

76 Serafeim.

77 Alex Edmans and Bruce Bolger, "Can Stakeholder Capitalism Save Capitalism? First We Must Define It," *Forbes*, August 26, 2020, https://www.forbes.com/sites/lbsbusinessstrategyreview/2020/08/26/can-stakeholder-capitalism-save-capitalism-first-we-must-define-it/?sh=1f68a6b41aa7.

78 Edmans and Bolger.

79 Martin Lipton, "The New Paradigm: A Toolkit for Balancing Conflicting Stakeholder Interests and Protecting Long-Term Business Value," Harvard Law School Forum on Corporate Governance,

August 30, 2023, https://corpgov.law.harvard.edu/2023/08/30/the-new-paradigm-a-toolkit-for-balancing-conflicting-stakeholder-interests-and-protecting-long-term-business-value/.
80 Lucian A. Bebchuk and Roberto Tallarita, "The Illusory Promise of Stakeholder Governance," *Cornell Law Review* 106 (February 26, 2020): 91–178 (Harvard Law School John M. Olin Center discussion paper no. 1052; Harvard Law School Program on Corporate Governance working paper 2020–21), https://ssrn.com/abstract=3544978.

Chapter 11: New Directors: Recruiting, Diversity, and Onboarding

1 "Requirements for Public Company Boards," Weil, January 3, 2022, https://www.weil.com/-/media/files/pdfs/2022/january/requirements_for_public_company_boards_including_ipo_transition_rules.pdf.
2 "2023 U.S. Spencer Stuart Board Index," Spencer Stuart, 2023, https://www.spencerstuart.com/-/media/2023/september/usbi/2023_us_spencer_stuart_board_index.pdf.
3 Dennis Carey and Joseph E. Griesedieck, "CEOs as Directors? Maybe Not," Korn Ferry, April 2, 2021, https://www.kornferry.com/insights/briefings-for-the-boardroom/the-decline-in-ceo-board-directors.
4 "The Big 3 and ESG: A Guide to Blackrock, State Street and Vanguard Proxy Voting Policies and Guidance on Key ESG Issues," Weil, May 2023, https://www.weil.com/-/media/mailings/2023/q2/the-big-three--esg--a-guide-to-blackrock-state-street--vanguard-proxy-voting-policies--guidance-on-k.pdf.
5 Bill Hayes, "Ted Kennedy Jr.: More People with Disabilities Are Needed in the Boardroom," Directors & Boards, July 28, 2023, https://www.directorsandboards.com/board-composition/ted-kennedy-jr-more-people-with-disabilities-are-needed-in-the-boardroom/.
6 Hayes.
7 Sundiatu Dixon-Fyle et al., "Diversity Matters Even More: The Case for Holistic Impact," McKinsey & Company, December 5, 2023, https://www.mckinsey.com/featured-insights/diversity-and-inclusion/diversity-matters-even-more-the-case-for-holistic-impact.
8 Katherine Klein, "Does Gender Diversity on Boards Really Boost Company Performance?," Knowledge at Wharton. May 18, 2017,

https://knowledge.wharton.upenn.edu/article/will-gender-diversity-boards-really-boost-company-performance/.
9. Klein.
10. Klein.
11. "2023 U.S. Spencer Stuart Board Index."
12. "2023 U.S. Spencer Stuart Board Index,"
13. "2022 U.S. Spencer Stuart Board Index."
14. "2023 U.S. Spencer Stuart Board Index."
15. Subodh Mishra, "Racial and Ethnic Diversity on U.S. Corporate Boards—Progress since 2020," Harvard Law School Forum on Corporate Governance, July 21, 2022, https://corpgov.law.harvard.edu/2022/07/21/racial-and-ethnic-diversity-on-u-s-corporate-boards-progress-since-2020.
16. Lyuba Goltser, Kaitlin Descovich, Bianca Lazar, and Julie Rong, "Governance and Securities Alert," Weil, 2023, https://www.weil.com/-/media/files/pdfs/2022/december/alert_2023_iss_and_gl_voting_policy_updates.pdf.
17. "Proxy Voting Guidelines: Benchmark Policy Changes for 2025: U.S., Canada, and Americas Regional," ISS Governance, December 17, 2024, https://www.issgovernance.com/file/policy/active/updates/Americas-Policy-Updates.pdf?v=2024.12.1.
18. Andrew Ramonas, "Contested Nasdaq Board Diversity Rules Take Effect: Explained," Bloomberg Law, December 21, 2023, https://news.bloomberglaw.com/esg/contested-nasdaq-board-diversity-rules-take-effect-explained.
19. Ramonas.
20. Alexander Osipovich, "Appeals Court Strikes Down Nasdaq's Board-Diversity Rules," *WSJ*, December 11, 2024, https://www.wsj.com/finance/stocks/appeals-court-strikes-down-nasdaqs-board-diversity-rules-0a2eb7ee?st=DcM1Dh&reflink=article_email_share.
21. Marie-Christine Valois, Stephen Erlichman, Dyna Zekaoui, and Paul Blyschak, "The Moving Target of ESG Diversity Disclosure," Fasken, June 12, 2023, https://www.fasken.com/en/knowledge/2023/06/the-moving-target-of-esg-diversity-disclosure-when-might-consensus-emerge-and-who-should-lead.
22. Daniel Kurt, "Corporate Leadership by Race," Investopedia, February 15, 2024, https://www.investopedia.com/corporate-leadership-by-race-5114494.

316 Notes

23. "Today's Boardroom: Confronting the Change Imperative: PwC's 2023 Annual Corporate Directors Survey," PwC, 2023, https://www.pwc.com/us/en/services/governance-insights-center/library/assets/pwc-gic-acds-2023.pdf.
24. "Today's Boardroom."
25. "Today's Boardroom."
26. Julian Ha and David K. Rehr, "Strengthening the Onboarding Practices of New Directors," Heidrick & Struggles, https://www.heidrick.com/en/insights/boards-governance/board-monitor-us-2023.
27. Sarah Kessler, "D.E.I. Goes Quiet," *New York Times*, January 15, 2024, https://www.nytimes.com/2024/01/13/business/dealbook/dei-goes-quiet.html.
28. Jonathan Richman, "Washington Federal Court Dismisses Derivative Challenge to Starbucks' DEI Initiatives," Corporate Defense and Disputes, September 13, 2023, https://www.corporatedefensedisputes.com/2023/09/washington-federal-court-dismisses-derivative-challenge-to-starbucks-dei-initiatives/.
29. Jason Schwartz et al., "Washington Judge Dismisses Challenge to Starbucks Diversity Policies in Decisive Order Upholding Business Judgment Rule," Gibson Dunn, September 14, 2023, https://www.gibsondunn.com/washington-judge-dismisses-challenge-to-starbucks-diversity-policies-in-decisive-order-upholding-business-judgment-rule/.
30. Stephen Foley, "PwC Drops Some US Diversity Goals to Meet Changed Legal Landscape," *Financial Times*, January 17, 2024, https://www.ft.com/content/20d1646d-2039-40de-abe1-f2270830b01f.
31. Foley.
32. Sarah Butcher, "Morning Coffee: Goldman Sachs, JPMorgan Quietly Did Away with Diversity Hiring Schemes. Prime Broking Is Where the Investment Is," eFinancialCareers, March 5, 2024, https://www.efinancialcareers.com/news/diversity-hiring-banks.
33. "Over a Third of Boards Lack an Onboarding Process for First-Time Directors, Survey Shows," Business Wire, October 16, 2023, https://www.businesswire.com/news/home/20231016632055/en/Over-a-Third-of-Boards-Lack-an-Onboarding-Process-for-First-Time-Directors-Survey-Shows.
34. Ha and Rehr, "Strengthening the Onboarding Practices."

Chapter 12: The Chief Executive Officer

1. Kyle Peterdy, "CEO (Chief Executive Officer)," CFI, https://corporatefinanceinstitute.com/resources/career/what-is-a-ceo-chief-executive-officer/; Ronald E. Marden, Randal K. Edwards, and William D. Stout, "The CEO/CFO Certification Requirement," *CPA Journal*, July 2003, http://archives.cpajournal.com/2003/0703/features/f073603.htm.
2. A. G. Lafley, "What Only the CEO Can Do," *Harvard Business Review*, May 2009, https://hbr.org/2009/05/what-only-the-ceo-can-do.
3. "The Leadership Traits of Successful CEOs," McKinsey & Company, July 23, 2023, https://www.mckinsey.com/featured-insights/mckinsey-guide-to-excelling-as-a-ceo/the-leadership-traits-of-successful-ceos.
4. Ruth Umoh, "The No. 1 Behavior That Transforms Ordinary People into Successful CEOs, According to a Study of 2,600 Leaders," CNBC, March 29, 2018, https://www.cnbc.com/2018/03/29/the-no-1-behavior-that-turns-ordinary-people-into-successful-ceos.html.
5. Richard Haythornthwaite and Ajay Banga, "The Former and Current Chairs of Mastercard on Executing a Strategic CEO Succession," *Harvard Business Review*, March–April 21, 2021, https://hbr.org/2021/03/the-former-and-current-chairs-of-mastercard-on-executing-a-strategic-ceo-succession.
6. Haythornthwaite and Banga.
7. Haythornthwaite and Banga.
8. Boris Groysberg, J. Yo-Jud Cheng, and Annelena Lobb, "CEO Succession at Cisco (A): From John Chambers to Chuck Robbins," Faculty & Research, Harvard Business School, August 2016, https://www.hbs.edu/faculty/Pages/item.aspx?num=51605.
9. Groysberg, Cheng, and Lobb.
10. Groysberg, Cheng, and Lobb.
11. Trey Williams, "A Record Number of CEOs Headed for the Exits in 2023," SHRM, July 11, 2023, https://www.shrm.org/executive-network/insights/record-number-ceos-headed-exits-2023.
12. Nicole Lobdell, "CEO Exits Fall in November 2024; 167 CEO Exits Add to Highest Number of CEO Moves on Record," Challenger, Gray & Christmas, Inc., December 20, 2024, https://www.challengergray.com/blog/ceo-exits-fall-november-2024-167-ceo-highest-number-moves-record/.

13 "Fortune 500 C-Suite Snapshot: Profiles in Functional Leadership," Spencer Stuart, December 2023, https://www.spencerstuart.com/research-and-insight/fortune-500-c-suite-snapshot-profiles-in-functional-leadership.
14 "2023 CEO Transitions," Spencer Stuart, January 2024, https://www.spencerstuart.com/research-and-insight/2023-ceo-transitions.
15 "Corporate Headhunters Are More Powerful Than Ever," *Economist*, February 6, 2020, https://www.economist.com/briefing/2020/02/06/corporate-headhunters-are-more-powerful-than-ever.
16 "Corporate Headhunters."
17 "Corporate Headhunters."
18 "2023 CEO Transitions."
19 Md Reiazul Haque et al., "Insider vs. Outsider CEO and Firm Performance: Evidence from the Covid-19 Pandemic," *Finance Research Letters* 47 (December 3, 2021): 102609, https://pmc.ncbi.nlm.nih.gov/articles/PMC9167990/.
20 Aaron Sorensen, "Risks and Rewards of Internal and External CEO Candidates," Directors & Boards, June 21, 2024, https://www.directorsandboards.com/board-duties/board-ceo-relationship/risks-and-rewards-of-internal-and-external-ceo-candidates/.
21 Alan Murray and Nicholas Gordon, "Insiders Are Beating Outsiders in the Race to Be CEO," *Fortune*, May 8, 2023, https://fortune.com/2023/05/08/ceo-succession-planning-insiders-outsiders/.
22 Murray and Gordon.
23 Sheryl Estrada, "More Big Companies Are Searching for a CFO to Eventually Become CEO," *Fortune*, June 13, 2023, https://fortune.com/2023/06/13/more-big-companies-searching-cfo-to-become-ceo/.
24 "2023 CEO Transitions."
25 Spencer Stuart.
26 Spencer Stuart.

Chapter 13: Risks and Crises

1 Nicholas J. Price, "3 Fundamental Components of Any Enterprise Risk Management Plan," Diligent, March 28, 2018, https://www.diligent.com/insights/entity-management/3-fundamental-components-of-any-enterprise-risk-management-plan/.
2 "What Is Cybersecurity?," Cisco, 2025, https://www.cisco.com/c/en/us/products/security/what-is-cybersecurity.html.

Notes 319

3 "2023 Was a Big Year for Cybercrime—Here's How We Prepare for the Future," World Economic Forum, November 11, 2024, https://www.weforum.org/agenda/2024/01/cybersecurity-cybercrime-system-safety/.

4 "Business Email Compromise: The $55 Billion Scam," FBI Internet Crime Complaint Center (IC3), Alert Number I-091124-PSA, September 11, 2024, https://www.ic3.gov/PSA/2024/PSA240911.

5 Wes Davis, "MOVEit Cyberattacks: Keeping Tabs on the Biggest Data Theft of 2023," The Verge, November 10, 2023, https://www.theverge.com/23892245/moveit-cyberattacks-clop-ransomware-government-business.

6 Craig A. Newman, "Lessons for Corporate Boardrooms from Yahoo's Cybersecurity Settlement," *New York Times*, January 23, 2019, https://www.nytimes.com/2019/01/23/business/dealbook/yahoo-cyber-security-settlement.html.

7 Kevin LaCroix, "Yahoo Data Breach-Related Derivative Suit Settled for $29 Million," The D&O Diary, January 21, 2019, https://www.dandodiary.com/2019/01/articles/cyber-liability/yahoo-data-breach-related-derivative-suit-settled-29-million/.

8 Sean Michael Kerner, "Colonial Pipeline Hack Explained: Everything You Need to Know," WhatIs, April 26, 2022, https://www.techtarget.com/whatis/feature/Colonial-Pipeline-hack-explained-Everything-you-need-to-know.

9 Jen Easterly and Tom Fanning, "The Attack on Colonial Pipeline: What We've Learned & What We've Done over the Past Two Years," Cybersecurity and Infrastructure Security Agency (CISA), May 7, 2023, https://www.cisa.gov/news-events/news/attack-colonial-pipeline-what-weve-learned-what-weve-done-over-past-two-years.

10 Kerner, "Colonial Pipeline."

11 John Vaillant, *Fire Weather: A True Story from a Hotter World* (New York: Knopf, 2023), 321.

12 "How to Set Up Effective Climate Governance on Corporate Boards: Guiding Principles and Questions," World Economic Forum, January 2019, https://www3.weforum.org/docs/WEF_Creating_effective_climate_governance_on_corporate_boards.pdf.

13 "Risks, Opportunities, and Investments in the Era of Climate Change," Salata Institute, July 19, 2023, https://salatainstitute.harvard.edu/risks-opportunities-and-investments-in-the-era-of-climate-change/.

14 "Risks, Opportunities, and Investments."
15 "How to Set Up."
16 Vaillant, *Fire Weather*, 409.
17 Didier Cossin and Abraham Hongze Lu, "Board Oversight of Geopolitical Risks and Opportunities," IMD Business School for Management and Leadership Courses, May 2021, https://www.imd.org/research-knowledge/corporate-governance/articles/board-oversight-geopolitical-risks-opportunities/.
18 "What Is Artificial Intelligence (AI)?," IBM, n.d., https://www.ibm.com/topics/artificial-intelligence.
19 Katherine Haan, "How Businesses Are Using Artificial Intelligence," Forbes Advisor, April 24, 2023, https://www.forbes.com/advisor/business/software/ai-in-business/.
20 Haan.
21 "The CEO Digital Divide," AND Digital, n.d., https://www.and.digital/and-accelerate-whitepaper.
22 Maya Dollarhide, "Social Media: Definition, Importance, Top Websites and Apps," Investopedia, July 31, 2024, https://www.investopedia.com/terms/s/social-media.asp.
23 Amanda Holpuch, "Behind the Backlash against Bud Light," *New York Times*, November 21, 2023, https://www.nytimes.com/article/bud-light-boycott.html.
24 Andrew Bary, "Bud Light Sales Fall 26% as Transgender Backlash Worsens," *Barron's*, May 1, 2023, https://www.barrons.com/articles/bud-light-sales-dylan-mulvaney-transgender-backlash-9d426f09.
25 Jura Liaukonyte, Anna Tuchman, and Xinrong Zhu, "Lessons from the Bud Light Boycott, One Year Later," *Harvard Business Review*, March 20, 2024, https://hbr.org/2024/03/lessons-from-the-bud-light-boycott-one-year-later.
26 "FINRA Cybersecurity Advisory—SEC Rules on Cybersecurity Risk Management, Strategy, Governance, and Incident Disclosure by Public Companies (Exchange Act Release No. 97989)," FINRA.org, n.d., https://www.finra.org/rules-guidance/guidance/cybersecurity-advisory-sec-rules-on-cyber-risk-mgmt-governance-incident-disclosures.
27 "FINRA Cybersecurity Advisory."
28 "Many Companies Struggle to Adopt Spirit of Amended SEC Risk Disclosure Rules," Deloitte and USC's Leventhal School of

Accounting's Risk Management Program, March 2021, https://uscmarshallweb.s3-us-west-2.amazonaws.com/assets/uploads/s1/files/deloitte_usc_risk_management_program_article_march_2021_1_ha0elhirhe.pdf.

29 Securities and Exchange Commission 17 CFR 229, 239, and 240, https://www.sec.gov/files/rules/final/2020/33-10825.pdf.

30 Dean Kingsley, Matt Solomon, and Kristen Jaconi, "SEC Risk Factors Disclosure Analysis," Harvard Law School Forum on Corporate Governance, December 3, 2023, https://corpgov.law.harvard.edu/2023/12/03/sec-risk-factors-disclosure-analysis/#20b.

31 Dean Kingsley, Matt Solomon, and Kristen Jaconi, "SEC Risk Factor Disclosure Rules," Harvard Law School Forum on Corporate Governance, December 22, 2021, https://corpgov.law.harvard.edu/2021/12/22/sec-risk-factor-disclosure-rules/.

32 Kingsley, Solomon, and Jaconi.

33 P. J. Himelfarb et al., "Need to Know: Disclosure Developments and 2023 Form 10-K Disclosure Locator," Weil, January 16, 2024, https://www.weil.com/-/media/mailings/2024/q1/need-to-know-disclosure-developments-and-2023-form-10-k-disclosure-locator.pdf.

34 Himelfarb et al.

35 Robert Tita, Dow Jones Newswires, "Nikola Awarded $165M in Case against Founder," *Barron's*, October 25, 2023, https://www.barrons.com/livecoverage/stock-market-today-102423/card/nikola-awarded-165m-in-case-against-founder-syg6GkiuIYAwzsj6kDJv.

36 Andrew J. Hawkins, "GM Acquires Stake in Electric Truck Maker Nikola, Will Help Make the Company's First Vehicle," The Verge, September 8, 2020, https://www.theverge.com/2020/9/8/21427009/gm-nikola-acquisition-electric-hydrogen-truck.

37 "Nikola: How to Parlay an Ocean of Lies into a Partnership with the Largest Auto OEM in America," Hindenburg Research, September 10, 2020, https://hindenburgresearch.com/nikola/.

38 Ben Foldy, "Wall Street's Pre-eminent Short Seller Is Calling It Quits," *WSJ*, January 15, 2025, https://www.wsj.com/finance/investing/wall-streets-pre-eminent-short-seller-is-calling-it-quits-aee48b64.

39 "Nikola."

40 John Rosevear, "Nikola Stock Surges 9% after Disgraced Founder Trevor Milton Ordered to Repay $165 Million," CNBC, October 24,

2023, https://www.cnbc.com/2023/10/24/nikola-nkla-trevor-milton-damages.html.
41. Natalie Sherman, "Nikola: Trevor Milton Sentenced to Prison after Fraud Conviction," BBC, December 18, 2023, https://www.bbc.com/news/business-67752125.
42. Ben Foldy, "Even a Fraud Conviction Won't Keep Nikola's Founder Away from the Company," *Wall Street Journal*, May 20, 2024, https://www.wsj.com/business/nikola-founder-trevor-milton-ownership-7124b1cd.
43. Emily Bary, "Nikola Made More Fuel-Cell Trucks in Q1 Than It Did in All of 2023; Stock Soars," MSN, April 4, 2024, https://www.msn.com/en-us/money/companies/nikola-produced-more-fuel-cell-trucks-in-q1-than-it-did-in-all-of-2023/ar-BB1l4i3d.
44. "Nikola Initiates Comprehensive Voluntary Chapter 11 Sale Process," PR Newswire, February 19, 2025, https://www.prnewswire.com/news-releases/nikola-initiates-comprehensive-voluntary-chapter-11-sale-process-302380185.html.
45. Joseph E. Griesedieck and Stuart S. Crandell, "Board Effectiveness: Stepping up or Not Stepping Enough?," Korn Ferry, April 2, 2021, https://www.kornferry.com/insights/briefings-for-the-boardroom/board-effectiveness--stepping-up-or-not-stepping-enough.
46. Jonathan F. Foster, "The Board's Role in Crisis Response," *CFO*, January 19, 2021, https://www.cfo.com/news/the-boards-role-in-crisis-response/655873/.
47. Paula Loop, "Pandemic Tests Boards' Crisis Management Skills," Corporate Compliance Insights, October 19, 2020, https://www.corporatecomplianceinsights.com/pandemic-tests-boards-crisis-management/.
48. "Section 1403 Organization Designation Authorizations (ODA) for Transport Airplanes: Expert Panel Review Report," FAA, n.d., https://www.faa.gov/newsroom/Sec103_ExpertPanelReview_Report_Final.pdf.
49. "Section 1403."
50. "Section 1403."

Chapter 14: Keeping a Board Fresh and Sharp

1. Jane Stevenson and Anthony Goodman, "Note to the Board: Should Someone Step Down?," Korn Ferry, September 27, 2023, https://www.kornferry.com/insights/this-week-in-leadership/note-to-the-board-should-someone-step-down.
2. "Making Board Refreshment a Reality," The Conference Board, March 9, 2023, https://www.conference-board.org/topics/board-practices-compensation/making-board-refreshment-a-reality-op-ed.
3. "10. How Americans View Proposals to Change the Political System," Pew Research Center, September 19, 2023, https://www.pewresearch.org/politics/2023/09/19/how-americans-view-proposals-to-change-the-political-system/.
4. Michael P. Olson and Jon C. Rogowski, "Legislative Term Limits and Polarization," *Journal of Politics* 82, no. 2 (October 11, 2019): 572–86, https://www.journals.uchicago.edu/doi/10.1086/706764.
5. Anthony Fowler, "Democracy Reform Primer Series: Term Limits," University of Chicago Center for Effective Government, January 25, 2024, https://effectivegov.uchicago.edu/primers/term-limits.
6. Grant Thornton https://www.grantthornton.com/insights/articles/nfp/2023/5-reasons-that-healthy-boards-need-term-limits.
7. "5 Reasons That Healthy Boards Need Term Limits," Grant Thornton, April 24, 2023, https://www.sciencedirect.com/science/article/abs/pii/S1062940821000474.
8. Hui Liang James, Thanh Ngo, and Hongxia Wang, "Independent Director Tenure and Corporate Transparency," *North American Journal of Economics and Finance* 57 (March 14, 2021): 101413, https://papers.ssrn.com/sol3/papers.cfm?abstract_id=2089175.
9. "2022 Policy Guidelines," Glass Lewis, 2022, https://resources.glasslewis.com/hubfs/2023%20Guidelines/2023%20United%20States%20Benchmark%20Policy%20Guidelines.pdf.
10. "Boards around the World: A Changing Landscape," Spencer Stuart, March 2024, https://www.spencerstuart.com/research-and-insight/boards-around-the-world-a-changing-landscape.
11. "Choosing a New Board Leader: Eight Questions," Wharton Executive Education, March 2023, https://executiveeducation.wharton

.upenn.edu/thought-leadership/wharton-at-work/2023/03/choosing-new-board-leader-eight-questions/.
12. "10. How Americans View Proposals."
13. Bob Woods, "From Disney to Target to Boeing, Retirement Is a Thing of the Past for CEOs," CNBC, December 13, 2022, https://www.cnbc.com/2022/12/11/from-disney-to-target-boeing-ceo-retirements-are-a-thing-of-the-past.html.
14. "Making Board Refreshment a Reality."
15. "2023 CEO Transitions," Spencer Stuart, January 2024, https://www.spencerstuart.com/research-and-insight/2023-ceo-transitions.
16. "Making Board Refreshment a Reality."
17. Maria Castañón Moats, Paul DeNicola, and Matt DiGuiseppe, "Using Transparency to Build Trust: A Corporate Director's Guide," Harvard Law School Forum on Corporate Governance, April 11, 2023, https://corpgov.law.harvard.edu/2023/04/11/using-transparency-to-build-trust-a-corporate-directors-guide/.
18. Maria Moats, Paul DeNicola, and Catie Hall, "Conducting Effective Board Assessments," Harvard Law School Forum on Corporate Governance, June 2, 2022, https://corpgov.law.harvard.edu/2022/06/02/conducting-effective-board-assessments/.
19. Holly J. Gregory, "Rethinking Board Evaluation," *Practical Law*, March 2015, https://www.sidley.com/~/media/publications/march15_thegovernancecounselor.pdf.
20. "Annual State of Board Evaluations in the U.S. 2024," Korn Ferry / Gibson Dunn, 2024, https://www.kornferry.com/content/dam/kornferry-v2/pdf/KornFerryGibsonDunnAnnualStateofBoardEvalutionsUS2024Final.pdf.
21. Moats, DeNicola, and Hall, "Conducting Effective Board Assessments."
22. Moats, DeNicola, and Hall.
23. "Making a Great Board," NYSE Governance Services, n.d., https://www.nyse.com/publicdocs/nyse/listing/Making_a_Great_Board_RHR_White_Paper.pdf.
24. Rich Fields and Rusty O'Kelley, "Is Your Board Effective?," Harvard Law School Forum on Corporate Governance, October 21, 2022, https://corpgov.law.harvard.edu/2022/10/21/is-your-board-effective/.

25 Fields and O'Kelley.
26 "NACD Directorship Certification," NACD, n.d., https://www.nacdonline.org/nacd-credentials/nacd-directorship-certification.
27 "Corporate Director Certificate," Harvard Business School, Executive Education, n.d., https://www.exed.hbs.edu/corporate-director-certificate.

Index

Ackman, Bill, 122–23, 128
activism, 12, 117
    governance considerations, 130–35
    history of, 119–23
    key players, 123–24
    modern, 125–30
advance notice provisions, 134
age diversity, 205
agendas, 41–42
AI. *See* artificial intelligence
Airgas, 101–4
Air Liquide, 104–5
Air Products, 102–4
Allen, Mike, 31–32, 34, 89, 108, 152, 194, 250, 263
Allen, William T., 30–31
antitakeover provisions, 98–99
AOL, 92
Apollo Global Management, 13, 20, 110, 162
Apple, 62, 165
artificial intelligence (AI), 234–35
audit committees, 45–52, 188–89
Avon letter, 140

Ballmer, Steve, 122, 127
Balsanek, Kristy, 183–85, 188, 193, 263
Banga, Ajay, 219
Bankruptcy Act (1898), 157
bankruptcy directors, 173–74
Bankruptcy Reform Act (1978), 157–58
Barra, Mary, 182
Bastian, Stanley A., 210
Bayh, Evan, 233–34, 263
Bear Stearns, 109–10
Bebchuk, Lucian, 129–30, 133–34, 196

Benham, Doug, 54–55, 213, 231, 263
Berg, Larry, 73, 263
Bergerac, Michel, 98
Berle, Adolf A., 9
Best Buy, 84
Black, Leon, 110
Black, Lewis, 30
BlackRock, 66, 80, 138, 143–46, 162, 181, 191–93
Blackstone, 13, 57, 110, 159
Blue Bell case. See *Marchand v. Barnhill*
board culture and chemistry, 253–54
board diversity, 65–67, 186, 204–10
board evaluations, 243
board leadership, 69–77, 79–82
board meetings, 41–42
board minutes, 29–30
board skills matrix, 199–201
Boeing, 22–23, 30, 37, 41, 58, 79, 242
Bogan, Vicki L., 65
Bogle, Jack, 142, 144
Bolger, Bruce, 195
bonuses, 53–54, 57–58, 62, 72
boomerang CEOs, 224
Botelho, Elena, 218
Bouchard, Andre, 28–30, 35, 238, 250, 256, 263
Boy Scouts, 175
Brandeis, Louis D., 9
Brandon, David, 71–72, 168, 263
Brown, Kathleen, 205, 209, 263
Buffett, Warren, 119, 142, 247
Bush, George W., 14
Business Roundtable, 182
Byrne, Robert, 71, 79, 221–22, 263

328 Index

Cadbury Committee, 80
Calhoun, Dave, 37, 79
Carbone, Mario, 23–25, 186, 218, 263
Caremark. See *In re Caremark Derivative Litigation*
Carlucci, Frank, 7
Carlyle Group, 7, 111, 208
Carney, John, 33
Carney, Mark, 233
Carstensen, Laura, 205, 247, 263
Casesa, John, 264
Catalano, Anna, 200, 213, 227, 250, 264
CEO. *See* chief executive officer
chair emeritus, 73–74
Chambers, John, 220
Chandler, William, 60
Chandler Act (1938), 157
Chapman, Shelley, 172, 177–78, 264
Chapter 11 restructuring, 3, 19, 22, 118, 155, 166–69, 172, 174, 176–78, 221
Chapter 7 liquidation, 166–67
charter, 33, 49, 63–64
Chemtura, 59
chief executive officer (CEO), 4, 14, 41, 43, 61–63, 69–70, 215–18
    board leadership and, 69–75, 79
    boomerang, 224
    compensation committees and, 47, 52–57, 60–64
    as directors, 201–2
    diversity of, 66–67
    evaluating, 254
    interacting with and evaluating, 226–28
    performance evaluation of, 80
    recruiting and hiring, 223–26
    succession planning for, 5, 80, 219–23
Church, John, 20
CISA. *See* Cybersecurity & Infrastructure Security Agency
Citrin, Jim, 70, 218–20, 223, 227–28, 264

classified boards, 133
Clayton, Jay, 149
Climate Action 100+, 193
climate change risks, 187, 232–33
Coates, John, 137–38, 141
Coller, Jeremy, 182
Colonial Pipeline, 232
combined chair and CEO, 70–71, 75, 83
community projects, 14
compensation committees, 45–46, 52–65, 188–89
compensation consultants, 58
compensation metrics, 64
conflict, 26, 39, 43, 90, 112, 203, 252
    distressed company advising and, 159–60
    duty of loyalty and, 27–29, 38, 106–7
    geopolitical risks from, 230, 233
    independent directors and, 171, 173–74
    of interest, 13, 28, 58, 171, 173
    between investors and managers, 8
    proxy advisors and, 149–50
    special committees and, 46–47
controlled companies, 32–33
controlling shareholders, 38–39, 105, 108
Cook, G. Bradford, 10
Cook, Tim, 62, 182
corporate governance. *See* governance
Corporate Governance Code (UK), 80
corporate strategy, 23–24, 113, 254
Corwin v. KKR Financial Holdings, 105–6
Coster, Philip, 45
Council of Institutional Investors, 13
COVID-19 pandemic, 224, 233, 241
crisis management, 237–38
Crist, Peter, 74, 216, 220, 228, 252, 264
Cybersecurity & Infrastructure Security Agency (CISA), 232
cybersecurity risks, 187, 230–32, 238

Darden Restaurants, 127–28
debtor in possession, 158, 166–67
debtor-in-possession financing, 158
DEI. *See* diversity, equity, and inclusion
Delaware Corporate Code, Section 203, 99
Delaware Court of Chancery, 29–31, 33–34, 38, 89–90, 95, 101, 106
   Blue Bell case, 36
   Boeing and, 22–23, 37
   on directors' responsibilities near insolvency, 171
   Disney case and, 60
   entire fairness and, 107–8
   Smurfit-Stone and, 19, 21–22
   on stakeholder versus shareholder debate and, 195
   Tesla case and, 60–61
   Trulia case, 89
   Van Gorkom case, 95–96
Delaware courts, 30–35
Delaware General Corporation Law, 106
Delaware Supreme Court, 29, 31, 33, 61, 102
   Blue Bell case, 36
   on directors' responsibilities near insolvency, 170
   on duty of care, 26
   on duty of loyalty, 27–28
   entire fairness and, 106–7
   on poison pills, 99
   Revlon standard and, 98, 105
   Unocal standard and, 101
   Van Gorkom case, 94–97
Deloitte, 56, 182, 189, 236
DeMott, Deborah A., 29
Devine, William, 78–79
Dimon, Jamie, 81, 85, 150, 182
Dingman, Michael, 4–5
direct lending funds, 162
directors
   agendas, questions, and meetings and, 41–42
   bankruptcy, 173–74
   CEOs as, 201–2
   ESG and, 193–94
   evaluations of, 243, 248–51
   good faith efforts by, 39–40
   identifying candidates for, 202–4
   indemnity and, 29
   liability protections for, 97
   licensing, 251–52
   management interactions with, 43–44
   mentoring for, 212
   nominating and governance committee and, 65
   orientation and onboarding, 211–13
   recruiting of, 65, 68, 199–202
   responsibilities of, 23–26
   standards for decisions by, 35–39
   See also independent directors
directors and officers insurance (D&O insurance), 23, 37, 90, 171
Disney, 59–60, 224
diversity, 65–67, 186, 204–10
diversity, equity, and inclusion (DEI), 146, 186–87, 210
Dodd-Frank Wall Street Reform and Consumer Protection Act, 45, 58, 61–63, 148
Dollar Thrifty, 101
Douglas, William O., 159
Drain, Robert, 164, 172–74, 177–78, 264
Drewry, Christopher, 118, 125, 129–32, 248, 264
due diligence, M&A process and, 113–14
duty of care, 13, 26–27, 37, 79, 107, 169
   indemnity and, 29
   Van Gorkom case and, 94–97
duty of loyalty, 13, 26–29, 34–35, 37, 106–8
Dysart, Ted, 199, 201–2, 208, 245, 250, 264
Dyson, Charles H., 109
Dyson, John, 109, 264

330　Index

Easterly, Jen, 232
Edmans, Alex, 195
Eisner, Michael, 60
Elbaum, Lawrence, 118, 128, 134–35, 264
Elhauge, Einer, 144
Elkington, John, 180
Ellias, Jared, 169, 173–74, 264
Ellison, Larry, 38–39
Elmore, Len, 24, 264
Elson, Charles, 37, 148, 150, 241, 264
　on board's responsibilities, 25–26
　on CEO and chair roles, 78
　on CEO evaluation, 228
　on director evaluations, 249
　on indexers and governance, 138
　on onboarding, 213
　on risk management, 230
　on Sarbanes-Oxley, 49
　on succession planning, 220
employee ownership, 56–57
Employee Retirement Income Security Act (ERISA), 140
enhanced scrutiny, 98–106, 112, 134
Enron, 13, 25, 45, 47, 148
entire fairness standard, 33, 38, 106–8
environmental, social, and governance (ESG), 5, 8, 179
　backlash against, 191–93
　BlackRock and, 145
　directors and, 193–94
　environment component, 183–85
　governance component, 187–89
　history, 180–83
　indexing firms and, 146
　institutional investors and, 139
　measurement and reporting challenges, 189–91
　nominating and governance committee and, 65
　social component, 185–87
　stakeholder versus shareholder debate, 194–96
environmental disclosures, 184

equity
　in compensation, 54
　forms of, 55
　long-term grants of, 53
equity receivership, 156–57
ERISA. *See* Employee Retirement Income Security Act
Ernst & Young (EY), 4, 50, 216
ESG. *See* environmental, social, and governance
EU. *See* European Union
European Union (EU), 184, 190
executive chair, 70–71, 73–74
executive search firms, 223, 225
"Expanded Role of the Compensation Committee, The" (Huang and Floersch), 64
external advisors, M&A process and, 113
Exxon, 123, 192
EY. *See* Ernst & Young

FAA. *See* Federal Aviation Administration
fairness opinions, 107
Favas, Matthieu, 223
Federal Aviation Administration (FAA), 242
Fidelity, 143–44
fiduciaries, 10, 23, 39, 60, 115, 172, 237
fiduciary duties, 19, 22, 106, 116, 140, 144, 194–95, 231, 240, 245
　to maximize shareholder value, 98
　reincorporation and, 34
　restructuring and, 169–71
　Van Gorkom case and, 96
fiduciary function, duty of care and, 27
financial crisis of 2007–9, 45, 126, 161–62
financial M&A deals, 91
financial restructuring, 155
financial statements, 49
Fink, Larry, 139, 145, 181, 192
Fisch, Jill E., 31, 61

Floersch, Richard R., 64
Floyd, George, 66, 207
Forstmann Little, 98, 100–101
Fox, Brian, 160, 264
fraudulent transfers, 167
Freeman, Ken, 44
Frerichs, Michael, 77
Frick, Walter, 119
Friedman, Milton, 11, 179
Furlow, Clark W., 101

Gartner, Steven, 122, 130, 264
gender diversity, 206
GenesisCare, 155, 175
Gensler, Gary, 125, 187
geopolitical risks, 233–34
Georgia-Pacific, 19
Gerace, Sam, 79
Geraghty, Joanna, 67
Gilbert, John, 120
Gilbert, Lewis, 120
Gillan, Stuart L., 139
Girsky, Steve, 78, 212, 238–41, 246–47, 264
Glass Lewis, 80, 138, 141, 146–51
    on board elections, 134
    board evaluations recommendations, 249
    diversity requirements, 207
    term limits and, 245
global financial crisis of 2007–9, 13
Goldberg, Arthur, 10
Goltz, Felix, 191
Goodman, Anthony, 243
Gorman, James, 73, 85
Gorsuch, Neil, 176
Gottlieb v. Heyden Chemical, 107
governance, 5, 8, 25
    activism and, 130–35
    BlackRock and, 145
    in ESG, 187–89
    first wave of reform in, 9–13
    indexing and, 138
    institutional investors and, 151–53
    lead independent directors and, 78–79
    postreorganization, 178
    proxy proposals and, 120
    second wave of reform in, 13–15
    separating CEO and chair roles and, 78
government pension plan assets, 139
Graham, Benjamin, 119–20
Grant, Adam, 43
Great Depression, 9, 91, 109, 157
Great Recession of 2007–9, 45, 126, 161–62
Greenberg, Scott, 170, 265
Griffin, Caleb N., 144
Gubler, Zachary, 100
Gursahaney, Naren, 243, 265
    on age limits, 247
    on board leadership models, 76
    on board's responsibilities, 24
    on CEO recruiting, 225
    on director evaluations, 250
    on separation of chair and CEO, 84
    on strategic planning, 42
    on term limits, 245
Guth, Charles G., 27, 106
Guth v. Loft, 27–28

Hansen, Dale, 141
Harkin v. Brundage, 157
Harris, Josh, 110
Haythornthwaite, Richard, 219
Heckes, Howard, 216–17, 220, 222, 227, 265
Heltebran, Laura, 165, 265
Hertz, 101
Hinchman, Brook, 265
Hindenburg Research, 123, 239
Hockaday, Ed, 246
Holland, Emily, 191
Horbach, Sandra, 111, 208, 255, 265
hostile takeovers, 98–99
Huang, Ani, 64
human capital management, 63–64

Humbach, John A., 97
Hunker, David, 117

Icahn, Carl, 12, 91, 123
Iger, Bob, 127, 224
in-court restructuring, 163–64, 166–69
independent auditing firms, 50–51
independent chair, 70–71, 75, 77–82, 84
independent directors, 10–11, 43, 94, 132, 238, 245
    committee requirements and, 46, 52
    conflict and, 171, 173–74
    debtor-in-possession system and, 158
    defining, 46
    identifying candidates for, 203–4
    lead, 41, 69–71, 75–80, 82, 85, 226
    recruitment and, 68
    restructuring and, 168, 171–78
    Smurfit-Stone and, 19–20, 22
    special committees of, 108, 112
index funds, 141–46, 153, 180
indexing, 138
individual director evaluations, 248–51
initial public offering (IPO), 13
In re Caremark Derivative Litigation (Caremark), 31, 36
In re Dollar Thrifty Shareholder Litigation, 101
In re MFW Shareholders Litigation, 108
In re Oracle Corporation Derivative Litigation, 38–39
In re Smurfit-Stone Shareholder Litigation, 19, 30, 108
In re Trulia Stockholder Litigation, 89
In re Walt Disney Derivative Litigation, 59–60
insolvency, 170–71
institutional investors, 13, 137, 139–41, 151–53
Institutional Shareholder Services (ISS), 80, 100, 138, 141, 146–51
    on board elections, 134
    board evaluations recommendations, 249
    diversity and, 187, 207
    term limits and, 245
IPO. *See* initial public offering
ISS. *See* Institutional Shareholder Services

Jacobs, Jack B., 31, 72
Jacobs, Ken, 71–72, 265
JetBlue, 67, 187
Jobs, Steve, 165
Johnson, Clem, 225
Johnson, Ron, 128
Joly, Hubert, 84, 224
Jordan, Michael, 83
JPMorganChase, 81, 85, 150, 193

Kamar, Ehud, 173
Kaplan, Steve, 115
Karakulova, Karina, 140
Kastiel, Kobi, 173
Kavanaugh, Brett, 176
Kennedy, Ted, Jr., 206
Key, Steve, 4, 213, 226, 265
Kindler, Rob, 102, 108, 265
KKR, 13, 56–57, 105, 109–11, 187
Klain, Ron, 25, 44, 218, 231–32, 238, 265
Klein, Ele, 126, 265
Klein, Katherine, 206
Klein, Rich, 266
Klemash, Steve, 117
Kohlberg, Jerome, 109–10
Kostin, David, 117
Krause, Ryan, 81
Kravis, Henry, 109–10

Lafley, A. G., 216
Lamb, Natasha, 77
Larcker, David F., 81, 84, 149
Laster, J. Travis, 33, 195
Lavin v. West Corporation, 106
Lazard, 3–5, 20–21, 71, 121, 160, 162

Index

LBOs. *See* leveraged buyouts
leadership, 79, 81–82, 218
   importance of, 69–70, 256
   models of, 70–77
lead independent director, 70, 75–76, 78–79
Lear, 118, 211, 225, 238
Lee, James B. ("Jimmy"), 161
Lemkau, Gregg, 116, 266
leveraged buyouts (LBOs), 7, 12, 91–92, 100, 108–12
Lewis, Bill, 20
liability management exercises (LMEs), 164
Lipin, Steve, 131, 195, 266
Lipschultz, Marc, 161–62, 266
Lipton, Marty, 12, 14, 75, 98–100, 128–29, 196, 266
Little, Royal, 109
LMEs. *See* liability management exercises
Loeb, Dan, 123
London Stock Exchange, board leadership disclosure requirements, 80
long-term equity grants, 53
Lorsch, Jay, 75
Lumbra, Ron, 40, 201–2, 207–9, 212, 225–26, 266
Lynch, Fred, 79, 201, 220–22, 226, 228, 266

Ma, Jenny, 117
Mace, Myles, 9
Malone, Leah, 191
management, director interactions with, 43–44
M&A. *See* mergers and acquisitions
Mandato, Joseph, 78–79
Manjoo, Farhad, 144
Manoff, Mark, 50–51, 216, 266
Manzo, Bob, 159–60, 165, 266
Marchand v. Barnhill (Blue Bell), 35–37, 41

Marmon Group, 94–95
Masonite, 3–4, 105, 217, 220–22, 228
Matt, Gary, 93, 266
Mattson, George, 165, 266
McCann, Jim, 8, 75, 83, 247, 266
McCausland, Peter, 27, 101–5, 266
McCormick, Kathaleen, 60–61
McKesson & Robbins, 45, 47
Means, Gardiner, 9
mergers and acquisitions (M&A), 7, 12, 20, 37–38, 89–93, 101, 112–16, 160
Meta, 77–78
Metzenbaum, Howard, 11
Microsoft, 122, 127, 165
Miebach, Michael, 219–20
Milken, Michael, 12, 161
Miller, Harvey, 159
Millstein, Ira, 76
Millstein Center, 76
Milton, Trevor, 239–41
Minow, Nell, 37
Miter Brands, 105
Modern Corporation and Private Property, The (Berle and Means), 9
Moelis, Ken, 33
Moran v. Household International, 101
Morgan Stanley, 73, 85
MSCI, 180
Muilenburg, Dennis, 79
Mullen, Admiral Mike, 14, 63, 212, 218, 220, 227, 266
   on audit committees, 48
   on diversity, 206
   on meetings, 41–42
Musk, Elon, 32, 34, 60–61, 148

NACD. *See* National Association of Corporate Directors
Nadella, Satya, 122
Naftalis, Gary, 60
Narasimhan, Laxman, 74
NASDAQ, 46, 52, 58, 76, 203–4, 207, 243

334 Index

National Association of Corporate Directors (NACD), 13–14, 56, 72, 75, 212–13, 232, 252, 258
Neff, Daniel, 104, 132–33, 266
Nelson, Gaylord, 183
Netflix, 62, 123
NetSuite, 39
Nevada, 33–35
Newman, Art, 159–60
Niccol, Brian, 74
Nikola, 238–41
nominating and governance committee, 46, 65–68, 188–89
nonfinancial metrics, 57–58
North American Catholic Educational Programming Foundation Inc. v. Gheewalla, 170
NYSE, 4, 11, 59, 90, 207, 243, 248
   audit committees and, 47–48
   committee requirements, 45–46
   compensation committees and, 52
   compensation consultants and, 58
   independent director rules, 203–4
   lead independent directors and, 76

Oberhelman, Doug, 24, 76, 81–82, 123, 183, 192, 196, 201–2, 213
Olive Garden, 127–28
onboarding, 211–13
O'Neill, Paul, 195
Oracle, 38–39, 90
orientation, 211–13
Orszag, Peter, 71
Ortberg, Kelly, 37
Other People's Money and How the Bankers Use It (Brandeis), 9
out-of-court restructuring, 163–66, 168
Ovitz, Michael, 59–60

Palia, Darius, 61
Pantry Pride, 98
Parker, Adam, 35
Parson, Richard, 71
Parsons, Donald F., 19, 22

Paterson, Muir, 131, 138, 149, 153, 193–94, 266
PCAOB. *See* Public Company Accounting Oversight Board
Peltz, Nelson, 124, 127
Penn Central, 10
pension funds, 139
Peregrine, Michael W., 49
Perelman, Mark A., 157
Perelman, Ronald, 98, 100–101
performance-based compensation, 53
performance stock units (PSUs), 55–56
Perot, Ross, 140
Peterson, Pete, 110
PGT Innovations, 105
Pick, Ted, 73
plans of reorganization, 166, 168
poison pills, 68, 99–100, 102
Polle, Gregg, 112, 212, 267
Popovich, Gregg, 83
postreorganization governance, 178
Potemkina, Ekaterina, 65
Powell, Kim, 218
prenegotiated bankruptcy filings, 168
Pritzker, Jay, 95
private credit, 161–62
private debt funds, 161
private equity firms, 12–13, 20, 57, 175
"problem of 12," 137–38
Protection of Shareholders Rights Act (1980), 11
proxy advisors, 146–51
proxy fights, 117, 147
PSUs. *See* performance stock units
Public Company Accounting Oversight Board (PCAOB), 47, 49
public pension funds, 120, 139–40
Purdue Pharma, 164, 175–77
Purpose and Profit (Serafeim), 195
PwC, 3, 45, 209–10, 248

Quadrant v. Vertin, 171
Quinn Emanuel, 29

Radin, Stephen, 96
receivership, equity, 156–57
recruiting, 65, 199–202
    board diversity and, 204–10
    of CEOs, 223–26
    identifying candidates, 203–4
    orientation and onboarding, 211–13
Red Lobster, 127
reincorporation, 33–34
Related Companies, 165
restricted stock, 55
restricted stock units (RSUs), 55–56
restructurings, 155
    categories of, 163–69
    directors' responsibilities in, 169–71
    history of, 156–63
    independent directors and, 168, 171–78
    retirement ages, 243, 246–48
Revlon case, 98–106
Revlon standard, 37
Revlon v. MacAndrews & Forbes, 21, 31
Rich, Jonathan, 82, 267
Ridings, Barry, 20, 162–63, 166, 177, 267
risk management, 229–30
risks, 51, 230–37
Robbins, Chuck, 220
Roberts, George, 109–10
Roberts, John, 176
Rock-Tenn, 19–22
Rohatyn, Felix, 92, 101
Romans, Donald, 94–95
Roosevelt, Franklin, 157
Rosenblum, Steve, 20
Rosenfeld, Jerry, 202, 267
Ross, Stephen, 165
Rossman, Andy, 29, 34–35, 250, 254, 267
Rouen, Ethan, 189
Rowan, Marc, 110
RSUs. *See* restricted stock units
Rubright, Jim, 20–21, 267

Sachdeva, Kunal, 189
Sackler family, 176–77
S&P 500
    board leadership models in, 70, 75
    diversity of boards in, 66
    index funds holdings of, 143
    retirement ages in, 247
    risk disclosures by members, 236
    staggered board in, 133
    sustainability reports by companies in, 190–91
    term limits in companies in, 243
    Vanguard holdings of, 139
Sarbanes-Oxley Act, 45, 47–49
SARs. *See* stock appreciation rights
SASB. *See* Sustainability Accounting Standards Board
Savage, Terry, 20
Say-on-Pay, 61–62, 68, 77, 147, 153
Schacht, Kurt N., 140
Schedule 13D, 124–25
Schedule 13G, 124
Schulman, Dan, 71
Schultz, Howard, 73–74, 224
Schulze, Richard, 84
Schwarzman, Steve, 110
Scott, Ray, 225
Section 220, 106
Securities and Exchange Commission (SEC), 7, 9–13, 64, 120, 139–41, 148, 158, 187, 189–90, 207, 211, 235
    activism and, 124–25
    audit committees and, 47
    board leadership disclosure requirements, 80
    committee recommendations, 45
    compensation and, 52, 58–59
    Enron and, 25
    environmental disclosure requirements, 184–85
    filings with, 49–50
    McKesson & Robbins investigated by, 45

Securities and Exchange
  Commission (*continued*)
  proxy advisory firms and, 149
  railroads and, 159
  risk disclosure requirements,
    236–37
  shareholder proposals and, 120
Securities Exchange Acts (1933 and
  1934), 9, 124
Semadeni, Matthew, 81
Seminara, Robert, 267
separation of CEO and chair, 77–82
Serafeim, George, 195, 232
Shapiro v. Wilgus, 157
shareholder activism. *See* activism
shareholder capitalism, 11
shareholder proposals, 120
shareholder rights plans, 68
shareholders, 7, 11, 13–14, 61–62,
  194–96
shareholder value, 7, 196, 224–25, 253
  activism and, 12, 118, 121, 126,
    132–35, 192
  board obligation to maximize, 20,
    98
  bonuses and, 54–56, 59
  ESG and, 192–94
  LBOs and, 112
  M&A process and, 113–15
  Nevada and, 34
Sharfman, Bernard, 97
Shekshnia, Stanislav, 70
Signal, 106–7
Simoncini, Matt, 225
Singer, Paul, 124
Skeel, David A., 156
skills matrix, 199–201
Skrmetti, Jonathan, 191
Slifkin, Daniel, 8, 28, 32, 35, 38, 40,
  194, 226, 267
Smith, Jeff, 123–24, 127
Smith, Roger, 141
Smith, Stephen, 148
Smith v. Van Gorkom, 26, 94–97

Smurfit-Stone, 19–21
Smurfit-Stone. See *In re Smurfit-Stone*
  Shareholder Litigation
Sneed, Paula, 24, 103, 143, 186, 208,
  255, 267
socially responsible investment indexes,
  180
social media, 235
social metrics, 185–86
"Social Responsibility of Business Is
  to Increase Its Profits, The"
  (Friedman), 11
Solomon, Steven Davidoff, 61
SPAC. *See* special-purpose acquisition
  company
SpaceX, 34
special committee, 46–47, 112, 175,
  223
  entire fairness and, 38, 108
  NetSuite acquisition, 39
  Smurfit-Stone sale, 20, 22
special-purpose acquisition company
  (SPAC), 239
special shareholders' meetings, 134
Spencer Stuart, 48, 52, 70, 72, 218,
  220, 222, 224
Sprayregen, Jamie, 158, 160–61, 267
staggered board, 104, 133–34
Starboard Value, 123, 127–28
Starbucks, 73–74, 210, 224
Starks, Laura T., 139
Statement on the Purpose of
  a Corporation (Business
  Roundtable), 182
State Street, 66, 139, 143–46, 193
Stavros, Pete, 56–57, 111, 255, 267
Sterrett, Steve, 73, 76, 78, 226, 267
Stevenson, Jane, 243
Stigler, George, 90
stock, compensation with, 55
stock appreciation rights (SARs), 55
stock options, 55
stock price metrics, 55
strategic activism, 126–27

strategic M&A deals, 90–91
strategic planning meetings, 41–42
Strine, Leo E., Jr., 29–30, 33–34, 252, 254, 267
   on activism, 129
   on CEOs, 226
   on directors' time, 42
   on separation of chair and CEO, 82
   on term limits, 246
succession planning, 80, 219–23
Supino, David, 160
Sussberg, Josh, 164, 169, 175, 178, 268
Sustainability Accounting Standards Board (SASB), 184–85, 190
sustainability metrics and reports, 189–91
Sutton, Michael H., 25

Target, 122–23
Tayan, Brian, 81, 84, 149, 189
term limits, 243–46
Tesla, 32, 34, 60–61, 90, 190
Thermo Fisher Scientific, 93
Thompson, Mark, 224
Time Warner, 92
Tonello, Matteo, 82
Torrisi, Rich, 23
total shareholder return (TSR), 54–56
ToysRUs.com, 50, 155, 168
transaction committee, 21, 47
TransUnion Corporation, 26, 94–95
Trans World Airlines (TWA), 10, 123
TripAdvisor, 32–33
Triple Bottom Line, 180
Trump, Donald, 66, 160, 193, 233
TSR. *See* total shareholder return
Turner, Matt, 58–59, 62, 268
TWA. *See* Trans World Airlines

Ullem, Beth Daley, 25, 268
Ullman, Mike, 128
Ultan, Bill, 140–41, 143, 149, 268

Ungerleider, Howard, 56, 203, 215, 226, 229–30, 247, 268
United Airlines, 5, 56–57
United Nations (UN), 180–81, 188, 233
universal proxy, 125
Unocal standard, 101
Unocal v. Mesa Petroleum, 31, 101
UOP, 106–7
Useem, Michael, 83
US Supreme Court, 157, 176

ValueAct, 122, 127
van Baal, Mark, 192
Van Gorkom, Jerome, 94–95, 97
Van Gorkom case, 26, 94–97
Vanguard, 61, 139, 142–46
VectoIQ Acquisition Corporation, 239
Velasco, Julian, 26
Versata v. Selectica, 101

Wachtell Lipton, 12, 20–21, 29, 98, 104, 128–29
Walt Disney Company, 59–60, 127, 224
Weinberger v. UOP, 38, 106–8
Weinstein, Boaz, 192
Wellington, 139, 142
West Palm Beach Firefighters' Pension Fund v. Moelis & Co., 33
Wheels Up, 165
Whoriskey, Neil, 151, 268
Why Corporations Choose Delaware (Black), 30
Williams, Harold, 11
Wise, David, 58–59, 62, 64–65, 268
Wolosky, Steve, 121, 124, 148, 268
Woodrum, Jim, 147
WorldCom, 13, 45, 47
World Economic Forum, 188, 232

Ying, David, 160
Yonker, Scott E., 65
Yoon, Aaron, 189

York, Jed, 23, 216, 268
YouTube, 235

Zalaznick, Jeff, 23
Zehnder, Egon, 219

Zelin, Steve, 163, 268
Zolfo, Frank, 159
Zuckerberg, Mark, 77–78
Zurn, Morgan T., 22–23
Zywicki, Todd J., 157

About the Author

Jonathan F. Foster is the founder and managing partner of Current Capital Partners, a mergers and acquisitions advisory, corporate management services, and private equity investing firm. He spent a decade at Lazard, primarily focused on M&A advisory work, ultimately as a managing director. Jon has been on more than 50 boards, including Fortune 500 companies, private companies, and companies involved in restructurings. He has served as chair, as lead director, and on the three major board committees as well as on special, transaction, CEO succession, and other committees. He has been chair of two Fortune 500 audit committees. Jon has also been an expert witness in corporate litigation in some 60 cases on various governance, M&A, and restructuring issues, having filed reports, been deposed, and testified in arbitrations and at trial.

With decades of experience, Jon has written, spoken, and been quoted frequently and has guest lectured at various universities. He lives in New York City with his wife and goldendoodle. He has two grown children.

What's Next?

Work with Jonathan F. Foster

Jon wrote *On Board: The Modern Playbook for Corporate Governance* to provide a clear, actionable guide for board members, executives, and business leaders who want to oversee with knowledge, confidence, and integrity. But beyond the pages of this book, his work continues. He is committed to helping boards and management teams make smarter decisions, build stronger companies, and drive long-term success and value.

Jon is available for board presentations, executive briefings, speeches, and other events. He shares informed, firsthand insights on corporate governance, leadership effectiveness, M&A strategy and execution, and other topics. Please be in touch at jff@jonathanffoster.com and visit www.jonathanffoster.com.